NB1

ART NOUVEAU

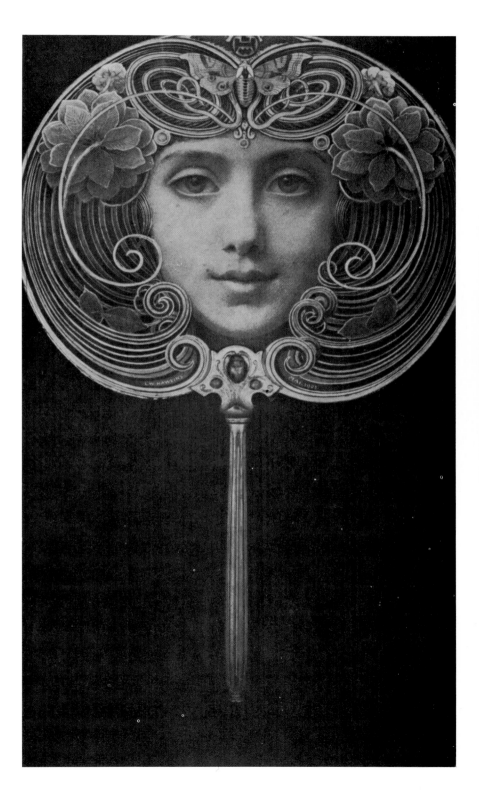

ART NOUVEAU

Lara-Vinca Masini

With 1093 illustrations,
297 in colour

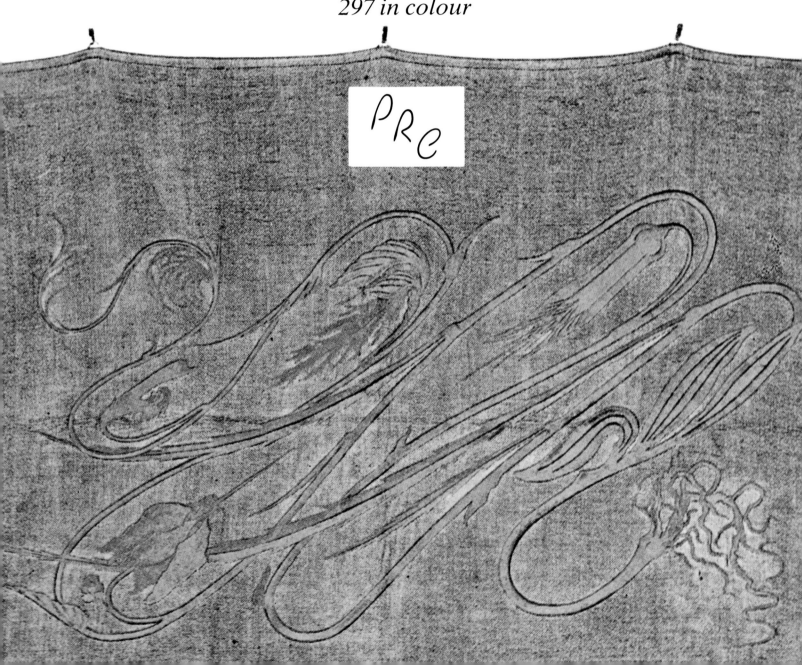

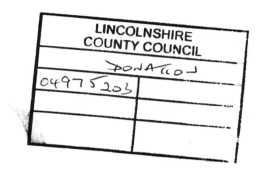
First published in Great Britain in 1984 by Thames and Hudson

English language edition © 1984 Patrick Hawkey & Company Ltd, London

Original Italian edition © 1976 Aldo Martello Giunti Editore SPA

This edition published 1995 by The Promotional Reprint Company Ltd,
Deacon House, 65 Old Church Street, Chelsea, London SW3 5RB
exclusively for Bookmart Limited, Desford Road, Enderby,
Leicester LE9 5AD Coles in Canada, Chris Beckett Limited
in New Zealand and A&R in Australia.

ISBN 1 85648 258 8

Printed in Malaysia

Contents

Preface

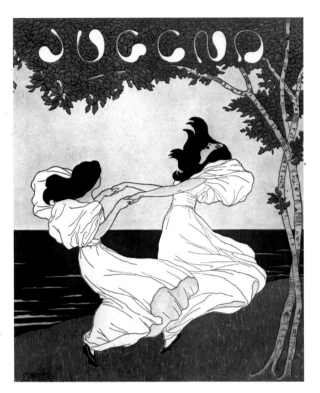

—LUDWIG VON ZUMBUSCH, cover of *Jugend*, n. 40, 1897.

The aim of this book is to present a reassessment of Art Nouveau as an international movement. Rather than examine in detail each nation's variation of the style in isolation, I have chosen to treat each as an aspect of the overall artistic fashion that took hold of Europe and America towards the end of the last century.

In recent years, the style has been popularized, even vulgarized, by the widespread commercial reproduction of many of its finest designs. This phenomenon, combined with the distaste with which it is viewed by those who would have art fulfil an ideological role in society, has led to its historical isolation. I believe that Art Nouveau still offers a rich area for scholarly examination and popular interest.

In my analysis of the stylistic features of Art Nouveau, I have ignored the traditional hierarchy of painting, sculpture, architecture and the applied arts into which studies on the Art Nouveau movement have often been divided. Rather, I have preferred to treat them as equal manifestations of a single aesthetic. For this reason, I have also drawn parallels between the plastic forms of Art Nouveau and contemporary literature and music. L.-V. M.

My particular thanks are due to Renzo Gherardini for his valuable collaboration in this work, especially for his generous information on the literary background to the period. I would also like to thank all those who have helped to assemble the photographic material. These include Wolfram Prinz of the University of Frankfurt, Nathan Schapira of the University of Los Angeles and Enzo Crestini, Massimo Becattini, Lilliana Martano and Guido Perocco of the Galleria d'Arte Moderna di Ca' Pesaro in Venice. I would especially like to thank Luigi Carlucco for making his archive of colour photographs available to me.

Introduction

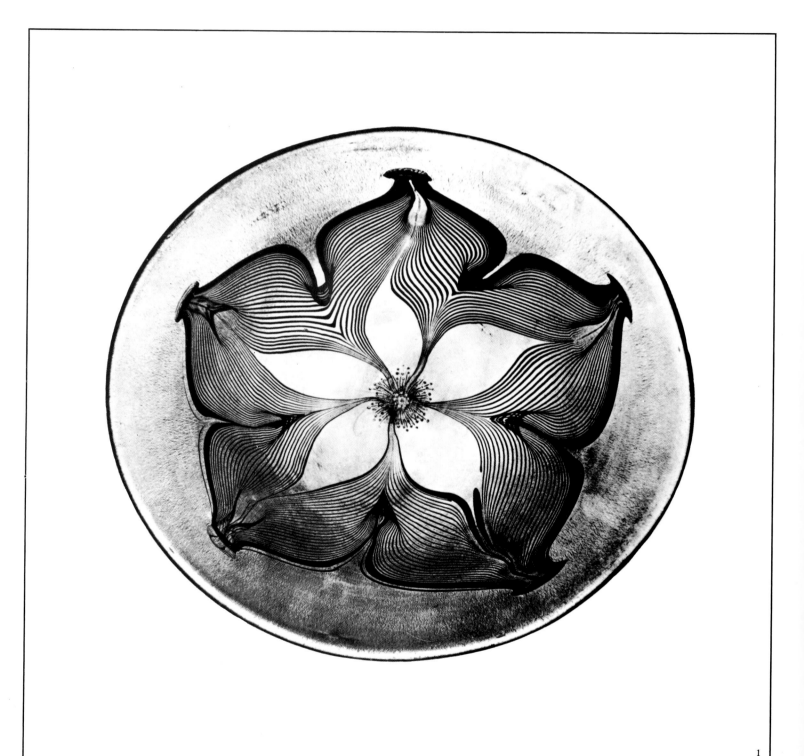

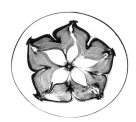

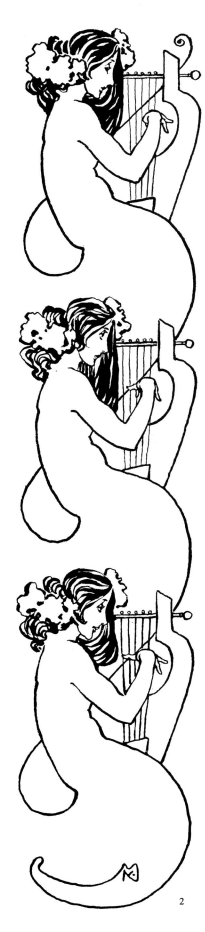

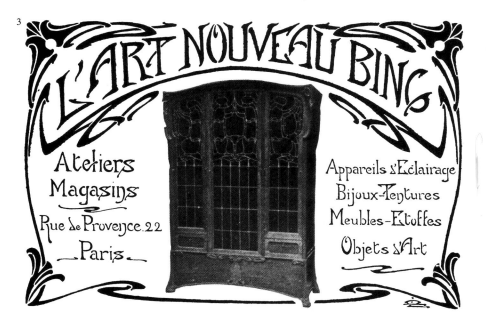

On the evening of 16 December 1895, a newly transformed gallery opened its doors at 22 rue de Provence in Paris. The owner was Samuel Bing, a German-born Jew, who was an established connoisseur, dealer and writer on Japanese art. His renovated gallery, however, was devoted to the work of leading young artists and exhibited not only fine art, but also works of applied art. Bing called his gallery L'Art Nouveau in order to emphasize the modernity of the works which he intended to show. In explanation of his intentions Bing wrote in 1902:

> L'Art Nouveau, at the time of its creation, did not aspire in any way to the honour of becoming a generic term. It was simply the name of an establishment opened as a meeting ground for all ardent young spirits anxious to show the modernity of their tendencies, and open to all lovers of art who desired to see the working of unrevealed forces of our time.

The inaugural exhibition presented a vast and bewildering array of paintings and decorative objects. There were stained glass panels designed by the Nabis and executed by Louis C. Tiffany; interiors designed by Henry van de Velde; a boudoir by Charles Condor; ceramics by Massier and Muller; glass by Emile Gallé and Tiffany; prints by Walter Crane and Aubrey Beardsley; sculpture by Auguste Rodin; as well as paintings in a wide range of styles by artists including Camille Pissarro and Jean-Baptiste Guillaumin, the Impressionists.

A visitor to the exhibition would have had difficulty in recognizing the coherent style which we would now call Art Nouveau in many of the exhibits. Nor did the opening of the gallery mark the beginning of

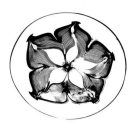

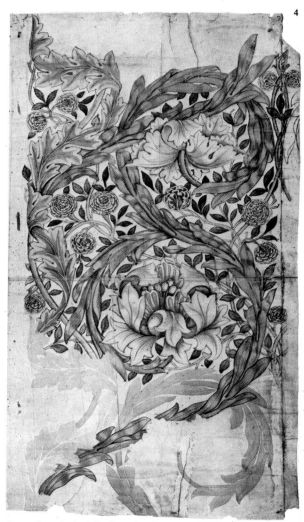

4

the new style. However, it gave its name to the international stylistic movement in the fine and decorative arts that flourished in the last decade of the nineteenth century and in the early years of the present century.

The series of international styles which we now call Art Nouveau were known by several names, many of which allude to artists or to the decorative features of the style. In France, Art Nouveau was also known as *Style Guimard* (a term coined by Hector Guimard himself) or *Style Métro,* an allusion to his design for the entrances to the Paris underground. Edmond de Goncourt referred to it disparagingly as *Yachting Style.* Other pejorative references to the style included *Style Nouille* (noodle style) in France, *Paling Style* (eel style) in Belgium, *Bandwurmstil* (tapeworm style) in Germany. Other more objective terms which are now generally accepted as descriptive names for the style are: *Style Horta* in Belgium (after the architect Victor Horta), *Stile Liberty* in Italy (after the famous London department store), *Sezessionstil* in Austria (after the Viennese Secession), *Modern Style* in France, and *Jugendstil* in Germany (after the periodical *Jugend* or youth).

1—and symbol of the Introduction, pp. 8-15 – LOUIS COMFORT TIFFANY, *Favrile* glass dish, c. 1896. New York, The Metropolitan Museum of Art.
2—KOLOMAN MOSER, *Suonatrici di lira* (The Lyre Players), typographical decoration.

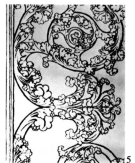

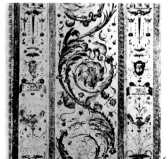

5

6

7

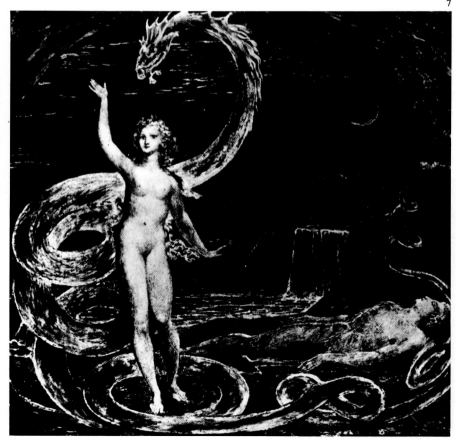

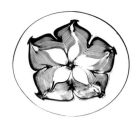

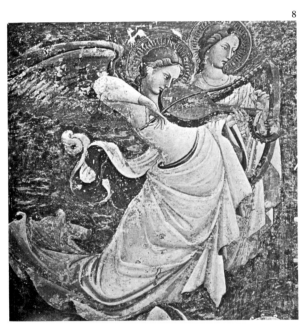

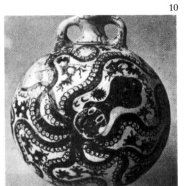

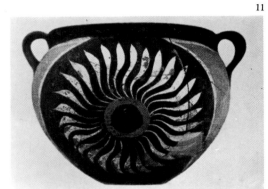

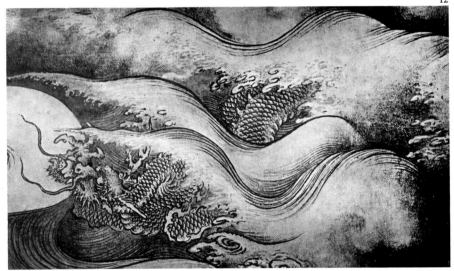

3—Publicity leaflet for Bing's L'Art Nouveau shops in Paris and Nancy.
4—WILLIAM MORRIS, design for chintz, 1876. Walthamstow, London, William Morris Gallery.
5—VILLARD DE HONNECOURT, grotesque, XIII century.
6—RAPHAEL, grotesque, after 1508, Rome, Vatican.
7—WILLIAM BLAKE, *Eve and the Serpent*, 1796.
8—PARRI SPINELLI, *Angel Musicians*, XV century. Arezzo, The Church of San Domenico.
9—GIOVANNI DA PAOLO, *Saint Clare Saves a Ship from Shipwreck*, XV century. Berlin, Staatliche Museum Gemäldegalerie.

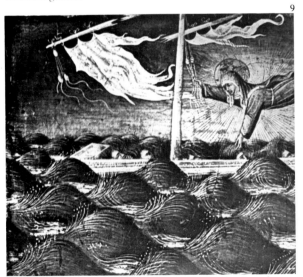

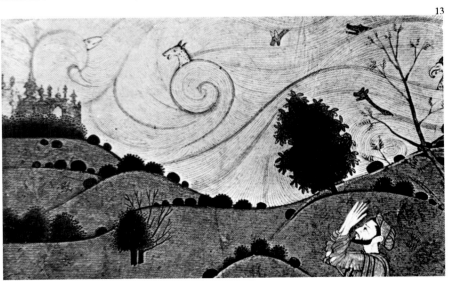

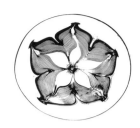

10—Minoan vase of the Guernia type ('new style'), from Paleocastro, c. 1580 BC. Heraklion (Crete), Archeological Museum.
11—Minoan vase of the Kamares type, c. 1800 BC. Candia (Crete), Archeological Museum.
12—CH'EN YUNG, *Screen of the New Dragons*, Sung dynasty, c. 1200 AD. Boston, Museum of Fine Arts.
13—*Sudama Approaches the Golden City of Krishna*, India, c. 1785 AD.
14—FRANCESCO BORROMINI, elevation and section of the lantern of Sant'Ivo della Sapienza, Rome, 1649-52. Vienna, Albertina.
15—Minaret of the mosque of Samarra, Iraq, IX century AD.
16—ATHANASIUS KIRCHER, *Turris Babel* (Tower of Babel), Amsterdam, 1679.
17—ETIENNE LOUIS BOULLÉE, spiral tower, 1784.
18—ANTONI GAUDÍ, enclosing wall at the Miralles Estate, 1901-02. Barcelona.

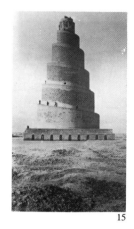

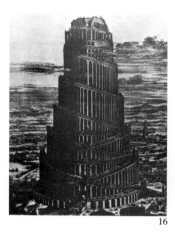

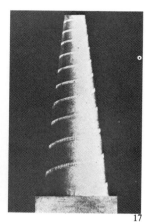

15   16   17

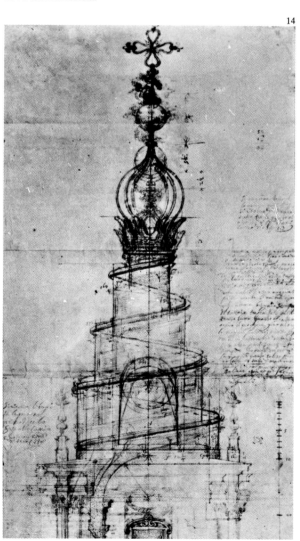

14

Regardless of the names of the individual groups, artists of all countries were united in their aim to dispense with the sober historicizing traditions of academic art, as well as the hierarchic division of the arts, which they felt had limited artistic production. Their aim was twofold: they wanted to avoid the endless repetition of earlier styles and subject matter, and they wanted to create a style which could shape the environment. They felt that this could be achieved by the synthesis of all the decorative arts.

The single characteristic of Art Nouveau which distinguishes it from any other contemporary style is that it makes the decorative elements autonomous within the work of art. In traditional styles of painting, architecture and the applied arts, formal, representational and emotional values had always overwhelmed decorative elements, while the Art Nouveau style attempted to liberate pure visual appeal from the restraint of meaning.

18

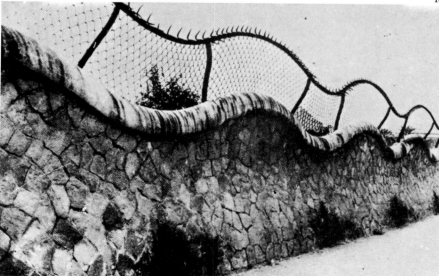

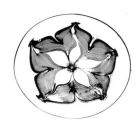

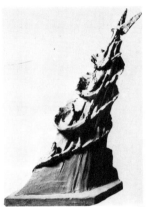
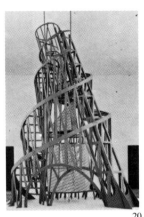

19   20

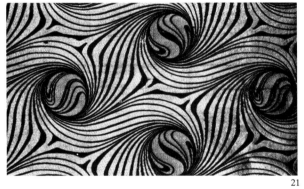

21

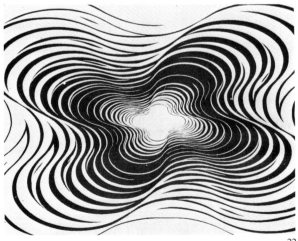

22

The freedom from what might be called wholly iconographic or practical considerations emerges most strongly in the Art Nouveau artist's use of line. In almost every example of the style there is a stress on the decorative values of floral motifs, arabesque and whiplash lines or complex linear rhythms. The treatment of the different types of linear ornament renders them independent within the work. In Art Nouveau it is the content of the work of art which follows the dictates of line; in earlier styles line is secondary to the demands of content.

A few examples of the way this process operates in an historical context will serve to illustrate the point. In architecture the simple example of the development of the spiral staircase demonstrates the peculiar position occupied by Art Nouveau within the history of the form. In both the East and West, towers containing a spiral staircase were conceived as primarily functional buildings in which the staircase leads to the top. From an early example, the ninth-century mosque at Samarra in Iraq, to the imposing model made by Etienne Boullée, the decorative quality of the spiral is ancillary to its function within the construction. When Hermann Obrist designed his project for a spiral tower monument in 1902, he broke with tradition. In his design, the spiral rhythm generates the structure of the tower. Vladimir Tatlin probably followed Obrist's example in his model for the Monument to the Third International (1919-20). However, Tatlin's version utilizes the freedom of line pioneered by Obrist to a new expressive purpose. Obrist's work is an exercise in the visually stimulating possibilities offered by the spiral, while Tatlin's is an experiment in the expressive use of form, used here to express the striving of the Russian people after the Revolution.

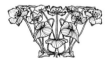

The development of the spiral was important to the Art Nouveau movement as a whole. In silhouette, Obrist's tower exhibits the same rhythmic line Gaudí used in his walls at the Miralles Estate (1901-02). Undulating rhythms similar to those of the Miralles Estate and Obrist's Monument were also exploited in the applied arts. The curvilinear rhythms which existed three-dimensionally in architecture were defined as patterns of colour in a variety of examples from Tiffany's *Favrile* glass (before 1906), to textiles by Obrist and the Viennese Koloman Moser (*c*. 1902). These examples may differ in the density of the patterns as well as in their relative success as works of art, but they are all based on the autonomous curve.

Again, we may illustrate how Art Nouveau differed from earlier styles which use similar decorative forms by comparing Tiffany's designs for a dish based on Minoan pottery with modern experiments

19—HERMANN OBRIST, project for a monument, 1902. Zurich, Kunstgewerbemuseum.
20—VLADIMAR TATLIN, model for the Monument to the Third International, 1919-20. Stockholm, Moderna Museet.
21—Furnishing textile, Austria, c. 1902.
22—JEFFREY STEELE, *Ilmatar*, 1967.
*—page 13, ornamental inset from *The Studio*.

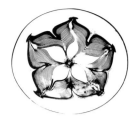

26

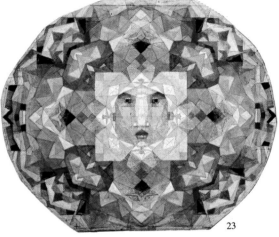

23

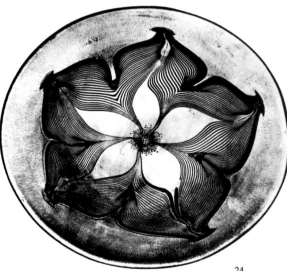

24

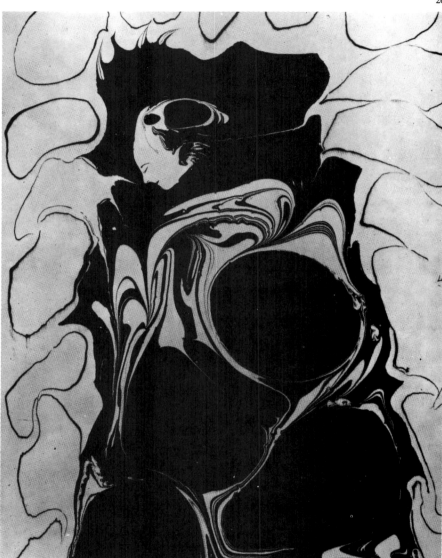

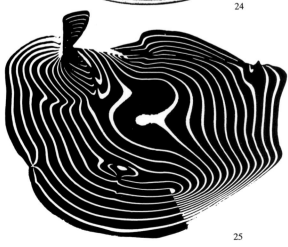

25

with repeated curves by Franco Grignani and Jeffrey Steele (in the late 1950s and early '60s). In the former, although there has been a shift from representational to purely decorative ornament, its shape is still subject to the form of the dish. In Grignani's and Steele's works, it is the illusion of the optical effect of pattern that makes them appealing, and they are as much psychological as visual works. In the dish by Tiffany it is the simple visual pleasure of the curve which excites us.

We can make similar generalizations about painting and the graphic arts. The spiral, arabesque, or repeated curve used as a decorative device can be found in the work of many painters from the earliest

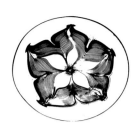

27

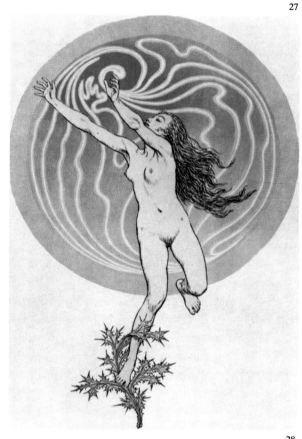

28

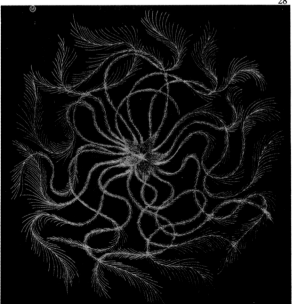

times. A brief glance at a range of examples from oriental painting, through the early Renaissance masters, to the Mannerists and to William Blake, shows how extensively these motifs were used. Yet in none of these cases do the decorative qualities achieve complete expression. They are always contained by the subject matter. Only when line and pattern are given an independent role in the work of art, for example in the posters designed by the English artists Ellen B. Houghton or Robert Anning Bell, do they fulfil their decorative potential. It is only in Art Nouveau that line and pattern were exploited in this way.

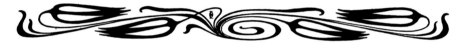

It should be said, however, that all these earlier artists were working in different materials and had quite different aims. Yet even when they worked in the decorative arts, for instance in architectural ornament or ceramics, their work is always representational and bound to the formal requirements of the object. In the designs of Villard de Honnecourt, or Raphael, and even in the early work of William Morris, line and pattern are at best only equal partners to natural or symbolic forms.

Art Nouveau style is important not only for its particular position within the history of art, and for its relationship to the art of the past; it must also be seen as having direct consequences for our own times. The highly sophisticated developments of Secessionist Art Nouveau, where curves, straight lines and different patterns all play a role within the same work of art, serve to illustrate how our visual experience has been influenced by it. If we compare the cover decorations designed by Emil Orlik for *Lafcadio Hearn* (1908) with a publicity leaflet for Bing's Art Nouveau gallery, we can see that in both there is an elegance which comes from a feeling for pattern and line as free elements in the composition. It is clear that Orlik's work provides a prototype for modern book cover design.

The Bing publicity leaflet was for an exhibition of furniture. The simplicity of construction and the clear vertical rhythm of Michele Achilli's sideboard (1959-60) suggest the influence of the furniture which was sold in Bing's gallery.

1-The Precedents of Art Nouveau

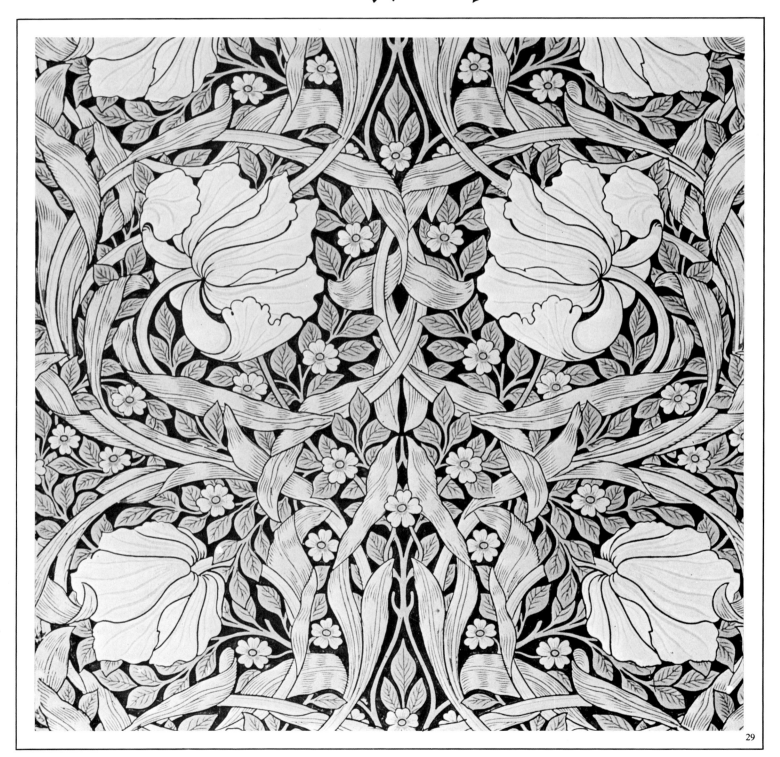

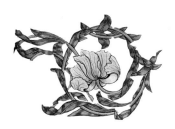

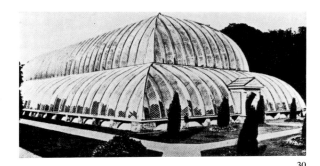

30

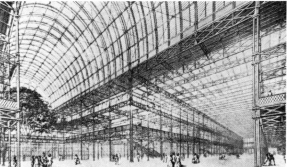

31

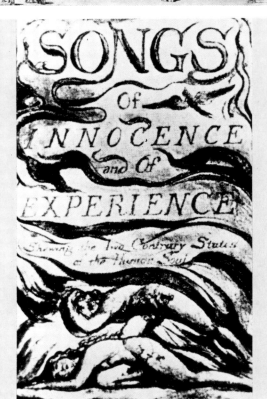

32

Although Art Nouveau was an international stylistic movement, most of its early development took place in Great Britain. England had been the first country to experience the Industrial Revolution and it continued throughout the nineteenth century to be the world's most advanced industrial nation.

Yet, running counter to the notion that industrial development was synonymous with progress, there was a growing ethical and aesthetic concern that enslavement to the machine and mass production was creating a world of ugliness and misery both at work and in the home. This anxiety found expression in the Gothic Revival: Pugin, Ruskin and later William Morris among others, looked back with admiration to the art and architecture of the Middle Ages. They thought that its beauty was a reflection of the society and of the crafts which had created it. At the same time, more aware industrialists, who had no intention of changing the system of production, realized that there was no adequate training in industrial design and that they would not be able to compete economically in the future with Europe if the design of their products was inferior. A Government Report of 1837 resulted in the establishment of Schools of Design in order to satisfy this need.

The visionary painter-poet, WILLIAM BLAKE (1757-1827), saw the 'dark Satanic mills' of the industrial townscape as a manifestation of materialist and rationalist ideologies. He turned his back on the world and spent his life investing his complex imagination in his art. In the rendering of his extraordinary visions, Blake created a style based on the decorative arrangement of curving forms which anticipates both Symbolism and Art Nouveau. In his art, the normal rules of the physical universe no longer apply. His figures become immaterial; defying gravity they float in space, a horse's mane bursts into an arabesque of flame, and entwining plant forms draw the surface into a dynamic rhythmic composition.

Few of his paintings were in oil; most were therefore not exhibited. This may account for their lack of influence during his lifetime. Early in his career (1775-78), Blake was planning a series of illuminated books which were written, illustrated, printed and hand coloured entirely by himself. The first of these, *Songs of Innocence*, was published in 1789. All his books are obviously inspired by medieval illuminated manuscripts; each page is conceived as an illustration or decorative border closely allied to and complementing the meaning of the lines. He achieved a greater degree of integration of the text and illustration than his medieval predecessors.

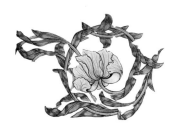

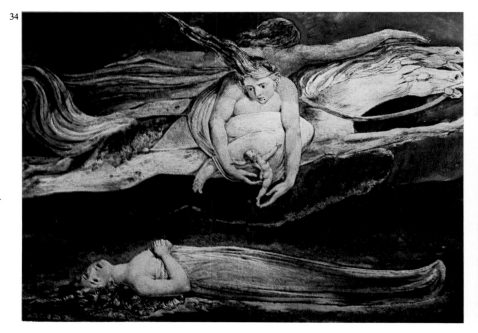

Blake was fundamentally influential to the Pre-Raphaelites, and through them he reached a wider audience. Furthermore, he prefigures the universal talents of Art Nouveau artists, because he tried to develop his art by working in a variety of media, at a time when industrial society was placing increasing emphasis on specialization.

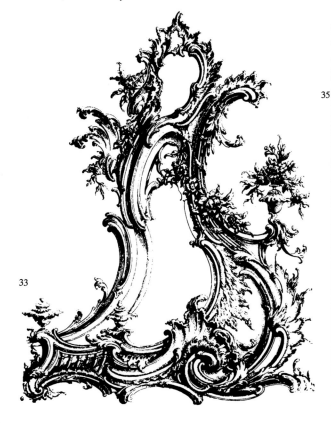

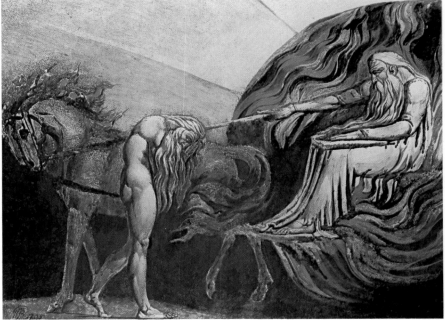

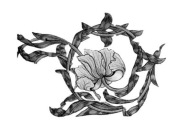

36

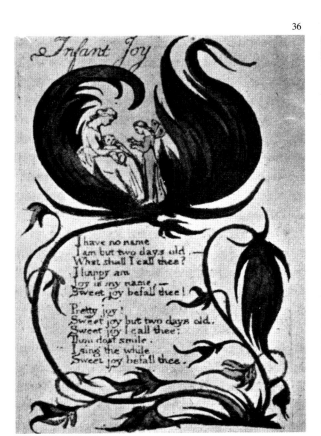

38

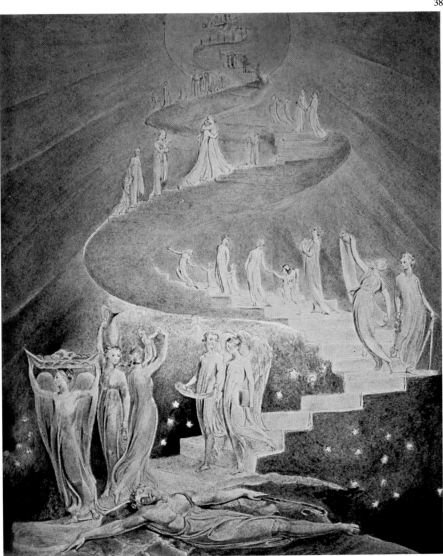

37

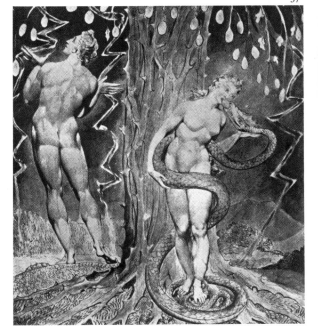

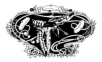

Other artists who influenced the Pre-Raphaelites and, later, Symbolism and Art Nouveau, were the Swiss JOHANN FÜSSLI (1741-1825) and the German CASPAR DAVID FRIEDRICH (1774-1840). Füssli, who later changed his name to Fuseli, spent the greater part of his career in England. He was a friend of Blake. He belonged to the Romantic tradition but his work has strong symbolic and psychologi-

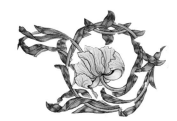

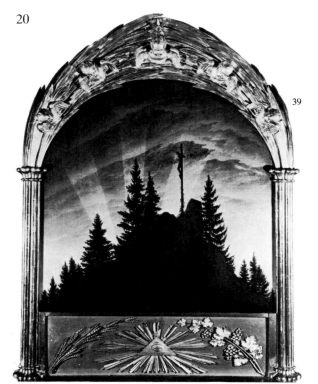

cal content. Many of his paintings contain either ethereal or dreaming figures, and their titles refer to dreams. His most famous painting, *The Nightmare*, is quite literally a haunted image. Friedrich's beautiful, melancholic paintings are meditations on the mysterious, unfathomable immensity of the universe. In his contemplation of infinity and eternity, natural elements in the landscape are used as religious allegories. Finally, the work of JEAN-AUGUSTE-DOMINIQUE INGRES, with its sensuous attention to detail and perfection of colour may also have been influential for the Pre-Raphaelites.

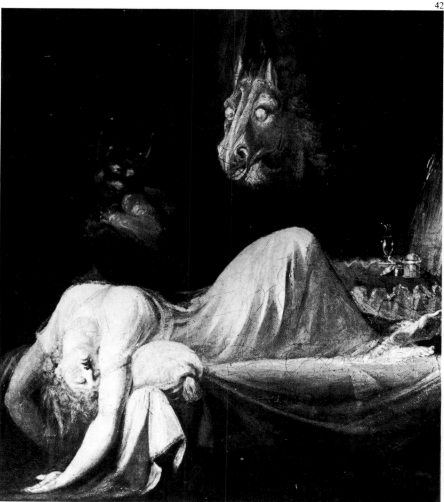

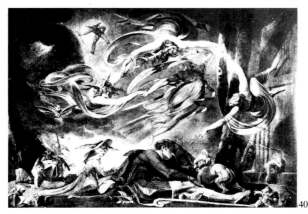

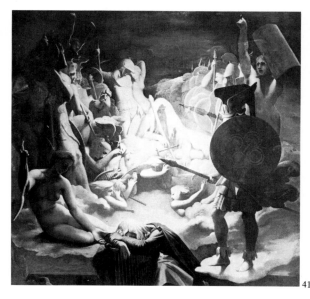

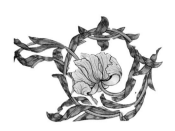

43

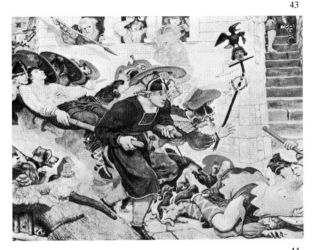

44

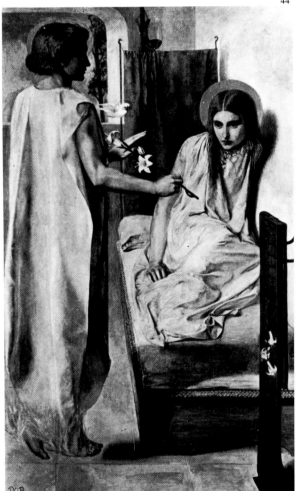

Blake never received any official recognition in his lifetime, and after his death he was completely forgotten for twenty years. However, in 1847, DANTE GABRIEL ROSSETTI (1828-82), who was interested in his work, bought a notebook of watercolours, sketches, notes and poems. This later came to be known as the *Rossetti Manuscript*. The notebook supported some of his artistic inclinations and it was one of the principal sources of inspiration for the Pre-Raphaelite Brotherhood, which was founded by Rossetti, together with two other young students at the Royal Academy Schools, William Holman Hunt (1827-1910) and John Everett Millais (1829-96), in 1848.

In 1849, Rossetti completed his first major painting, *The Girlhood of Mary*. The group received abusive criticism from the public at the Royal Academy exhibition of 1851, but they gained the support of the influential art critic JOHN RUSKIN (1819-1900).

Blake was not the only artist who aimed for a similar aesthetic to the Pre-Raphaelites. The ideals of the German Nazarenes, which were introduced into England by William Dyce (1806-64), were also influential with them. The Pre-Raphaelite Brotherhood has also been likened to the Salon de la Croix Rose, founded in 1892 by Sâr Péladan as an alternative and in opposition to the official Paris Salon. Although these groups are unrelated they shared an aversion to academic art, and both groups drew on religious or medieval legend for subject matter.

The Pre-Raphaelites, as their name implies, were inspired by the art which preceded Raphael. They rejected the academic tradition which had taken the perfection of the art of Raphael and his followers as the model to which all art should aspire. Instead they turned towards the pre-High Renaissance and medieval painting of Italy and Northern Europe. Their painting is characterized by a bright, overall luminosity of colour, sharply defined outlines and meticulous attention to detail. In order to achieve the brilliance of colour so characteristic of their work, they used an unusual technique – they painted on a pure white ground. Authenticity of detail was captured by working from life. Millais' *Ophelia* (1851-52) is a good example of how their painting could transcend the realism of its execution and create a world of evocative, hallucinatory beauty.

While Pre-Raphaelite subject matter in the early 1850s largely revolved around the fantasy world of medieval legend, inspired by Malory's *Morte d'Arthur* and the thirteenth-century Italian poet Dante (Blake had illustrated his *Divine Comedy*, and Rossetti had been named after him), pagan mythology later became a major source of inspiration. In contrast to the ethereal quality of these paintings, they developed other themes taken from modern life which dealt with contemporary social or moral problems. Although most of the Pre-Raphaelites produced paintings on these themes, Ford Madox Brown painted them most consistently.

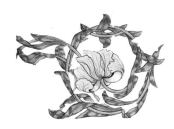

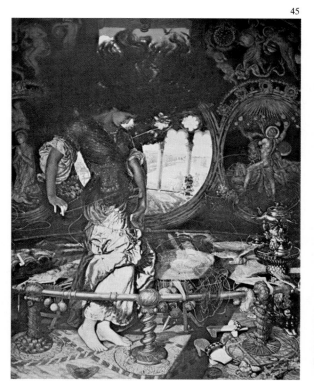

45

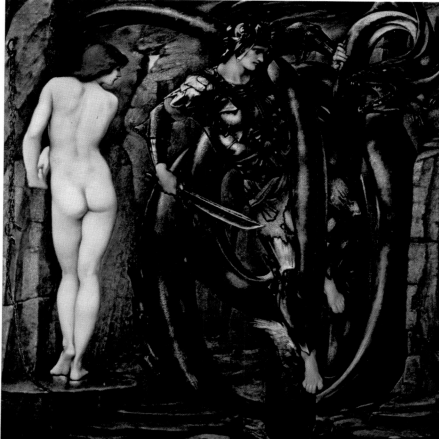

47

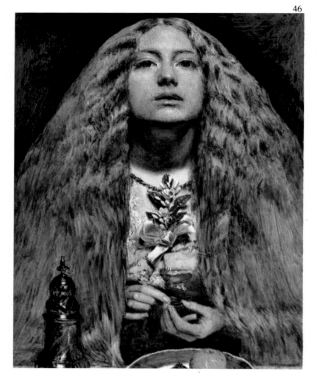

46

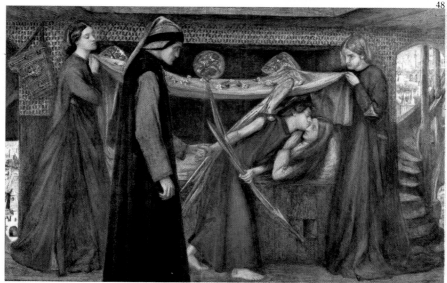

48

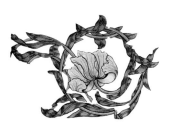

49

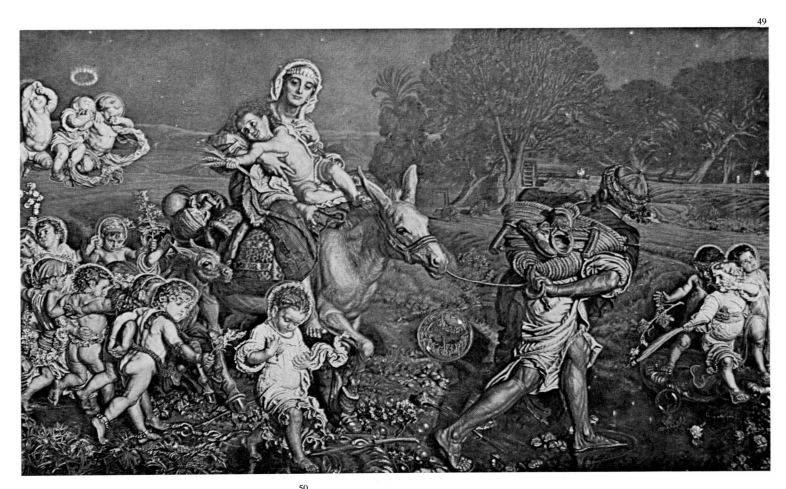

50

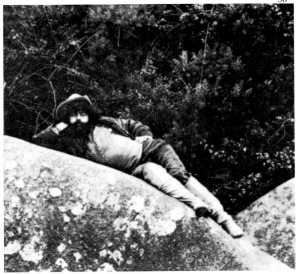

WILLIAM HOLMAN HUNT (1827-1910) is arguably the most representative of all the Pre-Raphaelites and he remained faithful, throughout his long career, to the technical precepts of early Pre-Raphaelitism. His departure for the Holy Land early in 1854 in order to paint biblical scenes in accurate settings, effectively marked the end of the Brotherhood.

Arguably the most gifted member of the group was JOHN EVERETT MILLAIS (1829-96), who later sold out to success and began producing works of cloying sentimentality to satisfy the demand for his work. At his best his paintings, which are essentially naturalistic and which evoke a contemplative lyrical and romantic atmosphere, are masterpieces of Pre-Raphaelitism.

When the Brotherhood were disbanding, Rossetti met two young students at Exeter College, Oxford: EDWARD BURNE-JONES (1833-98) and WILLIAM MORRIS (1834-96). Both were studying to enter the Anglican Church, but they were becoming increasingly aware that their real vocations lay elsewhere. During an art and architecture tour

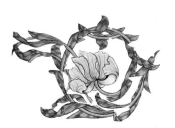

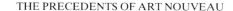

51

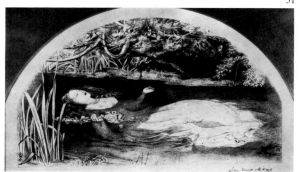

52

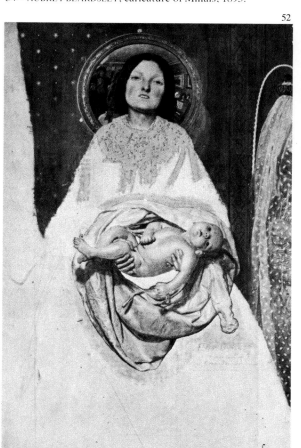

of France in the summer of 1855 (where, incidentally, they saw Pre-Raphaelite paintings in the Exposition Universelle in Paris), they decided to renounce the Church and devote their lives entirely to art.

Largely self-taught as a painter, Burne-Jones's early work is clearly influenced by Rossetti, both in subject matter and in execution. Like Rossetti he drew on Malory's *Morte d'Arthur* as a major source of

53

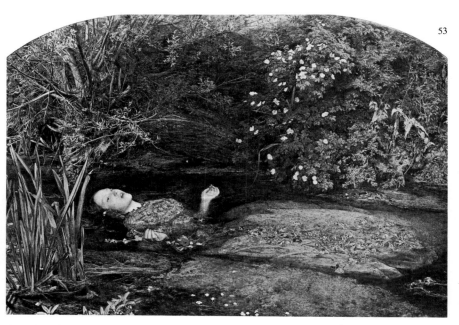

inspiration. Two visits to Italy, where he saw the art of Botticelli, Mantegna and Michelangelo, helped to develop the monumental and purely aesthetic style of his mature work. The subtle eroticism of his remote and ethereal figures, his delicate sensuous lines, which were admired by the Symbolists, provided a formative influence on the art of Aubrey Beardsley.

The friendship between Rossetti, Burne-Jones and William Morris underlies the influence of the Pre-Raphaelites on the decorative arts in what is now called the Arts and Craft Movement. After leaving Oxford, Morris studied briefly to become an architect and he also tried his hand as a painter. Realizing that he had no talent in either of these fields, he turned his attention to the arts of design, an area where his influence was crucial to the development of the Art Nouveau style over the next thirty years.

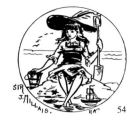

54

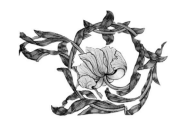

55

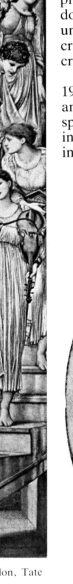

Morris was a socialist. His ideas on art, its function and diffusion in society were derived from Ruskin and Karl Marx. He believed that the industrial mass-production of goods was creating 'tons and tons of unutterable rubbish'. He saw art and design as part of everyday life, and he thought that the artist-craftsman should be a responsible participant in society, rather than isolated from it. He felt that the true designer could only learn the nature of his materials through the practice of the crafts. He learnt and mastered the technique of half a dozen crafts, including printing, joinery and glass blowing, in order to understand the qualities of his materials. For him the pleasure of creation was just as important as the beauty of the object. The craftsman's joy in making an object would in turn be felt by its owner.

Morris married in 1859 and he commissioned Philip Webb (1831-1915), whom he had met when he was studying architecture, to design and build him a house, the Red House at Upton. It was medieval in spirit and it was described by Burne-Jones as 'the beautifullest house in the world'. It contained furniture designed by Webb and the interior decoration was completed by objects designed by Morris's

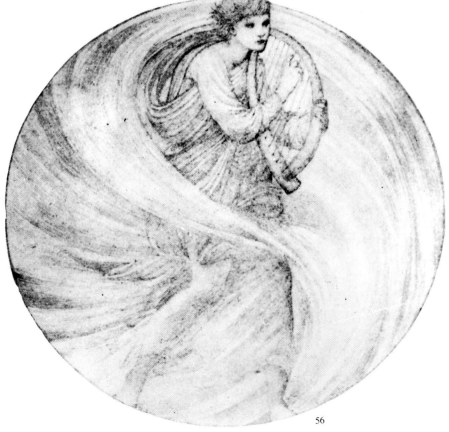

55—E. BURNE-JONES, *The Golden Stair*, 1880. London, Tate Gallery.
56—E. BURNE-JONES, *Orpheus*, 1875 (one of four designs on the theme of Orpheus and Eurydice). Oxford, Ashmolean Museum.

56

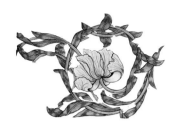

friends. The outcome of the collaboration on the interior design of the house was the foundation of the firm Morris, Marshall, Faulkner and Company. They described themselves as 'Fine Art Workmen in Painting, Carving Furniture and Metals'. Designs for the firm were produced by Webb, Madox Brown, Rossetti and Burne-Jones, along with many others. Morris bought out Marshall, Madox Brown and Rossetti in the mid 1870s and transferred his workshop in 1881 to Merton Abbey, where he founded the Kelmscott Press in 1890. The

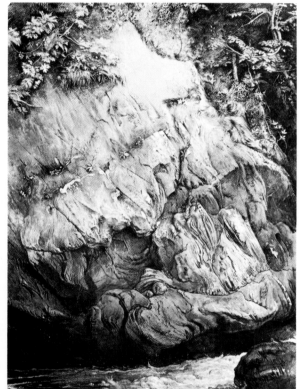

58

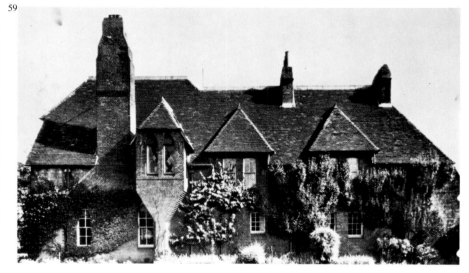

59

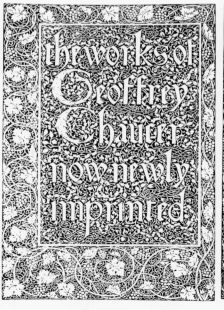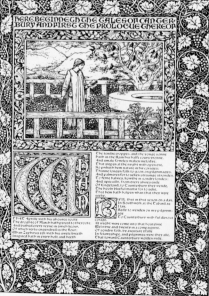

60

57—Trademark of the Morris Co., c. 1861.
58—JOHN RUSKIN, *The Rock of Gneiss at Glenfinlas*, 1853. Oxford, Ashmolean Museum.
59—PHILIP WEBB, The Red House, Bexley Heath, 1859.
60—E. BURNE-JONES. W. MORRIS, two pages from *The Works of Geoffrey Chaucer*, 1896.
61—WILLIAM MORRIS, wallpaper.
62—W. MORRIS, *The Evenlode*, furnishing chintz.
63—W. MORRIS, a blanket embroidered in silk, 1877.
64—JAMES MCNEILL WHISTLER, *Butterfly* (Whistler's signature), 1890.
65—J. MCNEILL WHISTLER, *Symphony in White n.4: The Three Maidens*, 1876-79. Washington, Smithsonian Institution.
66—J. MCNEILL WHISTLER, *Nocturne in Blue and Gold: the Old Battersea Bridge*, c. 1872-75.
67—J. MCNEILL WHISTLER, *Variations in Blue and Green*, c. 1868-69. London, Tate Gallery.

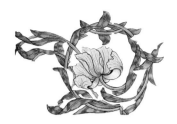

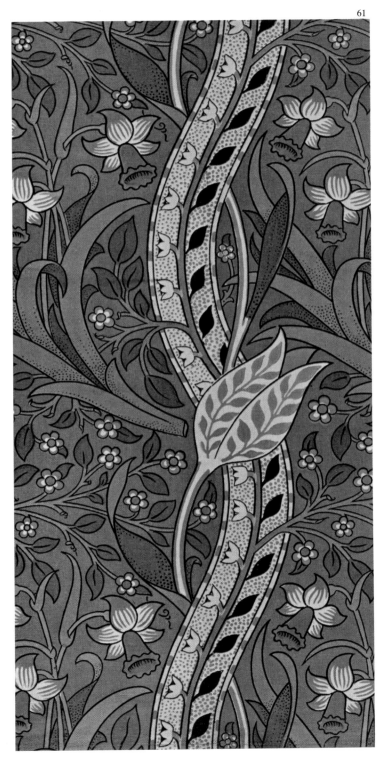

61

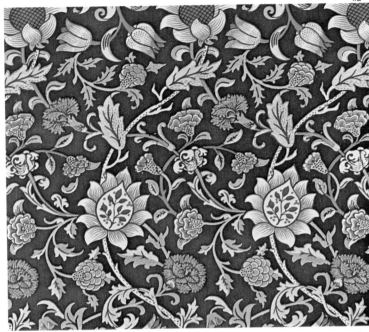

62

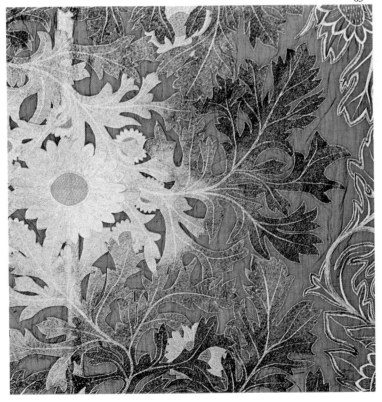

63

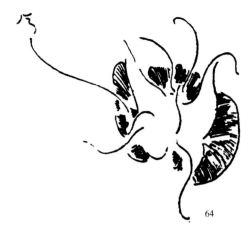

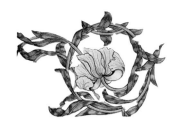

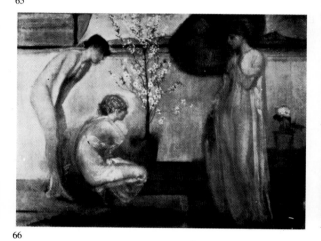

64

65

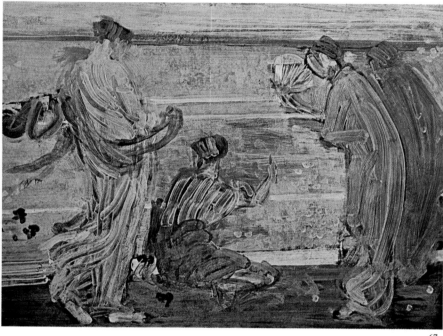

66

67

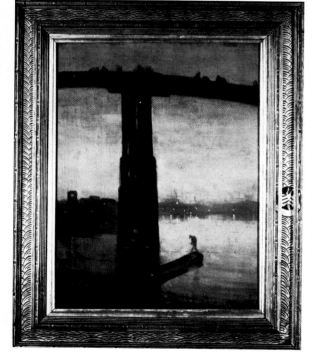

most magnificent book produced by the press is *The Works of Geoffrey Chaucer*; it has over 600 woodcut illustrations by Burne-Jones, Walter Crane and Arthur Gaskin and border designs by Morris himself. It took over five years to produce and was only completed a few months before Morris's death in 1896.

The International Exhibition in London in 1862 is something of a landmark. It introduced a wide audience to new elements which would shape artistic development in the second half of the nineteenth century. Firstly, there was the first public showing of the furniture, embroideries and stained glass which were inspired by the art of the Middle Ages and made by the newly formed Morris Company. These objects were highly acclaimed. Secondly, and perhaps more importantly, the first major exhibition of Japanese art in Europe was shown there. The impact of Japanese art on painting and the decorative arts was so profound and widespread that elements taken from it are often so fully integrated into the work that the source is indistinguishable.

After the exhibition, some of the Japanese *objets d'art* were sold off by Farmers and Rogers of Regent Street, a store managed by Arthur Lazenby Liberty. He founded his own store, Liberty and Co., in 1875, and he became the leading retailer in oriental goods of the best

68—A. BEARDSLEY, caricature of James McNeill Whistler (alluding to *L'Après-midi d'un faune* by Mallarmé).

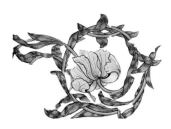

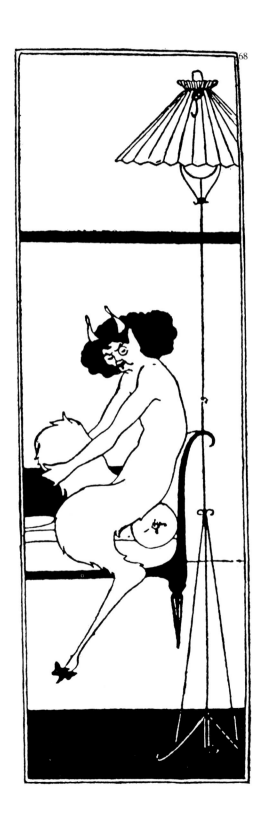

68

quality, as well as an important promoter of English Art Nouveau. He commissioned exclusive designs from Walter Crane, Jessie M. King, Charles Voysey and, above all, Archibald Knox.

A passionate collector of Japanese art, JAMES ABBOT McNEILL WHISTLER (1834-1903) was, not surprisingly, one of its most zealous advocates in London. He was possibly the first major artist whose style was directly influenced by it. American by birth, he had studied in Paris where he had good friends in the Impressionist circle. Having seen prints by Utamaro and Hokusai in Paris, he imported his

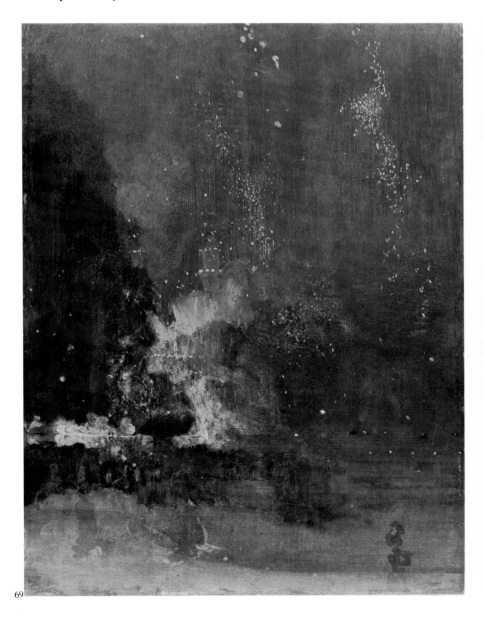

69

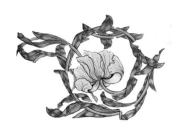

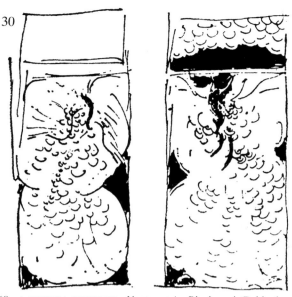

69—J. MCNEILL WHISTLER, *Nocturne in Black and Gold: the Fallen Race*, c. 1874.
70—J. MCNEILL WHISTLER, sketches for the decoration of the Peacock Room, 1876. Glasgow University Collection.

enthusiasm to London when he returned to live there in the late 1850s.

The White House, built for him by Godwin in Chelsea, was decorated according to Japanese taste, with only a few carefully hung pictures on white or yellow walls, and the furniture was arranged asymmetrically. Japanese mats, oriental white and blue china, and yellow table napkins embroidered with the Japanese-style butterfly monogram which Whistler used to sign his paintings completed the effect. His early paintings inspired by Japan, such as *Pink and Silver: the Princess from the Land of Porcelain* (1864), reproduced figures dressed in kimonos and other Japanese objects. Later he abandoned this practice and began to apply the principles of composition and structure taken from Japanese art to his own work (japonism).

71

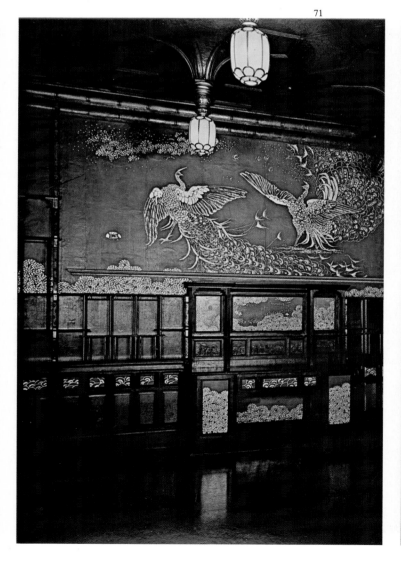

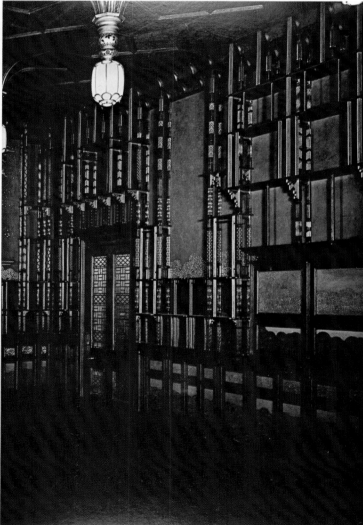

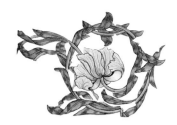

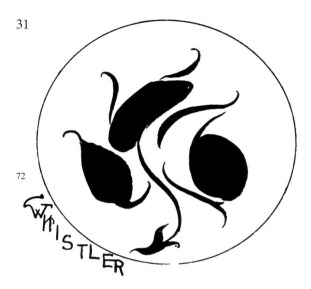

72

71—J. MCNEILL WHISTLER, The Peacock Room, 1876. Washington, Smithsonian Institution.
72—A. BEARDSLEY, caricature of Whistler's signature.
 *—J. MCNEILL WHISTLER, ornamental inset from *The Gentle Art of Making Enemies*, 1890.

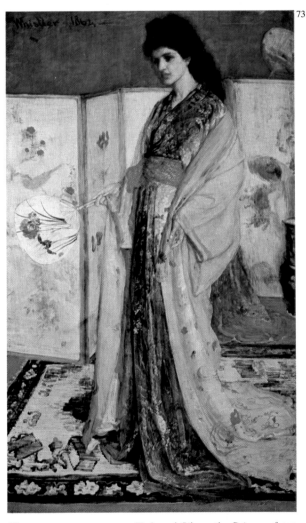

73

73—J. MCNEILL WHISTLER, *Pink and Silver: the Princess from the Land of Porcelain*, 1864.

Whistler, a wit and a dandy, has been proclaimed, with Oscar Wilde, as one of the heroes of Aestheticism. His role in the history of art as the artist who linked Japan with the Aesthetic Movement and Art Nouveau, is outstandingly more important than his own artistic production. His celebrated libel case against John Ruskin illustrates his fundamental break with Pre-Raphaelitism. Ruskin, the champion of the Pre-Raphaelites, thought that *Nocturne in Black and Gold: the Falling Rocket* (1874) lacked realism. He described it as 'a pot of paint flung in the public's face'. Whistler argued that his painting was 'an arrangement of line, form and colour'; it was purely aesthetic – a visual, decorative object devoid of narrative content.

This line of thinking is reflected in the musical titles and subtitles (harmonies, symphonies, variations) which he gave his paintings from about 1872. Similarly, his search for a complete visual harmony led him, like Rossetti, to design his own picture frames. In the design of frames Whistler far surpassed Rossetti. In *Nocturne in Blue and Gold: Old Battersea Bridge* (1872-75), the frame is decorated with a simple Japanese pattern in the dominant colours of the painting, and it is signed with his monogram on the right side of the frame.

Whistler's famous *Peacock Room* brings the search for decorative unity to its logical conclusion. Here the whole interior has been conceived as an extended picture frame. In 1876, Frederick Leyland commissioned from Thomas Jeckyll a design for the decoration of his dining room which would accommodate his porcelain collection and Whistler's painting, *The Princess from the Land of Porcelain*. Whistler felt that the colour of the flowers which were embossed on the expensive Russian leather panels clashed with his painting. He got permission to paint over them. In Leyland's absence he carried on painting until the whole room was decorated with blue and gold peacocks. When he realized that the colours on the border of the Persian rug did not harmonize with the overall scheme, he cut off the border.

In many ways, largely as a result of the original architectural work of Jeckyll, the *Peacock Room* now seems over-elaborate and claustrophobic. But the peacock motif became a major source of inspiration to Aubrey Beardsley. It was, together with the lily, the swan and maidens with long trailing hair, one of the principal motifs of Art Nouveau. Whistler was an intellectual élitist whose artistic theories excluded the social concerns of the Arts and Crafts Movement. This movement, however, did share his interest in oriental art.

One designer, Dr CHRISTOPHER DRESSER (1834-1904), took the unusual step of visiting Japan in 1875. This resulted in his book, *Japan: Its Architecture, Art and Art Manufactures* (1882). His artistic

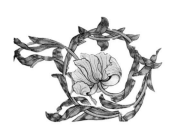

theories, developed in numerous books on ornamentation and design, were derived from his botanical studies. Dresser wanted to develop geometric and abstract qualities of design from natural forms, rather than return to historical styles for inspiration. His *Force and Energy* (c. 1870), while Gothic in feeling, is based on his idea that the inherent dynamic power of growth in organic matter should be evoked in a design. Frost patterns on a window pane inspired his design for a stained glass window (1873). Similar ideas had been developed by OWEN JONES (1809-74) in his *Grammar of Ornament* (1856). This manual was widely used by architects and designers (including Morris), and it was the basic textbook in the Schools of Design.

The ideas of Ruskin and Morris found their expression in the Arts and Crafts Movement through designers like ARTHUR HEYGATE MACKMURDO (1851-1942), WALTER CRANE (1845-1915) and CHARLES ASHBEE (1863-1942), and the organizations they were involved in founding. Ruskin's short-lived Guild of St George (1871) provided the model for Mackmurdo's Century Guild (1882-88) and the Art Workers' Guild, founded in 1884. The Arts and Crafts Exhibition Society was an offshoot of the Art Workers' Guild, formed to promote the craft and craft philosophy through a series of exhibitions. An exhibition was held annually for the first three years of its existence, but when it was noticed that the quality of the exhibits

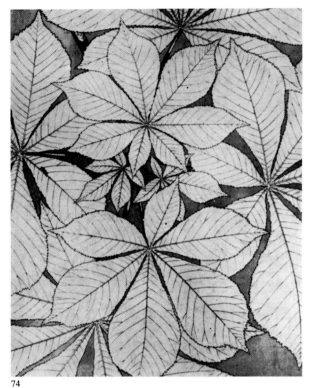

74

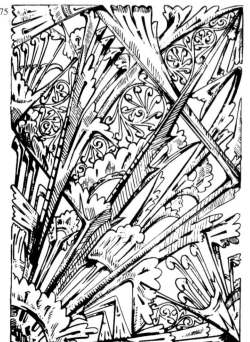

75

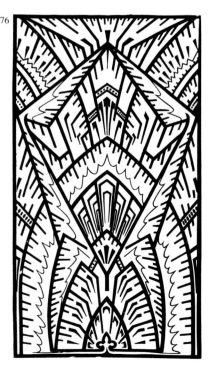

76

74—OWEN JONES, horse-chestnut leaf, c. 1895.
75—CHRISTOPHER DRESSER, *Force and Energy*, c. 1870.
76—C. DRESSER, design for stained-glass window, c. 1873.

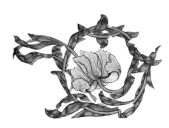

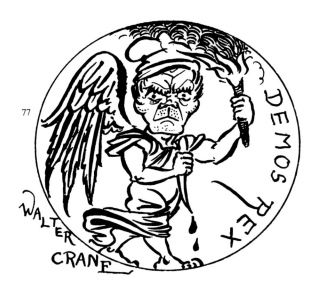

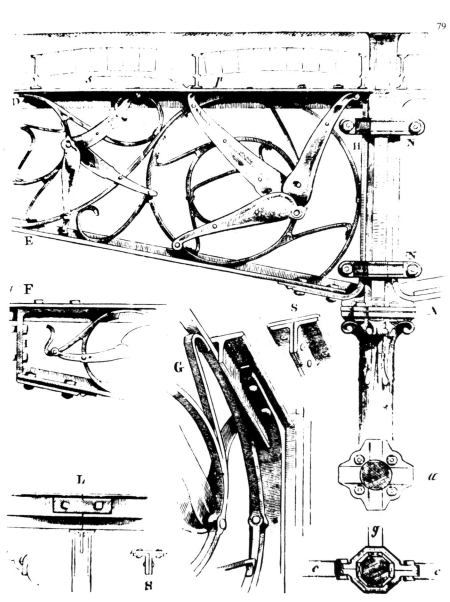

77—A. BEARDSLEY, caricature of Walter Crane, alluding to his socialist ideas, c. 1893.

78—EUGÈNE EMMANUEL VIOLLET-LE-DUC, design for wrought iron.

79—E. E. VIOLLET-LE-DUC, a page in *Entretiens sur l'Architecture*, 1872.

*—WALTER CRANE, ornamental inset.

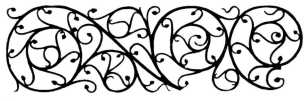

was declining, a triennial system was adopted. The exhibitions continued until the First World War.

In France, VIOLLET-LE-DUC (1814-79), architect, scholar and controversial restorer of medieval cathedrals and monuments, is the principal figure linking the Gothic Revival with Art Nouveau. He

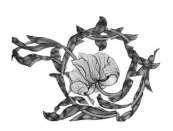

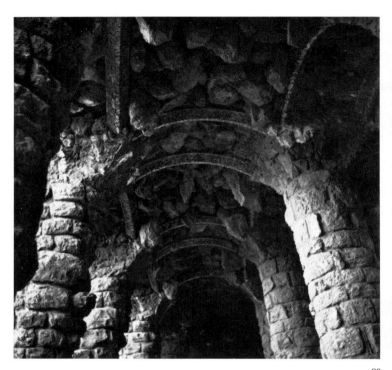

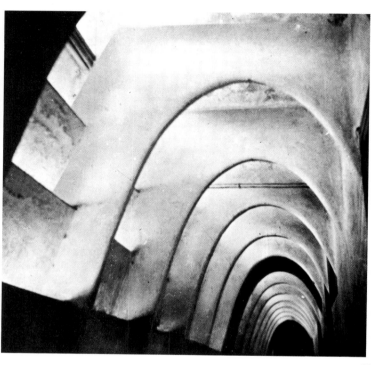

80

81

80—ANTONI GAUDÍ, Guëll Parco, Barcelona (detail).
81—A. GAUDÍ, Casa Battló, Barcelona (detail).

pioneered the undisguised use of iron in building. He evolved a style of ornament which was consistent with the material and the structural demands of buildings. Viollet-Le-Duc's writings and architecture were a point of departure for architects of international renown like Hector Guimard in France, Victor Horta in Belgium and Antoni Gaudí in Spain, all of whom were well acquainted with his *Entretiens sur l'Architecture* (1863, 1872).

The relationship between Britain and the Continent is complex. Although the Art Nouveau style emerged first in England, its influence on architecture was not very pronounced, and it never reached the level of adventurousness, or exotic exuberance, of other countries. The reserve and discretion of traditional Englishness is reflected in its coolness and restraint. Indeed, Walter Crane disassociated himself from 'this strange decorative disease known as l'Art Nouveau'.

Not surprisingly, Art Nouveau was developed first on the Continent in Belgium and France, and in crossing the Channel the English heritage was transformed. While some Art Nouveau designers, such as Henry van de Velde, shared Morris's socialist ideals, they did not share his distaste for industrial production. Indeed, they wanted to make beautiful objects which could be produced relatively inexpensively by industry. The majority of artists on the Continent were, however, in pursuit of individualism and the notion of 'Art for art's sake', which could only enrich the lives of the fashionable and wealthy

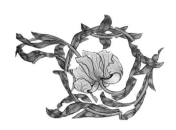

who could afford their objects even if they failed to understand them.

The Symbolist movement in painting, which is related to but distinct from Art Nouveau, similarly addressed itself to a sophisticated intellectual élite, who believed that little artistic merit could be ascribed to a painting if it could readily be appreciated by the public at large. The Art Nouveau artists, whether designing for industry or creating unique objects, all shared the belief that the traditional barriers between 'fine' and 'applied' art should be broken down, and that this could only be achieved by a synthesis of the arts.

In part this was a reaction to the fact that, in the nineteenth century, painting and the decorative arts had little in common. Training in the fine and decorative arts was, unlike in former times, completely separate. The development of the position of the dealer who had become responsible for the diffusion of art, created a situation where the former close relationship between the patron and the artist had broken down. The artist was in isolation. Except for portraits he no longer had any idea of the location where his work of art would be displayed. These artists felt that if they were to regain their position in society they had to take a revolutionary position in their art.

So, the search to impose overall unity and harmony on all the elements of interior decoration and architecture led to the appearance of the 'universal' artists, who were at home working in several different fields, and who characterize the Art Nouveau period. However, in their attempt to create a new art, a style which could regain classic status, and which genuinely belonged to late nineteenth-century society, artists in every major European capital inevitably responded to the problem in terms of their own personality and particular cultural traditions.

Two basic tendencies emerge from the bewildering range of styles which fall into the category of Art Nouveau style. The first shows a rectilinear, tightly composed interplay of straight horizontal and vertical lines, while the second is based on the organic dynamism of curvilinear form. In whatever manner the style manifested itself, essentially Art Nouveau is a reflection of artists' attempts to render the objects of everyday life beautiful.

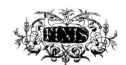

2-The Characteristics of Art Nouveau

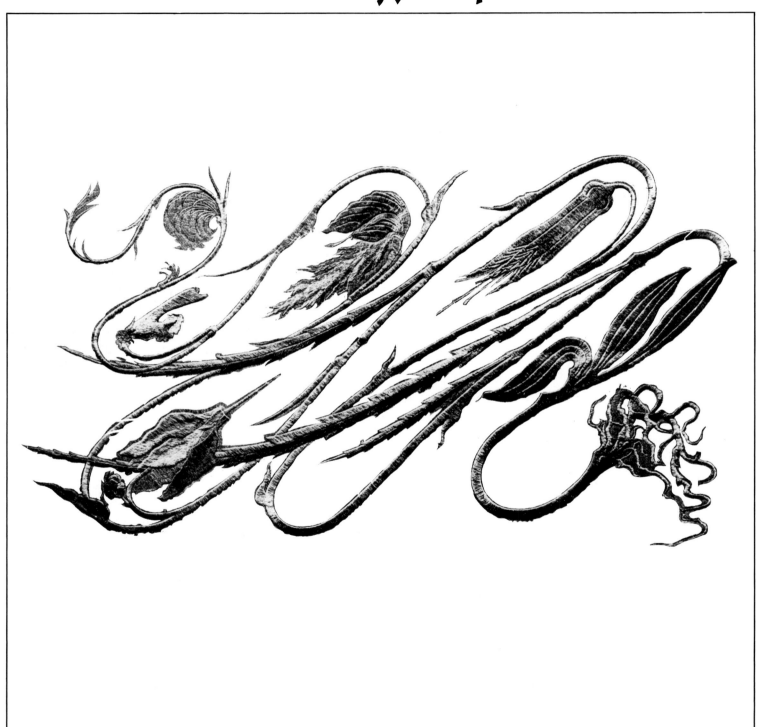

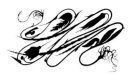

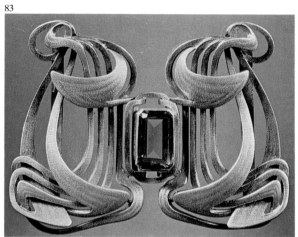

The range of ways in which Art Nouveau manifested itself is almost as diverse as the number of individual personalities involved. It is difficult, if not impossible, to formulate a simple definition of the style. However, some of the underlying characteristics may be discovered if one considers the problems that both painters and decorative artists faced and the kind of solutions they proposed.

82—and symbol of Chapter 2, pp. 36-53 – HERMANN OBRIST, *The Cyclamen* (*The Whiplash*), 1895 (wall hanging, silk embroidery). Munich, Staatsmuseum.
83—HENRY VAN DE VELDE, clasp in silver and amethyst, c. 1898.
84—LOUIS MAJORELLE, balustrade in wrought iron, c. 1900. Paris, Musée des Arts Décoratifs.

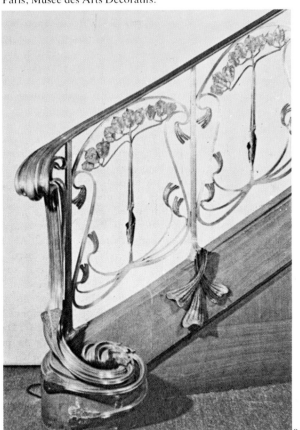

The Symbolist movement in painting was largely a reaction against the currents of realism and naturalism which had dominated art in the nineteenth century. Even the avant-garde Impressionists were part of this tradition.

Influenced by the Symbolist poets, who through the use of sound, rhythm and verbal imagery had tried to evoke emotional response and give shape to ideas, the Symbolist painters also wanted to go beyond realism and express in their work the mysterious and ambiguous realm of the imagination. Redon criticized the Impressionists for not having raised their sights high enough, and Gauguin, originally an Impressionist, quickly realized that they were trying to describe that which was 'round about the eye' rather than attempting to reach 'the mysterious centre of thought'.

Unfortunately, painters have to render visible things that poets only have to describe. They faced the problem of dealing with subject matter which comes from the imagination without resorting to the stock of traditional signs and symbols of academic mythology or allegory. Many artists continued to paint in a traditional realistic way rather than try to express their inner emotions on canvas.

Some groups of artists, like the Nabis, saw the problem of self-expression as essentially one of style. The Dutch Nabi, Jan Verkade (1868-1946), said that 'there are no paintings, only decoration'. And his fellow Nabi, Maurice Denis (1870-1943), wrote in 1890, 'a painting previously seen as the representation of an object, a war horse, a nude woman or an anecdote, is essentially a flat surface covered with colours arranged in a certain order'. For the Nabis, a painting was only successful when the artist had penetrated the external appearance of things and, using colour and contour, had transformed the objects in the painting, so that its decorative features became paramount and the artist's personality or style was expressed. While painting on canvas had been generally considered to be not *one* but

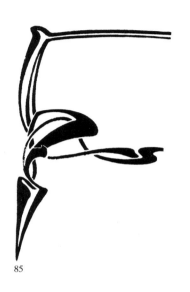

85

the *only* true art form, the Nabis considered it inferior to painting on panels which could then be inserted into a general decorative scheme incorporating objects from a wide range of media.

A similar act of conscious experimentation was taking place within the decorative arts. The Art Nouveau designers were trying to create a contemporary manner of expression avoiding the moribund plundering of historical styles. As a source of inspiration for ornamental design they turned to Nature.

The use of natural forms in decoration already had a long tradition in Western art, but they had largely been treated representationally. In Art Nouveau the approach was different. William Morris noted that the artist 'should not copy Nature, but recreate it, without losing its freshness'. The idea that fine art was not a mere first-hand copying of Nature, but an independent world of imaginative creation where Nature only supplied the raw material, was developed in the theories of Owen Jones, John Sedding, Selwyn Image and many others. Christopher Dresser in his *Modern Ornamentation* (1886) provided a geometric and psychological basis for the aesthetics of ornament of the Art Nouveau movement.

The evocative force and symbolic quality of line was used by Art Nouveau designers to convey rhythmic energy and organic growth.

86

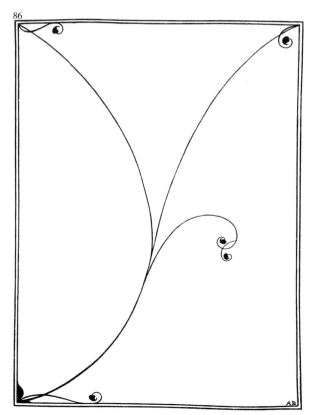

87

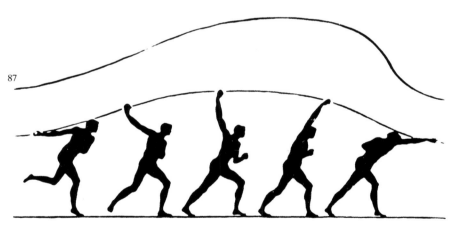

Line became delicate or aggressive, flowing, curving, undulating, rippling, dynamic. 'Line is a force which is active like all elemental forces', wrote Henry van de Velde. August Endell recognized the abstract implications of the new style, 'We stand at the threshold of an altogether new art, an art with forms which mean or represent nothing, recall nothing, yet which can stimulate our souls as deeply as the tones of music have been able to do.'

Once Nature had been reduced to essential lines, the artist could use them to design literally anything. Stems, leaves and petals could be twisted, elongated and curved according to the artist's requirements. The lily, iris, convolvulus and poppy were favourite plant

motifs, but sometimes they are abstracted or distorted so much that the original source of inspiration is no longer recognizable. The swan and the peacock were favourite birds, because of the sweeping curve of their bodies; while the *femme-fleur* with her long billowing hair could represent either idealized virginal beauty, or the exciting, emaciated, dark-eyed temptress who appears repeatedly in the work of Aubrey Beardsley, Jan Toorop, Georges de Feure, Gustave Klimt and the Glasgow Four .

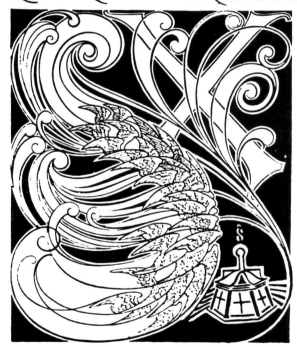

88

RICHARD · WALTER · ESSEX

HIS · BOOK

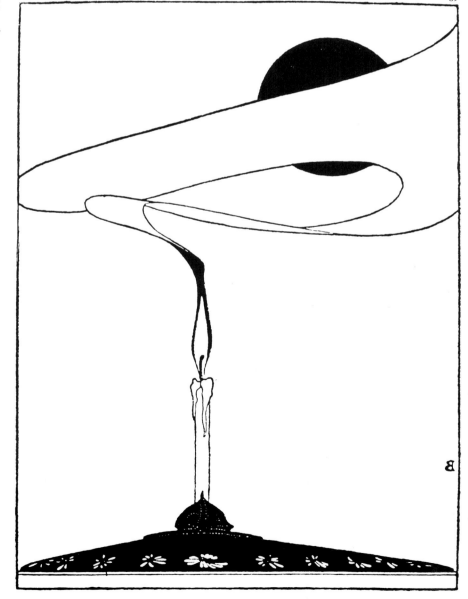

89

*—page 37, capital letter from *The Studio*.
85—H. VAN DE VELDE, margin design.
86—A. BEARDSLEY, design for the cover of a book of verses by Ernest Dowson, 1896.
87—WALTER CRANE, illustration from *Line and Form*, 1900.
88—CHARLES F. A. VOYSEY, cover of *His Book* by Walter Essex, c. 1896.
89—A. BEARDSLEY, design, 1894-95.

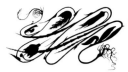

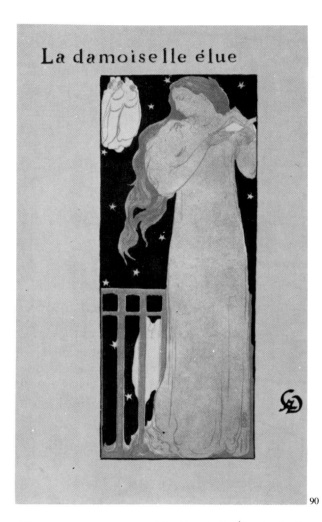

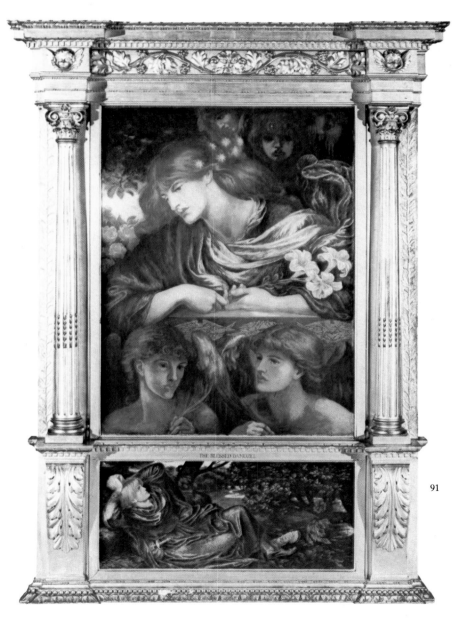

90—MAURICE DENIS, cover of *La Demoiselle Élue*, by D. G. Rossetti.
91—D. G. ROSSETTI, *The Blessed Damozel*, 1875-79. Port Sunlight, Lady Lever Art Gallery.

Since the Art Nouveau style is essentially two-dimensional, it was very well suited to the graphic arts, and especially book illustration and lithography, because both of these arts exploit line and flat areas of colour. Many of the Art Nouveau artists applied their style and talent to designing posters. Aubrey Beardsley shared the Nabis' distaste for easel painting – indeed, there is only one painting on canvas known to be by him. He limited his activity to book illustration and poster design. He developed similar theories to those of Walter

92—W. CRANE, linear interpretation of a ballerina's leap, illustration from *Line and Form*, 1900.
93—WILLIAM BRADLEY, design.
94—A. BEARDSLEY, *The Dreamer*.

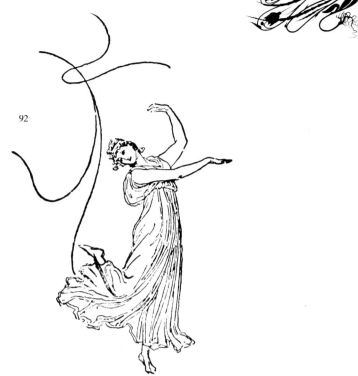

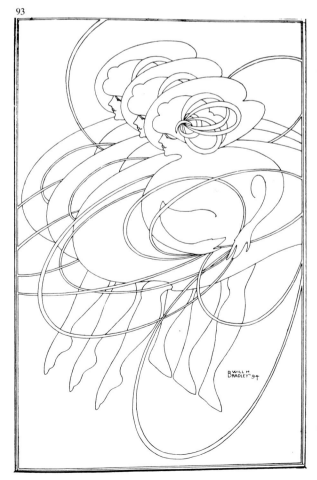

Crane on the importance of outline and expressed his genius almost entirely in black and white, in a medium where brushwork and modelling played no role in the process of reproduction. In his article 'The Art of the Hoarding', he attacked the idea of the supremacy of painting and suggested that the poster was a work of art which could 'take a part in everyday existence'. The artistic value of a poster (or of a book illustration for that matter) depended entirely on the quality of the design and not on the number of copies produced.

The imaginative and evocative subject matter of Symbolist paintings, the rhythmic tension in the Art Nouveau line, naturally led to

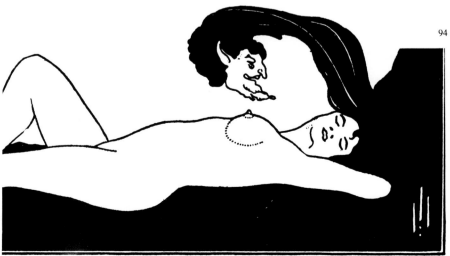

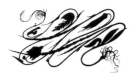

associations with music, the purest of art forms. In theoretical writing many artists spoke of the relationship between their art and music, while exhibition organizers consciously tried to demonstrate the connection. Erik Satie was specially commissioned to compose *Les Sonneries de la Rose + Croix* for the first of the Sâr Péladan's Salons, while Debussy's *La Demoiselle Elue*, inspired by Rossetti's poem and

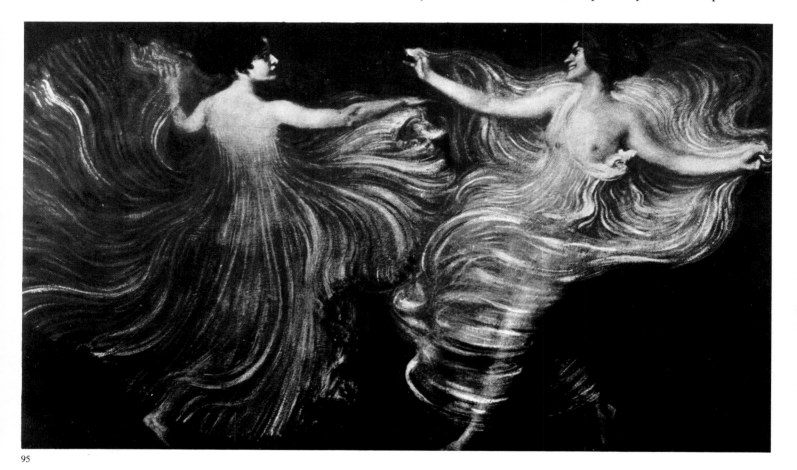

95

painting *The Blessed Damozel*, was played at the first exhibition of Le Livre Esthétique in Brussels in 1894.

Similarly, dance became one of the most recurrent motifs in Art Nouveau iconography, as diversely treated as in Beardsley's *Salomé* (1894) and Franz von Stuck's *Dancers* (1896). No dancer was as great a source of inspiration to so many artists or more frequently portrayed than the American dancer Loïe Fuller. Her performances in Paris at the Folies-Bergère were an immediate and spectacular success. Disappointingly, she was rather plain and plump in everyday life, but she underwent a transformation on stage. Wearing flowing diaphanous veils extended by hand-held batons, and dancing beneath a

95—FRANZ VON STUCK, *Dancers*, 1896. Schweinfurt, Private Collection.
96—A. BEARDSLEY, *The Belly Dancer*, illustration for *Salomé*, by Oscar Wilde. Shown at the International Exhibition, Paris, 1894.

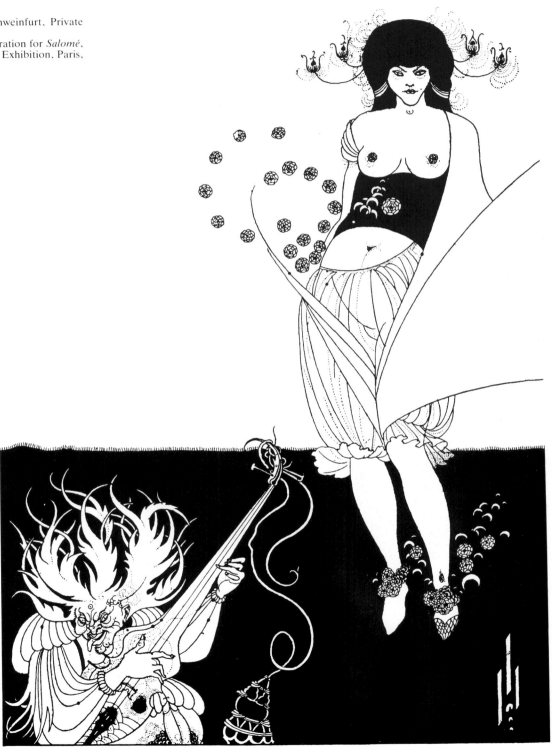

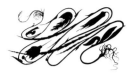

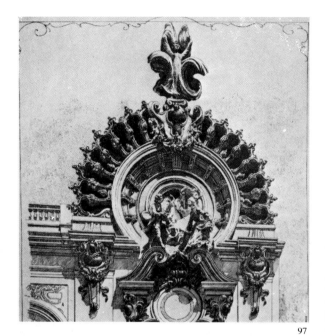

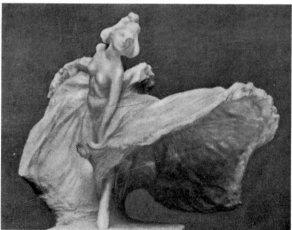

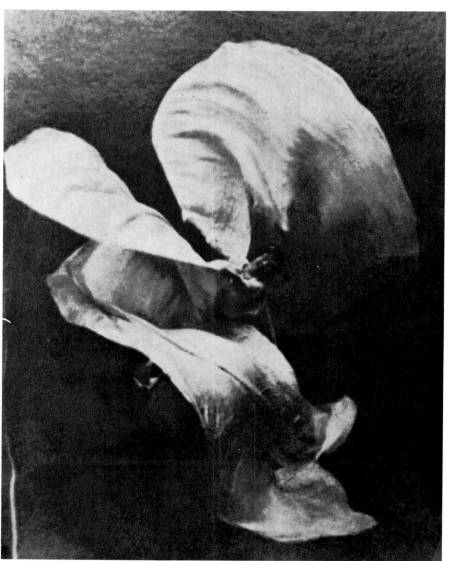

97—The Théâtre de la Danse with a statue of Loïe Fuller. Shown at the International Exhibition, Paris, 1900.
98—B. HOETZGER, *Loïe Fuller*, statuette.
99—Loïe Fuller.

flickering rainbow of constantly changing coloured electric lights, she was immortalized by such artists as William Bradley, Jules Chéret, Georges de Feure, Raoul Larche, Koloman Moser, Pierre Roche and Henri de Toulouse-Lautrec to name but a few. Isadora Duncan remembered her in her autobiography *My Life:* 'before our very eyes she turned to many coloured, shining orchids, to a wavering sea flower, and at length to a spiral-like lily, all the magic of Merlin, the sorcery of light, colour, flowing form . . . I was entranced . . . She transformed herself into a thousand colourful images before the eyes of her audience. Unbelievable. Not to be repeated or described.'

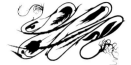

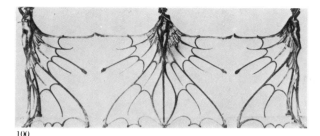

100

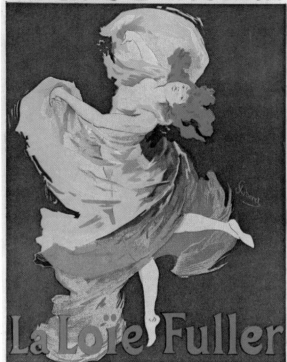

101

100—RENÉ LALIQUE, bronze parapet for the Loïe Fuller Theatre in Paris (destroyed), 1900.
101—JULES CHERET, *La Loïe Fuller, Folies Bergères*, poster, 1893. Paris, Bibliothéque des Arts Décoratifs.
102—HENRI DE TOULOUSE-LAUTREC. *Loïe Fuller*, I, 1893. New York, coll. Charell.
103—HENRI SAUVAGE, project for the Loïe Fuller Theatre in Paris.
104—K. MOSER, *Loïe Fuller*, poster. Vienna, Albertina.

103

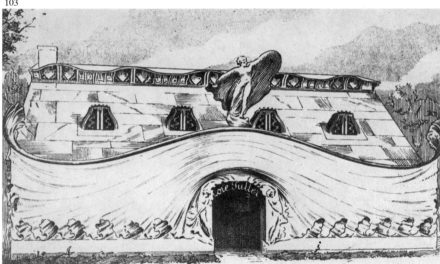

104

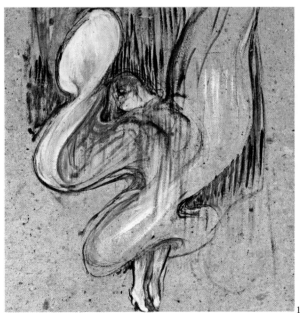

102

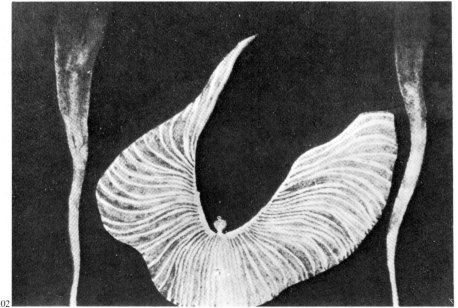

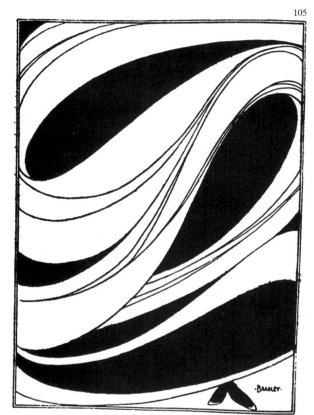

105

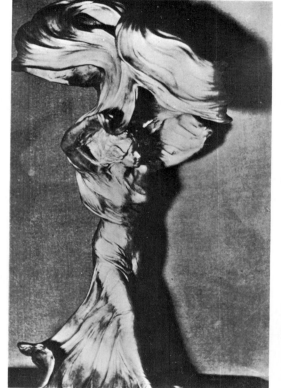

107

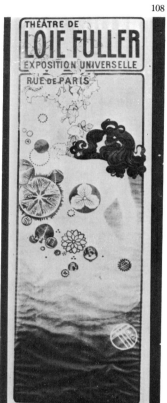

108

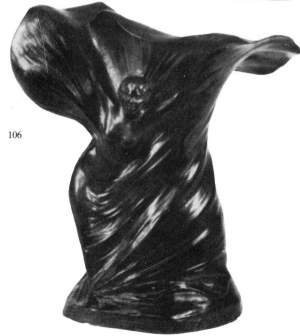

106

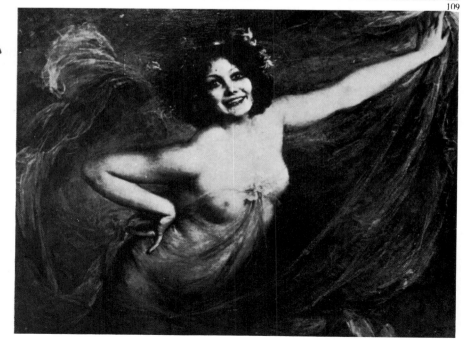

109

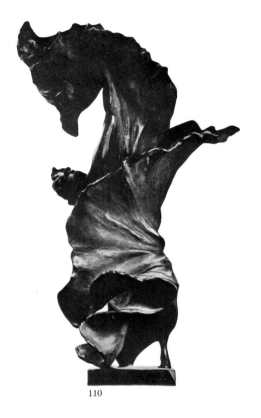

110

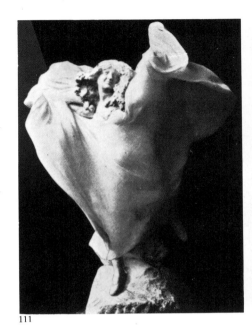

111

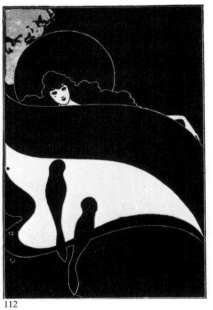

112

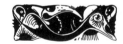

Faced with the daunting task of doing justice to the fleeting colour changes of the recently invented electric lights, some artists such as Chéret, de Feure and Orazi had their Loïe Fuller posters printed in different colour versions. Henri Sauvage presented a design for a theatre dedicated to her at the 1900 Exposition Universelle in Paris. The facade was decorated with flowing veils and her dancing figure surmounted the design. Her popularity with artists was probably due to the fact that the swirling draperies of her dance recalled the fluid arabesque line which Art Nouveau artists so loved.

The rhythmic, convoluted line pulsating with movement is the ultimate motif of the Art Nouveau style. It is most characteristically described by Hermann Obrist's large wall hanging *Cyclamen* (1895), nicknamed *Whiplash*. Here naturalistic detail is subordinated to line and an energetic S-shaped design of extraordinary strength is produced, which has the power of a prototype. The point of departure for this design is Arthur Mackmurdo's design for the title page of his book *Wren's City Churches* (1883), which in turn related to a design for a chair by him. These two designs come close to motifs present in the work of Blake, especially in *The Divine Image* (1789), as well as in furniture design (c. 1860) by Michael Thonet.

The motif later appeared in several disguises at different times and in many places, for example in Alfred Gilbert's Shaftesbury Memorial Fountain, commonly called the *Eros Fountain* (1887-93), in Victor Horta's Hôtel Solvay in Brussels (1895-1900), on the entrance gate of Antoni Gaudí's Güell Palace (1885-89), and in Louis Sullivan's ornament on the facade of the Carson Pirie Scott and Co. store in Chicago (1899-1904).

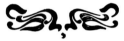

Art Nouveau is essentially a two-dimensional ornamental style which explores the possibilities of line and the forms which they describe, rather than perspective and depth. William Bradley's *The Serpentine Dancer* (1894-95) perfectly illustrates this quality in Art Nouveau. Here line and space are mutually defined and complemented by the use of black and white areas. The Art Nouveau style applied to architecture created the demand for the style to acquire body and substance and become three-dimensional. But many architects gave their details a flat and linear treatment, while expressing the forms cherished by Art Nouveau in their plans.

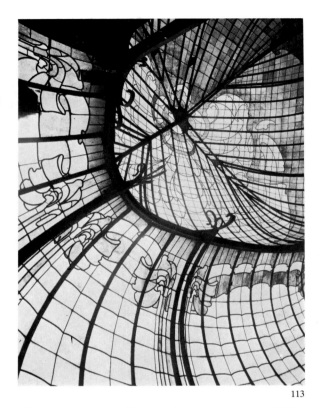

113

113—VICTOR HORTA, Hôtel Solvay, skylight, 1895-1900. Brussels.
114—A. GAUDÍ, Casa Milá, Barcelona.
 *—H. VAN DE VELDE, ornamental inset.

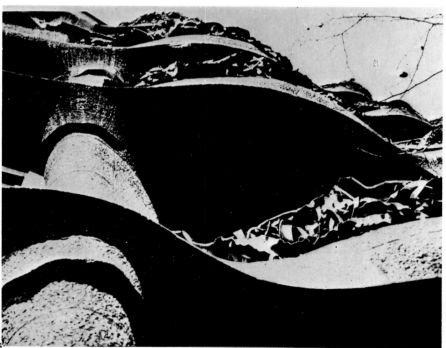

114

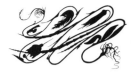

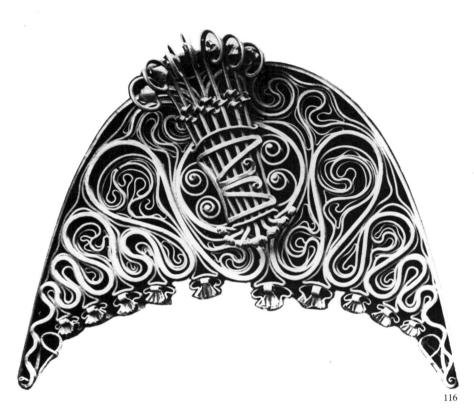

115—MICHAEL THONET, rocking chair in bentwood (beech), 1860. Frankfurt, coll. Helmut Goedeckemayer.
116—A. GAUDÍ, detail of the fanlight of the portal of the Guëll Palace, Barcelona, 1885-90.
 *—H. VAN DE VELDE, ornamental inset.

116

115

In Art Nouveau architecture the emphasis was on designing all the elements of an interior to produce a harmonious coherent unity, and the design process often began on the inside and then worked outwards. Clear distinctions between floors, walls and ceilings were minimalized by the unity of the design. The interior disposition of the rooms is often visible from the exterior and is reflected in the symmetrical arrangement of the facades. Structural elements are undisguised, although their decorative possibilities are exploited to gain the maximum effect.

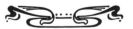

The intrinsic nature of the Art Nouveau movement as well as its role as the battleground of the avant-garde, contributed to its downfall. The aesthetic ideals of Art Nouveau were against standardization, which meant that each new commission, even of modest proportions, was considered unique and each element was designed from scratch. On a practical level, the design of a room in which all of the furniture and accessories from door handles to light fittings are co-

119—W. BLAKE, *The Divine Image*, in *Songs of Innocence*, 1789. London, British Museum.
120—ALFRED GILBERT, Shaftesbury Memorial Fountain, detail, 1887-93. London, Piccadilly Circus.
121—V. HORTA, Hôtel Solvay, 1894, Brussels.

117

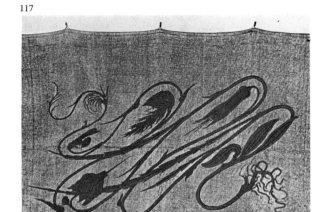

117—H. OBRIST, *The Cyclamen* (*The Whiplash*), 1895. See n.82.
118—C. RICKETTS, *Melancholy*, design for *The Sphinx*. London, private collection.

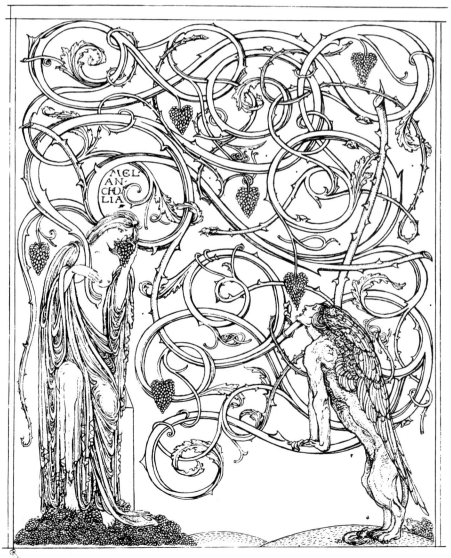

118

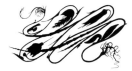

119

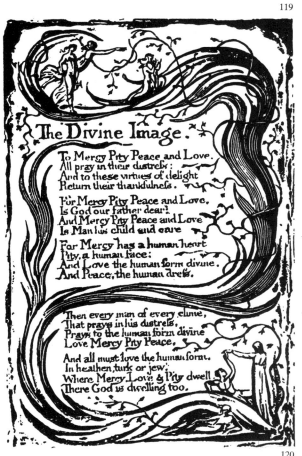

120

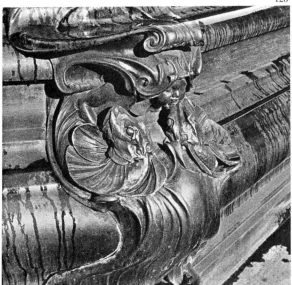

121

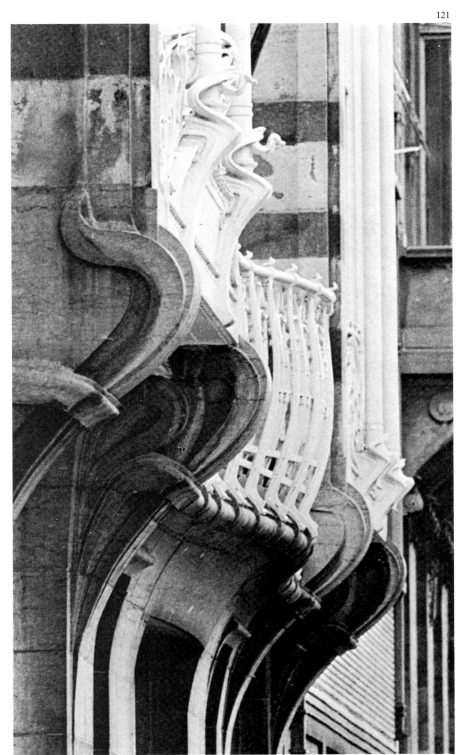

ordinated, demands an enormous amount of work from the architect, as well as large enonomic resources from the client. Many of the designers no doubt became tired of the impracticability of working under these constraints, as well as finding their powers of invention increasingly over-taxed.

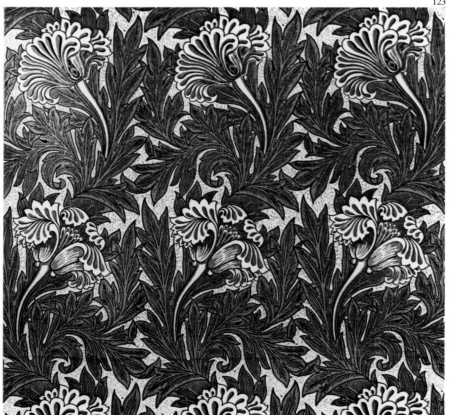

By 1900 most of the best Art Nouveau design had been produced, and the style had acquired a certain following from the fashionable élite. As it gained popularity it was commercially exploited and this was accompanied by a decline in quality and taste. The best designers lost interest and began to look for new means of expression. Meanwhile second-rate designers began to slap squiggles on to traditional (not specially designed) objects. Then the style began to founder under the weight of commercialism and its own excessive elaboration.

122—ARTHUR HEYGATE MACKMURDO, frontispiece for *Wren's City Churches*, 1883.

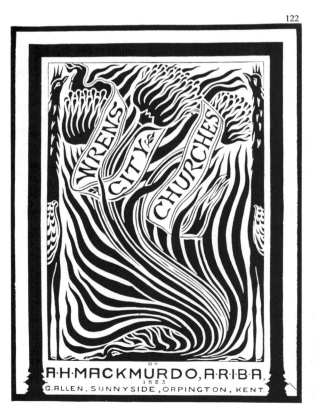

122

123—W. MORRIS, *Tulip*, furnishing fabric, 1875. London, Victoria and Albert Museum.

123

124

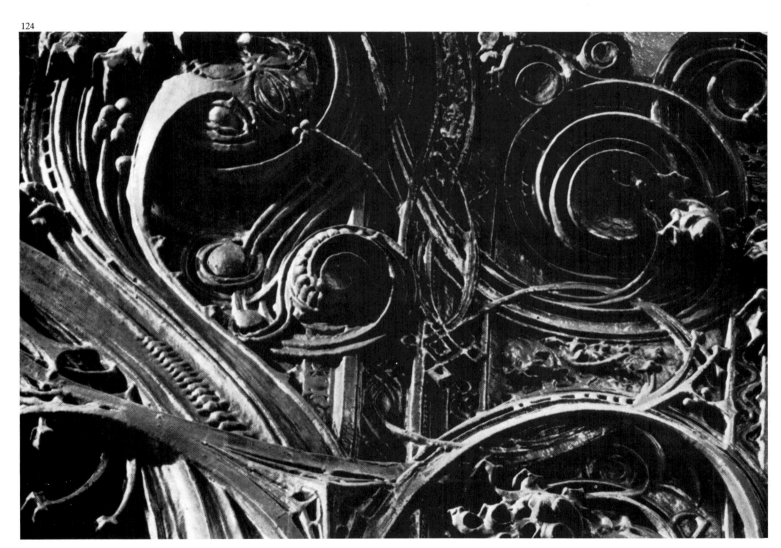

124—LOUIS SULLIVAN, Carson, Pirie, Scott & Co. store, Chicago, detail, 1899-1904.
*—H. VAN DE VELDE, ornamental inset.

The international character and wide diversity of Art Nouveau style means that it is difficult to plot the different lines of development and national variations on an annual basis. However, on stylistic considerations, the style can be broadly divided into 'early' and 'late' phases. Rather than provide such a chronology or treat each branch of the arts – poster and book illustration, glasswork, jewellery, textiles, furniture, architecture, etc. – in successive chapters, a country by country approach has been adopted in order to provide a comprehensive view of each nation's particular contribution.

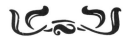

3-England

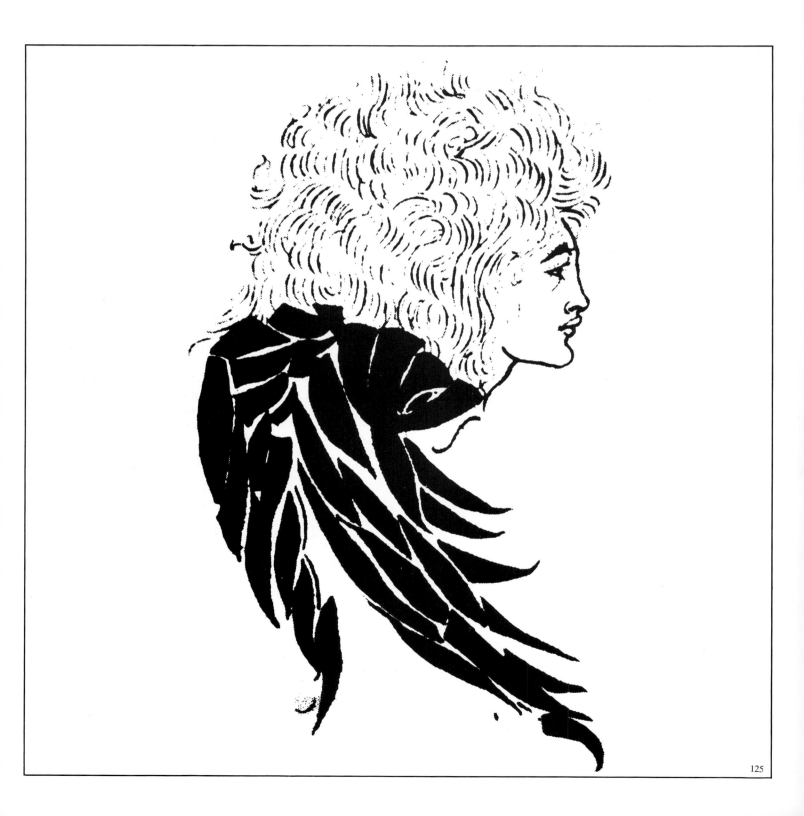

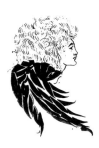

126

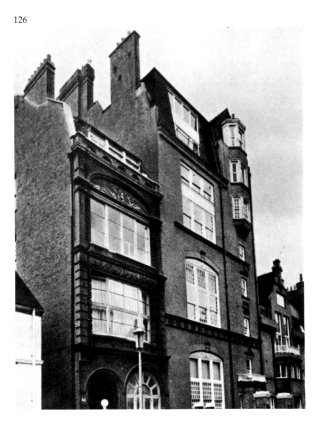

125—and symbol of Chapter 3, pp. 54-73 – A. BEARDSLEY, vignette in *Bon Mots* by Smith and Sheridan, 1893.
126—EDWARD WILLIAM GODWIN, The Tower House, 46 Tite Street, London, 1885.
127—E. W. GODWIN, Whistler's White House, London, 1879; elevation and section.
*—HORNE, ornamental inset from *The Hobby Horse*, 1890.

127

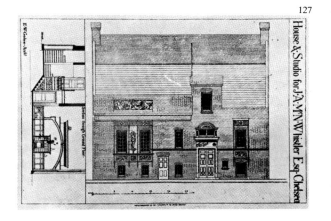

Although it received so much of its initial impetus from the Pre-Raphaelites and from the Arts and Crafts Movement, it is ironic that in England Art Nouveau was never as widespread, nor did it appear as revolutionary, as in other countries.

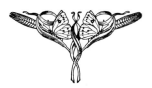

WALTER CRANE (1845-1915) was not alone in his condemnation of Art Nouveau. Indeed, the majority of the English designers whose work had provided the inspiration for later Continental developments shared his aversion and rejection of Continental Art Nouveau. The starting point for the English designers had been the aesthetics of Morris and the Arts and Crafts Movement, based on the 'honesty' and 'fitness' of Gothic architecture and the idea that good design sprang from an understanding of the function of the object and the nature of the materials employed in its manufacture.

More than a quarter of a century of gradual and continuous development founded on these principles and the early assimilation of Japanese art (in the 1860s) meant that by the 1890s English designers had made considerable advances towards the creation of a new style, which was more restrained, functional and simpler in conception than their European counterparts' style.

Fully aware of their dominant position in the field of design, it is understandable that they were wary of the developments on the Continent. They considered Art Nouveau as an unwholesome and unwanted foreign style, a fashionable aberration which distorted their ideas and ideals in a manner never intended by them.

EDWARD WILLIAM GODWIN (1833-86) was, like his friend Whistler, enthusiastic about Japanese art and he produced furniture designs which are usually described as 'Anglo-Japanese'. At the White House (1879) which he built for Whistler, rather than borrowing any clearly recognizable Japanese forms, he uses their simplicity and sober functionalism to blend traditional aspects of English domestic architecture with a subtle, diffuse Japanese spirit.

Despite his critical view of the style, much of Walter Crane's early work can be defined as Art Nouveau. A dedicated socialist like his friend Morris, he was a leading figure in the Arts and Crafts Movement and developed his theories on the unification of the arts in numerous books and articles. He produced many designs for wallpapers, fabrics and ceramics, but he is probably best remembered today, with Randolph Caldecott and Kate Greenaway, as an illustrator of children's books.

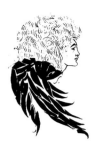

128

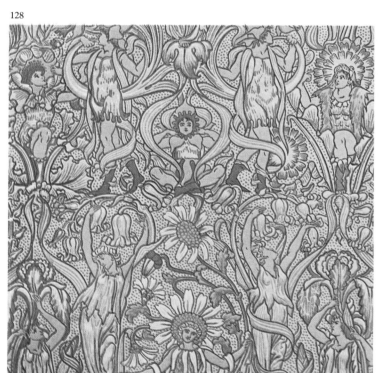

130

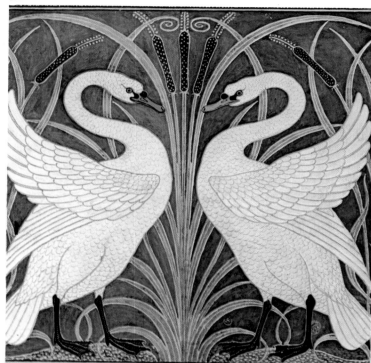

129

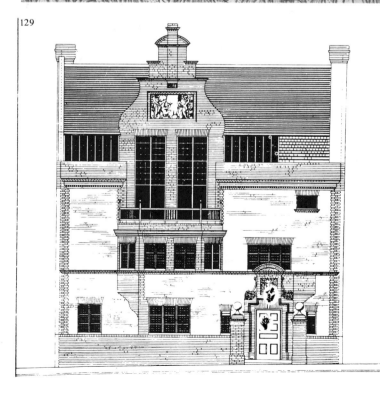

131

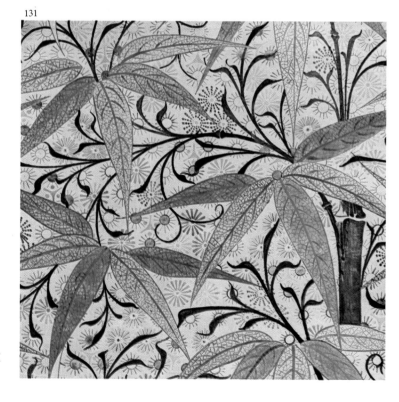

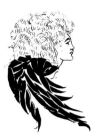

132

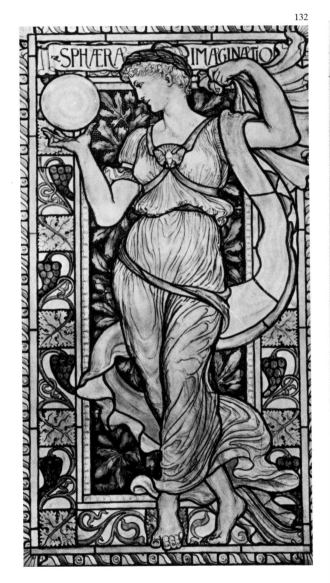

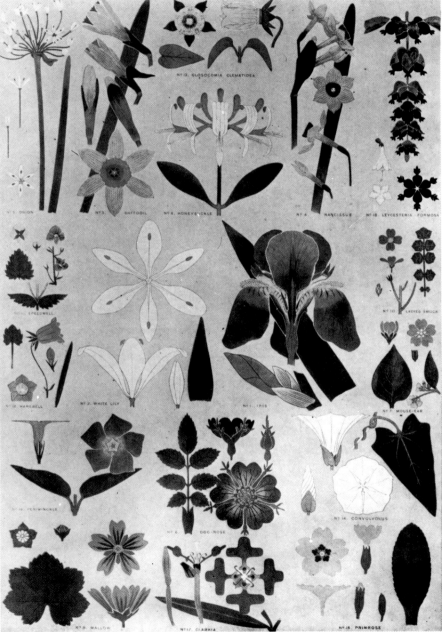

134

133

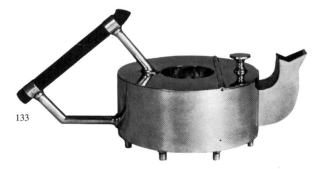

The theorist and industrial designer, CHRISTOPHER DRESSER (1834-1904), believed that 'the first aim of the designer of any article must be to render the object that he produces useful'. His work, which is simple in construction and which has undecorated surfaces, reveals a functional purism atypical of the time.

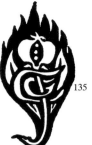

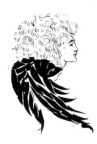

128—W. CRANE, furnishing fabric.
129—E. W. GODWIN, elevation of the studio-house in Tite Street, London, 1879.
130—W. CRANE, *Swans and Iris*, tile, 1877. London, Victoria and Albert Museum.
131—E. W. GODWIN, design for wallpaper, 1872.
132—W. CRANE, cartoon for stained-glass window. Waltham-stow, London, William Morris Gallery.
133—C. DRESSER, teapot, c. 1800. Sheffield, James Dixon and Sons.
134—C. DRESSER, *Study of Flowers*.
135—A. H. MACKMURDO, trademark of the Century Guild, 1884.
136—A. H. MACKMURDO, cover for *The Hobby Horse*, 1893.

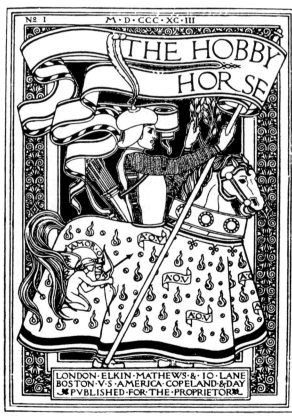

136

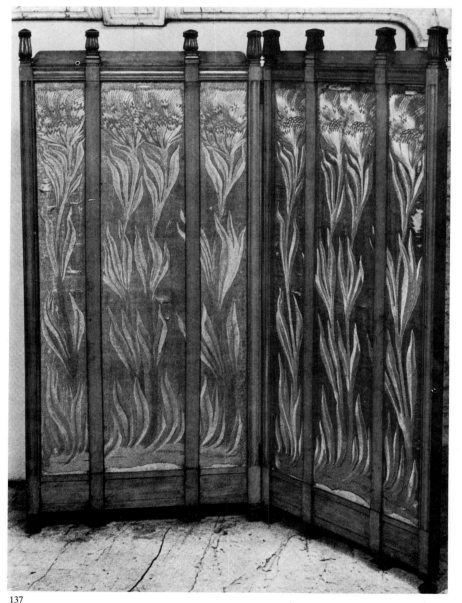

137

137—A. H. MACKMURDO, screen, 1884. Walthamstow, London, William Morris Gallery.
138—A. BEARDSLEY, *The Black Cape*, design for *Salome* by Oscar Wilde, 1894.
139—A. BEARDSLEY, a full page initial 'A' for *Le Morte d'Arthur*, by Malory, 1893-94.
140—A. BEARDSLEY, *How Sir Tristan Drank of the Love Drink*, illustration for *Le Morte d'Arthur*, 1893-94.
*—page 59, A. BEARDSLEY, ornamental inset for *Salom* by Wilde, 1894.

Like many other personalities in the Arts and Crafts Movement, ARTHUR HEYGATE MACKMURDO (1851-1942) was both an architect and a craft designer. A friend of William Morris, he visited Italy with Ruskin in 1874. He founded the Century Guild in 1882 in order to restore architecture and the crafts 'to their rightful place beside painting and sculpture'. In 1884 he launched *The Hobby Horse*, a quarterly art-oriented literary magazine, which, because of the emphasis it placed on the synthesis of the arts and its serious

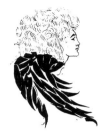

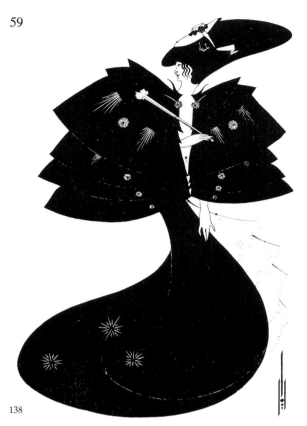

138

treatment of typography, influenced international publications like Charles Ricketts' *The Dial* (1889-97) and Henry van de Velde's *Van Nu en Straks* (1892-1901).

Important as these artists were for the development of Art Nouveau both in England and on the Continent, the graphic genius of AUBREY VINCENT BEARDSLEY (1872-98), whose short career (he died at twenty-six from tuberculosis) made him without doubt the most influential artist in the 1890s and arguably the most representative of the whole Art Nouveau movement. As a child he had shown some artistic talent as a musician and he had copied Kate Greenaway drawings to sell. His talent as a draughtsman received unequivocal encouragement and praise from Burne-Jones, who told him 'I seldom

139

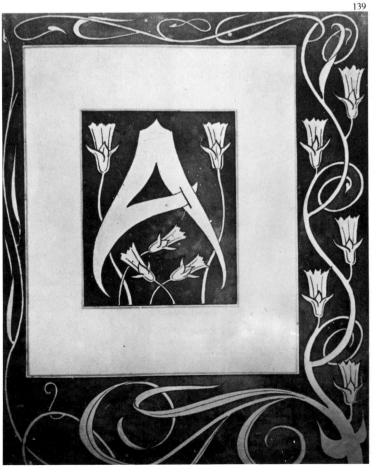

140

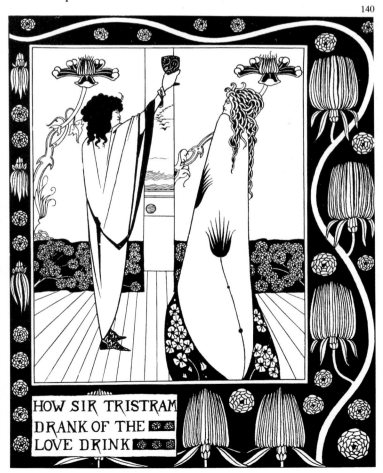

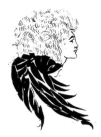

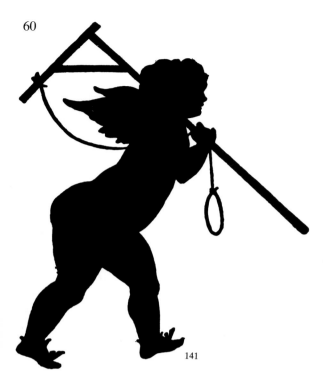

141

141—A. BEARDSLEY, border for the poem by Beardsley, *The Ballad of a Barber*, 1896.
142—A. BEARDSLEY, cover of *The Studio*, vol. I, n. I, April 1893.
143—A. BEARDSLEY, cover of *The Yellow Book*, 1895.

or never advise anyone to take up art as a profession, but in your case I can do nothing else.'

Burne-Jones thought that the drawings he had seen were preparatory sketches for paintings, but Beardsley considered them to be complete in themselves. Indeed, conscious that time was limited because of his illness, he deliberately confined his effort to the 'minor' medium of illustration and worked almost entirely in black and white. Unlike other artists of the period he was not afraid of technology. He realized that not only was his style perfect for photographic reproduction, but also that this method saved time and permitted the wide diffusion of his work.

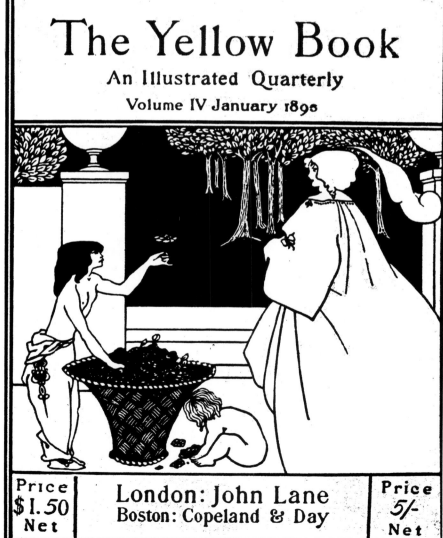

143

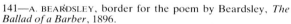

142

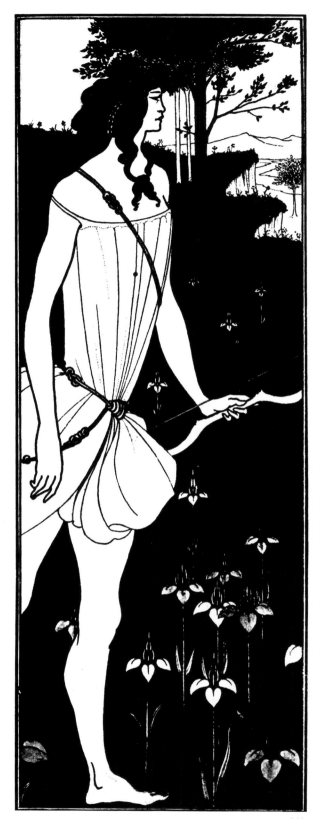

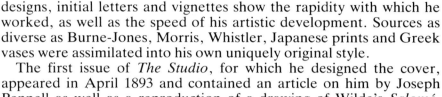

His first major commission came in 1892 when he was asked to illustrate Malory's *Morte d'Arthur*. The 550 or so illustrations, border designs, initial letters and vignettes show the rapidity with which he worked, as well as the speed of his artistic development. Sources as diverse as Burne-Jones, Morris, Whistler, Japanese prints and Greek vases were assimilated into his own uniquely original style.

The first issue of *The Studio*, for which he designed the cover, appeared in April 1893 and contained an article on him by Joseph Pennell as well as a reproduction of a drawing of Wilde's *Salomé*, which had been written in French especially for Sarah Bernhardt. Wilde's appreciation of the drawing resulted in him asking Beardsley, whom he had met through Burne-Jones, to illustrate the English translation. Its publication (1894), which contained images like *The Peacock Skirt*, brought him overnight fame as well as notoriety: his

145

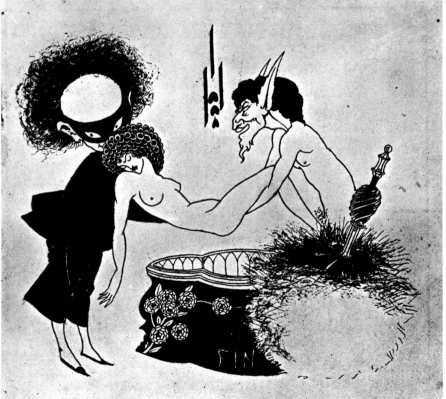

144

144—A. BEARDSLEY, *Atlanta and Calydon*, illustration for the poem by Algernon Charles Swinburne, 1895. London, British Museum.
145—A. BEARDSLEY, *The Burial of Salome*, vignette for *Salome* by Wilde, 1894.

vehement critics found his drawings 'grotesque, unintelligible. . . repulsive'.

With *Salomé*, Beardsley's art enters the first phase of his mature style. All naturalistic representation is stripped away, leaving the bare

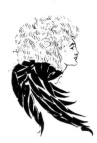

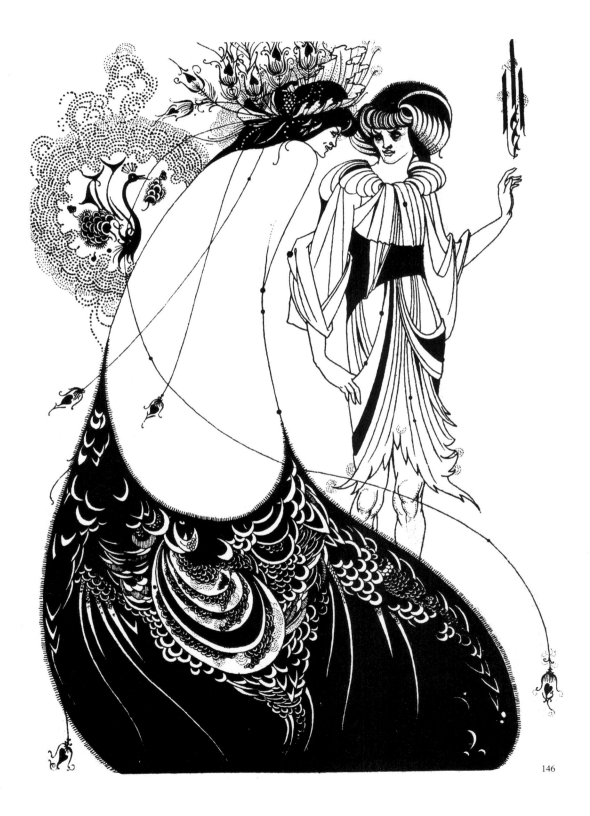

146

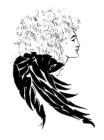

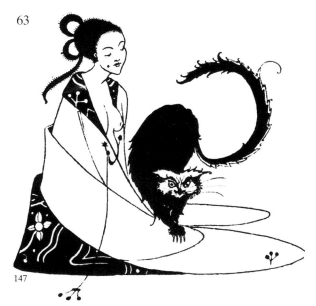

147

146—A. BEARDSLEY, *The Peacock Skirt*, design for *Salóme* by Wilde, 1894.
147—A. BEARDSLEY, vignette in *Bon Mots* by Smith and Sheridan, 1895.
148—A. BEARDSLEY, *The Climax*, illustration for *Salome* by Wilde, 1894.
149—A. BEARDSLEY, *The Dancer's Reward*, illustration for *Salome* by Wilde, 1894.

bones of a two-dimensional decorative surface. His elegantly distorted figures, by the contrast of highly ornamental and abstract lines with solid areas of pure black, become simultaneously the content and the form of these perversely imaginative compositions.

Shortly after the publication of *Salomé*, the first issue of *The Yellow Book* appeared. It was financed by Wilde and Beardsley was the art editor and most frequent illustrator. When the Wilde scandal broke in April 1895, the magazine stopped appearing. Beardsley quickly found another patron. In 1896 *The Savoy*, a magazine for collectors and bibliophiles was launched. It was financed and run by Leonard Smithers almost exclusively as a showcase for Beardsley's talents. The magazine ceased publication on the artist's death in 1898. In *The Savoy* he published the beautiful and classically inspired illustrations for Catullus's poem number CI *Ave atque Vale* which are inspired by antique art, as well as the illustrations for *Under the Hill* (1896), which

148

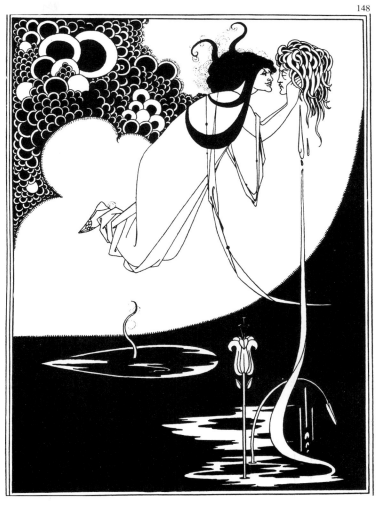

149

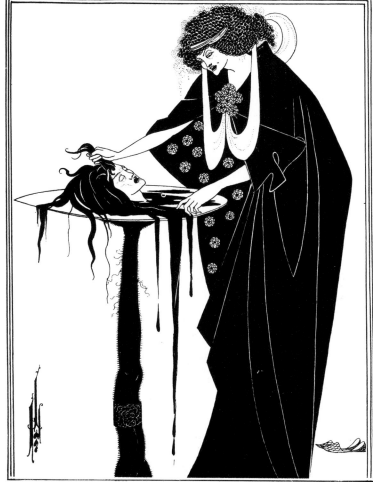

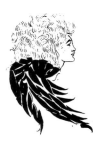

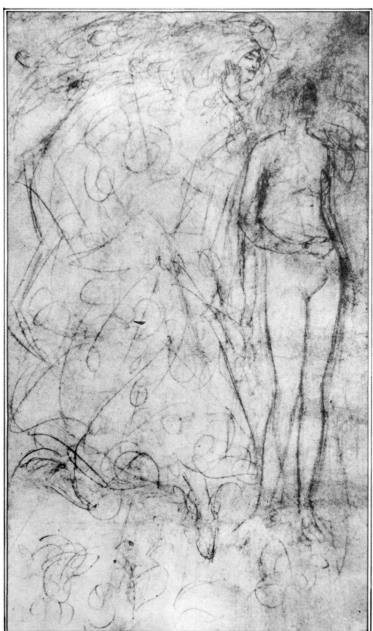

150

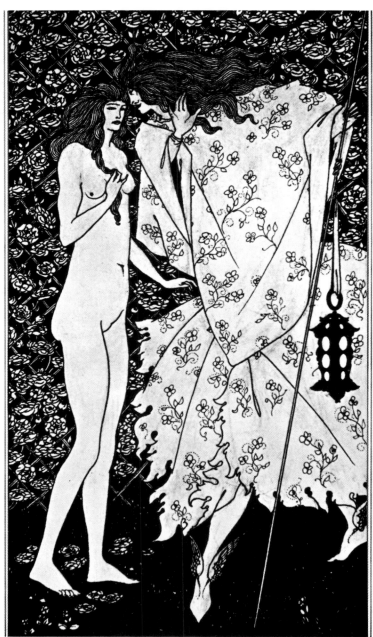

have the rich tonal quality of engraving that can be observed in his illustration *The Abbot* (1896).

In *The Yellow Book* Beardsley had begun to publish his often bitingly satirical modern life subjects. Like his work which is inspired by literature and the Middle Ages, they are preoccupied with eroticism. The public became aware of his sexual nature which had

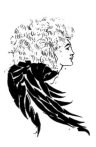

150—A. BEARDSLEY, sketch for *The Mysterious Rose Garden*
published in *The Yellow Book*, 1895.
151—A. BEARDSLEY, *The Mysterious Rose Garden*, 1895.
152—A. BEARDSLEY, *Ave Atque Vale*, illustration by Beardsley
of canto CI by Catullus, 1896.

hitherto been 'suppressed, consciously or otherwise'. But Beardsley's refined and detached rendition prevented his work from being perceived as pornographic.

Like Des Esseintes, the hero of Huysmans' decadent novel *A Rebours* (1884), Beardsley shunned nature. He preferred to work at night in his black–painted room, hung with erotic Japanese prints. By

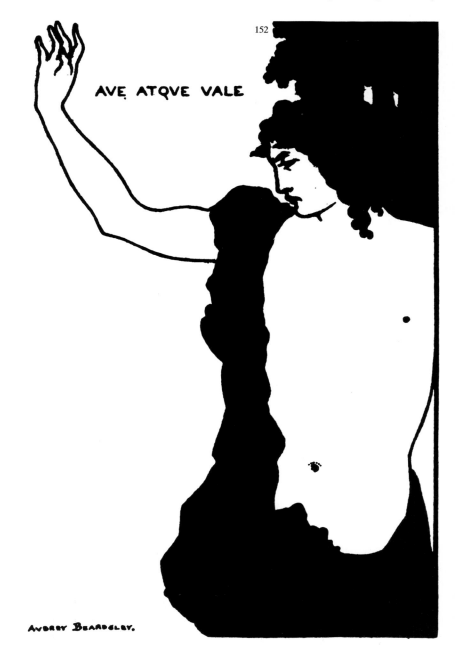

AVE ATQVE VALE

AVBREY BEARDSLEY.

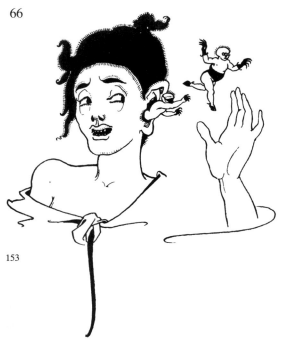

153

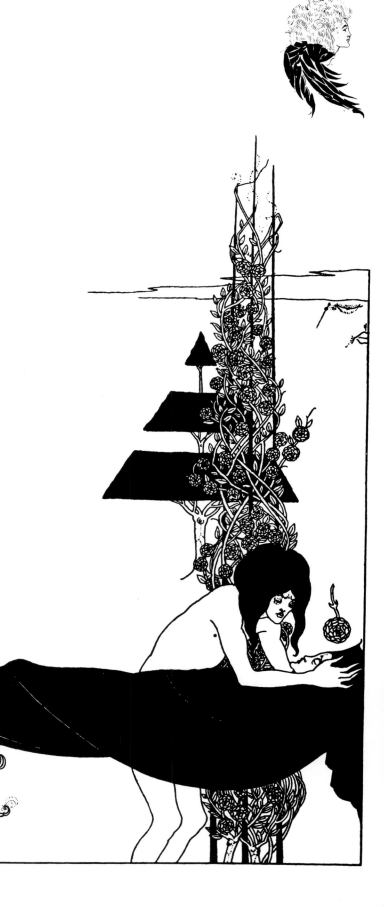

153—A. BEARDSLEY, vignette for *Bon Mots* by Sheridan and Smith, 1895.
154—A. BEARDSLEY, *Platonic Lament*, for *Salome* by Wilde, 1894.
155—A. BEARDSLEY, *John and Salome* (detail), in *Salome* by Wilde, 1894.
156—A. BEARDSLEY, *The Abbé*, illustration for *Under the Hill* by Beardsley, 1896.

154

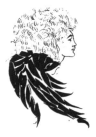

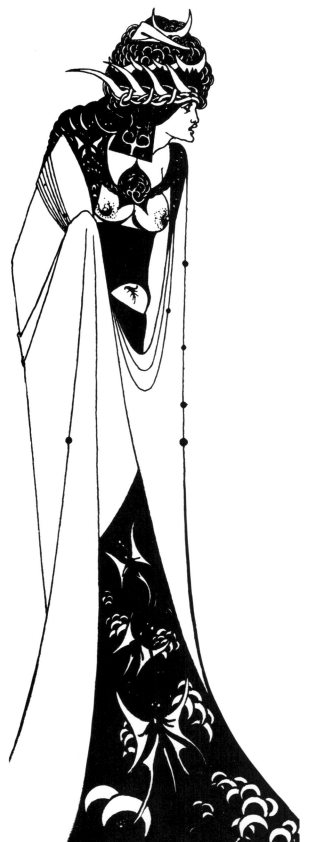

day the curtains remained closed and he worked by the light of 'two altar candles in gilt bronze Empire candlesticks on a rococo table which was also black, and of the type priests used'.

Increasingly 'shattered and incapable of working' because of haemorrhages, Beardsley was converted to Catholicism a little less than a year before his death. He wrote from France to his editor asking him to destroy 'by all that is holy *all* obscene drawings'. Needless to say, his dying wish was not complied with.

156

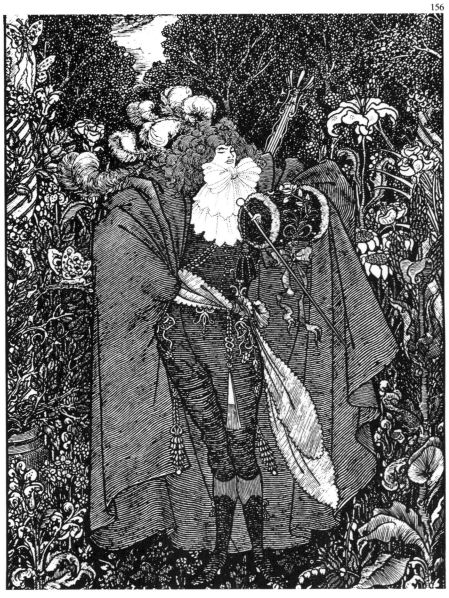

155

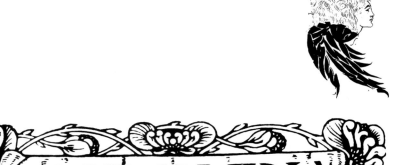

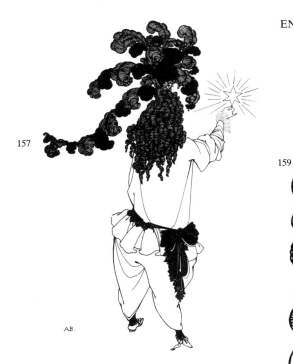

157

A.B.

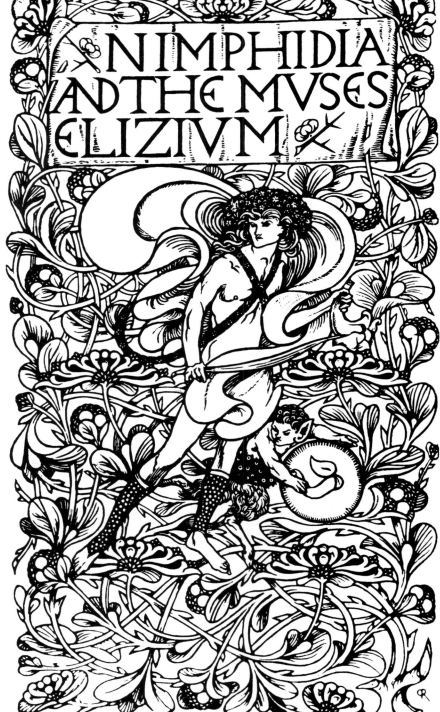

159

157—A. BEARDSLEY, *The New Star*, illustration for *The Rape of The Lock* by Alexander Pope, 1896.
158—CHARLES RICKETTS, binding for Sarah Prideaux. London, Victoria and Albert Museum.
159—C. RICKETTS, frontispiece for *Nimphidia and the Muses Elizium* by Michael Drayton, 1896. London, Victoria and Albert Museum.
160—A. BEARDSLEY, caricature of Gordon Craig, sketch for *Beckett*.

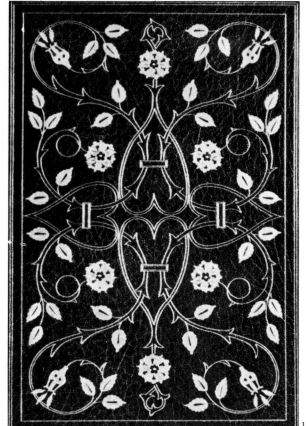

158

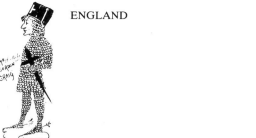

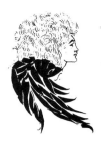

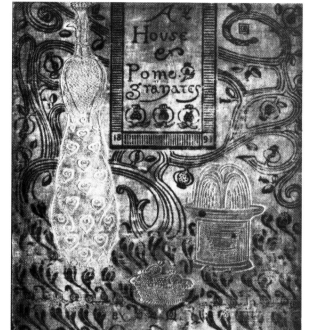

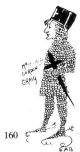

Despite being overshadowed by Beardsley's renown, CHARLES RICKETTS (1866-1931) was a draughtsman of great merit. He was a much closer associate of Wilde's, providing illustrations and bindings for most of his works, including *A House of Pomegranates* (1891). He was a painter, sculptor, craftsman designer of stage sets and costumes as well as the founder and chief illustrator of *The Dial* and the Vale Press.

The Beggarstaff Brothers, James Pryde (1872-1949) and William Nicholson (1869-1949), developed a highly original poster art of flat pattern by using paper cut-outs. Their first poster portrayed EDWARD GORDON CRAIG (1872-1966) in the role of Hamlet. Craig, who went on to become the theorist and pioneer of modern stage design in Britain, worked as an artist primarily in the more unusual field of woodcut. Clearly influenced by the Beggarstaffs, his outlines became broader and assumed volume in contrast to the two-dimensional linearity of Beardsley's and Ricketts' work, while the work of Lautrec and Félix Vallotton inspired the way that he foreshortened space.

161—C. RICKETTS, binding for *A House of Pomegranates* by Wilde, 1891. London, British Museum.
162—GORDON CRAIG, woodcut illustration for *King Lear*, 1920.
163—G. CRAIG, *Irving as Robespierre*, lithograph.
 *—C. RICKETTS, ornamental inset for *A House of Pomegranates* by Wilde, 1891.

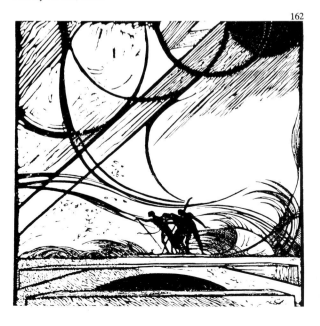

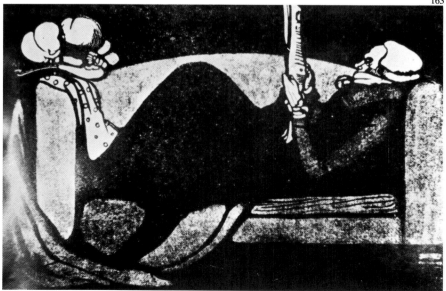

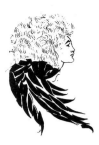

164

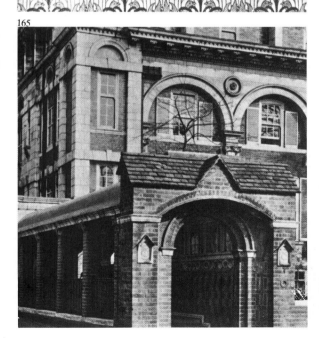

CHARLES ANNESLEY VOYSEY (1857-1941) set up his own practice as an architect in 1882. A pupil of Mackmurdo, he was first an interior decorator, designer of furniture, wallpaper, textiles and metalwork. He built his first house in 1888. He was influenced by the architecture of Philip Webb (the architect of Morris's Red House) and by Richard Norman Shaw. He shared his master's, Mackmurdo's, taste for Japanese art and added elements like screens and grilles borrowed from Japanese architecture to these influences. He specialized in designing country and surburban houses in which he developed his own characteristic linear style, which is uncluttered by ornament and prefigures the Modern Movement.

166

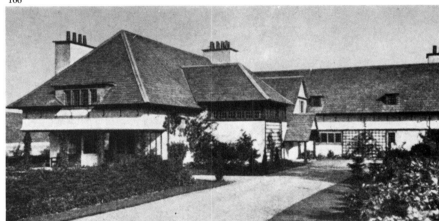

165

167

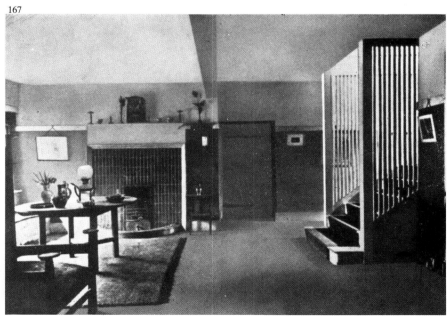

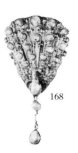

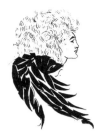

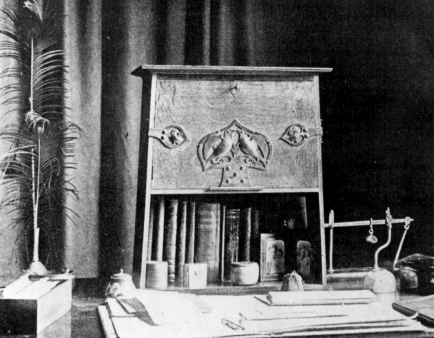

164—CHARLES ANNESLEY VOYSEY, design for furnishing fabric, *Bird and Tulip*, 1896.
165—C. F. A. VOYSEY, 14-16 Hans Road, London, 1891.
166—C. F. A. VOYSEY, Broadleys, Lake Windermere, 1898.
167—C. F. A. VOYSEY, CHARLES WOOD, the living room at The Orchard, Chorley Wood (Voysey's own house), 1900.
168—CHARLES ROBERT ASHBEE, pendant, 1900. Letchworth, private collection.
169—C. R. ASHBEE, mustard pot and spoon, c. 1900. Zurich, Kunstgewerbemuseum.
170—C. R. ASHBEE, 38 Cheyne Walk, London, 1899-1901.
171—C. F. A. VOYSEY, portable writing desk, illustrated in *The Studio*, 1896.
172—C. H. TOWNSEND, church at Great Warley, Essex, 1904.

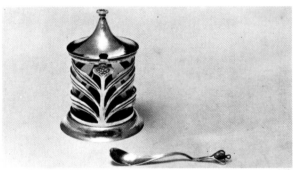

169

171

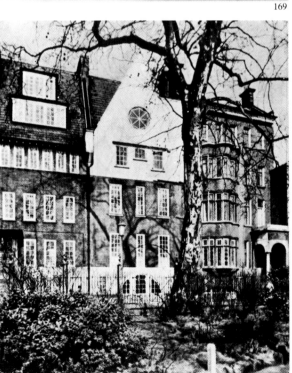

170

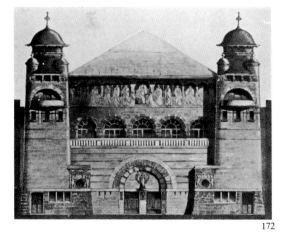

172

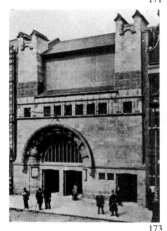

173

CHARLES ROBERT ASHBEE (1863-1942) was also an architect and decorator who produced 'controlled, understated' designs for all aspects of interior decoration. A founder member, with Crane and Mackmurdo, of the Arts and Crafts Movement and chief designer of the Guild of Handicrafts, he later came to believe in the rationally applied use of machinery.

Although CHARLES HARRISON TOWNSEND's (1852-1928) use of asymmetry and surface ornament in buildings, for example in the Whitechapel Art Gallery (1897) and the church at Great Warley in

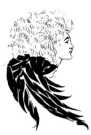

173—CHARLES HARRISON TOWNSEND, Whitechapel Art Gallery, London, 1891.

174—ALFRED GILBERT, table centrepiece for Queen Victoria, c. 1880. London, Royal Institute of Painters in Watercolour.

175—A. GILBERT, Shaftesbury Memorial Fountain, detail, 1887-93. London, Piccadilly Circus.

*—page 72, HERBERT GRANVILLE FELL, ornamental inset in *The Book of Job*, 1896.

176—A. GILBERT, presidential badge and chain, 1891-96. London, Royal Institute of Painters in Watercolour.

177-179—HUGH BAILLIE SCOTT, three designs for interiors, 1900-02.

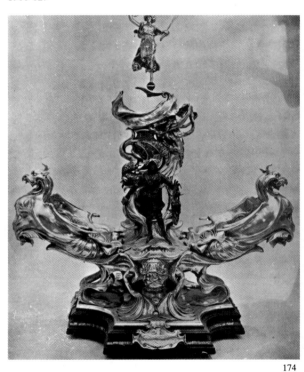

174

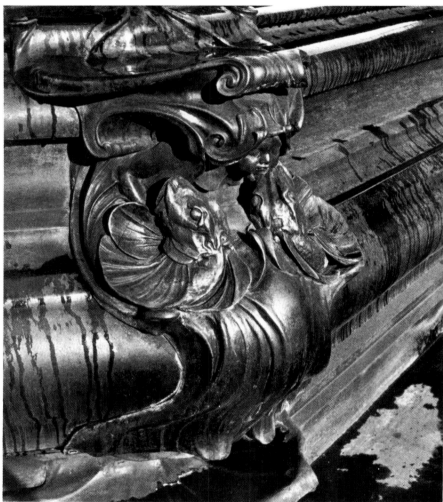

175

Essex (1904), make him the English architect closest in spirit to the European Art Nouveau movement, HUGH BAILLIE SCOTT (1865-1945) was probably the most well-known English architect on the Continent. In 1897, Baillie Scott, together with Ashbee, was commissioned to provide the furniture and interior decoration for the drawing and dining rooms of the Grand Duke of Hesse at Darmstadt. In 1901 in the German 'House for an Art Lover' Competition, Baillie Scott's design was awarded the highest prize in preference to a design submitted by Charles Rennie Mackintosh. The sculptor ALFRED GILBERT (1854-1934), whose early European training and contact with the Baroque is betrayed in the flamboyant ornamentation of his silver table centre for Queen Victoria's Jubilee (1887), and the Shaftesbury Memorial Foundation (1887-93) in Piccadilly Circus, was also linked to the Continent.

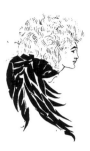

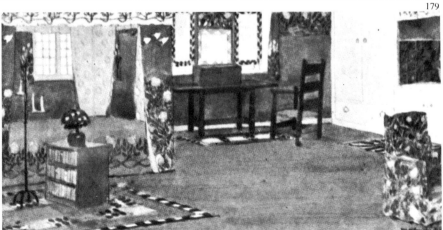

England's fundamental role in the development of the Art Nouveau style was in the preparation of the style rather than in expounding it. The early development of a Proto-Art Nouveau style and the insularity of the Arts and Crafts generation meant that apart from Beardsley, there were no major English practitioners of the international Art Nouveau style comparable to the European variations in the last years of the nineteenth century. Similarly, the tendency of the later Arts and Crafts designers to build on the heritage of their immediate predecessors made it difficult for them to take the necessary steps to establish a full working relationship with industry, in contrast to their European counterparts.

176

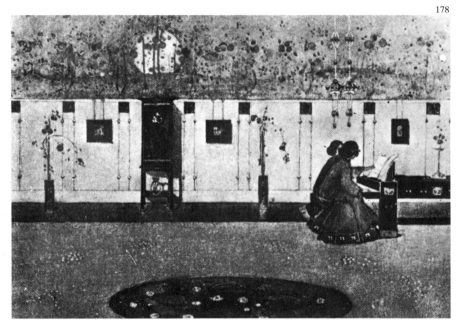

177

178

179

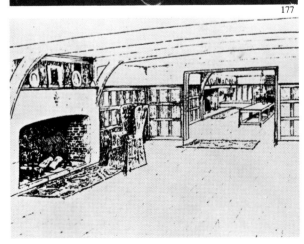

4-France

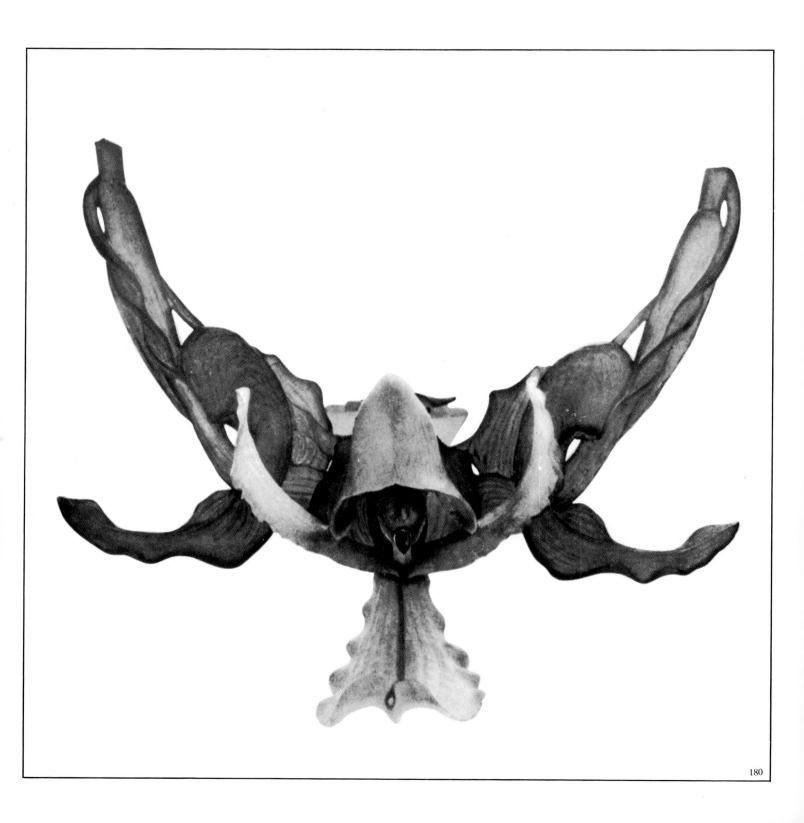

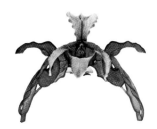

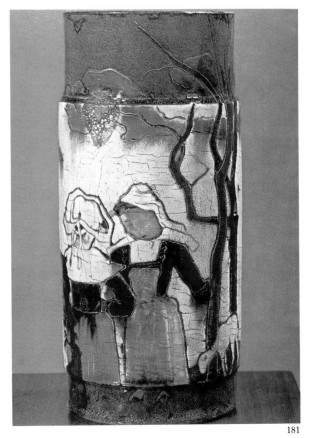

181

In France, the Art Nouveau movement found its most direct expression in architecture and the applied arts. This in part was due to the influence of Samuel Bing, whose gallery L'Art Nouveau had opened in 1895 attracting considerable artistic and popular interest in contemporary arts. Art Nouveau was also enormously influential in the fields of advertising and publishing. Its elegant and decorative synthesis of word and image was ideal for an arresting poster or a beautifully illustrated book.

The development of Art Nouveau painting is complex. The seeds of the style were contained in the 'cloisonnisme' of Emile Bernard (1864-1941) and Louis Anquetin (1861-1932), which was formulated in the late 1880s. The cloisonnist technique was named after its resemblance to *cloisonné* enamels; the style was based on strong forms painted in flat colours surrounded by dark contours. Paul Gauguin (1848-1903) experimented with cloisonnisme. His use of hard contours demonstrates this, but in his later work there is often a hint of the pleasing arabesque line characteristic of Art Nouveau. Odilon Redon (1840-1910) and Gustave Moreau (1826-98), although at times close to the style, are too concerned with spatial mysteries and ambiguities to be included in the category of Art Nouveau artists.

Henri de Toulouse-Lautrec (1864-1901) is an example of an artist whose style was at times wholly Art Nouveau. This is especially noticeable in his later work where he responds most strongly to the desire for an integrated surface rhythm, and he allows his line complete decorative freedom.

The relationship between Art Nouveau and Symbolism was profitable. Both groups of artists shared an interest in an iconography

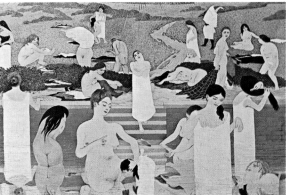

182

180—and symbol of Chapter 4, pp. 74-95—RENÉ LALIQUE, orchid in ivory and horn, 1897-1900.
181—PAUL GAUGUIN, vase with a Breton design, c. 1888. Brussels, Musées Royaux d'Art et d'Histoire.
182—FÉLIX VALLOTTON, *Summer, Women Bathing in an Open Swimming Pool*, 1892. Zurich, Kunsthaus.
183—ODILON REDON, *Portrait of Violette Heymann*, 1909-10. Cleveland, Museum of Art.

183

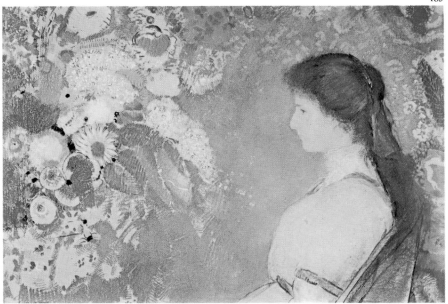

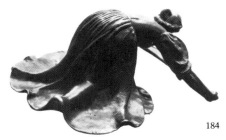

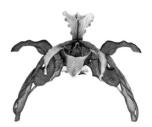

184

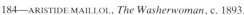

184—ARISTIDE MAILLOL, *The Washerwoman*, c. 1893.
185—MAURICE DENIS, *The Muse*, 1893. Paris, Musée Nationale d'Art Moderne.
186—GUSTAVE MOREAU, *Salome*, c. 1876. Paris, Musée Moreau.
187—WASSILY KANDINSKY, *Moonrise, 1902-03*. Munich, Staatliche Galerie.
188—F. VALLOTTON, *La paresse*, 1896.
189—PABLO PICASSO, *Woman in Blue*, 1901. Madrid, Museo Nacional de Arte Moderna.
*—page 77, A. MAILLOL, illustration in *Daphnis and Chloë*, 1937.

186

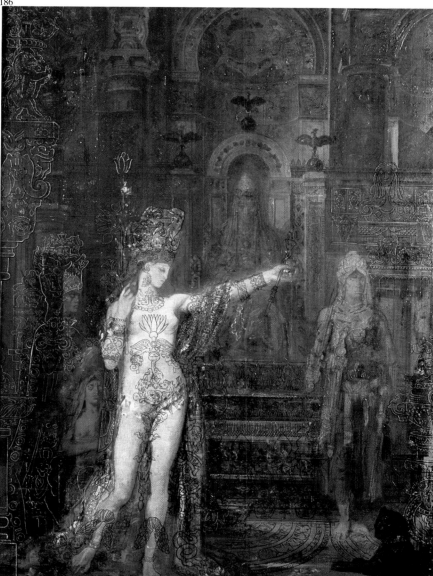

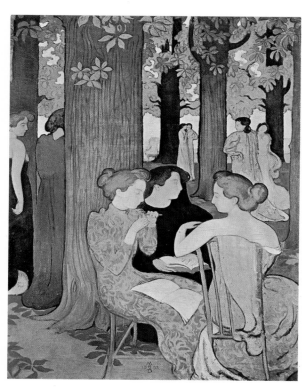

185

drawn from exotic, mysterious and erotic subjects. They also shared many technical preferences and their style can often be described only by reference to characteristics of both movements. Such artists as Edmond Aman-Jean (1860-1935), Lucien Lévy-Dhurmer (1865-1953) and Georges de Feure (1868-1943) were equally attracted to both movements.

In sculpture, the influence of Art Nouveau on Gauguin is very evident in the period. The arabesques which decorate his vases and wood carvings are reminiscent of Art Nouveau, although they have a quality of primitivism and savagery entirely lacking in Art Nouveau.

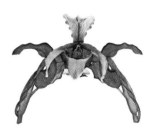

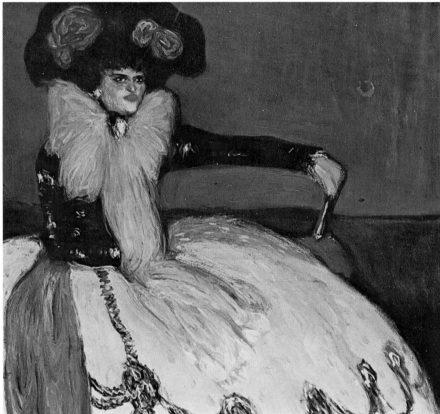

189

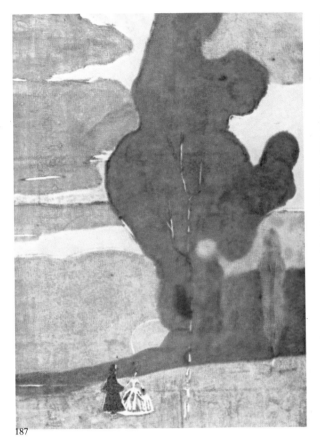

187

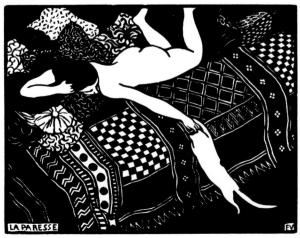

188

In Aristide Maillol's work (1861-1944) there is a closer stylistic parallel. His line is more gentle and refined but it is never as entirely decorative as the Art Nouveau line. Undoubtedly, PIERRE ROCHE (1855-1922) comes closest to the definition of Art Nouveau sculpture. His design for the sculpture on the facade of the theatre designed by Henri Sauvage and dedicated to the dancer Loïe Fuller in 1900, describes the fluid and sinuous arabesque movement of the dancer's drapery in an entirely decorative manner.

On pages 78-79
190—LUCIEN LÉVY-DHURMER, *Eve*, 1896. Paris, private collection.
191—EDMOND AMAN-JEAN, *Girl with Peacock*, 1895. Paris, Musée des Arts Décoratif.
192—EDGARD MAXENCE, *Peacock-Profile*, c. 1896. Paris, private collection.
193—A. MAILLOL, *Profile of a Girl*, c. 1895-1906. Perpignan, Musée Hyacinthe Rigaud.
194—GEORGES DE FEURE, watercolour (from *Art and Decoration*), 1901.
195—PIERRE PUVIS DE CHAVANNES, *Summer*, 1889-93.
196—HENRI DE TOULOUSE-LAUTREC, *Jane Avril at the Jardin de Paris*, poster, 1893. Albi, Musée Toulouse-Lautrec.

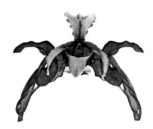

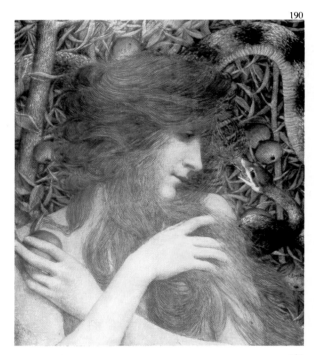

190

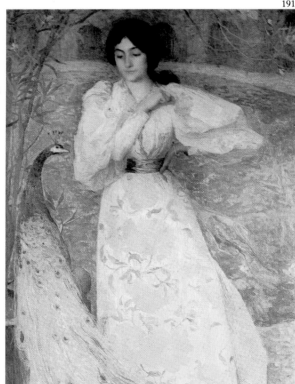

191

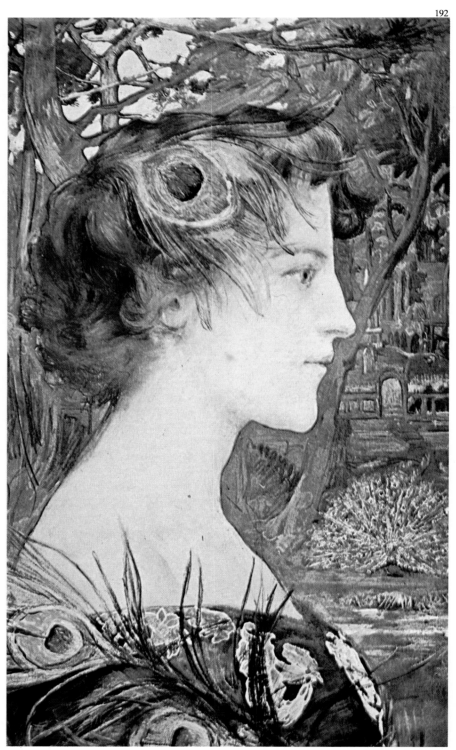

192

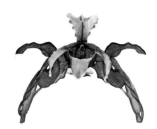

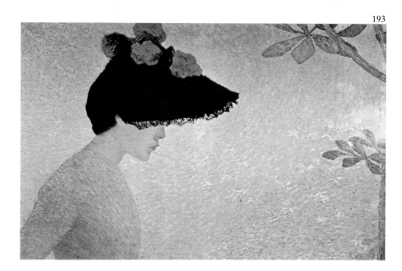

193

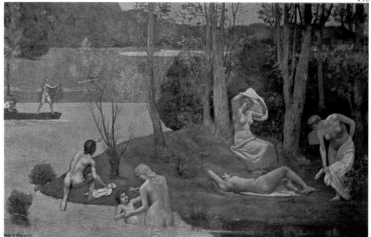

195

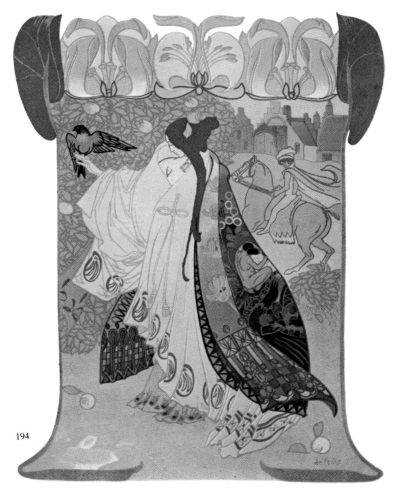

194

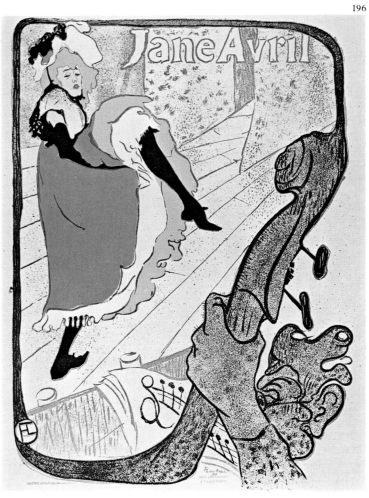

196

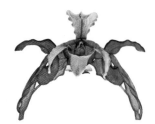

197

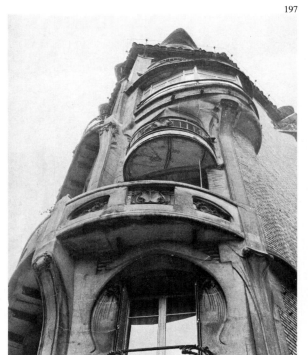

199

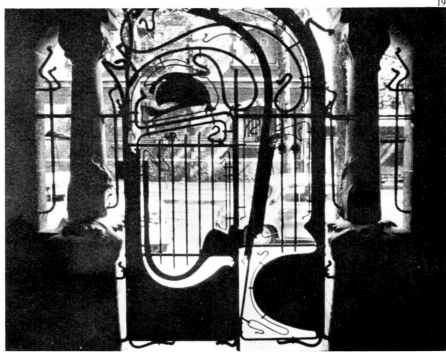

198

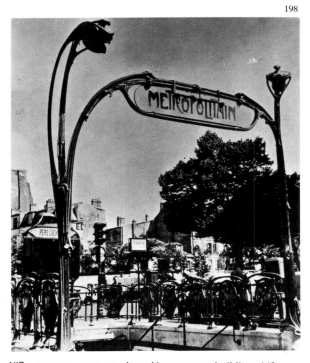

197—HECTOR GUIMARD, Jassedé apartment building, 142 rue de Versailles, Paris, 1903-05.

200

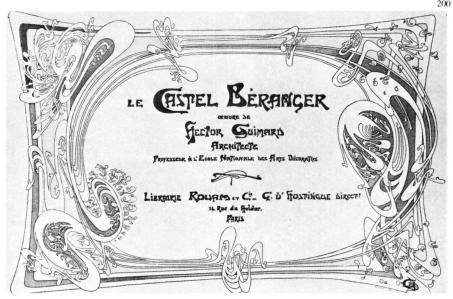

The most prestigious achievements of Art Nouveau architecture in France are those of HECTOR GUIMARD (1867-1942). He built the capricious Castel Béranger (1894-97), and also designed the distinctive ironwork entrances for the Paris Métro. His metalwork incorporates floral motifs and lettering designed with an extraordinary degree

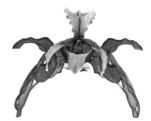

201

202

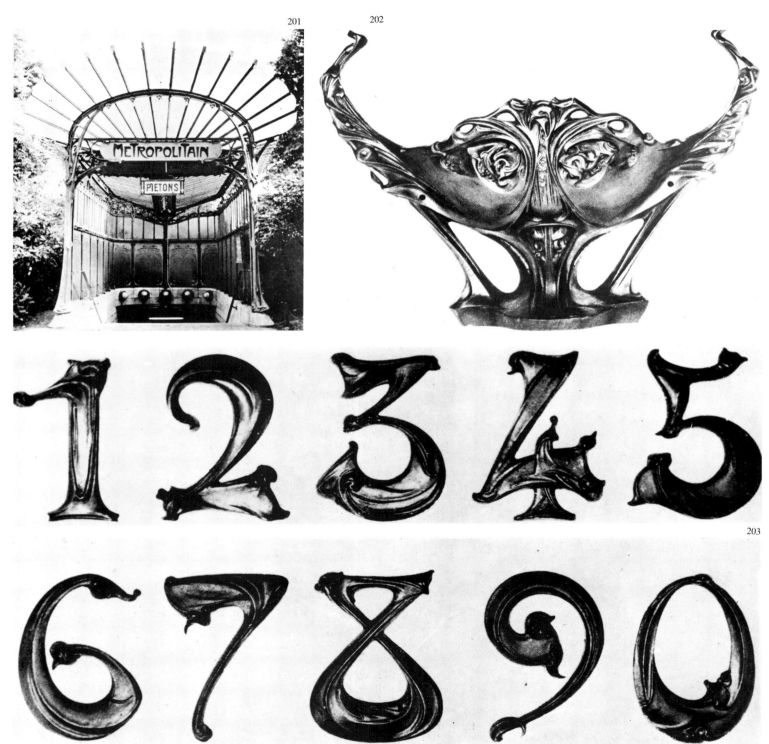

203

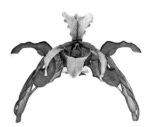

198—H. GUIMARD, Monceau Station, the Paris Métro, c. 1900.
199—H. GUIMARD, Castel Béranger, 16 rue de la Fontaine, Paris, 1894-97. Detail of a gate.
200—H. GUIMARD, frontispiece of the publicity album for Castel Béranger, 1898. New York, The Museum of Modern Art.
201—H. GUIMARD, Port Dauphine Station, the Paris Métro, c. 1900.
202—H. GUIMARD, metal cup, c. 1900.
203—H. GUIMARD, glazed house numbers; designed in 1893, executed at Ivry by Emile Muller.

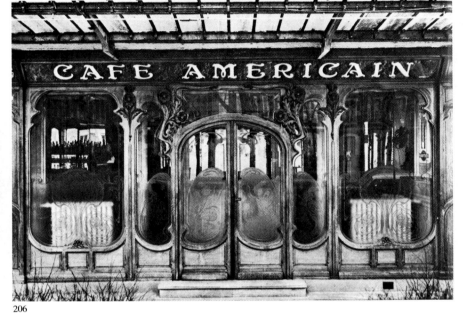

206

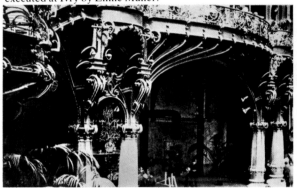

204

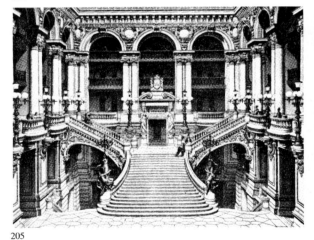

205

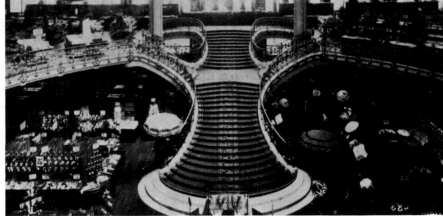

207

204—L. A. LOUVET, Grand Palais, Paris, c. 1890 (detail).
205—TONY GARNIER, staircase at the Opéra, Paris, 1875.
206—A. MOULINS, Café Américain, Paris, 1900.
207—GEORGES CHEDANNE, Galeries Lafayette, Paris, 1900.
208—HENRI SAUVAGE, C. SARAZIN, Café de Paris, Paris, c. 1895 (demolished).
209—LOUIS MARNEZ (in collaboration with LÉON SONNIER), Chez Maxim restaurant, Paris, 1899.
210—RAPIN, reading room with motif of the salamander on the wood and ceramic fireplace.
211—L. MARNEZ (in collaboration with L. SONNIER), Chez Maxim restaurant, Paris, 1899; detail of the salon.

of delicacy. Their green enamelled surfaces suggest real plant forms.

No other French architect of the period reached the same level of decorative freedom as Guimard, although a few approached his level of distinction. GEORGES CHEDANNE's (b. 1861) Galeries Lafayette (1900) are notable for the economic and imaginative use of line which here defines the plan and elevation of the stair. The staircase is clearly based on Tony Garnier's staircase at the Paris Opéra (1875).

There are plenty of isolated examples of highly resolved and successful Art Nouveau buildings in France. In designs like Jules Aimé Lavirotte's facade for the Lycée Leonardo de Vinci (12 rue Sedillon, Paris) and Xavier Schollkopf's design for Yvette Guilbert's

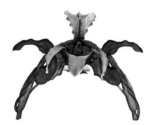

208

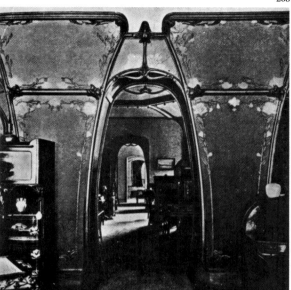

210

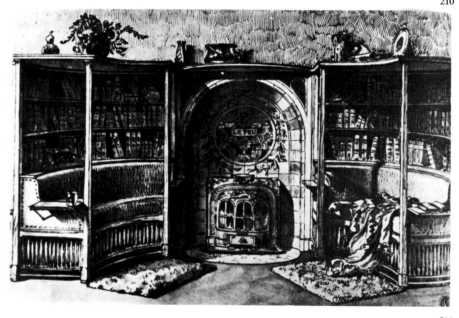

209

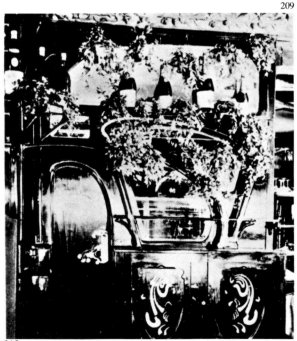

211

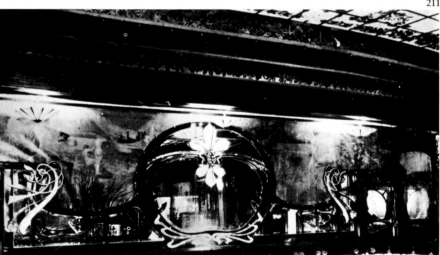

212—JULES AIMÉ LAVIROTTE, house, Avenue Rapp, Paris, 1901.
213—WAGON, house, rue Franklin, Paris, 1903; detail of the portal.
214—AUGUSTE PERRET, apartment block, rue Franklin, Paris, 1903; detail of the facade.
*—page 85, EUGÈNE GRASSET, illustrations for *Méthode de Composition Ornamentale*, 1905.

house (23 bis boulevard Berthier, now demolished), the style reaches lyrical confidence.

Many architects, including Henri Sauvage, Louis Bonnet, Charles Plumet, Gustave Rive, remained on the periphery of the Art Nouveau movement. Anatole de Baudet's work on the church of St Jean de Montmartre, shows the influence of the movement clearly. But this building is important because of the choice of the material rather than for its decorative qualities. The building is in reinforced concrete, used here for the first time in a religious building. His

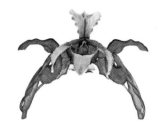

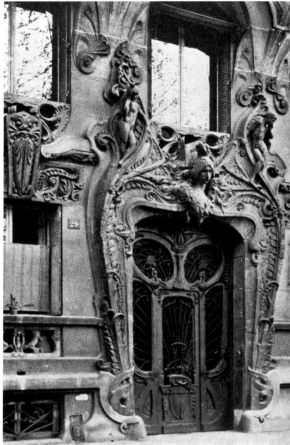

212

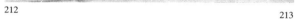

213

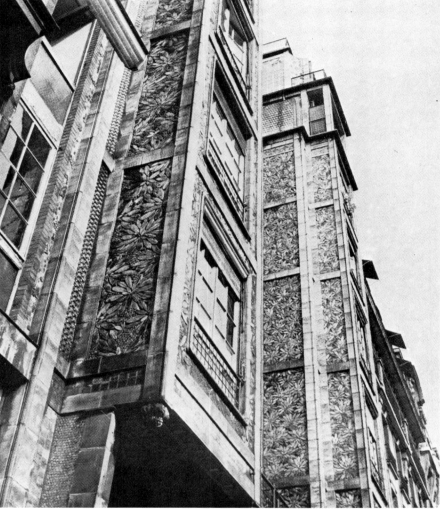

214

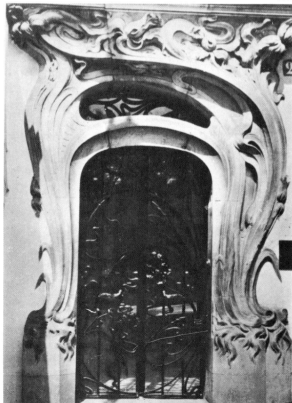

example was followed by AUGUSTE PERRET (1874-1954), who utilized the idea of exposing the structural metal support, thereby anticipating the aesthetics of the Modern Movement.

French Art Nouveau architecture aimed at a vital and decorative synthesis of line and space. In an entirely modern way it transforms its Gothic and Rococo sources. The impact of the new aesthetic was felt particularly in the field of interior design. The finest examples of Art Nouveau interiors in France were in the work executed by Louis Marnez and the painter Leon Sonnier at Chez Maxim (1899).

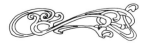

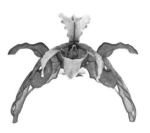

215

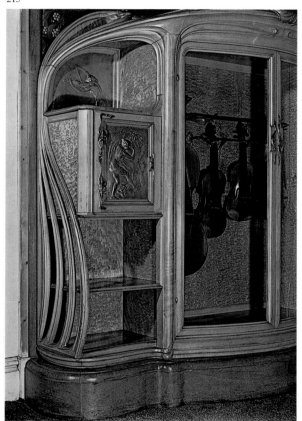

*—page 84, EUGÈNE VALLIN, design for door handle.
215—ALEXANDRE CHARPENTIER, cabinet for musical instruments, c. 1901; detail. Paris, Musée des Arts Décoratifs.
216—CHARLES PLUMET, firescreen (photograph from *The Studio*), 1897.

216

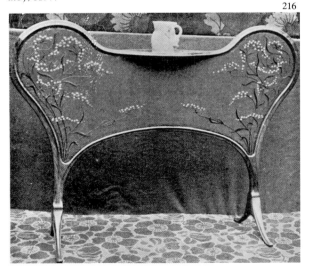

The favourable market conditions in France ensured the success of Art Nouveau in the applied arts. There was a demand for unique objects of refined taste. An important centre for the diffusion of the taste for Art Nouveau objects was the exhibition of the Union Centrale des Arts Décoratifs of 1884. In 1889 they inaugurated their annual international exhibitions. The new taste was also catered for by the Salon du Champ de Mars in 1891, and by the foundation of the Groupe des Cinq (Charpentier, Dampf, Aubert, Selmersheim and Moreau-Mélaton; Plumet joined in 1896 and Nocq and Sauvage in 1897). In 1897 the German critic Julius Meier-Graefe opened his gallery La Maison Moderne ('the modern house') in Paris.

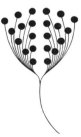

The establishment of a School of Nancy in 1901 reflects the fact that the interest in the new style was not merely metropolitan, but was also an indication of the rapid growth of the taste for Art Nouveau objects. Although the products by this group of artists are more traditional and figurative than Parisian Art Nouveau products, their works are none the less of the highest decorative quality. At the Paris Exposition Universelle (1900) the furniture designs of Hector Guimard were acclaimed as a triumphant adaptation of his architectural style. His use of rhythmic sinuous lines was shared by other members of the School, notably Gaillard and Louis Majorelle. However, it is above all in the work of EMILE GALLÉ (1846-1904), already a leading exponent of Art Nouveau in 1890, that we can identify the School of Nancy. His work exhibits a particularly successful marriage of elements drawn from Rococo and Oriental art with those of Art Nouveau itself.

Gallé founded the School and became its first director. The DAUM brothers (Auguste 1853-1909 and Antonin 1864-1930), LOUIS MAJORELLE (1859-1926) and Eugène Vallin (1856-1922) worked with him. Gallé had studied and gained considerable knowledge of botany, philosophy and design. He also had the experience of running his

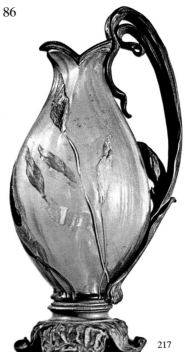

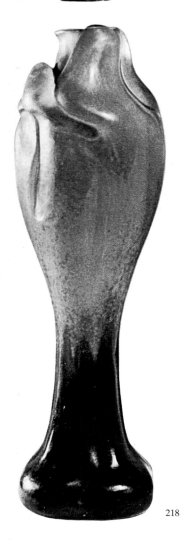

217

218

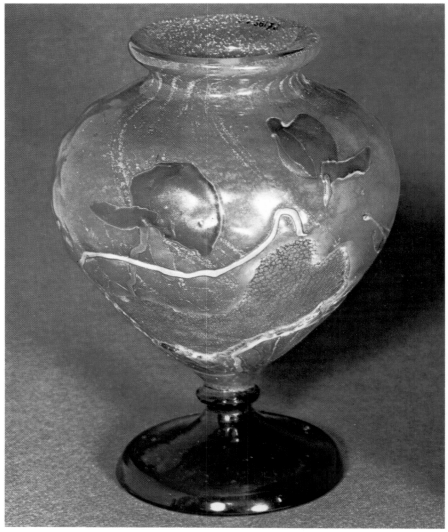

219

father's glass works in 1874. His glass objects show particular freedom in the treatment of floral motifs. He also used strong colour with great sensitivity, to produce opalescent effects. He often inscribed these objects with quotations from Symbolist poets like Baudelaire or Maeterlinck. Their organic and almost biomorphic quality comes from Gallé's deep commitment to Nature expressed in his motto 'our roots lie in the soil of the woods, in the moss by the rim of the pool'.

Gallé also made furniture, but these works are seldom as successful as his work in glass which was a more familiar material to him. In the famous Butterfly Bed of 1904 the butterfly motif overwhelms the function of the bed. The work of the Daum and Muller brothers shares Gallé's plastic inventiveness and colourist subtlety.

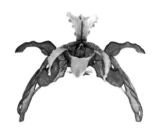

220

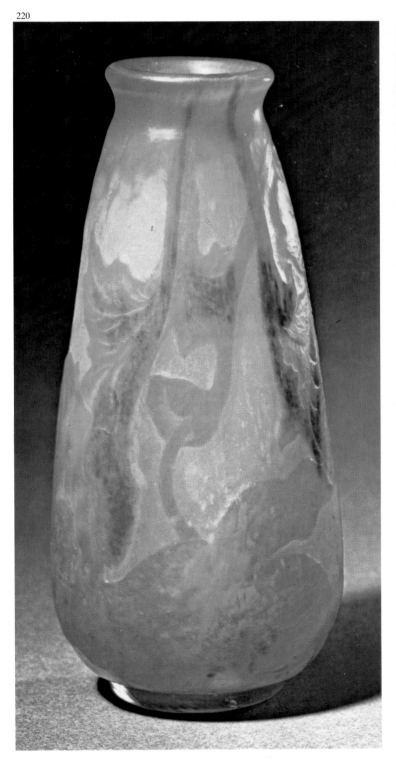

221

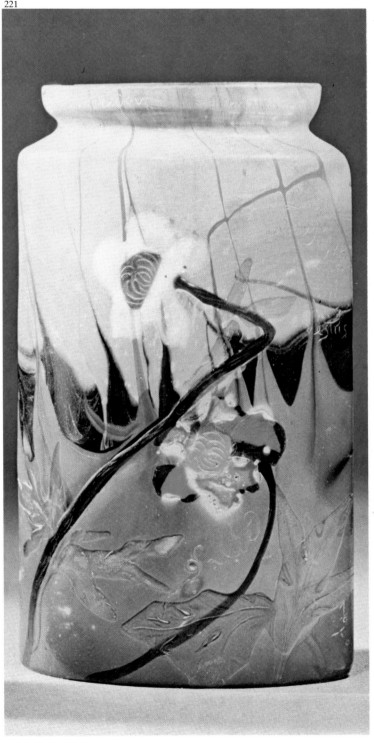

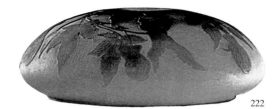

222

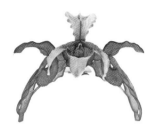

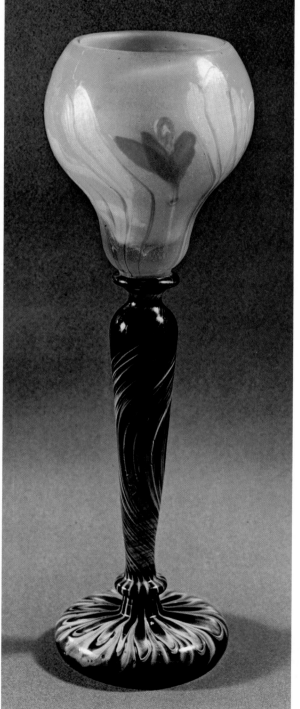

217—EMILE GALLÉ, iris vase in yellow and polychrome glass, bronze mounting.
218—E. GALLÉ, 'bursaire' vase, c. 1900.
219—E. GALLÉ, vase, 1889-95.
220—E. GALLÉ, vase, 1890-95.
221—E. GALLÉ, *The Woodland Anemone*, vase, 1900.
222—Workshop of E. GALLÉ, detail of base for a lamp, c. 1895.
223—E. GALLÉ, chalice, 1903.
224—E. GALLÉ, *The White Vine*, dining-room cabinet, c. 1900.

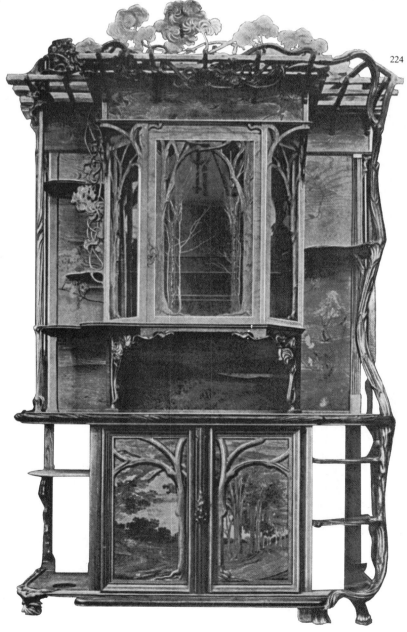

224

223

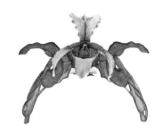

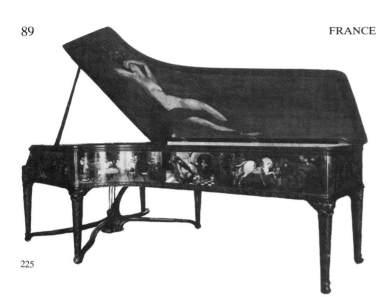

225

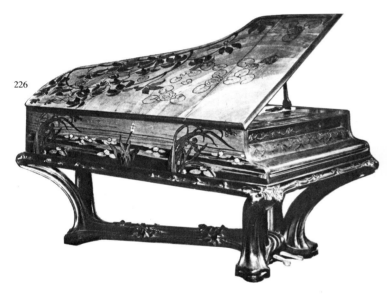

226

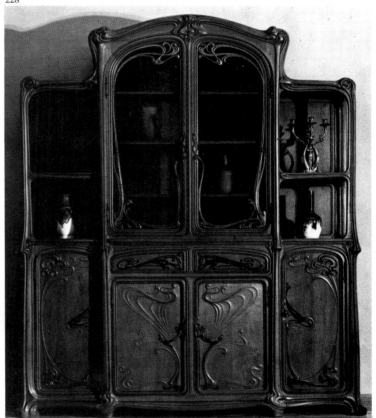

228

227

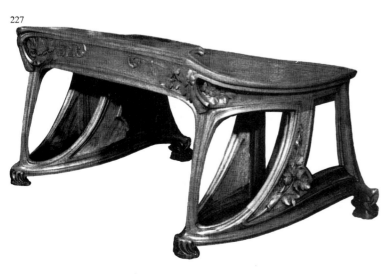

229

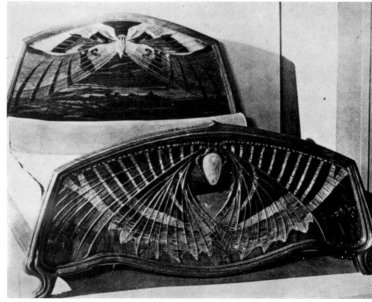

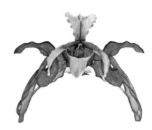

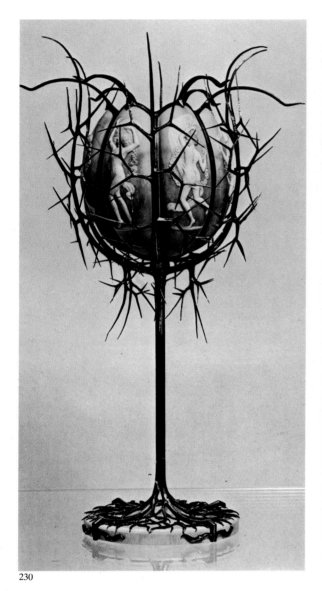

230

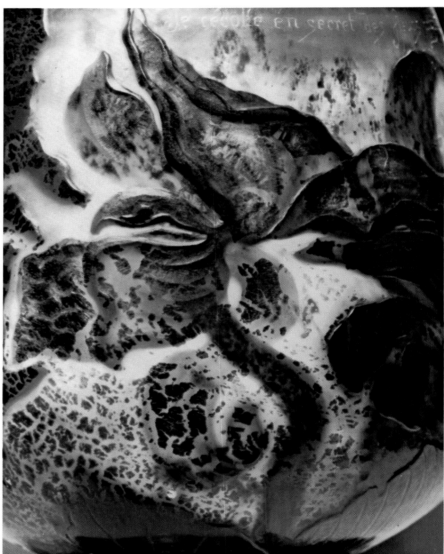

231

Louis Majorelle is possibly the next most important figure from the School of Nancy. His works are very plastic and their function is subordinated to his decorative intention. This is particularly true of his furniture designs. Other prolific furniture and interior designers associated with the School are Alexandre Charpentier and Eugène Vallin. Their success was probably due to their awareness of spatial and formal problems which they had encountered in their architectural work.

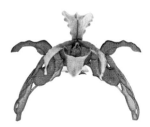

230—ALBERT DAMMOUSE, School of Nancy, *Damas' chalice*, by Félix Gilon; iron mounting by the Nics brothers. Nancy, Musée de l'Ecole de Nancy.
231—E. GALLÉ, *The Flesh-eaters*, c. 1889; detail bearing a verse by Alfred de Musset, *Je récolte en secret des fleurs mystérieuses*. Nancy, Musée de l'Ecole de Nancy.
232—Signatures of the brothers Daum from 1890 to 1903.
233—DAUM BROTHERS, cyclamen vase, c. 1900. Florence, private collection.

232

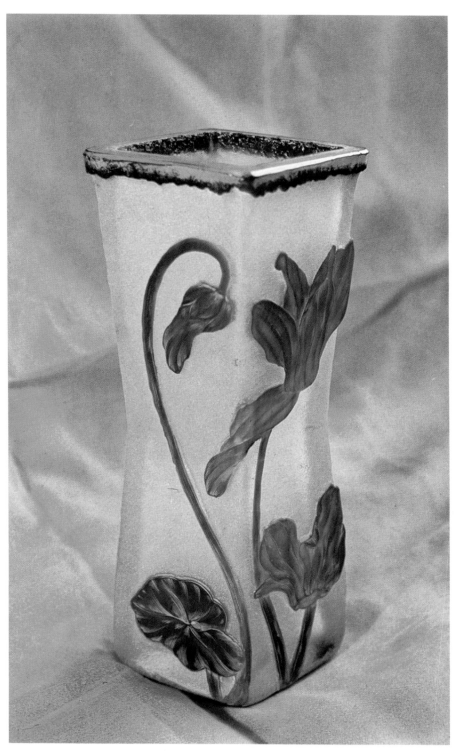

233

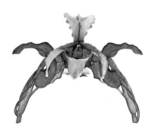

234

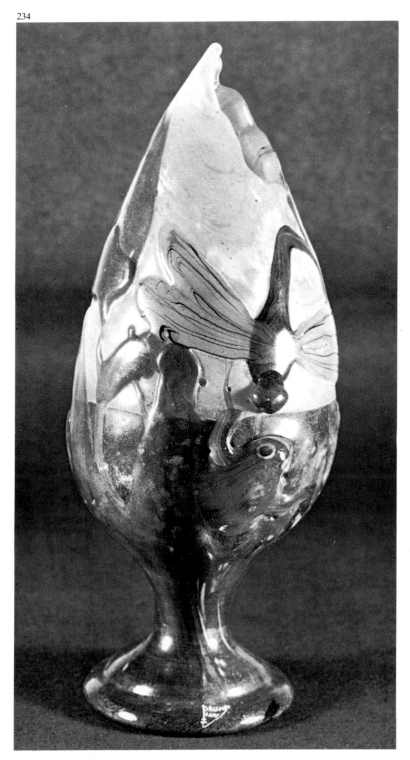

235

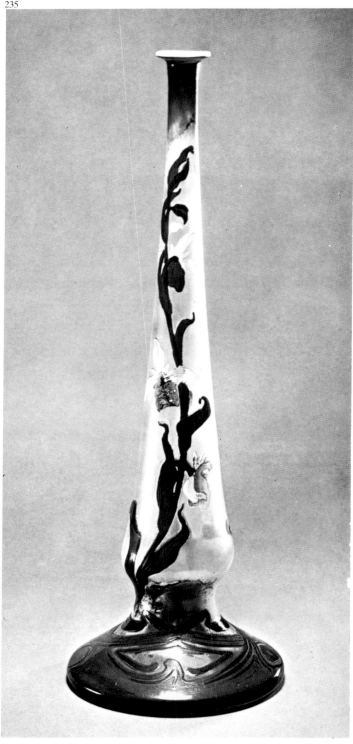

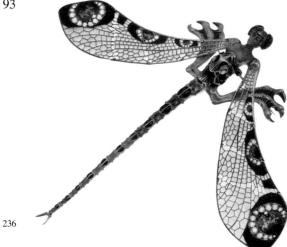

236

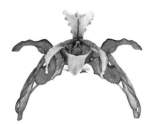

238

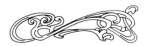

234—DAUM BROTHERS, vase with dragonfly and toad, c. 1900, Nancy, Musée de l'Ecole de Nancy.
235—MULLER BROTHERS, vase with floral decoration, c. 1910. Nancy, Musée de l'Ecole de Nancy.
236—R. LALIQUE, brooch with a flexible dragonfly, 1898.
237—ANDRÉ, house at Nancy, rue Claude Lorraine, c. 1900.
238—Nancy, pavilion adjacent to the Musée de l'Ecole de Nancy, 30, rue du Sergent-Blandau.

237

In the field of jewellery design the name of RÉNÉ LALIQUE (1860-1945) reigns supreme. Lalique began his studies in Paris and then went to London for further training. Upon his return to Paris in 1885 he opened a workshop. In 1894 he made his first jewels for Sarah Bernhardt. The patronage of the famous actress made him instantly famous and ensured his becoming the most sought-after jeweller in Europe.

Lalique's work shows his complete understanding of the techniques of traditional goldsmiths. This can be seen not only in his reproduction jewellery but also in the confidence with which he turned the principles of his art into the novel forms of his mature style. His jewels represent luxurious, possibly parasitic, plants brilliantly coloured and often inhabited by insects. Another of his favourite themes is woman. She is portrayed with minute accuracy as a disturbingly irresistible being. Flowers or insects which function as symbolic attributes are also present in these jewels.

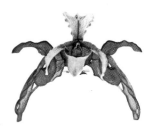

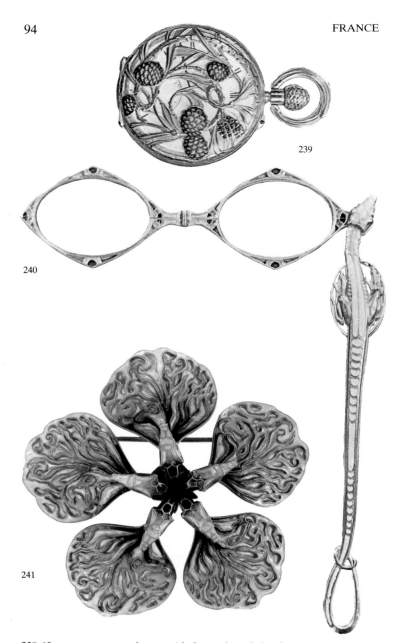

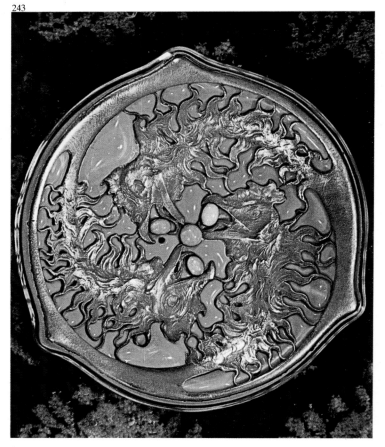

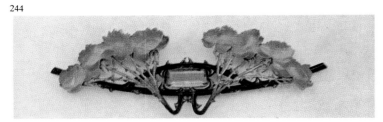

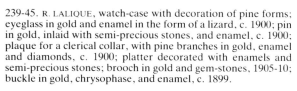

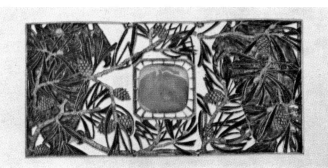

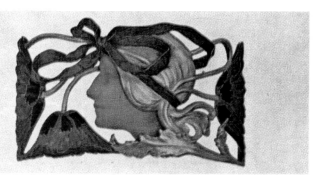

94 FRANCE

239

240

241

243

244

245

242

239-45. R. LALIQUE, watch-case with decoration of pine forms; eyeglass in gold and enamel in the form of a lizard, c. 1900; pin in gold, inlaid with semi-precious stones, and enamel, c. 1900; plaque for a clerical collar, with pine branches in gold, enamel and diamonds, c. 1900; platter decorated with enamels and semi-precious stones; brooch in gold and gem-stones, 1905-10; buckle in gold, chrysophase, and enamel, c. 1899.

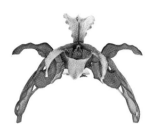

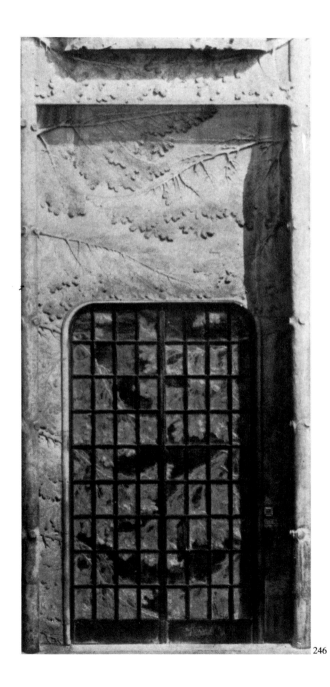

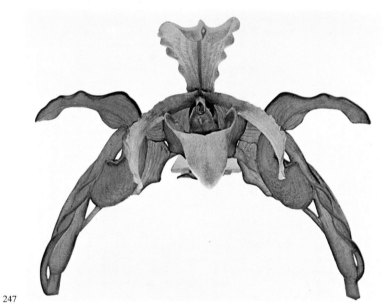

247

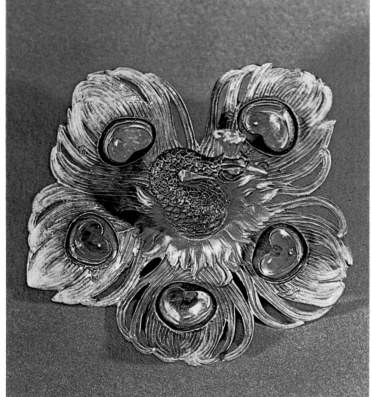

246—R. LALIQUE, the artist's house, Paris; detail of the facade.
247—R. LALIQUE, orchid in ivory and horn, 1897-1900.
248—R. LALIQUE, peacock pin in gold, enamel and semi-precious stones. Darmstadt, Hessische Landesmuseum.

246

248

5-Belgium

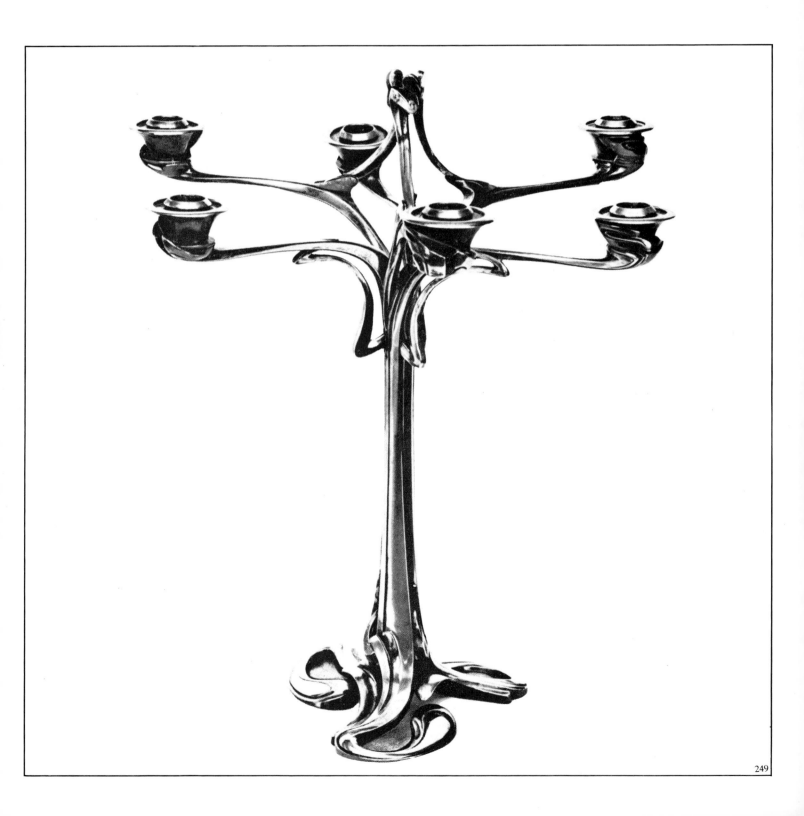

249

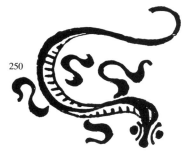

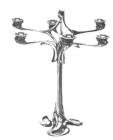

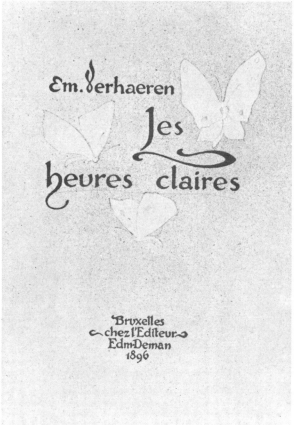

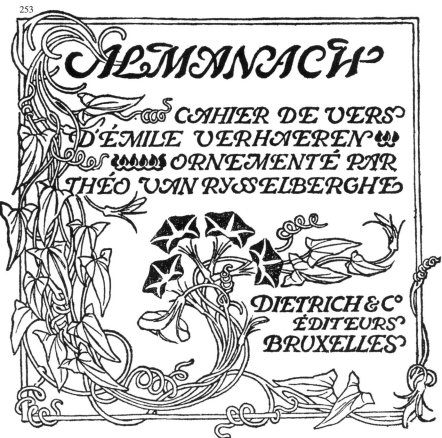

249—and symbol of Chapter 5, pp 97-125—HENRY VAN DE VELDE, six-branched candelabra, 1900. Brussels, Musées Royaux d'Art et d'Histoire.
250—THEO VAN RYSSELBERGHE, lizard design in *Les Villes Tentaculaires* by Emile Verhaeren, 1895.
251—T. VAN RYSSELBERGHE, cover of *Les Heures Claires*, by E. Verhaeren, 1896.
252—T. VAN RYSSELBERGHE, *Portrait of Octave Maus*, 1885. Ixelles, Musée des Beaux Arts.
253—T. VAN RYSSELBERGHE, title page for E. Verhaeren's *Almanach, cahier de vers*, 1985.

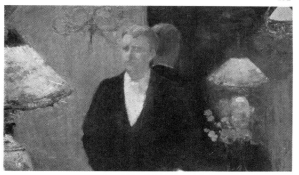

The singular position of Brussels as a cultural and artistic centre in the 1890s is due mainly to the activities of a group of writers and artists of the previous decade, who had established connections with the Parisian avant-garde. One of the most important of these was Emile Verhaeren, who secured Georges Seurat's participation in the 1887 exhibition of the Société des Vingt (Les XX) with the showing of his *Sunday on the Island of La Grande Jatte*. The presence of this revolutionary painting not only established the Society as the most progressive exhibiting organization in Europe, but it also stated their intention of establishing a political role for the arts in opposition to the stultifying role which they felt that bourgeois society had imposed on the arts.

Seurat's pointillist style was soon adopted by many of the Belgian members of Les XX, for instance Theo Van Rhysselberghe and Anna Boch. The style was adopted not just as a compliment to the Parisian painter, but as a means of expressing the desire of the Belgians to be in the forefront of artistic development.

The Société des Vingt had been established in 1884 under the auspices of its secretary Octave Maus, who from 1881 was the founder

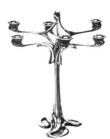

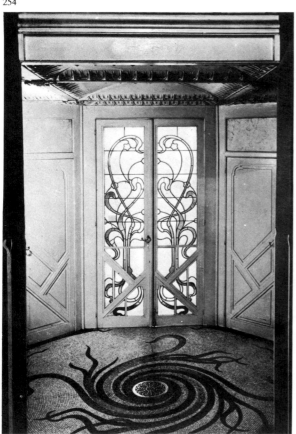

254

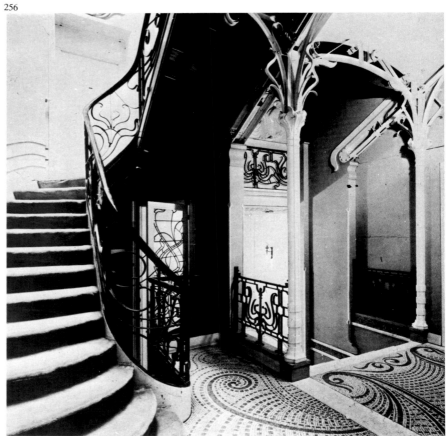

256

254—VICTOR HORTA, Hôtel Tassel, Brussels, 1893.
255—V. HORTA, chandelier for the Hôtel Solvay at Brussels, 1895-1900.
256—V. HORTA, Hôtel Tassel, vestibule and staircase.
257—V. HORTA, Hôtel Wissinger, Brussels, 1894.
258—V. HORTA, Hôtel Tassel, staircase.
259—V. HORTA, Hôtel Wissinger, bay window.
*—page 99, MAX ESKAMP, vignette, c. 1900.

255

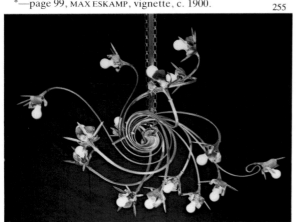

of the progressive journal *L'Art Moderne*. The range of artists attracted to Les XX mirrored Verhaeren's international taste. In 1883 Ford Madox Brown exhibited with the group, and in 1884 Rodin, Ashbee, Image, Morris and Beardsley were all showing their work in Brussels. In 1886 Pierre-Auguste Renoir, Claude Monet, Odilon Redon and Georges Minne had an exhibition at Les XX. Between 1887 and 1891 Les XX saw works executed by the majority of the leading figures from the English and French avant-garde, many of whom were grateful for the opportunity to show in an environment where their work would receive critical understanding. Among these were Paul Signac, Paul Cézanne, Camille Pissarro, Toulouse-Lautrec, Whistler, Crane, Gauguin, Vincent van Gogh, Chéret and the Norwegian, Thaulow.

Brussels was one of the first centres where Art Nouveau was accepted as an international style because of the number of artists from other countries who were encouraged to work and exhibit there. Local artists quickly achieved success because of the particularly active cultural life of the city. Among them are the artists whose names are synonymous with the European expansion of Art Nouveau

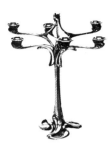

257

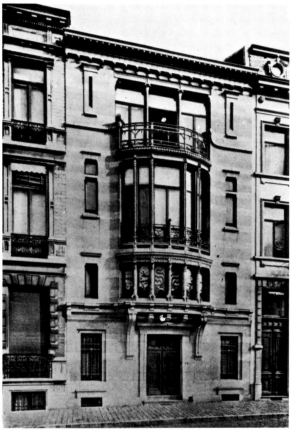

259

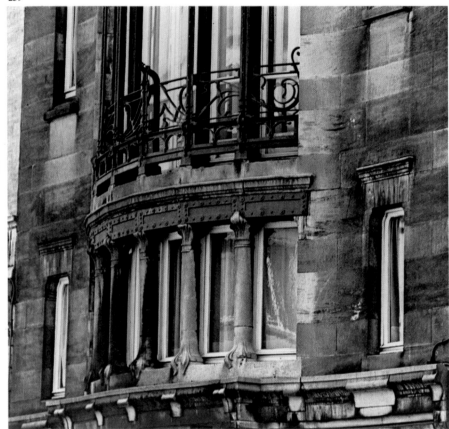

258

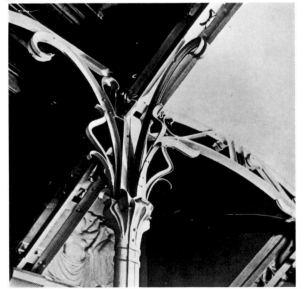

– Henry van de Velde, Paul Hankar and Victor Horta, whose work represents the first truly mature expression of the movement.

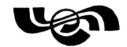

If van de Velde represents the success of Art Nouveau in Belgium as a wide-ranging style, the architect VICTOR HORTA (1861-1947) is the most successful exponent of Art Nouveau architecture. Horta had been exposed to the most recent developments in French architectural thinking. The theoretical basis for his works lies in the work of Viollet-le-Duc and Vaudrener. Horta's most important early work is the Hôtel Tassel (1892-93), built in Brussels. At this early stage in the development of the movement, the building was already a remarkably mature statement of the new architectural style. It is both free from historicism and it is perfectly coherent in its details.

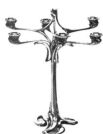

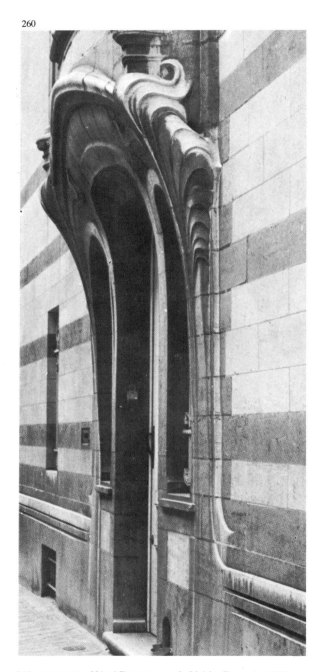

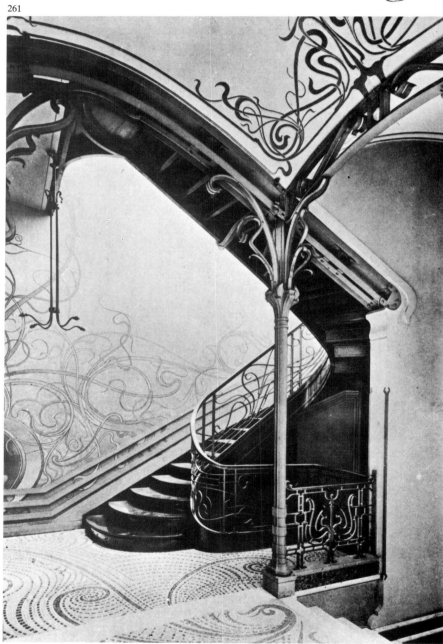

260—V. HORTA, Hôtel Deprez-van de Velde, Brussels, 1896.
261—V. HORTA, Hôtel Tassel, Brussels, 1893, staircase.

The Hôtel Tassel is important because Horta has successfully transformed a common Belgian building type (namely the single family house) into a novel and harmonious composition. The basis of the design is the springing movement of the whiplash arabesque motif, which originates in the facade and controls the luminous entrance hall. The hall is dominated by a brightly-lit stair supported

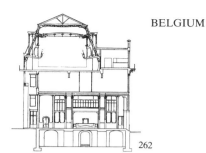

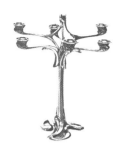

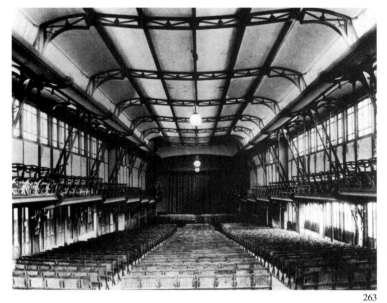

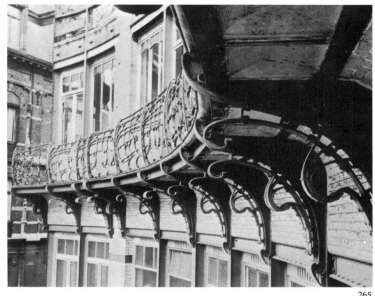

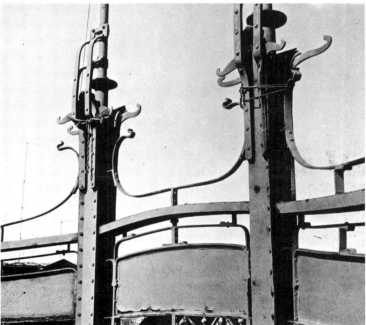

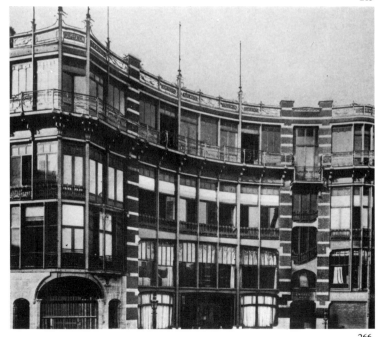

262—V. HORTA, Maison du Peuple, Brussels, 1895 (now demolished), section.
263—V. HORTA, Maison du Peuple, Brussels, the conference hall and theatre.
264—V. HORTA, Maison du Peuple, exterior balustrade.
265—V. HORTA, Maison du Peuple, balcony.
266—V. HORTA, Maison du Peuple, balustrade and flagstaffs.

on a cast iron column and impost with whiplash capitals. These generate all of the decorative elements from the treatment of the wall surfaces to the banister rail and the mosaic floor.

In Horta's Maison du Peuple (1896-99) – built for the Union of Socialist Workers – the architect makes radically inventive use of iron and glass. Here the iron supporting columns project out beyond the

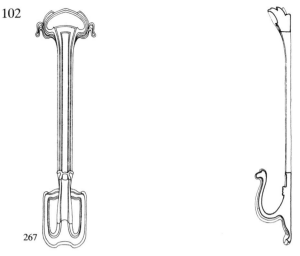

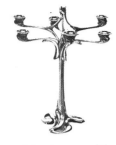

plane of the glass window. Horta thus endows structural features with ornamental values. The large expanses of glass and the delicate iron grid supports produce an almost diaphanous effect. Two other remarkable buildings designed by Horta are the Hôtel Solvay (1895-1900) and the Hôtel van Eetvelde (1895). In the former the structural and decorative properties of the cast iron skeleton are used to make the windows in the stone building appear much larger. The combina-

267

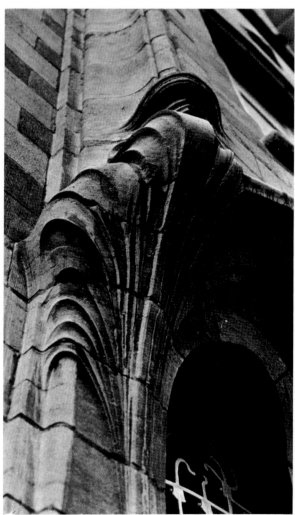

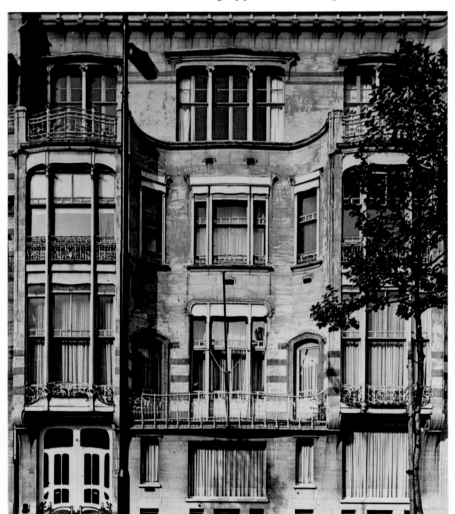

268

269

267—v. HORTA, door handle and letter-box for the atelier Horta, Brussels.
268—v. HORTA, Hôtel Deprez-van de Velde, Brussels, 1896; detail of the facade.
269—v. HORTA, Hôtel Solvay, Brussels, 1895-1900; facade (demolished)..
270—v. HORTA, Hôtel van Eetvelde, Brussels, 1895; skylight.

tion of the two materials used here is very successful and gives a rhythmic alternation of wall and aperture. The result is an elevation which is highly articulated, rhythmic and monumental. In the Hôtel Eetvelde (1895), Horta used iron to support glass, creating large transparent areas which are related by their rhythmic composition. Slender iron piers and beams now support web-like arabesque

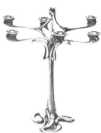

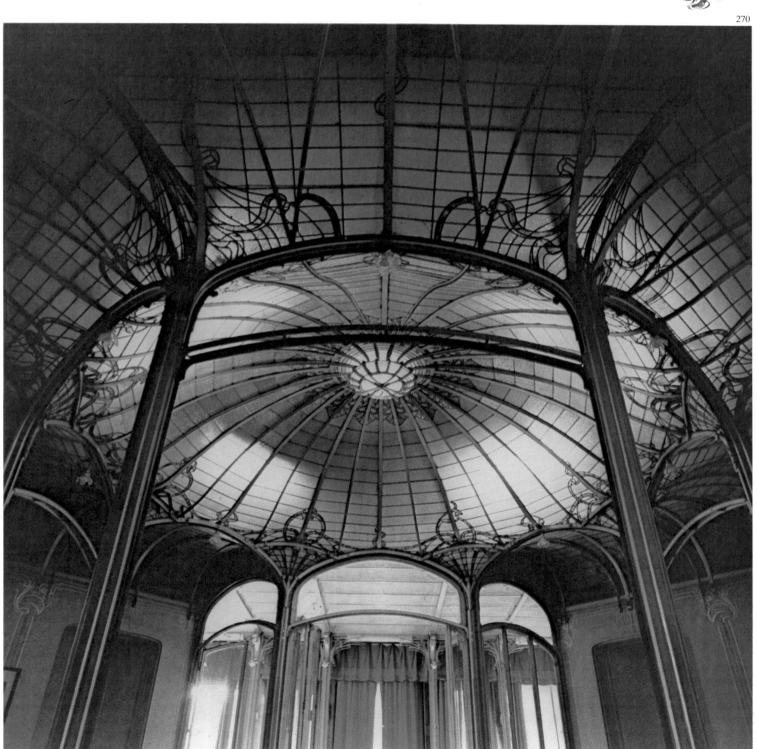

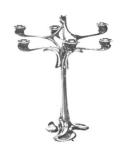

271

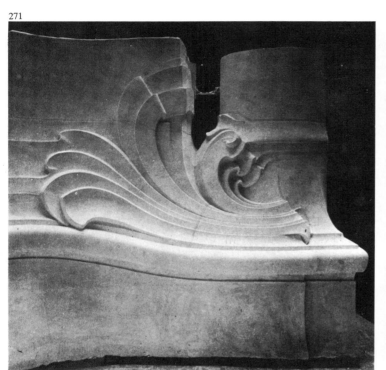

273

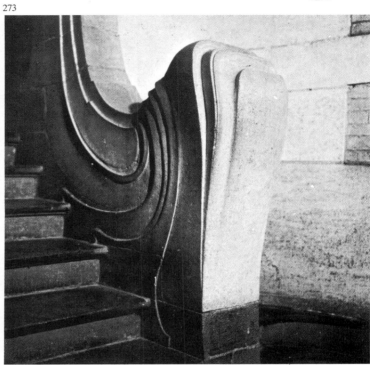

272

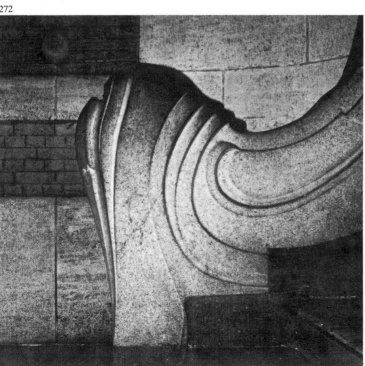

274

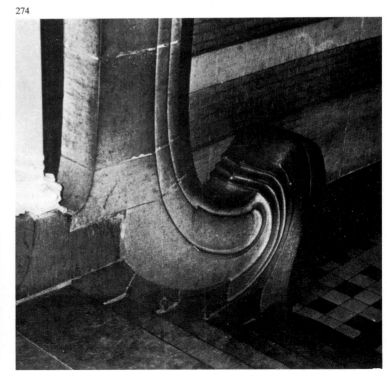

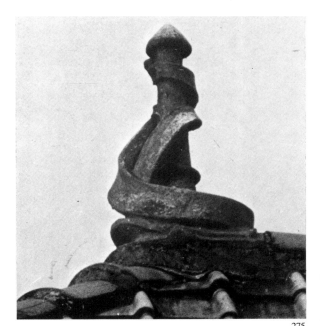

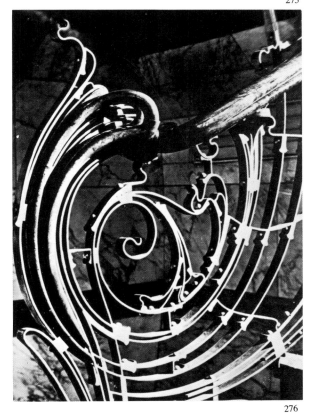

275

276

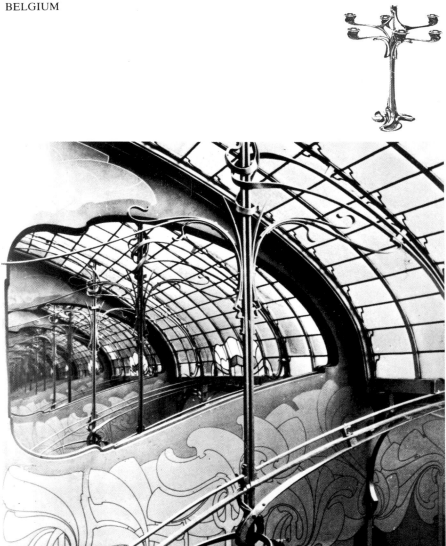

277

ironwork whose thin members in turn support large areas of glass, allowing the maximum penetration of light and spatial fluidity. The effect is one of great decorative fantasy in which the eye is led continually from one transparent space to another, guided by the rhythms of the supporting iron structure.

271—V. HORTA, a model for a base of a column on the facade of the Museum at Tournai, 1911.
272-274—V. HORTA, The Maison du Peuple, 1895; details of the staircase.
275—V. HORTA, Villa Carpenter at Renaix, chimney.
276—V. HORTA, Hôtel Solvay, 1895-1900; detail of the staircase.
277—V. HORTA, Hôtel van Eetvelde, Brussels; skylights.
*—page 105, HORTA's seal.

Whereas Horta's work represents the highest development of curvilinear Art Nouveau architecture in Brussels, PAUL HANKAR (1861-1901), who was also a member of the Art Nouveau movement, is his stylistic opposite. His work is characterized by a tendency to stress the volume and equilibrium of his buildings while simplifying the linear elements. Hankar shared with Horta an interest in the work

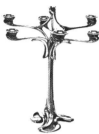

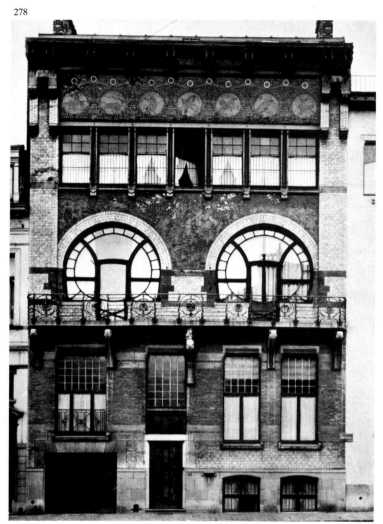

278

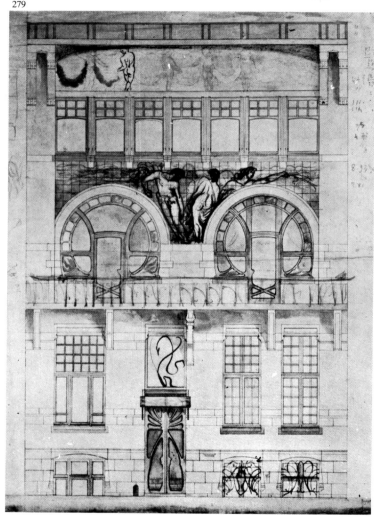

279

278—PAUL HANKAR, The Ciamberlani House, Brussels, 1897 (demolished); facade.
279—P. HANKAR, project for the facade of the Ciamberlani House in Brussels (the painted figures are by Ciamberlani).
280—P. HANKAR, the door to Maison A. Niguet, Brussels, 1899 (demolished).
281—P. HANKAR, a door in the Ciamberlani House, 1897.
282—P. HANKAR, pavilion, ethnographic section at the Colonial Exhibition in Terveuren, 1897.
283—P. HANKAR, Maison A. Niguet, Brussels, 1899 (demolished).
284—P. HANKAR, stool. Brussels, coll. Hankar.
285—P. HANKAR, New-England, shop in Brussels (demolished).
286—P. HANKAR, small table. Brussels, coll. Hankar.
287—P. HANKAR, Grand Hôtel, Brussels, 1896 (demolished); facade of the restaurant in rue l'Evêque.
  *—page 108—P. HANKAR, project for a window-frame for the Ciamberlani House.

of Viollet-le-Duc. He was attracted to revivalism and many of his works have a flavour of late Renaissance architecture. He was also particularly impressed by the linear ornament used by the architects of the English Arts and Crafts Movement. These features are evident in his Ciamberlani House (1897), designed for the painter Ciamberlani and now destroyed. The mixture of ornate surface decoration and near symmetry in the overall design defines Hankar's own particular range.

The Maison Niguet (1899 and also now destroyed) is an arguably more successful synthesis of structural and decorative features. In the shop facade of this building there is a restraint of articulation and a respect for symmetry. However, within this framework the architect has achieved a highly developed ornament which also supports the large area of glass. This ornament, which both carries load and

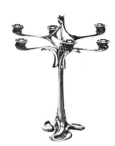

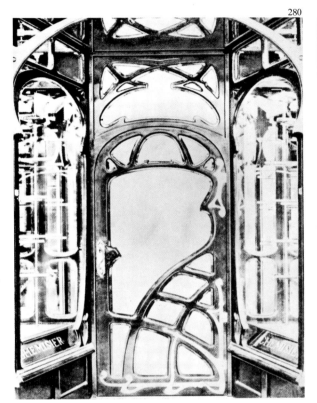

280

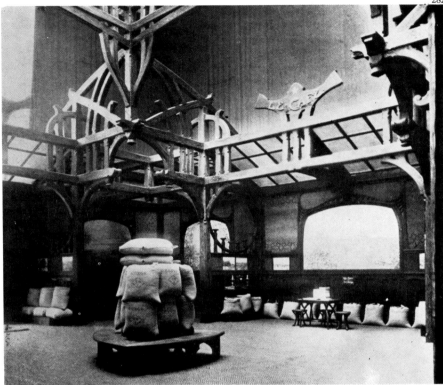

282

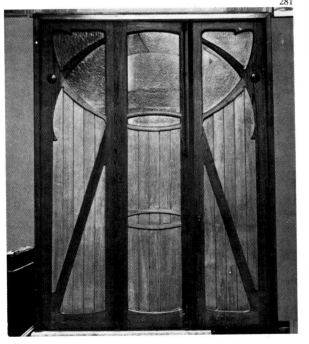

281

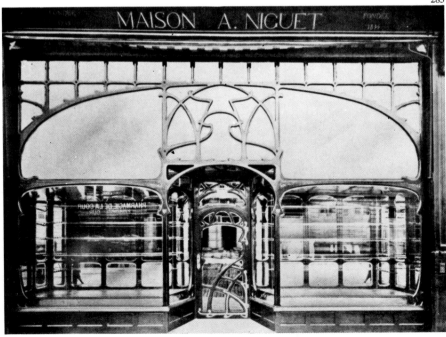

283

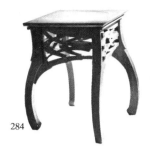

284

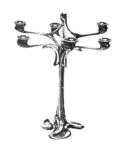

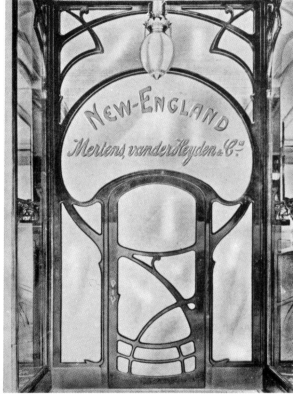

285

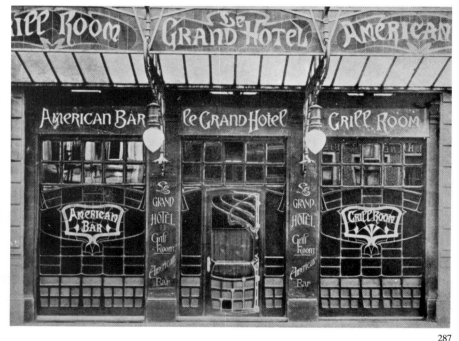

287

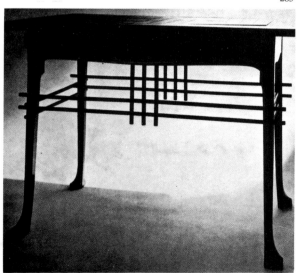

286

expresses the surface rhythm, is firm in its appearance and it asserts a major role within the scheme of the building as a whole.

By the mid-1890s there were developments in Brussels which would turn whole areas of the city into unified Art Nouveau neighbourhoods. Both private, middle-class housing and public buildings were built in this style. Art Nouveau became the official style of urban renewal in Brussels and dispensed with the traditional use of architectural hierarchy to define the function of different types of buildings. Between 1900 and 1910 a whole generation of Brussels architects took part in the renovation of the city. Gustave Strauven, whose work combines quotations from Gothic and Baroque architecture with Art Nouveau itself, built the house of the painter de Saint-Cyr in 1900. Paul Vizzavona worked on several private housing projects, as did his contemporaries Ernest Blerot, Emile van Averbeke and Paul Cauchie, whose own atelier, built in 1905, has strong affinities with Hankar's Ciamberlani House of the previous decade.

By 1893, Les XX was showing a tendency to include work which was not exclusively 'fine art'. Crane's illustrated book designs and Chéret's posters are just two examples. In the following year the society was dissolved and reconstituted itself as Le Livre Esthétique.

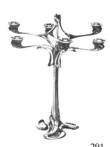

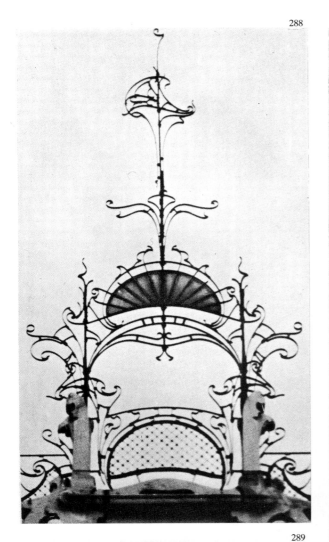

288

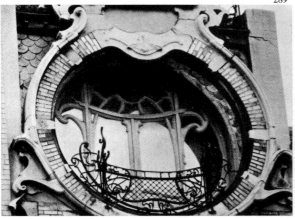

289

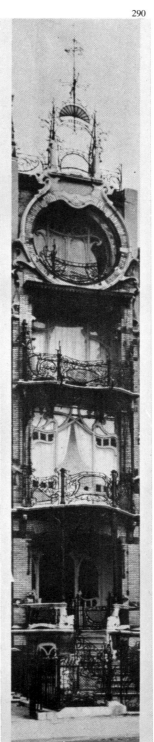

290

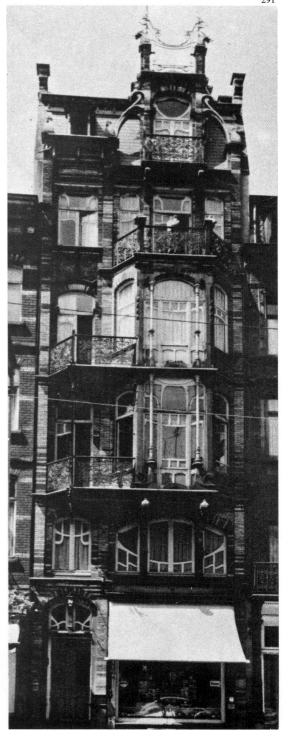

291

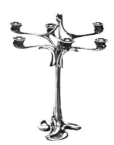

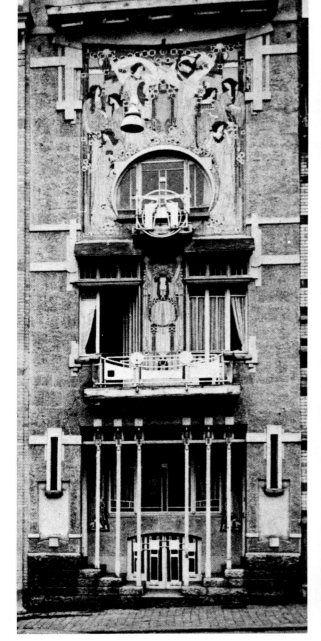

292

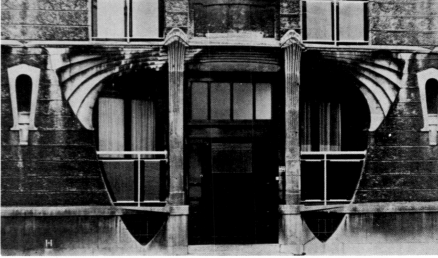
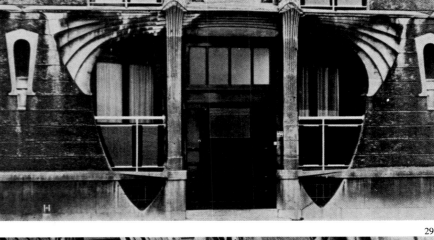
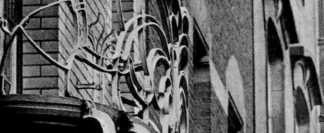

293

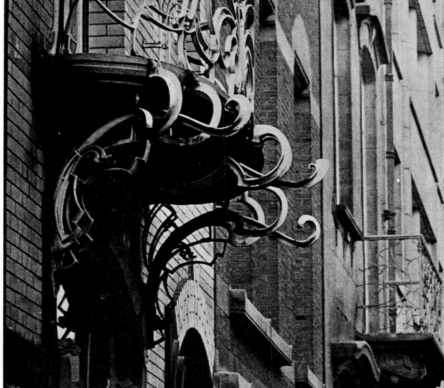

294

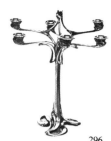

295

296

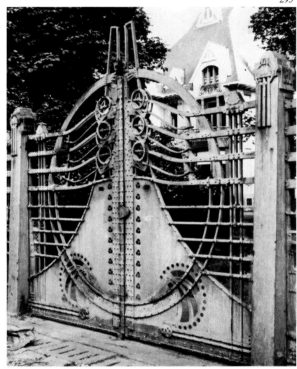

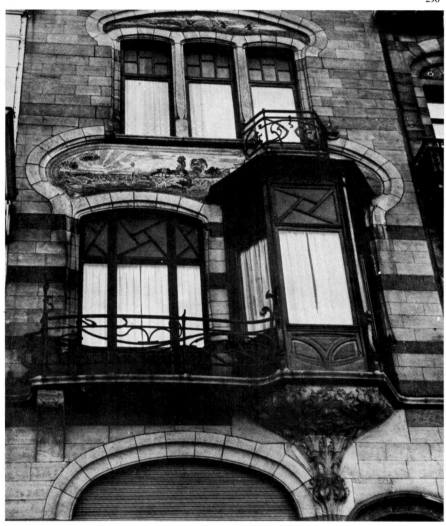

288—GUSTAVE STRAUVEN, house of the painter de Saint-Cyr, Brussels, 1900; wrought-iron pinnacle on the facade.
289—G. STRAUVEN, house of the painter de Saint-Cyr, 1900; attic window and grille.
290—G. STRAUVEN, house of the painter de Saint-Cyr, 1900; facade.
291—G. STRAUVEN, apartment block, Saint-Gilles, Brussels, 1902-09.
292—PAUL CAUCHIE, his house and studio, Brussels, 1905.
293—Public housing, Forest (Brussels); entrance.
294—PAUL VIZZAVONA, private house, Ixelles, Brussels, 1903; detail of the balcony.
295—EMILE VAN AVERBEKE, Villa Cortenbergh, Brussels, 1903; gate.
296—E. BLÉROT, private house, Saint-Gilles, Brussels, 1900.
297—E. BLÉROT, townhouses; project for Brussels, 1900.

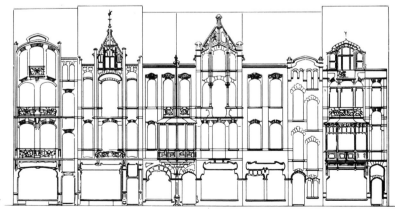

297

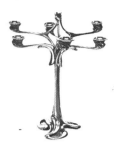

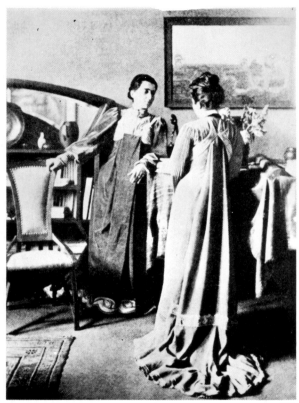

The aim of the new society was close to that of the earlier one, but its scope was broadened to promote work from all areas of artistic production without hierarchical divisions between them. The most prominent member of this new society was HENRY VAN DE VELDE (1863-1957). After his brief flirtation with 'pointillism' influenced by Seurat and Signac, van de Velde began to produce a wide range of artifacts in the new style. The aesthetic, or even ethical impetus behind this change of direction came directly from Morris and socialist art theory. Van de Velde saw his products as having a directly beneficial effect on society. They could give ordinary people an opportunity to enjoy beautiful objects which were created by artists' involvement with the manufacturing process. Van de Velde always viewed art as a means of social regeneration which could release society from the bonds of an economic system which he felt tended to dissociate its members from the environment.

Van de Velde's own house Bloemenwerf (1895) which he built and furnished himself, is a manifestation of his vision of the relationship between man and his environment. Although he was not formally trained as an architect, the building very successfully reconciles functional demands and decorative intentions within the structure. The architecture is in the vernacular idiom; it already shows the soft uninterrupted rhythms which were to dominate Art Nouveau architecture in the coming years.

Bloemenwerf is remarkable for its overall design. The house was conceived as a complete entity; the furniture, decorations, even the

298

298—H. VAN DE VELDE, lady's gown, c. 1896.
299—H. VAN DE VELDE, Bloemenwerf house, Uccle, Brussels, 1895; facade.
300—H. VAN DE VELDE, silver candlestick, 1906-07.
301—H. VAN DE VELDE, bronze ink-pot, 1898.
302—H. VAN DE VELDE, silver cutlery, 1902-03.

On pages 114, 115
303—H. VAN DE VELDE, portrait of his wife in a dress designed by him.
304-306—H. VAN DE VELDE, three pendants in silver, gold and precious stones, c. 1900.
307—H. VAN DE VELDE, writing desk, c. 1900.
308—H. VAN DE VELDE, samovar, c. 1903. Zurich, Kunstgewerbemuseum.
309—H. VAN DE VELDE, *Tropon*, 1898, poster.
310—H. VAN DE VELDE, binding for *Stampe e libri* by Beraldi, c. 1897.
311-312—H. VAN DE VELDE, chair and triangular table, 1903, 1902.

299

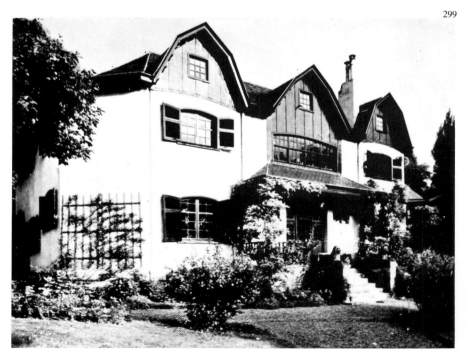

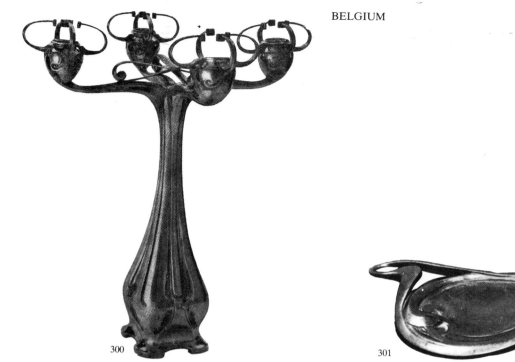

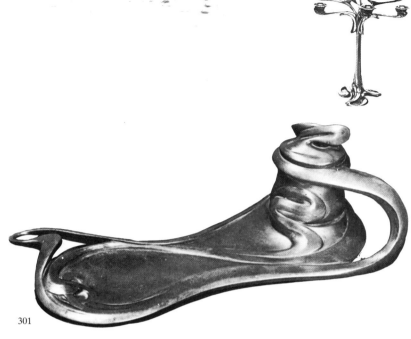

300

301

302

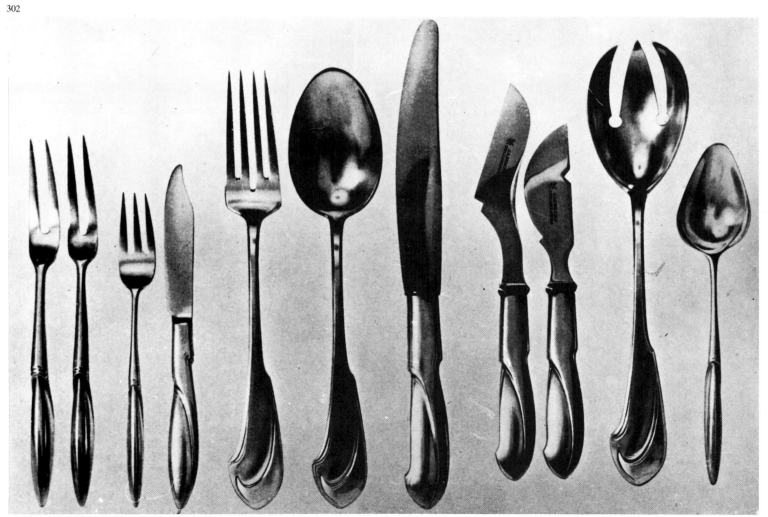

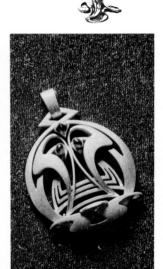

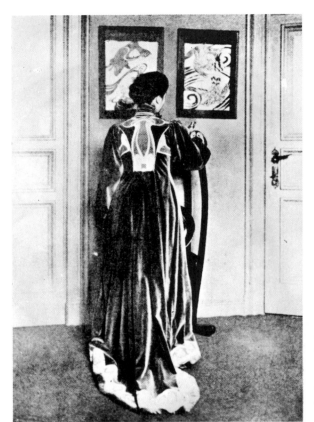

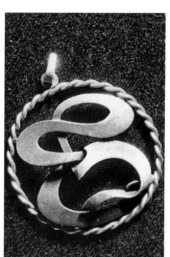

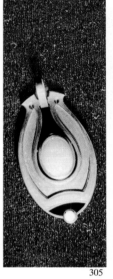

303

304

305

306

307

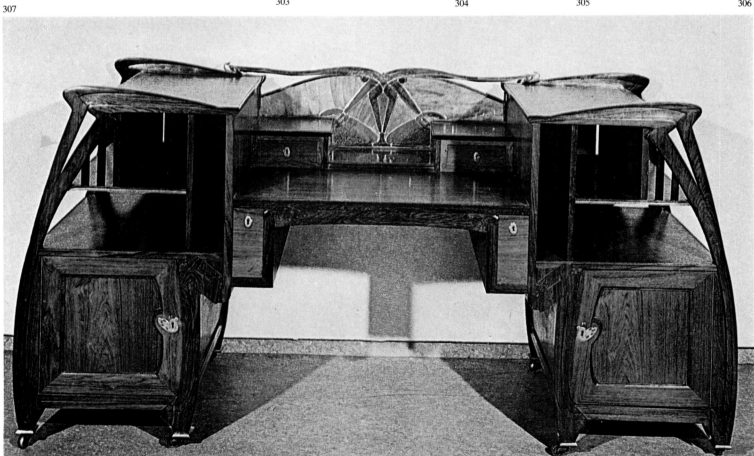

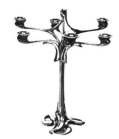

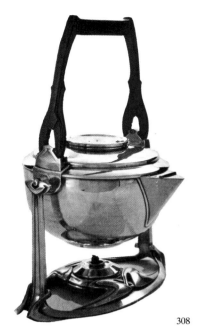

308

310

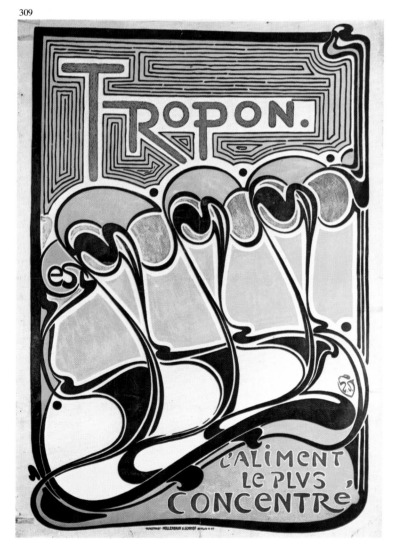

309

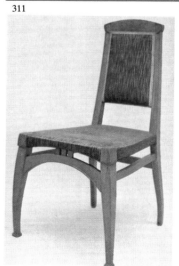

311

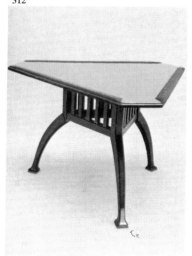

312

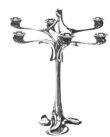

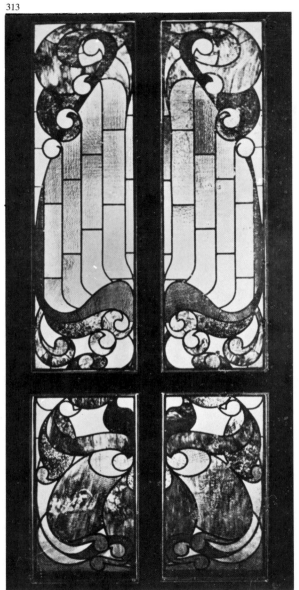

313

314

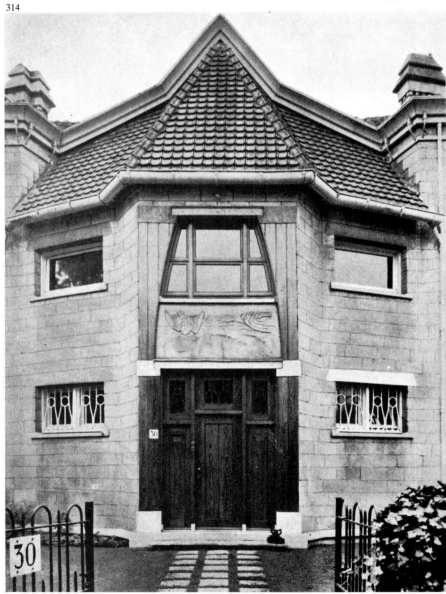

313—H. VAN DE VELDE, stained-glass window, 1900.
314—H. VAN DE VELDE, Lauring House, Scheveningen, Holland, 1903; the facade.
315—H. VAN DE VELDE, Hohenhof House for K. E. Osthaus, Hagen; Germany, 1906.
316—H. VAN DE VELDE, Rudolf Springman House, Hagen, 1906; garden facade.
317-318—H. VAN DE VELDE, Hohenhof House, Hagen, 1906; staircase and hall with frescoes by Hodler.

clothes to be worn by those living there, were all part of a floral arabesque decorative system and an overall colour scheme which was dominated by the light tone wood and copper of the furniture. The scheme soon attracted interest. Samuel Bing invited van de Velde to design similar schemes to show in his gallery L'Art Nouveau, and Julius Meier-Graefe, the influential editor of *Pan*, published his designs in this important periodical.

As a result of this publicity, van de Velde spent most of his time working for German patrons and from 1899 worked only in Germany.

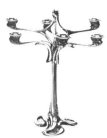

315

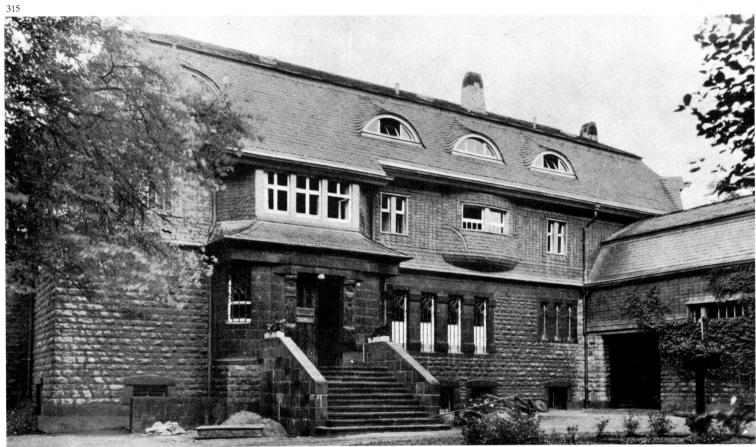

316

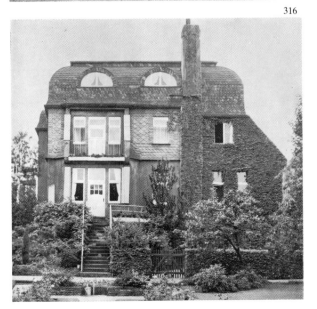

317

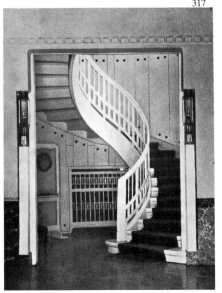

318

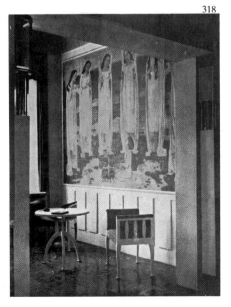

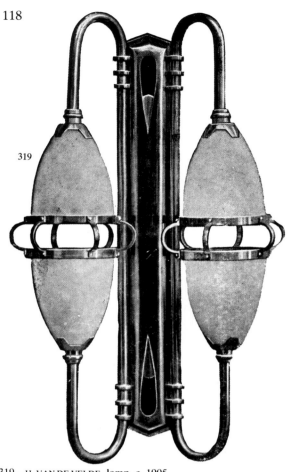

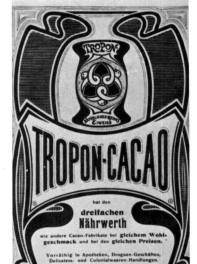

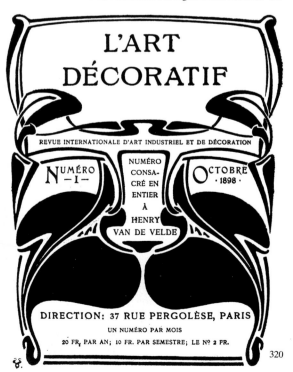

319—H. VAN DE VELDE, lamp, c. 1905.
320—H. VAN DE VELDE, cover of the first number of *L'Art Décoratif*; Paris, 1898.
321-322—H. VAN DE VELDE, posters for the Tropon company.
323—H. VAN DE VELDE, ornamental design for fabric, 1905-06.

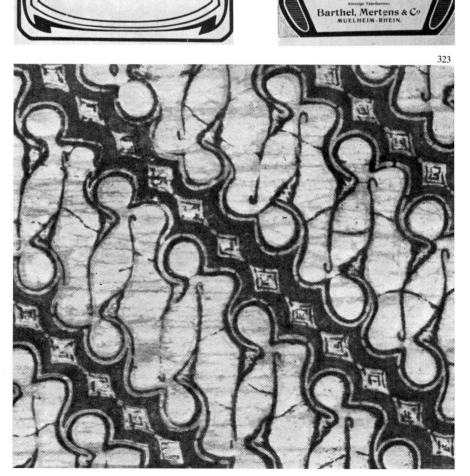

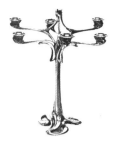

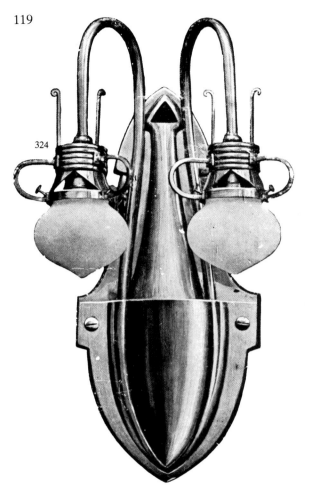

He is most readily identified with his work in the applied arts. He worked in almost the whole range of these arts: he made restrained yet dynamic designs for bookbindings, a famous poster for *Tropon*, remarkably vital furniture, as well as delicate and sophisticated cutlery and kitchenware. Even the language which van de Velde used in his theoretical and polemical writings, such as his *Débaillement d'Art* (1894), retains the feeling of Art Nouveau rhythm and dynamism which are the main features of his plastic work.

324—H. VAN DE VELDE, bracket lamp, 1905-10.
325—H. VAN DE VELDE, hanging lamp, 1905.
326—H. VAN DE VELDE, staircase at the Folkwang Museum, The Hague, 1902.

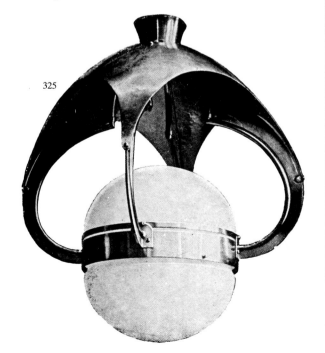

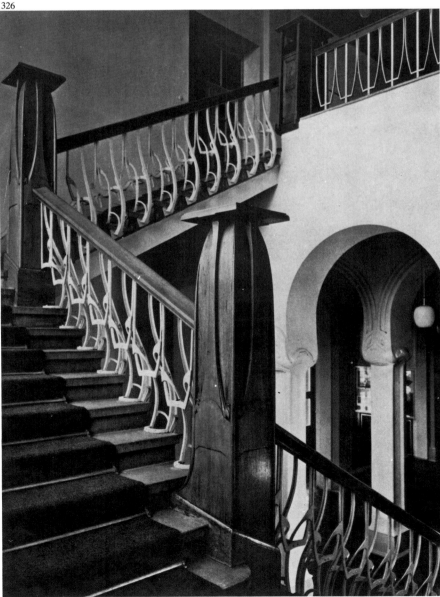

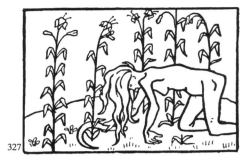

327

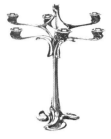

328

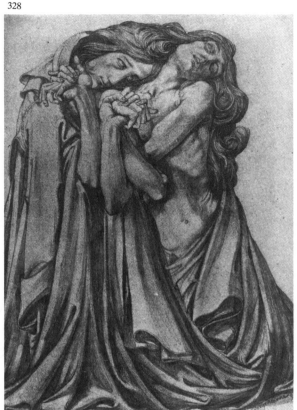

329

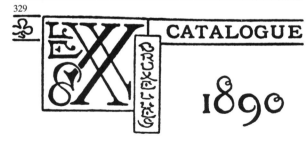

DE LA VIIe EXPOSITION ANNUELLE

327—GEORGES MINNE, illustration for *Serres Chaudes* by Verhaeren, Paris, 1889.
328—G. MINNE, *The Reprobates*, 1898. Brussels, Bibliothèque Royale.
329—FERNAND KHNOPFF, catalogue cover for *Les XX*, Brussels, 1890.
330—G. MINNE, *Fountain of the Kneeling Youths*, 1898.
331—F. KHNOPFF, *Portrait of his Sister*, 1887; detail. Brussels, coll. B. Thibaud de Maisières.
332—F. KHNOPFF, *Incense*, 1898; detail. Brussels, coll. B. Thibaud de Maisières.

Despite the enormous popularity that Art Nouveau enjoyed as an architectural style, it influenced only a very few painters and sculptors. In sculpture, the only exponent of the style was Georges Minne (1866-1941). Meier-Graefe described his fragile and delicate rhythms as 'plastic ornament'. Minne's work, however, is too complex to be fully admitted to the Art Nouveau canon. His fundamentally mystical approach is evident in his illustrations for Verhaeren's *Serres Chaudes* (1889) and his group *Fountain of the Kneeling Youths* (1898). If he sometimes assumes the surface features of Art Nouveau rhythmic organization, as he does in later work, these are submerged by an aim that is altogether more tense and searching.

330

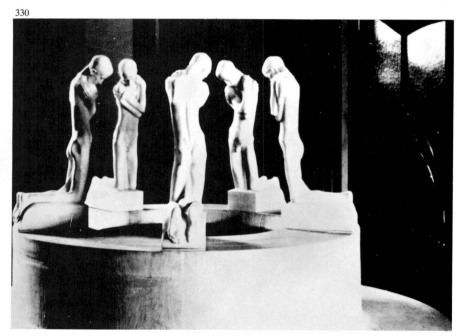

The work of the painter and critic, FERNAND KHNOPFF (1858-1921) is similarly ambiguous in its relationship to Art Nouveau. Khnopff's first works, like the *Portrait of the Artist's Sister* (1887) show the marriage of English Pre-Raphaelite influences with Seurat's synthetic style of drawing. In later works, Khnopff combines the other-worldly qualities of Burne-Jones' and Rossetti's female figures with decorative, almost Byzantine, settings. *Incense* (1898) is typical of this; the image is at once compelling for its psychological 'mystery' and evocative of splendour in its use of rich and exotic drapery. Khnopff learnt the decorative value of exotic surfaces from Gustave Moreau, one of his heroes (a bronze ring inscribed with his name hung on a Japanese brocade tapestry in Khnopff's home).

Khnopff's Art Nouveau work emerged in his association with the Viennese Secession. In the first year of the appearance of the

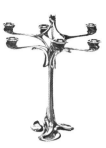

331

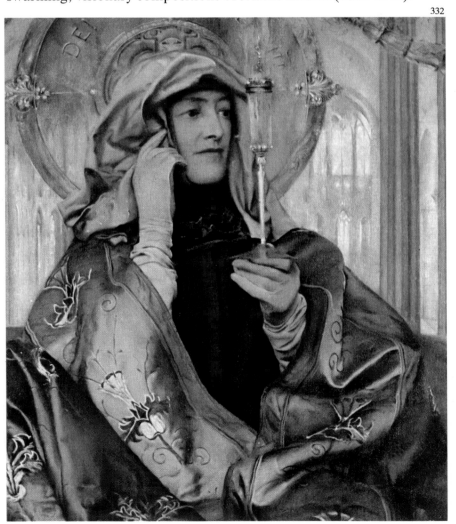

Secessionist magazine *Ver Sacrum* (1898), a whole issue was devoted to him. The surviving pieces of his graphic Art Nouveau work are, however, the designs and illustrations for the Société des Vingt exhibitions and catalogues. The cover for the 1890 catalogue is a small yet perfect marriage of calligraphy and arabesque line, worthy of the finest achievements in this field.

Curvilinear rhythms and highly developed decorative surfaces also occur in the work of Khnopff's contemporaries Jean Delville (1867-1953) and Emile Fabry (1865-1966). But their work, which is too steeped in evocative and mysterious imagery, cannot be called Art Nouveau. Rather than design the pure and limpid decorative work that had characterized the style in 1900, the Belgian painters began to develop anxieties which found their most powerful expression in the swarming, visionary compositions of JAMES ENSOR (1860-1949).

332

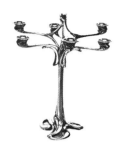

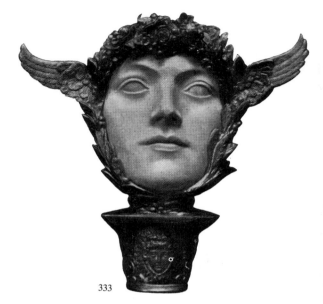

333

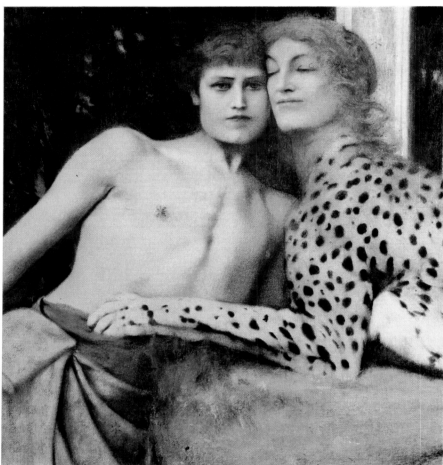

334

335

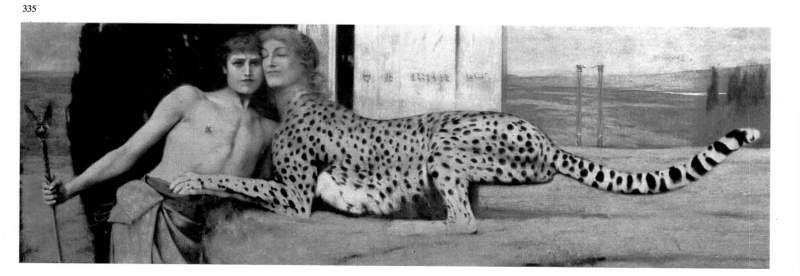

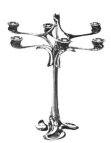

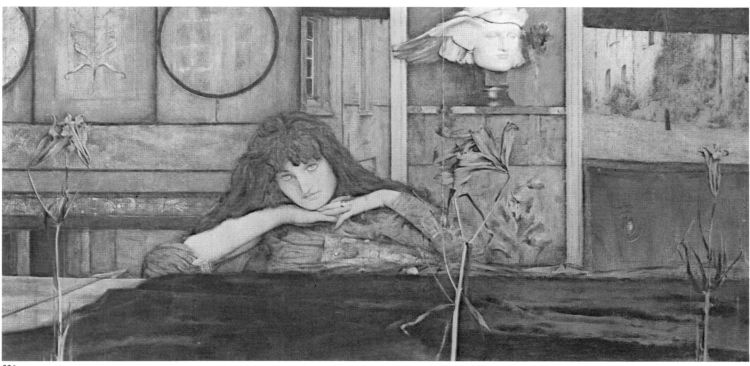

336

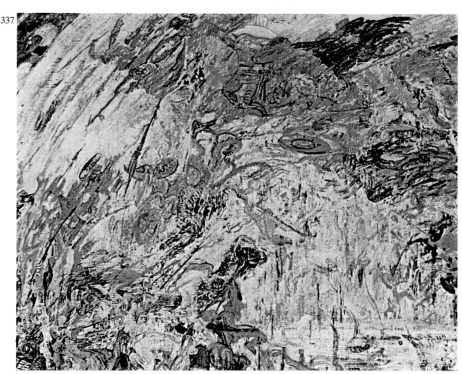

337

333—F. KHNOPFF, a mask in painted ivory, bronze and enamel.
334—F. KHNOPFF, *The Caresses of the Sphinx*, 1896; detail.
Brussels, Musées Royaux d'Art et d'Histoire.
335—F. KHNOPFF, *The Caresses of the Sphinx*, 1896. Brussels,
Musées Royaux d'Art et d'Histoire.
336—F. KHNOPFF, *I Closed the Door Behind Me*, 1891. Munich,
Bayerische Staatgemäldesammlungen.
337—JAMES ENSOR, *The Fall of the Rebellious Angels*, 1889;
detail. Antwerp, Musée Royale des Beaux Arts.

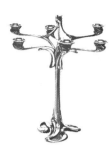

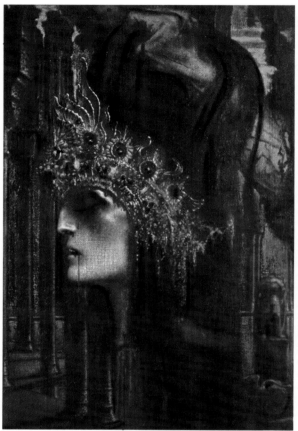

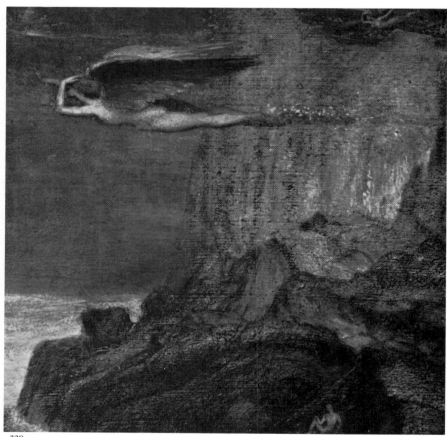

338

339

340

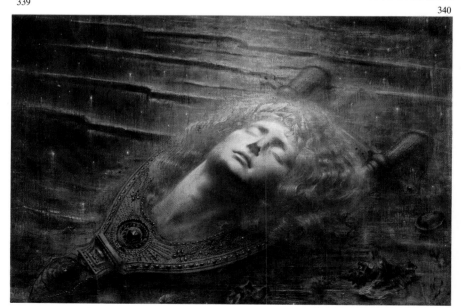

338—JEAN DELVILLE, *The End of a Reign*, 1893. Paris, private
collection.
339—EMILE FABRY, *The Poet and the Chimera*, 1916.
340—J. DELVILLE, *Orpheus*, 1893. Brussels, coll. Delville.

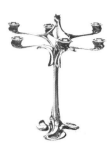

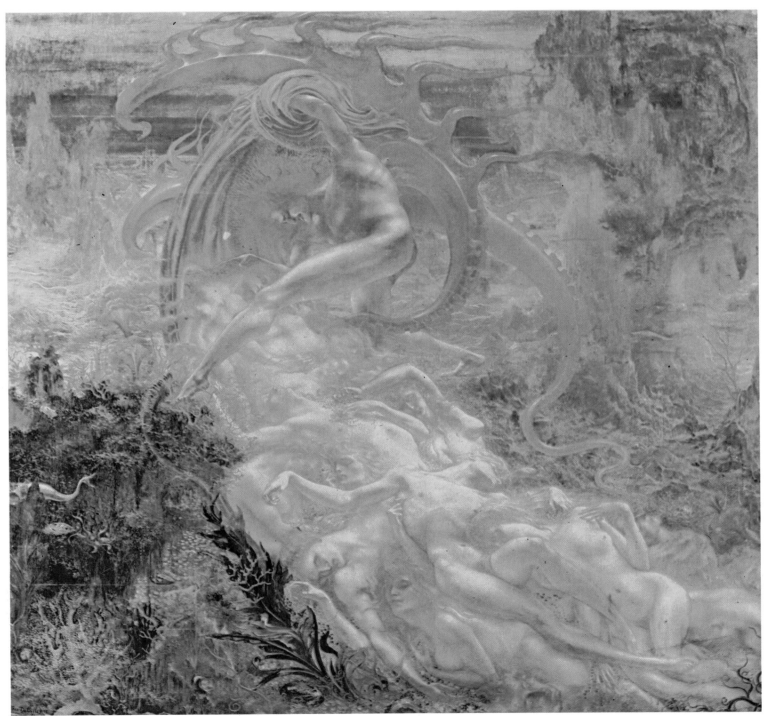

341—J. DELVILLE, *The Treasures of Satan*, 1895.

6-Spain

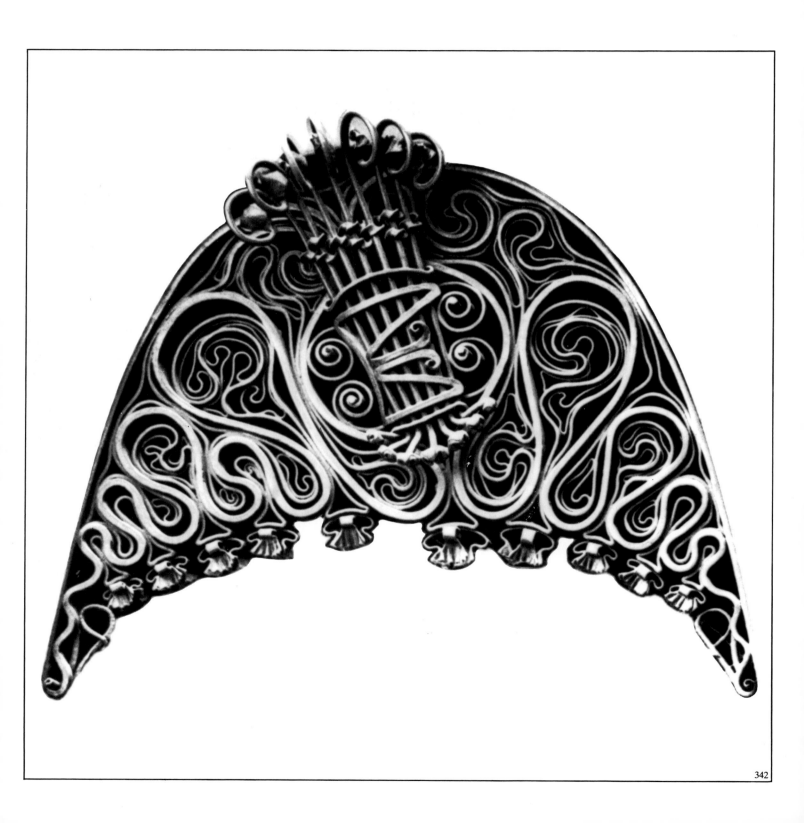

SPAIN

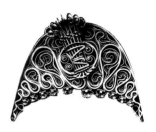

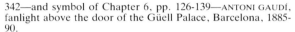

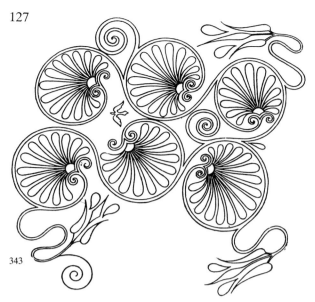

343

342—and symbol of Chapter 6, pp. 126-139—ANTONI GAUDÍ, fanlight above the door of the Güell Palace, Barcelona, 1885-90.
343—drawing of the decoration on the handle of a nolan amphora, the Nicostene group, late black-figure period.
344—A. GAUDÍ, Casa Vicens, Barcelona, 1878-80; detail of the gate.
345—A. GAUDÍ, Casa Vicens, Barcelona; drawing of the metalwork in the gate.
346—A. GAUDÍ, Casa Vicens, Barcelona; facades.

In Spain, the most powerful and successful Art Nouveau works were those of the architect ANTONI GAUDÍ (1852-1926). Gaudí's work was the product of a complex and rich set of cultural circumstances. Towards the end of the last century his native Barcelona was enjoying a renaissance of its artistic traditions. The Catalan language and traditions were being revived after centuries of Castilian domination. Although this revival initially recreated regional and traditional art forms, the cultural climate in Barcelona soon became very cosmopolitan as people flocked there. A wide range of ideas and opinions were expressed and exchanged there. This as much as anything was at the root of Gaudí's swift and personal reaction to Art Nouveau. He is known to have been interested in illustrated English art periodicals and in the writings of Ruskin and Pater, and this alerted him to the decorative possibilities of the new arabesque forms which were also present in the Moorish architecture of Spain.

In Gaudí's architecture this is expressed in an uncannily organic manipulation of form. His work took on the quality of natural

346

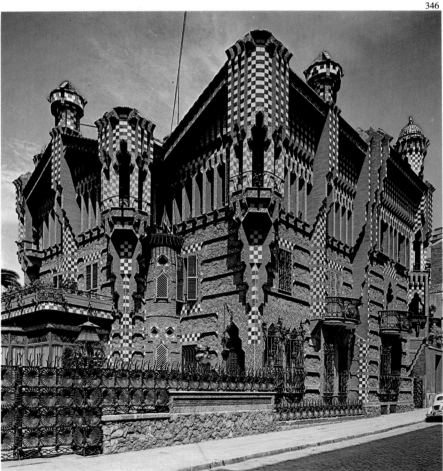

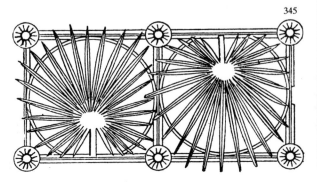

344

345

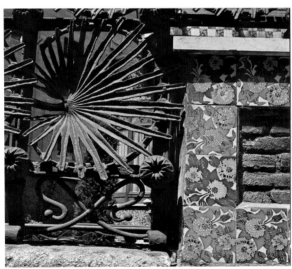

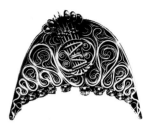

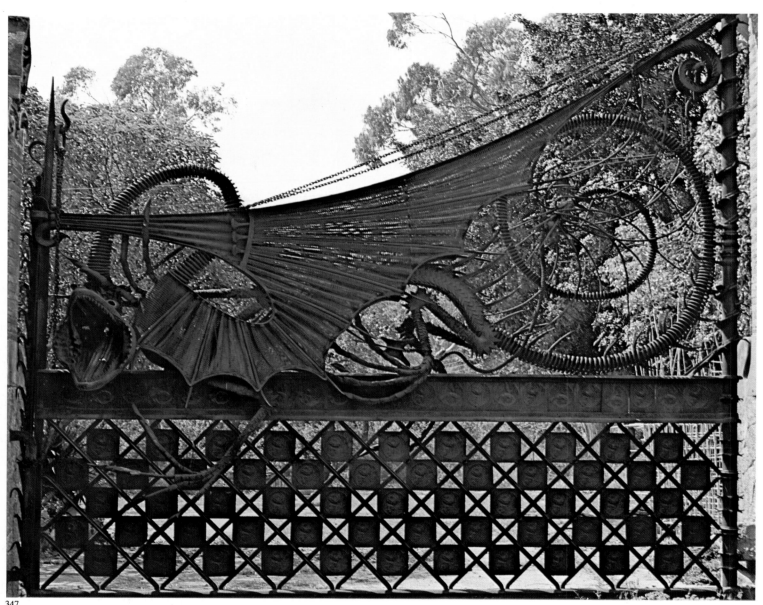

347

phenomena. This effect is less apparent in his early work, but even then there is still a highly charged emotional current operating in his work which is visible in his use of tight rhythmic repetitions. In one of his earliest works, the Casa Vicens (built between 1878 and 1880), Gaudí's later lyricism is absent. He has treated the house in a capricious and ostentatious manner; forms push outwards, forming serried and linear patterns. The idiom of this building is clearly that of the Moorish *mudéjar*, its exoticism heightened by an effervescent use of tiles. Black and white patterns are offset by orange and green tiling.

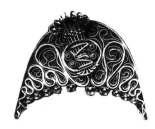

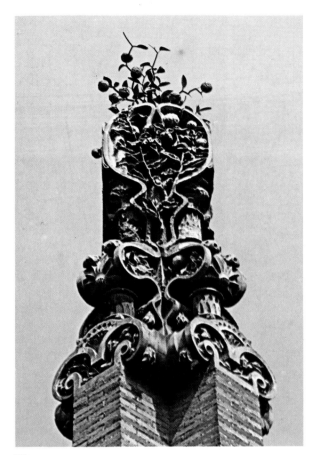

The overall effect is very exciting but the building lacks the unity characteristic of his later work. His treatment of the balconies on the street facade and in the iron railings however, shows some sign of his preference for Art Nouveau motifs. These are designs based on palm leaves set in square frames.

Moorish patterns are again evident in Gaudí's decoration of the Güell Palace (1885-89). The building derives from the Moorish tradition in the use of the colonnade, the minaret and many ornamental features like the surface ornament and corner details. Here the curvilinear plan, the arched entrances and the arabesque ironwork indicate the influence of Art Nouveau.

347—A. GAUDÍ, Güell Estate, near Barcelona, 1887; the dragon gate.
348—A. GAUDÍ, Güell Estate, near Barcelona; pinnacle.
349-350—A. GAUDÍ, Güell Estate, 1887; corner of the wall.

348

349

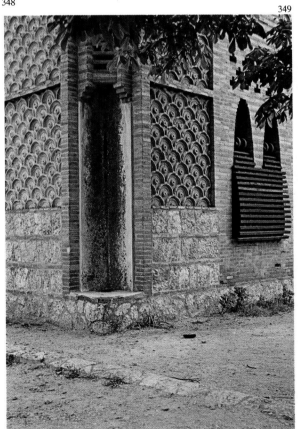

350

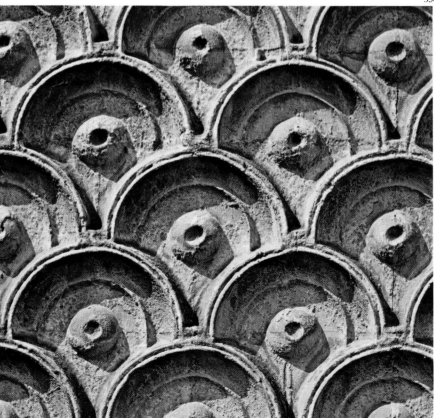

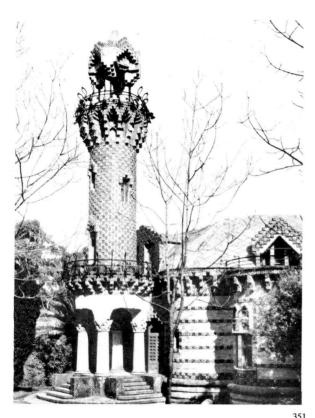

351

351—A. GAUDÍ, Villa El Capricho (1883), Comillas (Santander).
352—A. GAUDÍ, Villa El Capricho; detail.

The Güell Park (1900-14) is probably Gaudí's first statement in his fully mature style. It is a kind of Garden of Mysteries, and Moorish reminiscences are obvious in the treatment of the pinnacles and crenellations on top of the park's buildings as well as in the use of polychrome inlays. However, these designs have a monumentality entirely new to his work. The roof-lines suggest rows of massive volcanic craters whose fluid curves have been produced by some enormous natural force. Gaudí broke wholly with Moorish tradition in his daring use of curved forms. All parts of the building rhyme with each other and the individual units are integrated into the larger scheme. In his treatment of surface decoration, Gaudí has abandoned the autonomous ornament used in his earlier work in favour of an almost random application of tiling which creates a serpentine pattern across the sweeping, fluid curves.

At the Casa Batlló (1905-07) biomorphism gives way to a more urbane and sophisticated treatment. While respecting the planar surface of the upper storeys, Gaudí interpolates rhythmic window units on the lower storeys. These seem to grow out of the wall, and create a rippling surface. This motif is further developed in the Casa Milá (1905-10), where the facade is treated as a mass of horizontal undulations. Here Gaudí has exploited the corner site and produced a design where the vertical thrust of the multi-storey building has been balanced by undulation. The apartment block seems to have been carved out of an enormous sedimentary deposit. The balustrades look like shellfish clinging to rocks. Gaudí's defiance of traditional

352

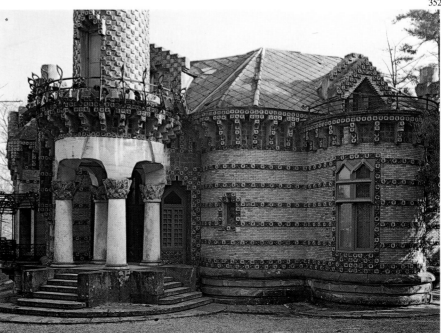

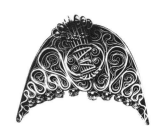

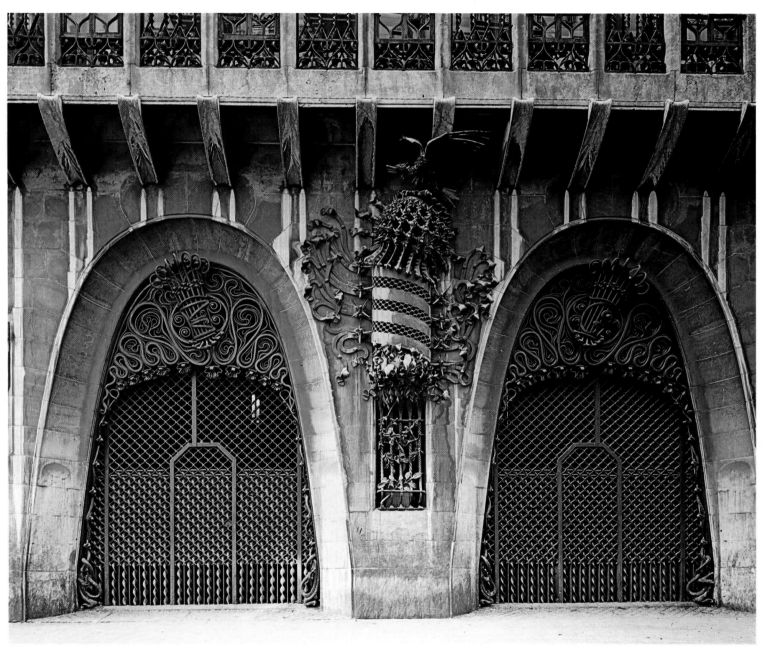

353

353—A. GAUDÍ, Güell Palace, 1885-89, Barcelona; portals and
wrought-iron gates.
354-357—A. GAUDÍ, Güell Park, Barcelona, 1900-14; details.
358—Section showing the incline of the vaults at the Güell
Park by A. Gaudí, Barcelona.
359-363—A. GAUDÍ, Güell Park, Barcelona; details and entrance pavilion.

354
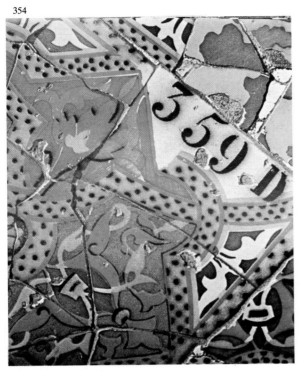

356
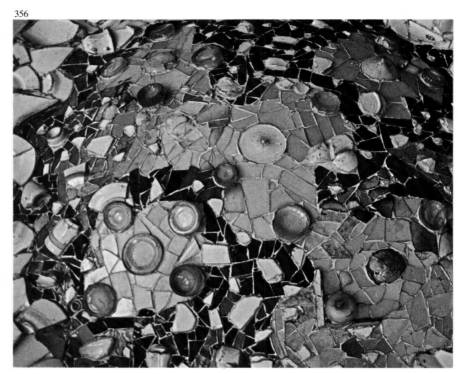

355
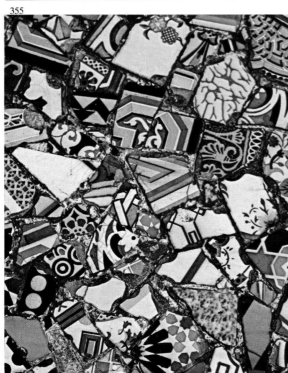

357
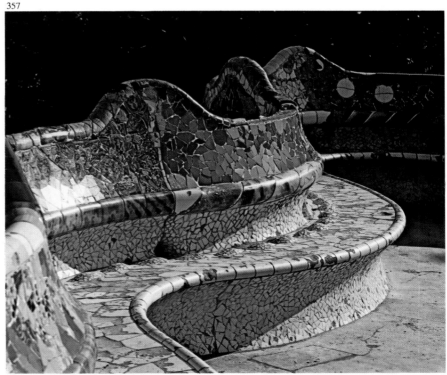

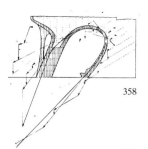

358

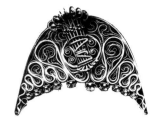

359

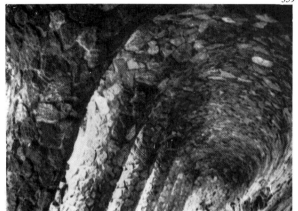

362

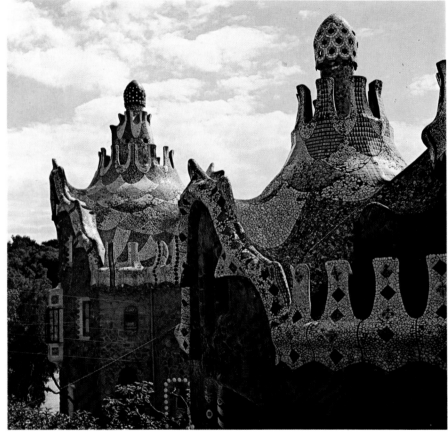

360

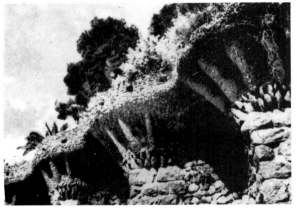

361

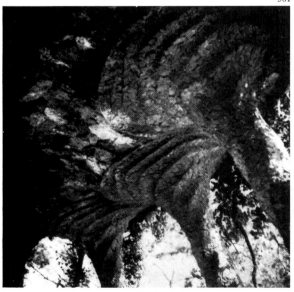

363

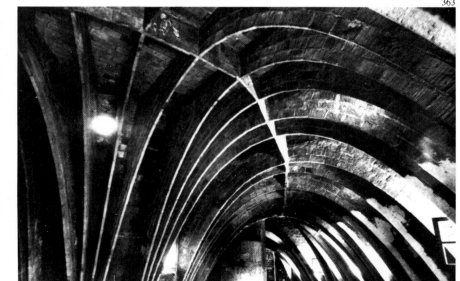

364

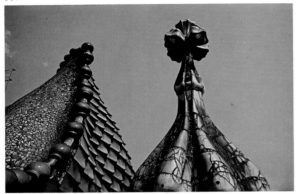

366

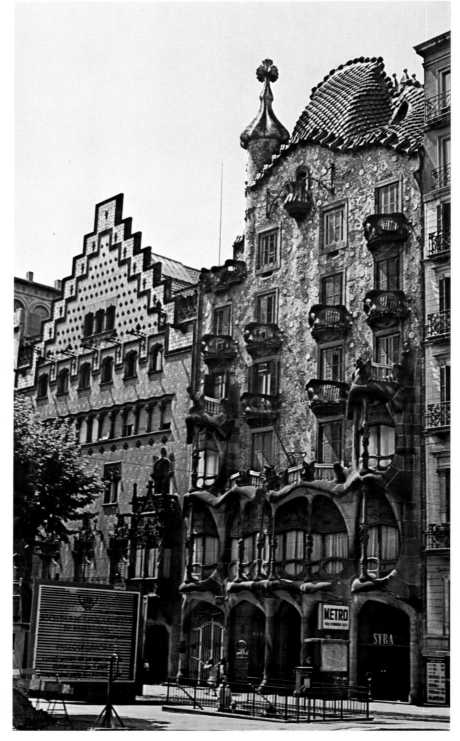

364—A. GAUDÍ, Casa Batlló, Barcelona, 1905-07; detail of the
roof.
365—A. GAUDÍ, Casa Batlló; chimney.
366—A. GAUDÍ, Casa Batlló (to the left Casa Amatller by Puig i
Cadafalch).
367—A. GAUDÍ, Casa Milà, detail of the facade.
368—A. GAUDÍ, Casa Milà detail of the roof and chimneys.
369—A. GAUDÍ, Casa Milà, facade.
  *—drawing of the ironwork at the Casa Vicens.

On page 136
370—Barcelona, mural decoration in ceramics on a staircase,
c. 1905.
371—'Modernist' furniture, c. 1900.
372—Barcelona, house in calle Llansá, c. 1900; detail of the
butterfly gable.
373—A chemist's shop in Barcelona; entrance and stained-
glass window.

365

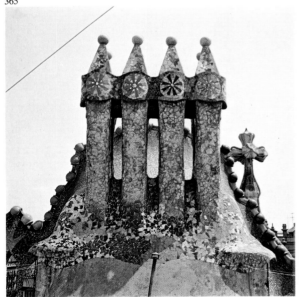

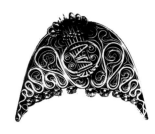

367

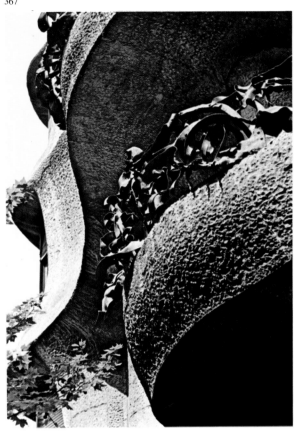

369

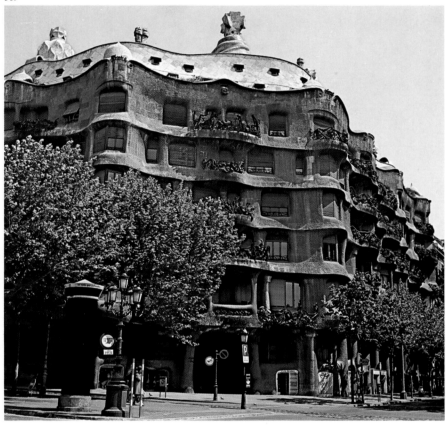

368

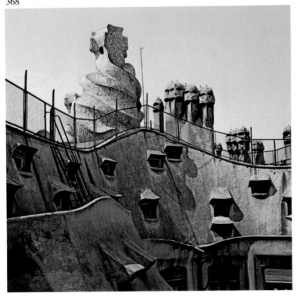

religious architecture reaches its peak with this building. The effect is one of massive living form which anticipates the emotional effects which Expressionist architecture aimed for later.

Other Catalan architects contemporary with Gaudí never quite achieved his level of personal expression, but they were successful in grafting the features of Art Nouveau style onto national traditions. Many architects designed successful variations of the Moorish *mudéjar*, among them were Francesc Berenguer i Mestres and Joan Rubio i Bellver. However, their work does not break with the rectilinearity of the traditional buildings in the way that Gaudí's architecture does. More successful from this point of view, is the work of Lluís Domènech i Montaner, whose decoration for the Casa Sola (1913-16) achieves three-dimensional fluidity.

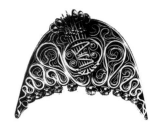

370

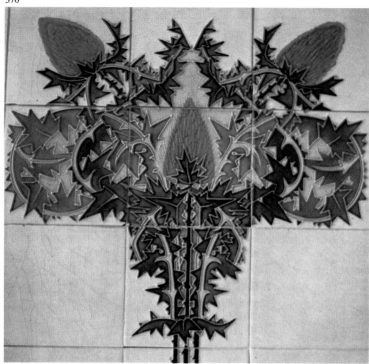

372

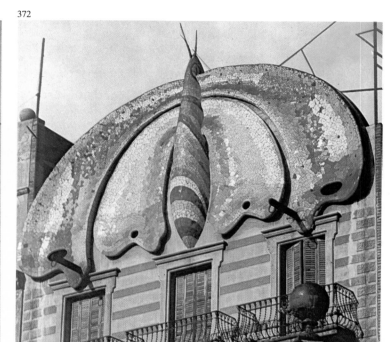

371

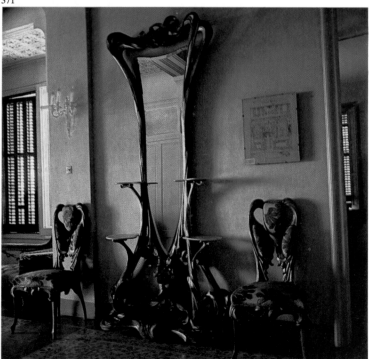

373

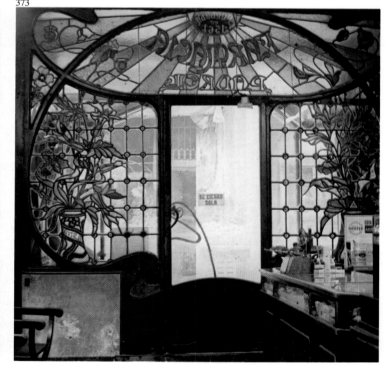

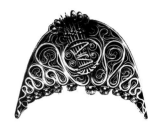

374

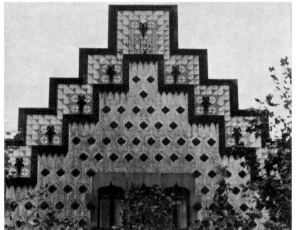

375

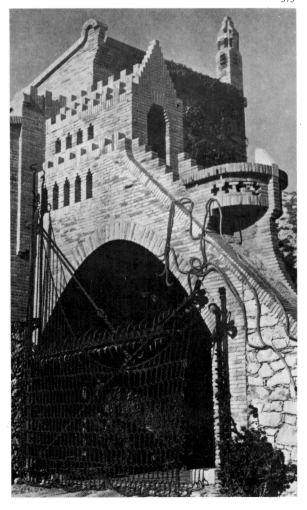

376

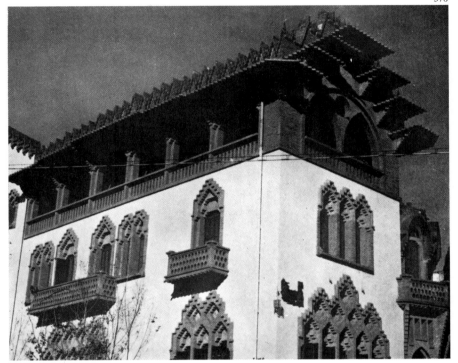

377

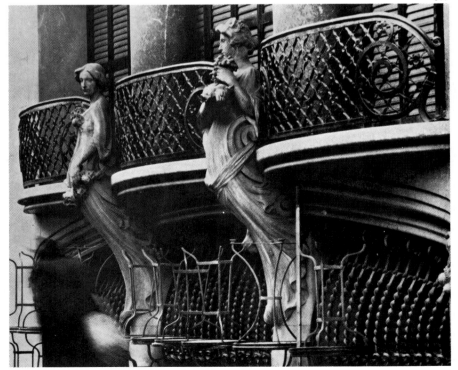

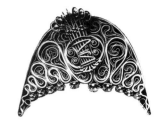

378

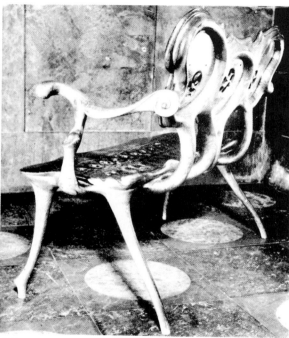

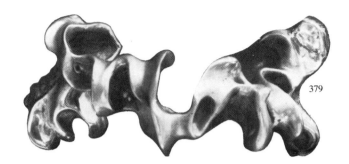

379

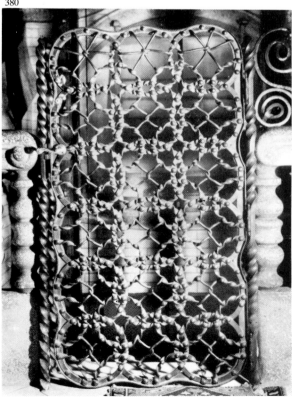

380

381

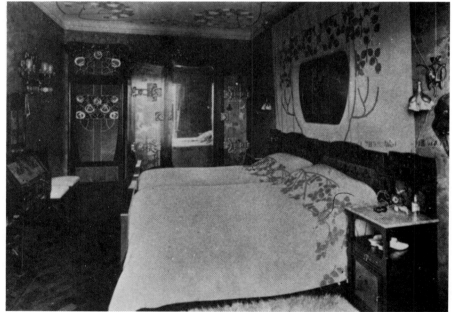

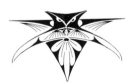

On page 137
374—JOSEF PUIG I CADAFALCH, Casa Amatller, Barcelona, 1900; detail of the gable.
375—FRANCESC BERENGUER I MESTRES, Güell wine cellar, Garraf, c. 1888-90.
376—JOAN RUBIO I BELLVER, Casa Roviralta, Barcelona.
377—LLUÍS DOMÈNECH I MONTANER, Casa Sola in the Firal, Olot, 1913-16; detail of the balconies.

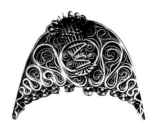

378—A. GAUDÍ, seat for the study in the Casa Calvet, c. 1906.
379—A. GAUDÍ, Casa Calvet, Barcelona, 1898-1904; bronze door handle.
380—A. GAUDÍ, Casa Calvet, Barcelona, 1898-1904; elevator gate.
381—GASPAR HOMAR, bedroom in the Casa Rosés, Barcelona, 1891.
382—L. DOMÈNECH I MONTANER, table in the bar of the Palace of Catalan Music, Barcelona.
383—GASPAR HOMAR, bedroom in the Oller House, Barcelona.
384—JOAN BUSQUET, dining room in the Arnuz House, Barcelona.
    *—page 139, ornamental inset from *The Studio*.

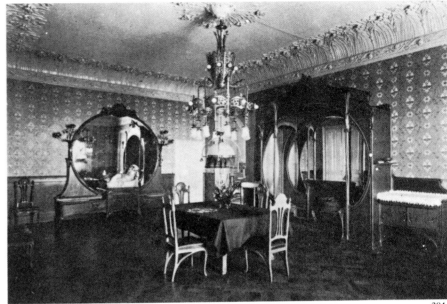

384

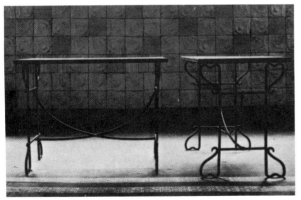

382

383

Two furniture designers stand out as the equals of Gaudí in their own field; they are GASPAR HOMAR (1870-1953) and JOÀN BUSQUET (1874-1949). Their designs lack the organic and monumental qualities of Gaudí's work, but they use arabesque lines with sophistication to decorate plane surfaces. Homar's work at the Casa Oller and Busquet's at the Casa Arnúz are both examples of their method of radically simplifying details in order to achieve a harmonious relationship between the elements of their interiors. However, the power of Gaudí's furniture designed for the Casa Calvert (1898-1904) suggests an entirely different aesthetic. Its forms are bold and solidly plastic and — like his architecture — suggestive of organic growth.

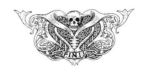

7-Scotland

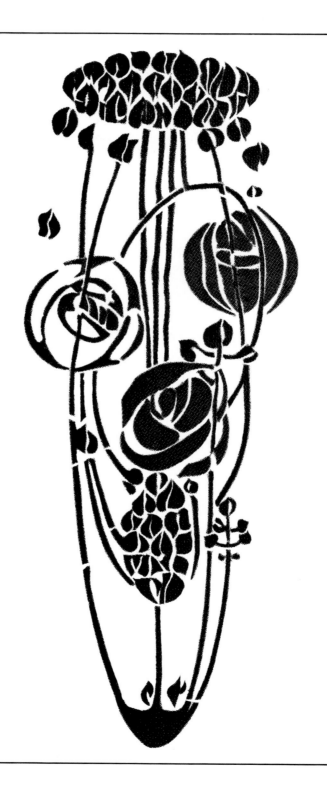

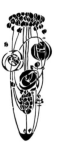

385—and symbol of Chapter 7, pp. 140-157 – CHARLES RENNIE MACKINTOSH, painted decoration on the back of an armchair exhibited at the Turin Exhibition, 1902.
386—C. R. MACKINTOSH, fabric design, watercolour, 1916-20. Glasgow University Collection.
387—C. R. MACKINTOSH, the Art School, Glasgow, 1896-99; main entrance on the north facade.

Inside Great Britain there was both the decadent or sensual Art Nouveau style characteristic of Beardsley and his associates, and the more refined, ordered work of the Glasgow School. The major representatives of this style were HERBERT MCNAIR (1870-1945), CHARLES RENNIE MACKINTOSH (1868-1928) and the MacDonald sisters, later their respective wives, Frances (1874-1921) and Margaret (1865-1933). The predominant characteristics of their style derive in part from national and Continental motifs. They introduced a new interplay between curvilinear and harder, more elegant vertical lines.

The activity of the so-called 'Group of Four' was preceded in Scotland by the work of the 'Glasgow Boys' – James Guthrie, John Lavery and George Walton – artists who had exhibited in London in

387

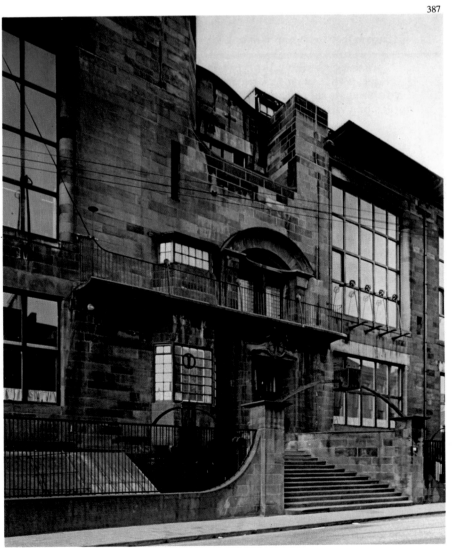

386

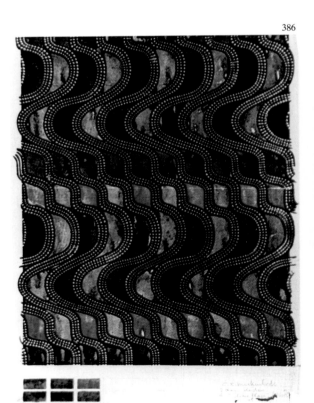

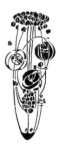

388

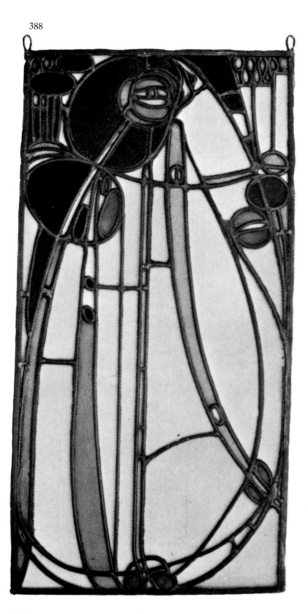

389

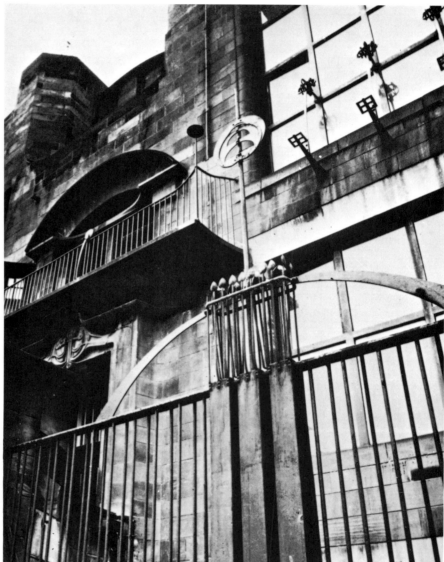

388—C. R. MACKINTOSH, decorative panel, 1902. Glasgow
University Collection.
389—C. R. MACKINTOSH, the Art School, Glasgow, 1897-99;
detail of the north wing.
390—C. R. MACKINTOSH, project for the Art School, Glasgow;
elevation of the north facade.
391—C. R. MACKINTOSH, decorative panel, c. 1893-96; Glasgow
University Collection.
392—C. R. MACKINTOSH, the Art School, Glasgow, 1897-99;
buttresses at the corners of the studio window frames.

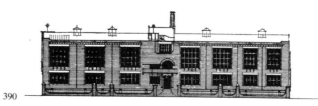

390

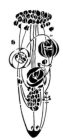

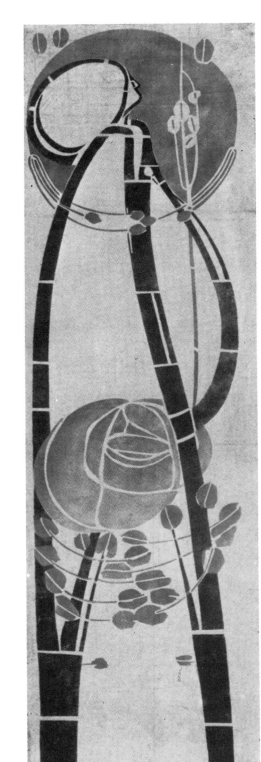

391

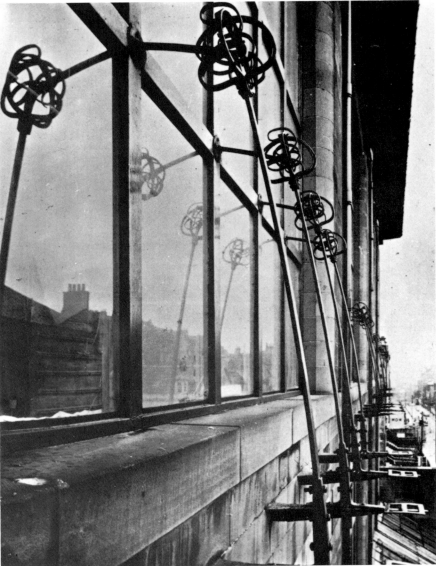

392

1890. The Mackintosh group also exhibited their work in London at the Arts and Crafts exhibition of 1890, an annual event founded in 1888 by Crane, Mackmurdo, Ashbee and Morris. Attracted by their work on show at the exhibition, the editor of *Studio* magazine, Gleeson White, devoted an article to their work. This article, with others, established their artistic reputation and commercial viability. In 1897 Mackintosh received important commissions for the new School of Art in Glasgow and the Cranston Tea Rooms.

The MacDonalds and McNair worked in a variety of media ranging from small book and magazine illustration to decorative panels, as

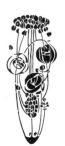

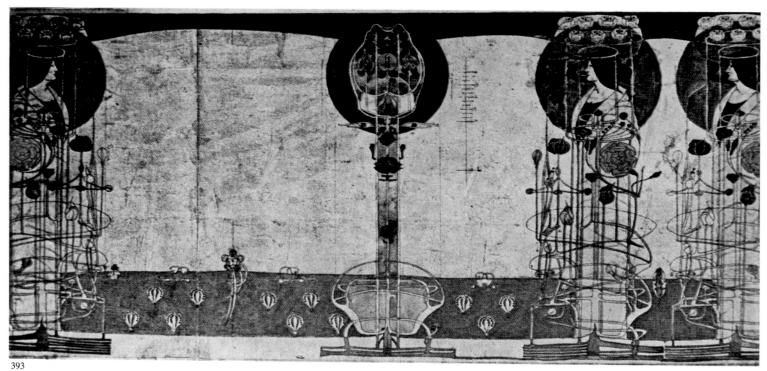

393

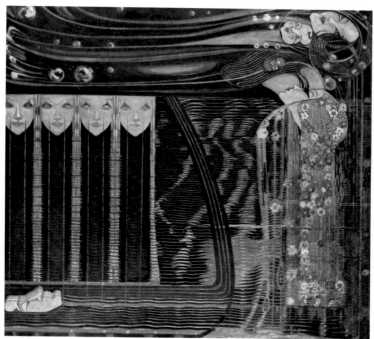

394

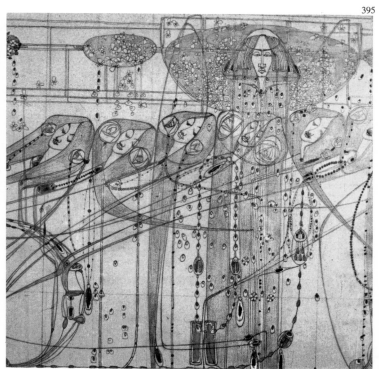

395

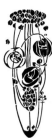

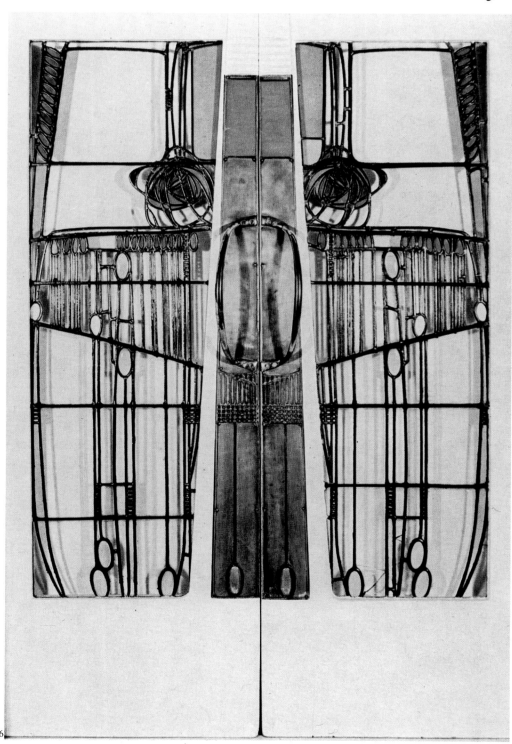

396

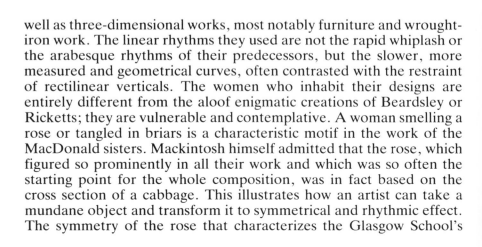

398

399

397

well as three-dimensional works, most notably furniture and wrought-iron work. The linear rhythms they used are not the rapid whiplash or the arabesque rhythms of their predecessors, but the slower, more measured and geometrical curves, often contrasted with the restraint of rectilinear verticals. The women who inhabit their designs are entirely different from the aloof enigmatic creations of Beardsley or Ricketts; they are vulnerable and contemplative. A woman smelling a rose or tangled in briars is a characteristic motif in the work of the MacDonald sisters. Mackintosh himself admitted that the rose, which figured so prominently in all their work and which was so often the starting point for the whole composition, was in fact based on the cross section of a cabbage. This illustrates how an artist can take a mundane object and transform it to symmetrical and rhythmic effect. The symmetry of the rose that characterizes the Glasgow School's

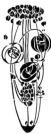

401

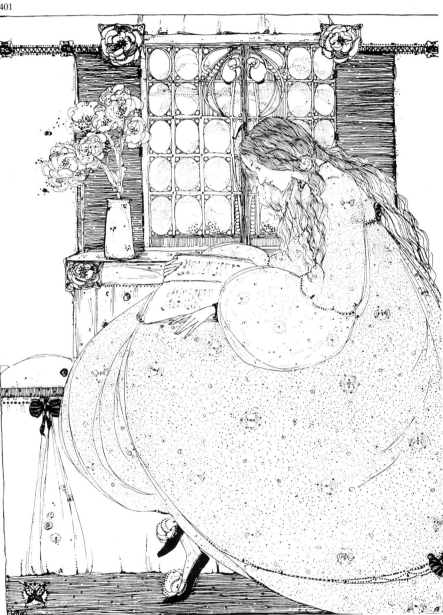

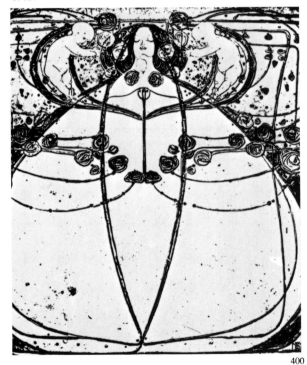

400

production, endows it with an unusual perfection and sense of harmony.

This feature is present in most of the larger decorative panels by the group. The motif draws the spectator into a reverie on the work, a vision of a world devoid of the harshness and imperfection of everyday life. One of the best examples of this are the panels for Frau Wärndorfer's Musical Salon designed by Mackintosh and Margaret

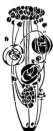

402

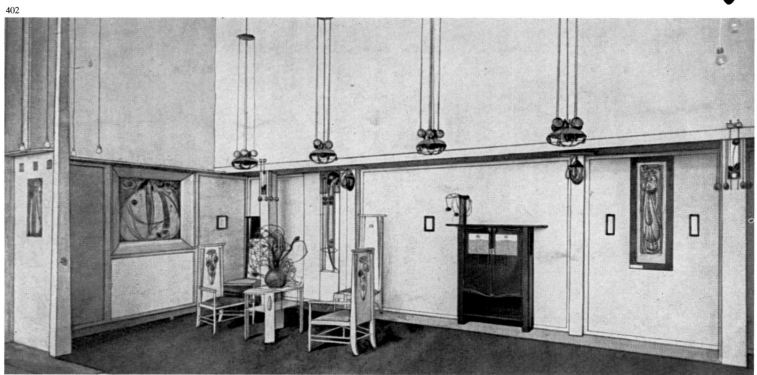

403

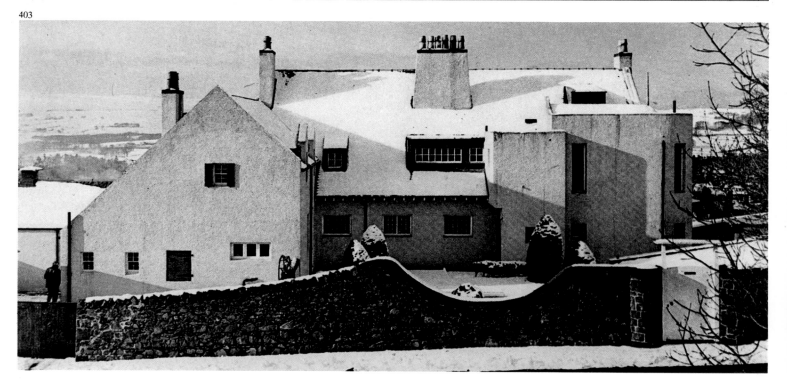

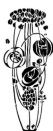

404

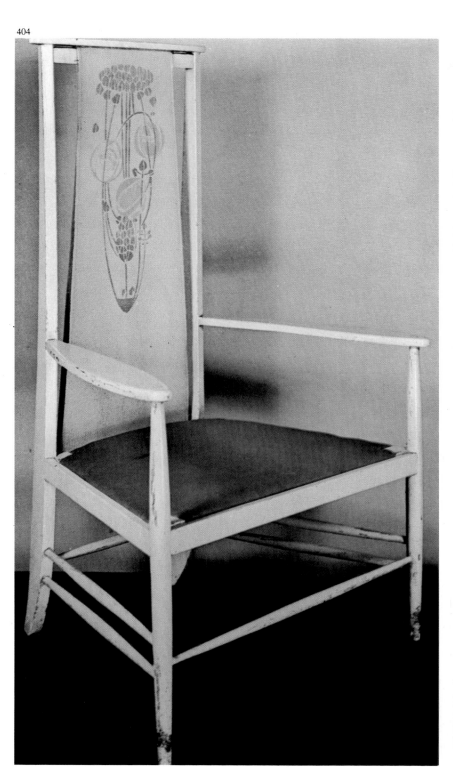

405

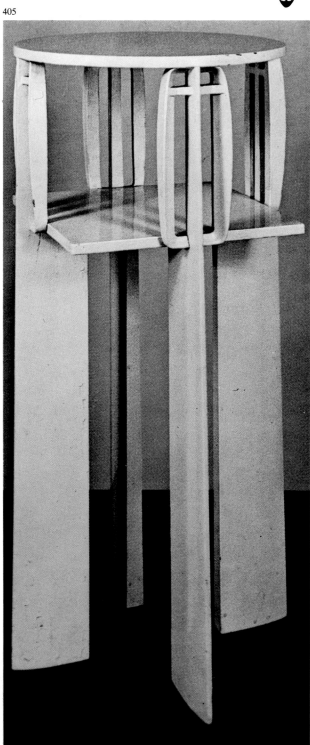

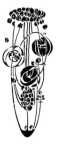

MacDonald. One of these, *The Opera of the Sea* (1902), is based on Maeterlinck's *The Dead Princess*. The princess is drawn into the sequence of waving rhythms which are expressed in the lines of the water and which flow like the hair of the sea nymphs.

In architecture and the applied arts, Charles Rennie Mackintosh succeeded in providing a range of solutions whose simplicity and clarity make him rank among the outstanding artists of the Art

406

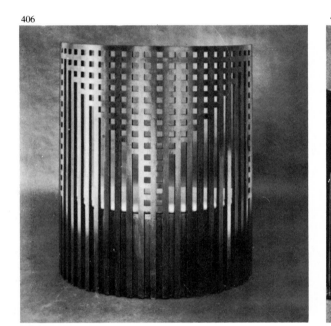

408

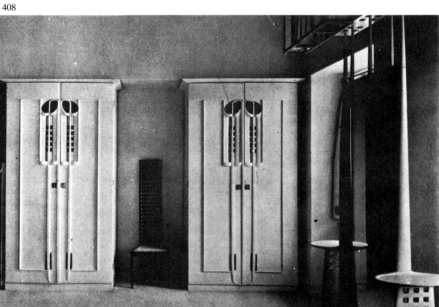

407

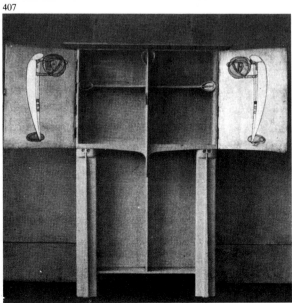

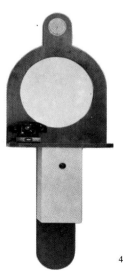

406—C. R. MACKINTOSH, armchair, 1904. Glasgow University Collection.

407—C. R. MACKINTOSH, cabinet, c. 1902. Glasgow University Collection.

408—C. R. MACKINTOSH, Hill House, Helensburgh, 1902; interior of the bedroom and wardrobes.

409—J. R. ETTORE SOTTSASS, *Tempus*, 1966.

410—C. R. MACKINTOSH, the Art School, Glasgow, west wing, 1907-09.

411—C. R. MACKINTOSH, the Art School, Glasgow, section through the library and reading room.

412—C. R. MACKINTOSH, Hill House, Helensburgh, 1902; view of the south-east facade.

409

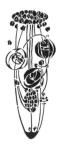

410

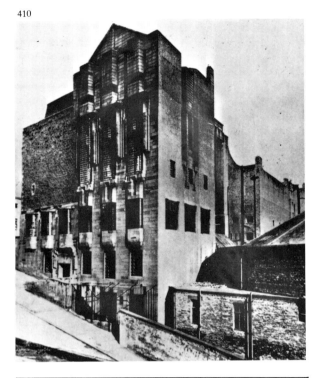

412

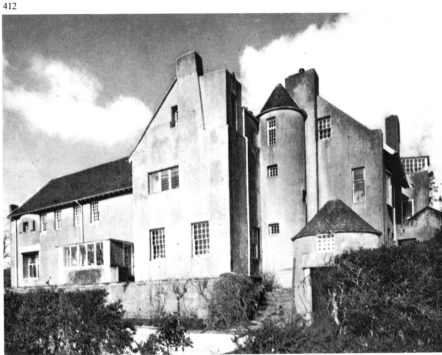

411

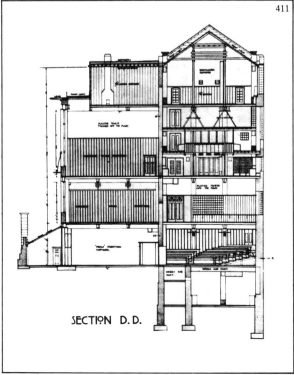

SECTION D.D.

Nouveau style. These solutions were later adapted for use by succeeding generations of architects who, although they did not share his aesthetics, found his solutions of considerable practical value. A glance at the clean intersections of the window frames in the Glasgow Art School, confirms their similarity with Russian Constructivism and even De Stijl.

The refined and authoritative treatment of Mackintosh's furniture has made them classics. These pieces are free of Continental organic content, they are subtle statements of a developed almost aesthetic intention. For instance, an elegant two-tier table shows an ingenious combination of Art Nouveau taste with a Japanese decorative quality. The distinct sources are overlaid with a new feeling for the austerity of the vertical line.

Mackintosh's architectural sources are similarly complex, and his work in this area is a successful amalgam of diverse elements. It is based on the tradition of Scottish baronial architecture, which Mackintosh saw as the only style which could be defined as wholly indigenous to Scotland. His work was also influenced by the study of Italian Renaissance architecture, which he saw when he visited Italy in 1892 and 1902. His conception of rhythm has a Japanese quality. He absorbs all of these influences in an entirely personal way to create his own Art Nouveau language.

The School of Art in Glasgow is generally considered to be Mackintosh's most important work. This was completed in two

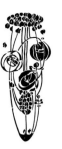

phases, from 1897-99 and from 1907-09. The imposing structure is composed on a system of receding planes. The symmetrically and assymmetrically organized components are massed with great equilibrium.

The interior of the building is no less considered and measured. In the library the walls which carry books are recessed behind slender structural beams supporting the upper storey, which in this case is a bright clerestory. In this way, the practical need for space for books and light for study is resolved.

At times Mackintosh's architectural language has a calligraphic quality. In the treatment of details he often achieves a very high level of decorative beauty. The door of the Willow Tea Rooms in Glasgow (1904) has a linearity that resembles calligraphy, and the interplay of forms is both free and restrained. Their charm lies in the simplicity of elaboration.

413—C. R. MACKINTOSH, project for a music room.
414—C. R. MACKINTOSH, leaded glass panel for the de-luxe room at the Willow Tea Rooms, Glasgow, 1904. Glasgow University Collection.
415—C. R. MACKINTOSH, the Art School, Glasgow, wing of the library.

413

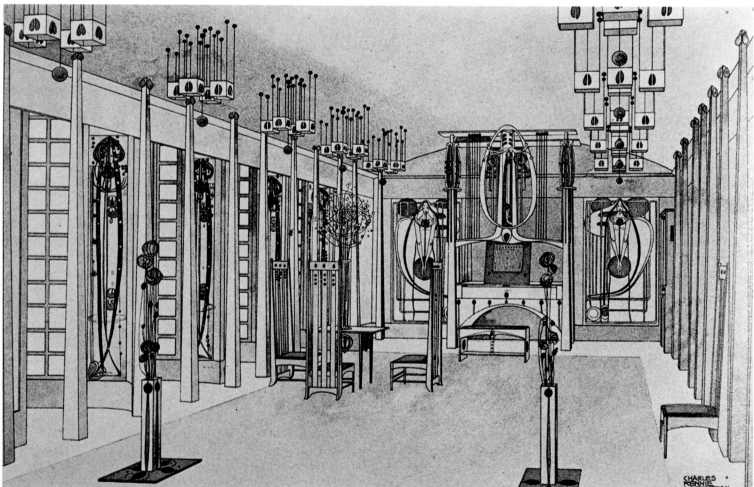

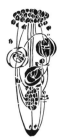

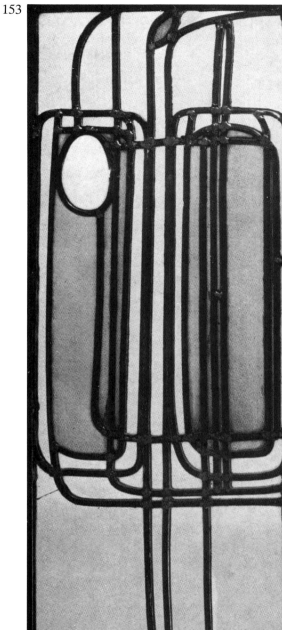

414

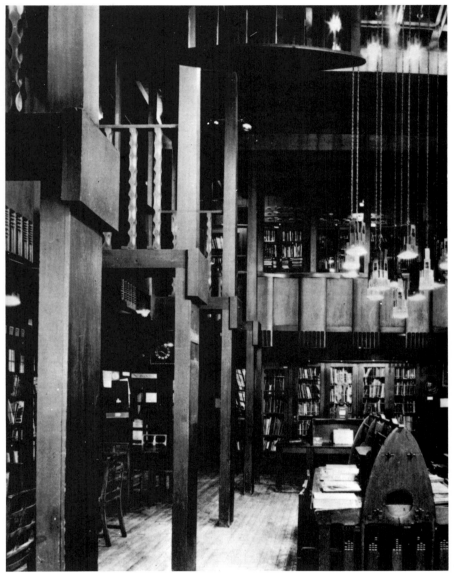

415

Mackintosh was successful both at home in Scotland and on the Continent. He was invited to exhibit in Paris in 1896, in Lyons and Vienna in 1900, and in Turin in 1902. He also showed his work between 1903 and 1913 in Budapest, Munich, Dresden, Venice and in Moscow following an invitation from Diaghilev. Unfortunately, he never felt appreciated by his own society and in 1903 he retired to Suffolk, where he devoted himself to painting. The Suffolk paintings beautifully integrate the subject with the demand for a rhythmically organized surface.

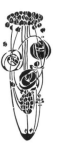

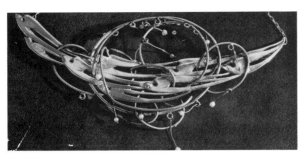

416

416—C. R. MACKINTOSH, necklace, 1902.
417—C. R. MACKINTOSH, textile design; watercolour, 1916-20. Glasgow University Collection.
418—C. R. MACKINTOSH, *Cabbages in an Orchard*, 1894.
419—C. R. MACKINTOSH, *The Street of the Sun*, 1927. Glasgow University Collection.
420—FRANCES MACDONALD-MCNAIR, *The Prince and the Sleeping Princess*, c. 1895. Glasgow University Collection.
421—C. R. MACKINTOSH, *Aconite*, c. 1894-1900. Glasgow University Collection.
422—M. MACDONALD-MACKINTOSH, menu for Miss Cranston's Tea Rooms, Glasgow, 1901. Glasgow University Collection.

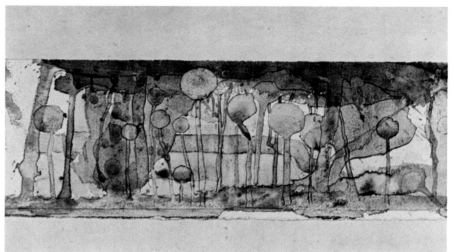

418

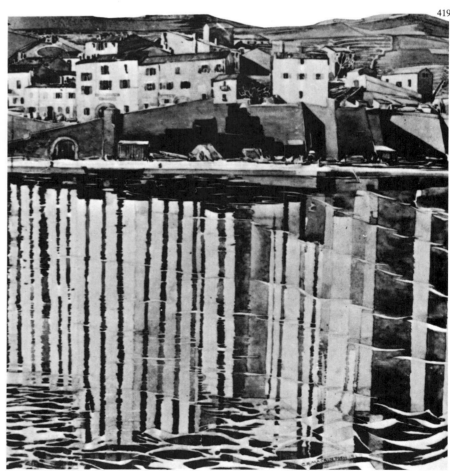

419

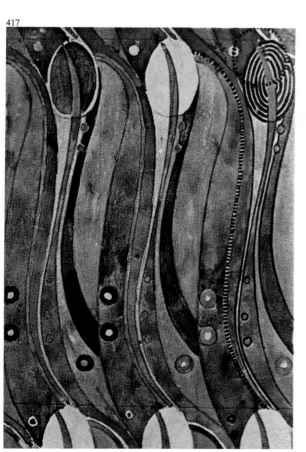

417

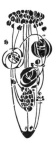

420

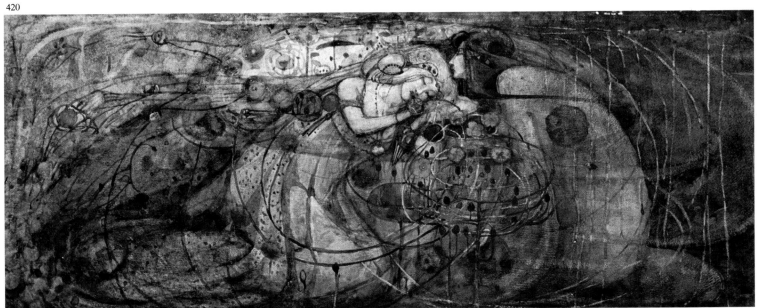

421

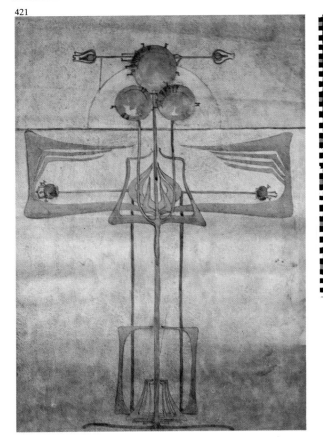

422

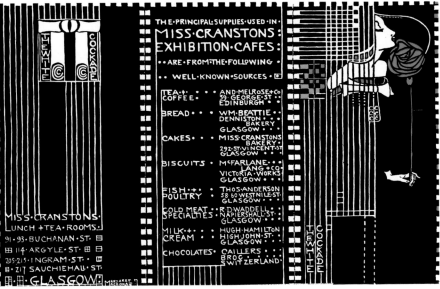

His personal life was unhappy. In 1915, while living in Chelsea, Mackintosh received commissions for buildings which he never completed. In 1920 he began planning a theatre which was never realized. He lived in isolation and drank heavily. His final creative effort was a remarkable series of oil paintings and watercolours painted after his departure for Port Vendres in France. Mackintosh developed cancer of the mouth and died in 1928.

The Glasgow Four were also interested in book illustration, and the

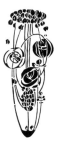

English-born illustrator Jessie King was closely associated with them. She worked in a similar style to McNair and Margaret MacDonald. Her jewel-like technique, which often incorporated small flashes of colour within slowly unfolding lines, made her illustrations possibly the most popular and commercially successful products of the genre. The gentle fantasy of her technique was ideally suited to poetry and

423

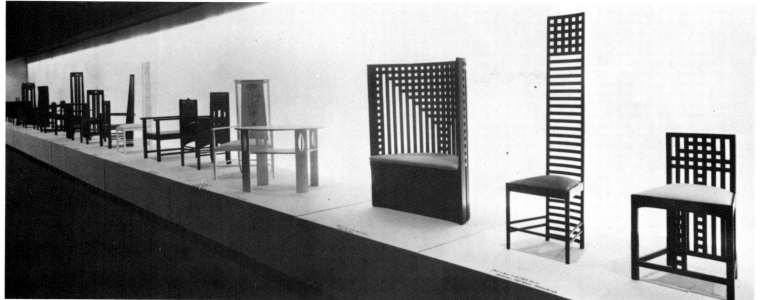

423—Milan Triennale, 1973; exhibition of chairs by C. R. Mackintosh, presented by F. Alison.
424—HERBERT MCNAIR, dustjacket, c. 1896, for Herbert McNair, *His Book*.
425—H. MCNAIR, pedestal bookcase, exhibited at the Turin Exhibition, 1902.
426—H. MCNAIR, F. MACDONALD-MCNAIR, small sitting room, exhibited at the Turin Exhibition, 1902.
427—H. MCNAIR, smoker's cabinet, c. 1897.

424

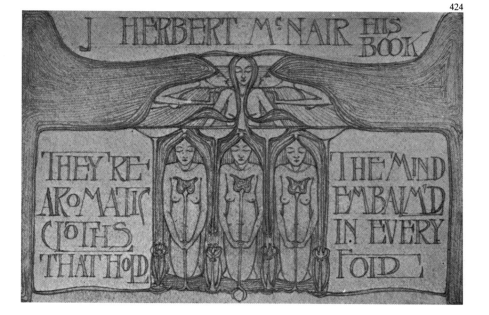

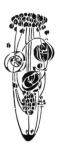

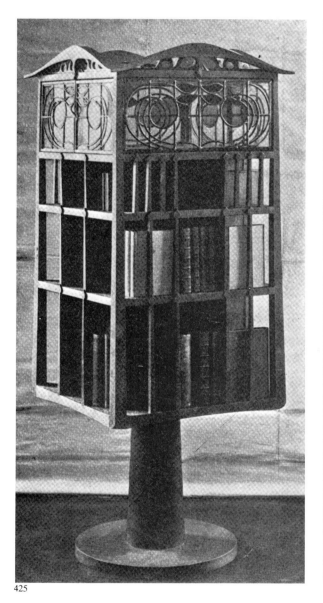

425

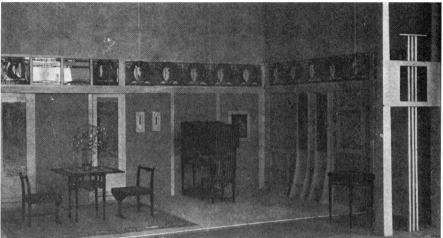

426

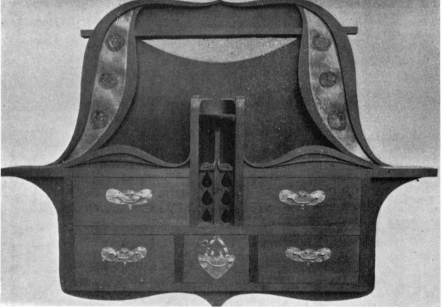

427

fairy-tale illustration and this accounts for her considerable success with many publishers in the first decade of this century.

However, Jessie King, like the other exponents of the Glasgow style, was not popular for long. This may be because their work lacked theoretical or ideological motive, or possibly simply because the members of the original four were quickly separated and the group and its work rapidly faded from public view.

8-Holland

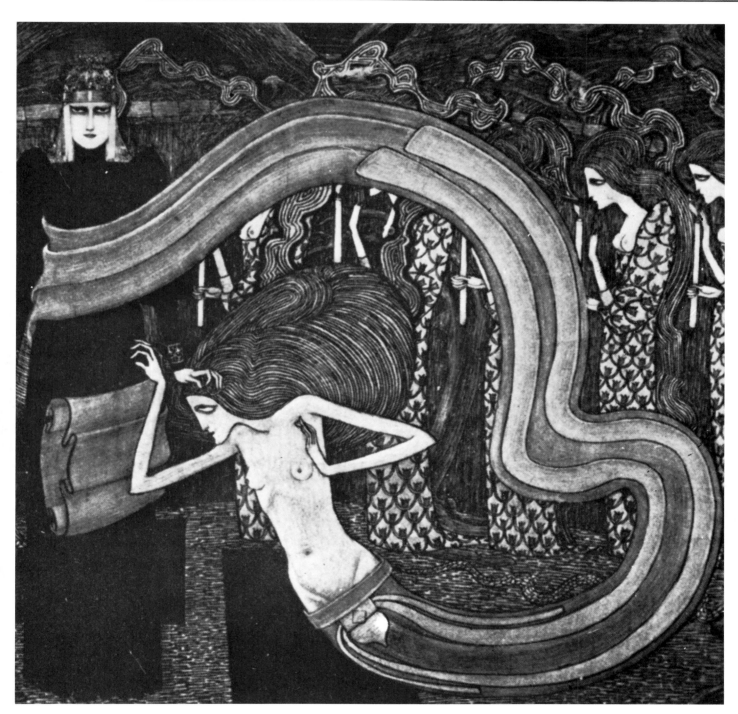

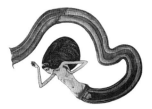

The cultural circumstances that allowed the widespread and lyrical expression of Art Nouveau in Belgium and France did not exist in Holland. The style was for the most part absorbed into the mainsteam of middle-class taste, which produced hybrid although intimate art.

A similar limitation handicapped the development of architecture in Holland. The traditional building material used in domestic architecture was brick. This made architecture subservient to the modular construction that the material imposed. However, this limitation induced a simplicity and purity of structure. Nowhere is this more evident than in the work of HENDRIK PETRUS BERLAGE (1856-

429

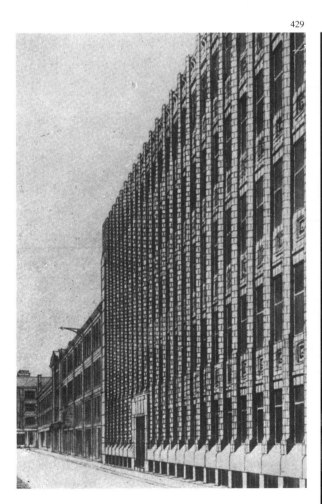

430

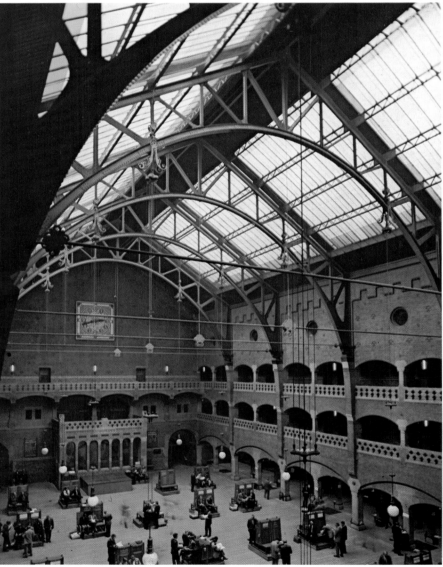

428—and symbol of Chapter 8, pp 158-171 – JAN TOOROP, *Fate*, 1893; detail. Otterlo, Kröller-Müller Museum.
429—HENDRIK PETRUS BERLAGE, Holland House, London, 1914.
430—H. P. BERLAGE, The Stock Exchange, Amsterdam, 1897-1903; interior.

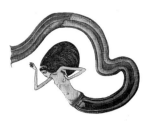

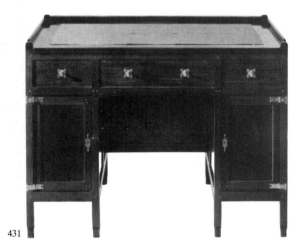

431—H. P. BERLAGE, desk, c. 1900. Berne, coll. A. C. Strasser-
Berlage.
432—H. P. BERLAGE, The Stock Exchange, Amsterdam, 1897-
1903; exterior.
433—H. P. BERLAGE, typographical letters.
434—H. P. BERLAGE, The Diamond Workers' Union building,
Amsterdam, 1899-1901.
435—H. P. BERLAGE, aerial view of urban redevelopment in
Amsterdam.
436—H. P. BERLAGE, insurance company headquarters, The
Hague.

432

431

1934), whose intuitive feeling for rational and geometric forms
distinguished his work. A major influence on Berlage's style was
Romanesque architecture. The clear and functional spaces of this
architecture found a new and wholly modern expression in his work.
He was also influenced by the American modernist architecture of the
Chicago School and Henry H. Richardson.

These features are present in Berlage's Amsterdam Stock Exchange (1898-1903). The exterior is based on a Romanesque cathedral: it is symmetrically disposed, has an entrance portico with
sculptural decoration and a clock tower (adapted from the bell tower
of its prototype). In the interior there is a more lucid application of
the expressive possibilities of the Neo-Romanesque style. The
building has a graceful glass roof carried on iron arches which run
down to the top of the lower arcade. Two superimposed galleries run
the length of the building above the ground floor arcade, and the
ornament is simplified to geometric forms. The atmosphere is calm
and grand. The building is a radical reinterpretation of a Romanesque
cathedral into a secular idiom. Here the architecture of the Stock

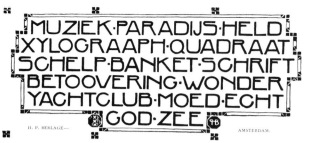

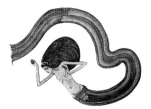

433

Exchange represents stability rather than the Divine Power of its prototype.

The exterior of Holland House (1914) on the other hand, is highly modelled. It has giant rusticated piers which run continuously the whole height of the building. The wall plane is expressed in the modelled panels below the tall elegant windows. Here Berlage created a personal and unhistoricizing style, which heralds modernism.

434

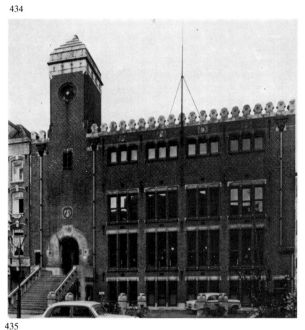

435

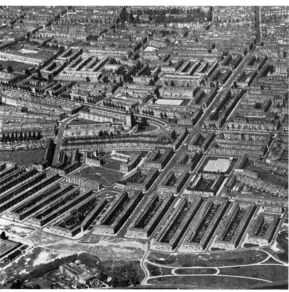

436

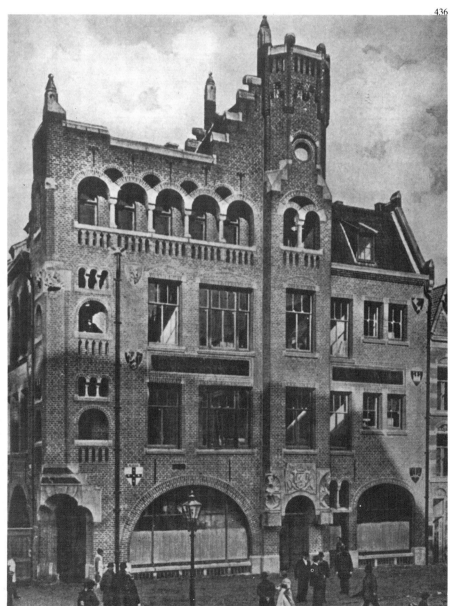

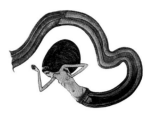

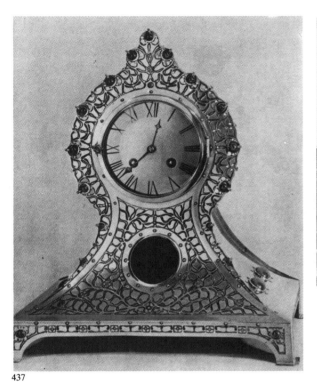

437

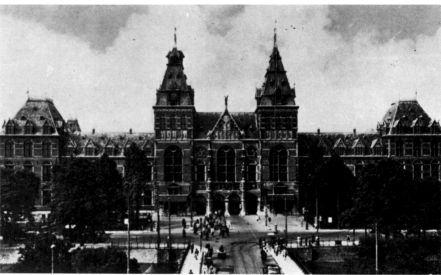

438

Berlage also produced furniture designs, which are aesthetically close to this architecture. A writing desk made by him (c. 1900) shows the clarity of conception and proportions which are found in his architecture, but because of its small scale the power of his architecture is replaced by the intimacy of an everyday functional object.

The Neo-Romanesque style that features in many examples of Berlage's architecture – for example, the Diamond Workers' Union building (1899-1900) and his insurance building in The Hague – was

437—THEO NIEUWENHUIS, pendulum clock. The Hague, Gemeentemuseum.
438—P. J. H. CUYPERS, Rijksmuseum, Amsterdam, 1877-85.
439—MENDES DE COSTA, decorated plate with Javanese designs. The Hague, Museum of the Decorative Arts.
440—Teapot manufactured by Rozenburg, c. 1900. Amsterdam, Stedelijkmuseum.
441—GERRIT WILLEM DIJSSELHOF, The Dijsselhof Room, Amsterdam, 1890-1902. The Hague, Gemeentemuseum.

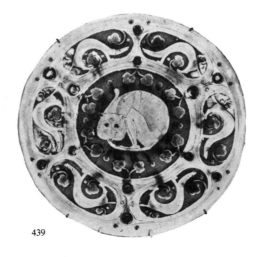

439

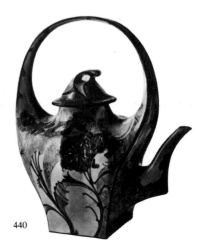

440

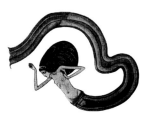

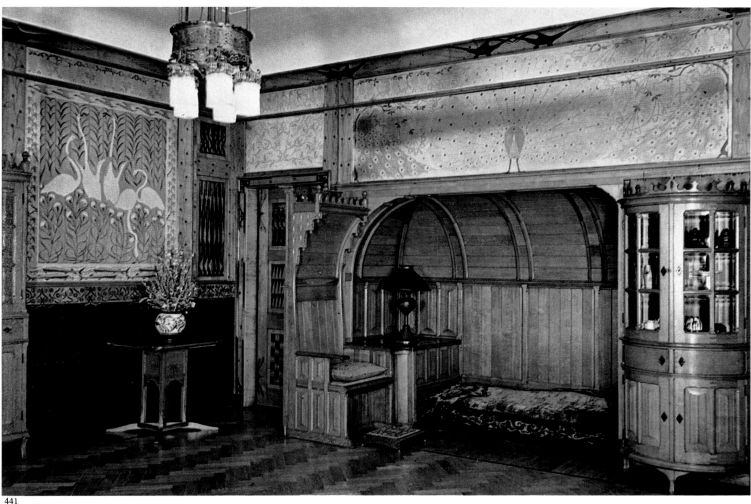

441

also characteristic of other Dutch architects of the period. The mixture of traditional and modern building styles can be found in the work of Hermann Pieter Mutters, William Kromhout and Peter Joseph Cuypers, who had designed the Rijksmuseum (1877-85). This building derives from a variety of architectural styles: it contains quotations from late Dutch Baroque architecture as well as Parisian architecture (note the Mansard roof). The elements are clearly disposed following the contemporary demand for rational and readily understood forms. It is the prototype for Berlage's architecture.

Holland was a more favourable climate for the blossoming of the crafts than for architecture. Works produced in this field exhibit a much greater freedom of conception and fantasy than was possible in architecture. The Government commissioned a report in 1871 on the applied arts. In 1881, the National School of Applied and Decorative Arts (Rijkschool voor Kunstnijveheid) was opened. In 1884 the Arts

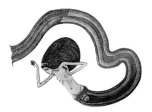

442

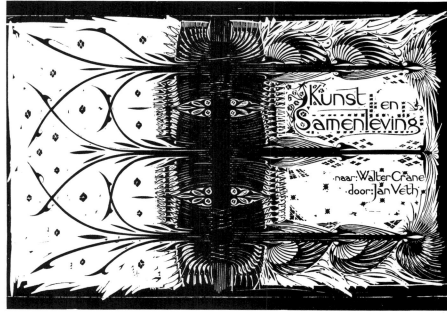

and Industries Association was founded, which aimed at promoting contact between artists, artisans and industry. In 1885 the Labor et Ars Association was formed, and members of this influential group included Willem Dijsselhof, who designed the so-called Dijsselhof Room (1890-1902), and Mendes de Costa, who produced remarkable ceramics in an idiom which combined Art Nouveau with Javanese influences. Dutch periodicals also helped the dissemination of Art Nouveau taste in the decorative arts. In 1888 *Bouw en Sierkunst* was inaugurated, and it was soon followed by *Arts and Crafts* (from 1898) under the artistic direction of Jan Thorn Prikker.

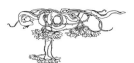

The graphic arts in Holland were perhaps the most successful in their development of a truly Art Nouveau style. The influence of publications like the translations of the English *Studio* magazine and of Walter Crane's illustrated books, provided a stylistic impetus. This was accompanied by the impact of primitive art, in particular that of Java, a Dutch colony at this time.

443

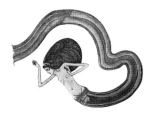

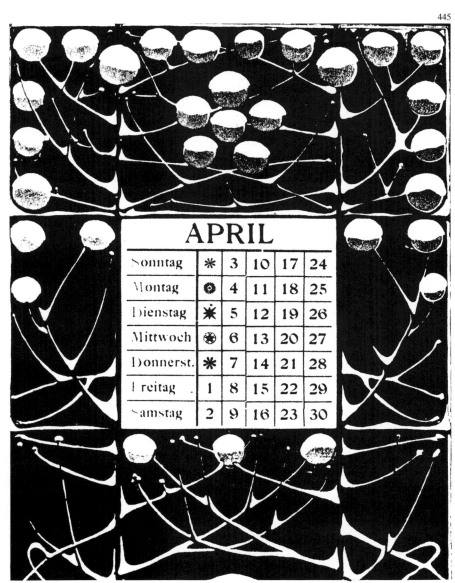

445

APRIL

Sonntag	✳	3	10	17	24
Montag	◉	4	11	18	25
Dienstag	✳	5	12	19	26
Mittwoch	✱	6	13	20	27
Donnerst.	✳	7	14	21	28
Freitag		1	8	15	22	29
Samstag		2	9	16	23	30

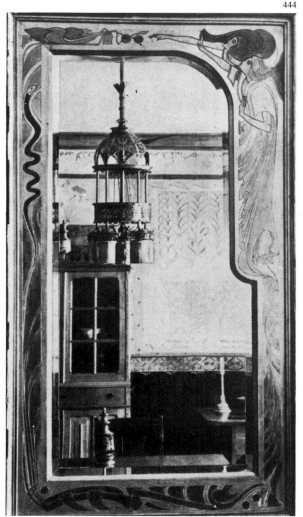

444

442—Haar Castle, Holland; detail of a door.
443—G. W. DIJSSELHOF, book cover for the Dutch translation of Walter Crane's book, showing Javanese influences.
    *—page 164, ornamental inset from *The Studio*.
444—JAN TOOROP, painted mirror frame. The Hague, Gemeentemuseum.
445—T. NIEUWENHUIS, a calendar.

On pages 166, 167
446—J. TOOROP, *Song of the Ages*, 1893.
447—J. TOOROP, *The Three Brides*, 1892. Otterlo, Kröller-Müller Museum.
448—J. TOOROP, study for *The Three Brides*. Otterlo, Kröller-Müller Museum.
449—J. TOOROP. *Delftsche Slaolie*, c. 1897, poster. Krefeld, Kaiser Wilhelm Museum.

JAN TOOROP (1858-1928) was born in Java. His work shows the influence of Javanese shadow-puppets, which have the elegant and sinuous silhouettes so characteristic of his work. Toorop's artistic development was complex. He began painting in a decorative Neo-Impressionistic style, and was later influenced by Khnopff, whose work he knew from Les XX (Toorop was a member of the society). However, the highly rhythmic and hard-edged linearity of Toorop's designs is predominantly influenced by the English.

The variety of sources unite in Toorop's personal, mystical style, evidenced in two works: *Song of the Ages* (1893) and the *Three Brides* (1892). By 1897, when he produced the remarkable poster, *Delftsche*

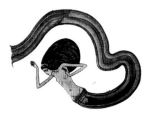

446

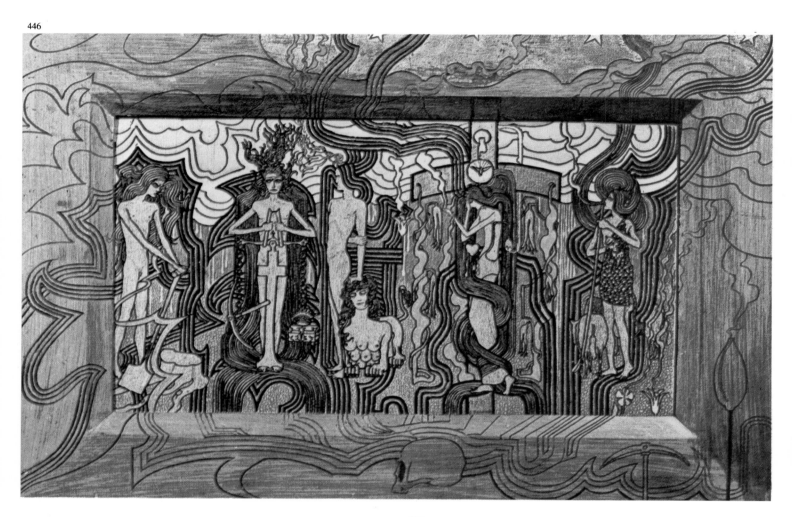

447

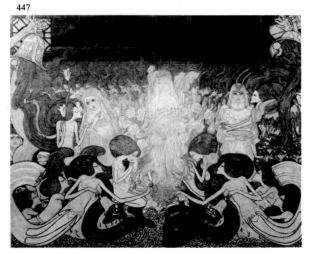

448

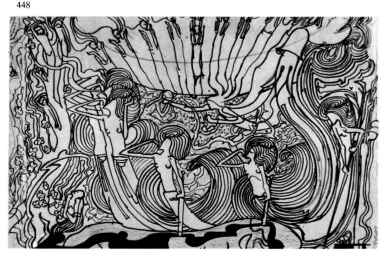

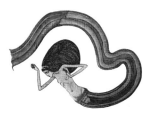

449

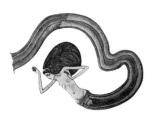

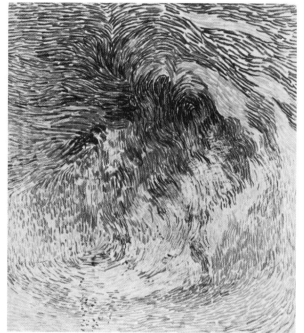

450

453

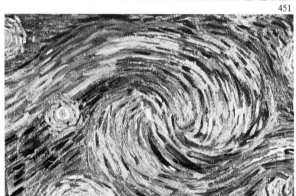

451

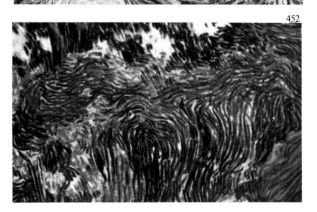

452

Slaolie, Toorop's style had become more elegant and decorative. The broad rhythms of Celtic art, which at one stage influenced Beardsley, and which may have been known to Toorop through his Irish wife, is recalled in this work.

The other dominant figure in Holland in the fine and graphic arts was JAN THORN PRIKKER (1868-1932). His work is even more mystical and Symbolist than Toorop's. The broken spiral brush strokes, recalling van Gogh, are present in his early work. Later he became more concerned with strong contours reminiscent of the Pont-Aven group and the Nabis. This is evident in works like *Christ on the Cross with the Virgin* (1891-92). The painting also shares the mystical, religious feelings of these painters, especially those of Emile Bernard and Maurice Denis. In *The Madonna of the Tulips* (1892) and *The Bride* (1893), these qualities find a completely personal expression. Flat forms are shaped by curvilinear contours, and the surface shimmers with opposing complementary colours, applied in small brush strokes. In the latter painting all distinguishing features of the figures are abolished and the figures are united by a plant which twines around the bridal heads. The marriage is expressed by the whiplash line which joins the couple.

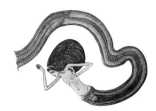

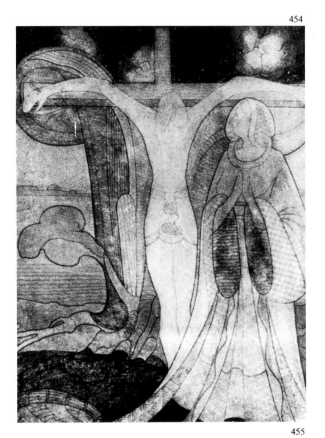

454

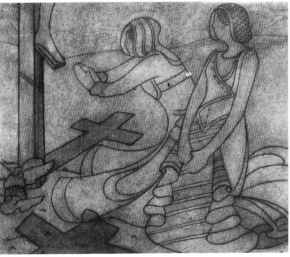

455

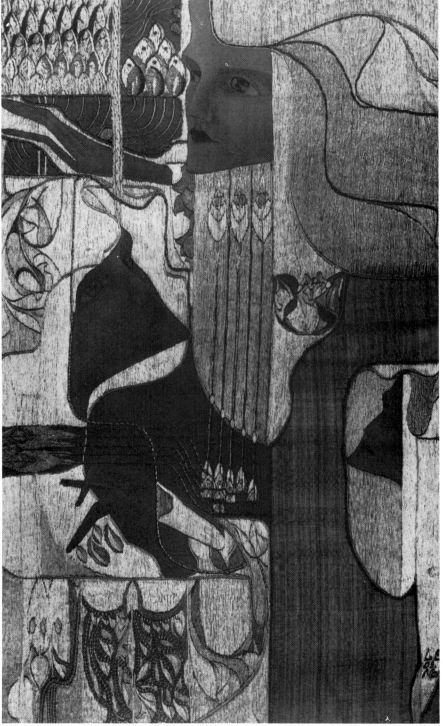

456

450—JAN THORN PRIKKER, detail of brushstrokes.
451—VINCENT VAN GOGH, detail of brushstrokes.
452—H. VAN DE VELDE, detail of brushstrokes.
453—J. TOOROP, *Fate*, 1893. Otterlo, Kröller-Müller Museum.

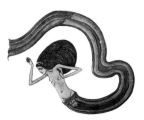

454—J. THORN PRIKKER, *Christ on the Cross with Mary*, c. 1891-92. Otterlo, Kröller-Müller Museum.
455—J. THORN PRIKKER, *The Holy Women at the Cross*, c. 1891-92. Otterlo, Kröller-Müller Museum.
456—CHRISTOPHE KAREL DE NERÉE TOT BABBERICH, *The Blessed*, c. 1909.
457—J. THORN PRIKKER, *The Madonna of the Tulips*, 1892. Otterlo, Kröller-Müller Museum.
458—J. THORN PRIKKER, *The Bride*, 1892-93.

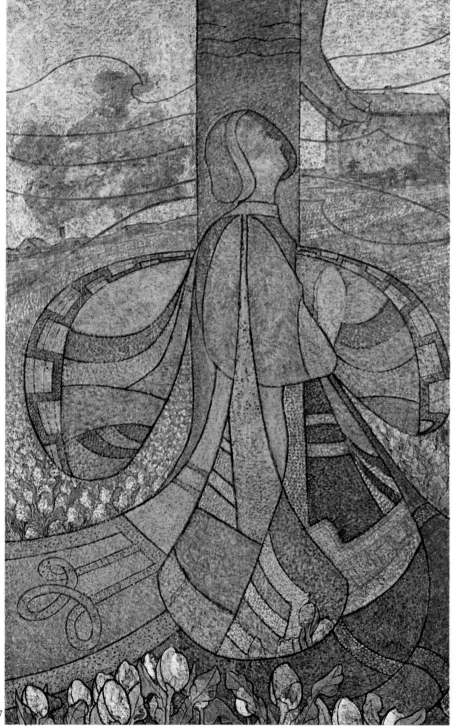

457

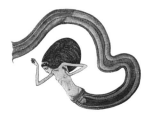

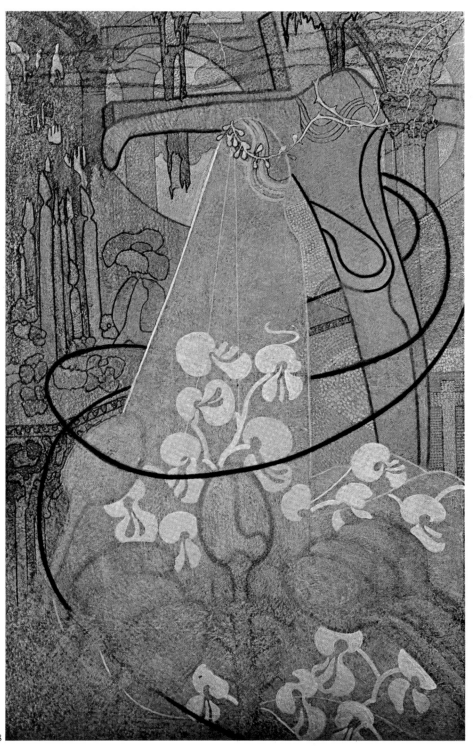

458

9-Germany

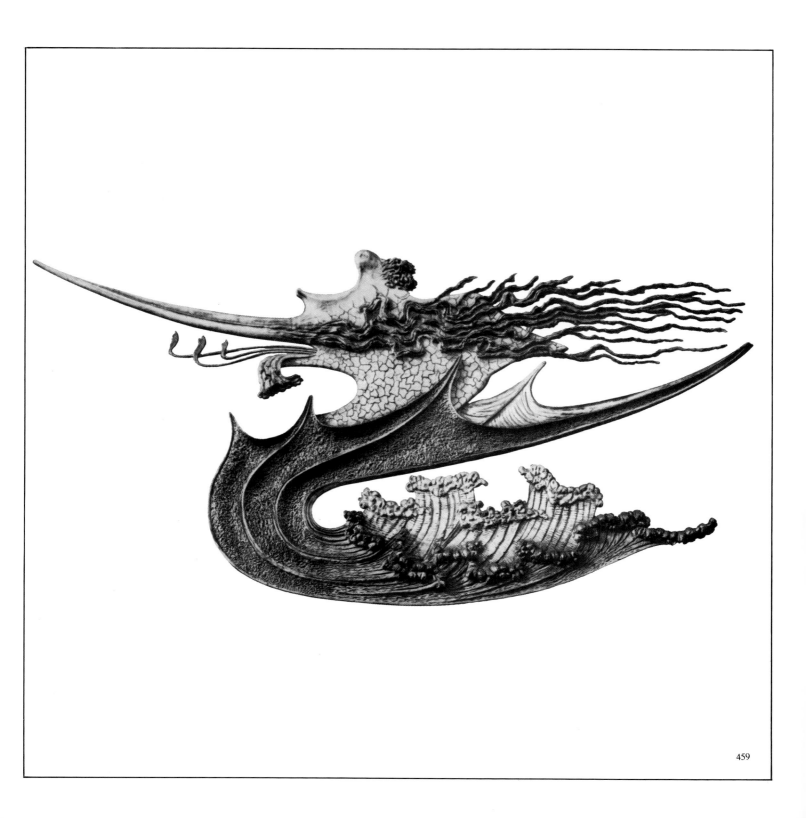

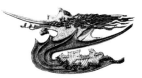

The strong national Rococo tradition resisted the proliferation of Art Nouveau in Germany. In the second half of the 1890s Rococo elements began to appear in the German Art Nouveau style. The immediate stimulus for the development of the style was the presence in Germany of Henry van de Velde. There were two distinct phases in the development of the style. An early floral style was gradually replaced after 1900 by a more geometric abstract style.

Education and publishing in the second half of the 1890s also stimulated the development of Art Nouveau in Germany. In 1895 van de Velde gave a course at the Textile Museum in Krefeld. In 1897 the association Vereininigten Werkstätten für Kunst im Handwerk was founded in Munich, followed a year later by the Werkstätte für Handwerkkunst in Dresden. The influential German Art Nouveau magazines were also published in this period. In 1896 *Die Jugend* began publication, followed in Munich in 1897 by *Kunst und Handwerk*. In Darmstadt, *Deutsche Kunst und Dekoration* and *Dekorative Kunst* began to appear in 1897.

HERMANN OBRIST (1863-1927) began his career by studying ceramics. In 1892 he opened a textile factory which he transferred to Munich in 1894. Obrist is famous for his 'Whiplash' tapestry (1895), which defines one of the central motifs of Art Nouveau art. Later in his career Obrist produced a series of remarkable sculptures, which seem to demonstrate a German taste for abstraction. In the Column Monument (1898), the change to a more abstract and geometric style can be observed in the way the plain column emerges from the stone block.

460

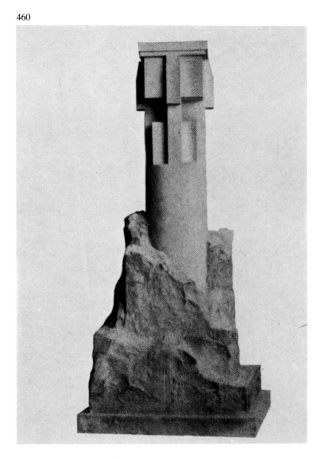

459—and the symbol of Chapter 9, pp. 172-193 – AUGUST ENDELL, Atelier Elvira, Munich, 1897-98 (demolished); detail of the ornament on the facade.
460—HERMANN OBRIST, *Column Monument*, 1898.
461—H. OBRIST, chair, c. 1898.
462—A. ENDELL, table. Munich, Staatsmuseum.
 *—page 173, OTTO ECKMANN, ornamental inset from *Pan*, 1896.

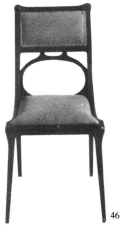

461

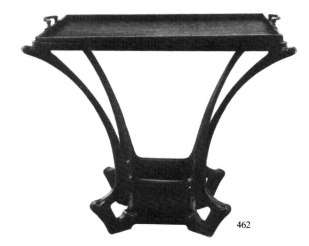

462

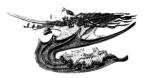

The floral expression of the Art Nouveau style in Germany is called Jugendstil (named after the magazine *Jugend*). In architecture the Bavarian Jugendstil aesthetic was highly successful and produced some very distinguished buildings. Prominent among the architects of the period was AUGUST ENDELL (1871-1925), who for a time was also associated with the Berlin Secession.

One of the first buildings designed and built by Endell was the Atelier Elvira (1897-98). This was destroyed by the Nazis, who saw it as degenerate, probably because of the sheer exuberance of the ornament which Endell applied to the building. The facade and gate are decorated with luxurious forms which ultimately derive from

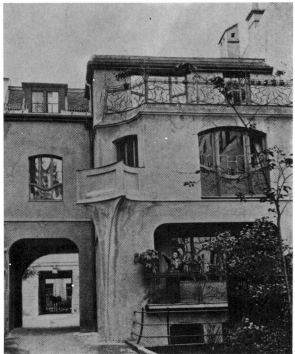

463

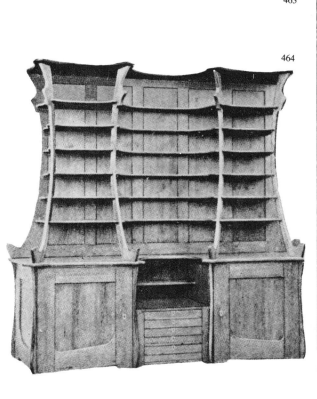

464

465

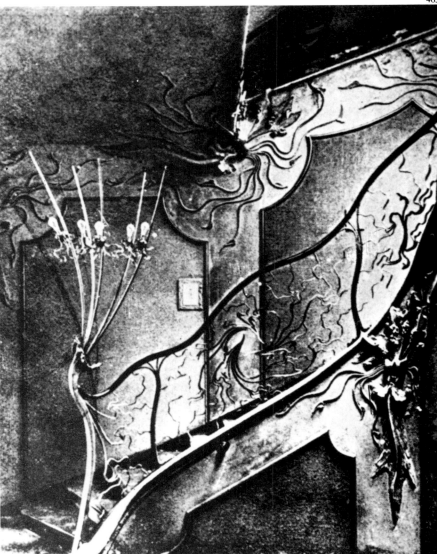

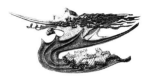

466

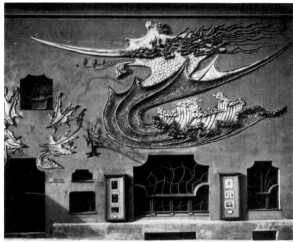

467

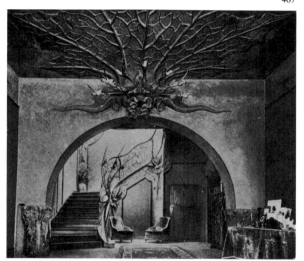

468

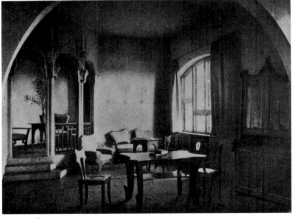

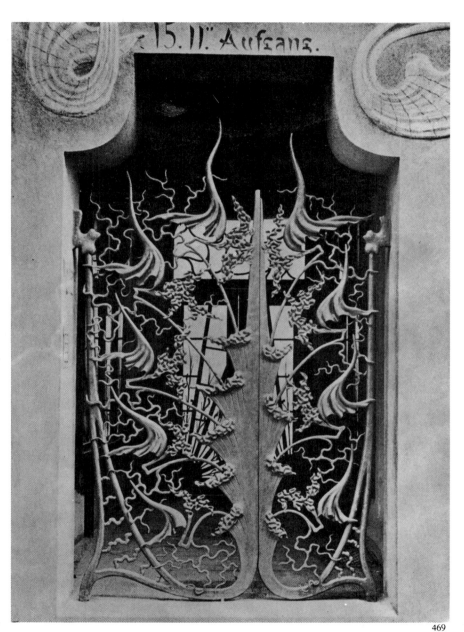

469

463—A. ENDELL, Atelier Elvira, Munich, 1897-98 (demolished); garden facade.
464—A. ENDELL, dresser made for the Industrial Art Workshops in Dresden.
465—A. ENDELL, Atelier Elvira, Munich, 1897-98; staircase.
466—A. ENDELL, Atelier Elvira, facade.
467—A. ENDELL, Atelier Elvira, entrance hall.
468—A. ENDELL, Föhr, Sanatorium, c. 1900; sitting room.
469—A. ENDELL, Atelier Elvira, Munich, 1897-98; main gate.

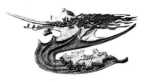

Chinese and Japanese decorative arts. The interior is similarly decorated. The staircase and photographic studio are treated organically. A series of branches or roots are modelled in three dimensions on the walls and ceiling—this creates a sense of abundance as well as a disturbing ambiguity of meaning.

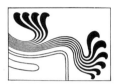

OTTO ECKMANN (1865-1902) is considered the leading exponent of Bavarian Jugendstil. After a brief period as a painter, Eckmann devoted himself almost entirely to the graphic and applied arts. He was one of the principal illustrators of *Die Jugend* and of the most

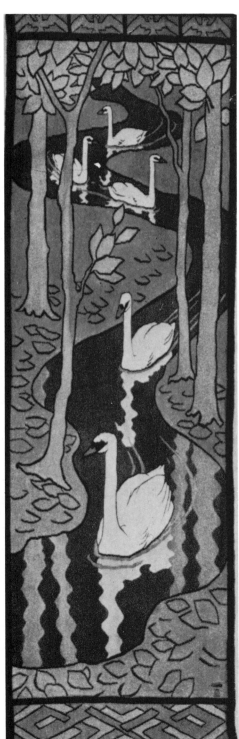

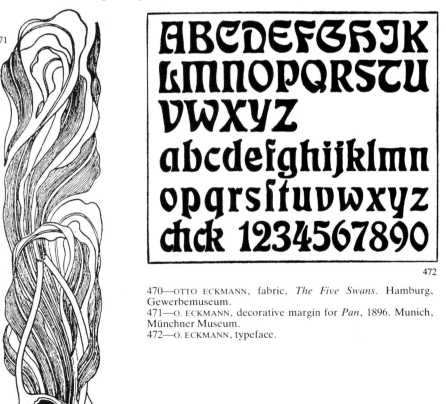

470

471

472

470—OTTO ECKMANN, fabric, *The Five Swans*. Hamburg, Gewerbemuseum.
471—O. ECKMANN, decorative margin for *Pan*, 1896. Munich, Münchner Museum.
472—O. ECKMANN, typeface.

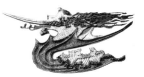

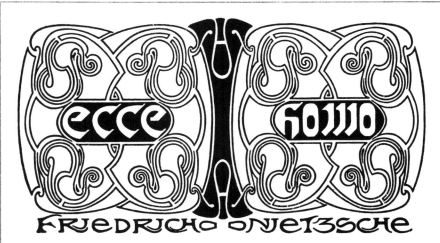

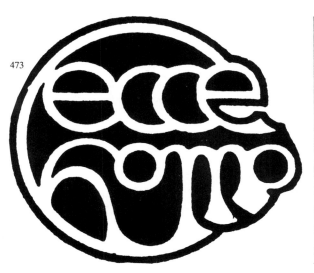

473—HENRY VAN DE VELDE, graphic decoration for *Ecce Homo* by F. Nietzsche, 1908.
474—O. ECKMANN, illustration.
475—H. VAN DE VELDE, flyleaf of *Ecce Homo* by F. Nietzsche, 1908.
476—O. ECKMANN, binding of *Der Sänger* by A. Wildbrand, 1899.

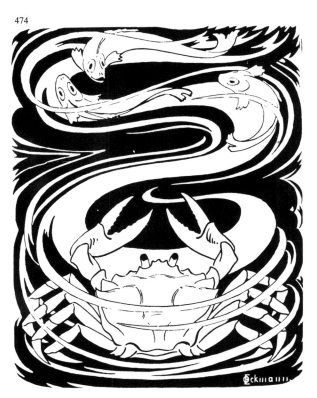

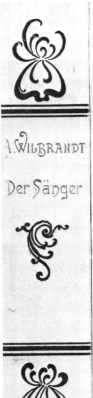

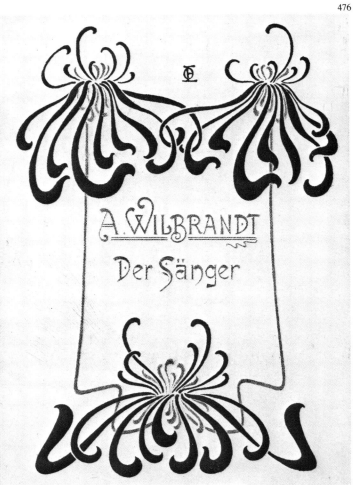

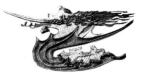

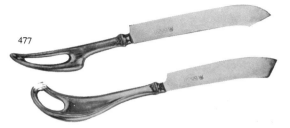

477

477—RICHARD   RIEMERSCHMID,   cutlery,   Hamburg, Gewerbemuseum.

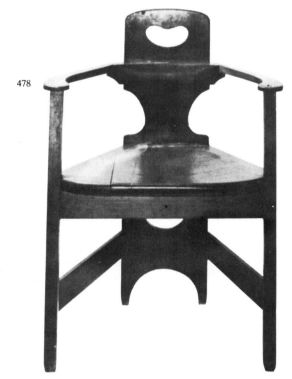

478

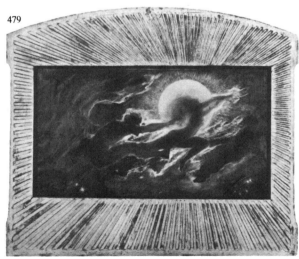

479

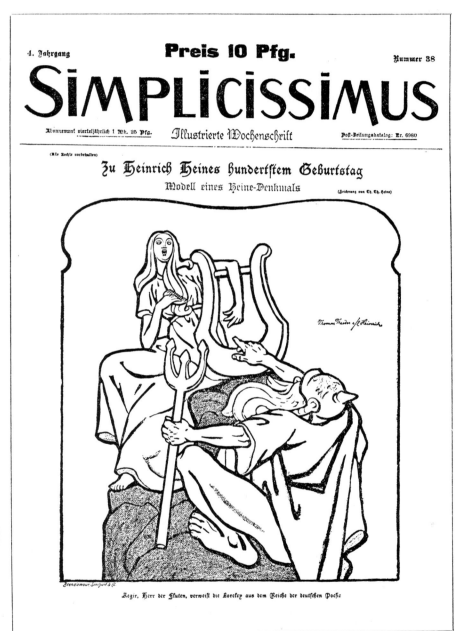

480

influential German Art Nouveau Magazine *Pan*. His illustrations in these magazines and his designs for bindings like the one he designed for Wildebrand's *Der Sänger* (1899) are highly condensed and decorative, and in their thick curving lines and contrasting areas of black and white they resemble van de Velde's work.

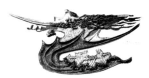

478—R. RIEMERSCHMID, armchair, c. 1900. Zurich, Kunstgewerbemuseum.
479—R. RIEMERSCHMID, *Wolkengenpenster*. Munich, Staatliche Galerie.
480—Cover of the journal *Simplicissimus*, 1899.

481—BERNHARD PANKOK, glass-fronted cabinet.
482—R. RIEMERSCHMID, foyer of the theatre at the Munich Exhibition, 1901.
483—B. PANKOK, reception room, c. 1900. Munich, Staatmuseum.

481

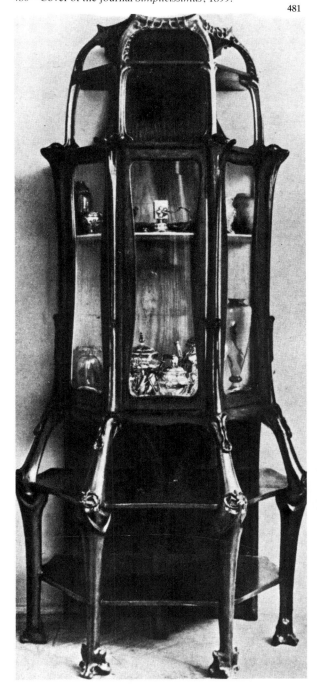

482

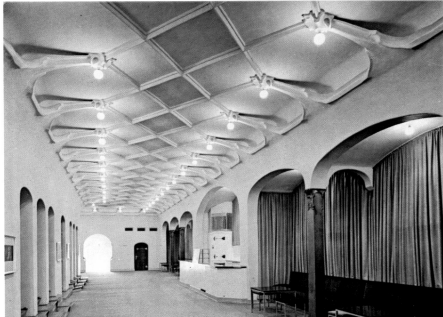

483

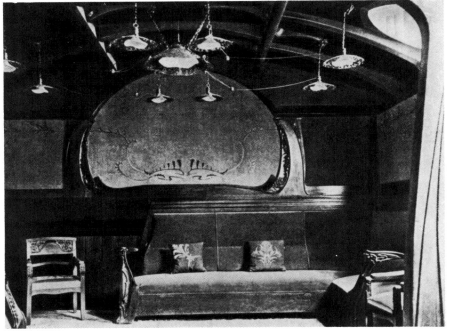

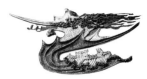

484—P. BEHRENS, two teapots, 1912.
485—P. BEHRENS, catalogue cover of the AEG.
486—R. RIEMERSCHMID, public housing for the Krupps Company, Essen, c. 1905.
  *—page 180, KOLOMAN MOSER, decorative inset.

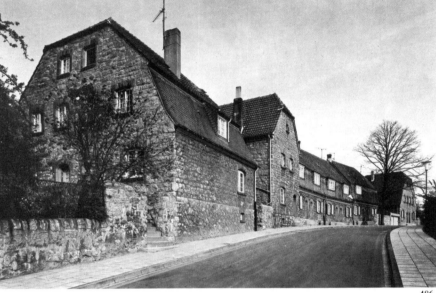

486

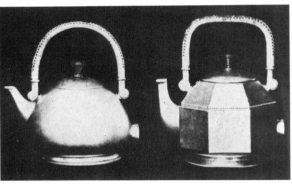

484

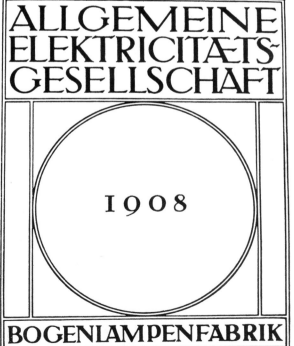

485

487-8—P. BEHRENS, lamps designed for the AEG.
489—P. BEHRENS, stained glass.

BERNHARD PANKOK'S (1872-1943) development was parallel to that of Eckmann's. Orginally a painter, Pankok moved into the decorative arts. Pankok's furniture and interior designs are close to the work of van de Velde in their firmness of line and volume. The foyer of the theatre he designed for the Paris International Exhibition (1900) is probably the best example of his well ordered interiors. These features are also found in the furniture and interior designs of Richard Riemerschmid (1878-1957). His pictorial work contains the more complex rhythms of Symbolism.

The most important architect of the Art Nouveau movement in Germany was PETER BEHRENS (1868-1940). He was one of the founders of the Munich Secession in 1892. He later moved to Darmstadt to join the community of artists housed in the village built by Joseph Maria Olbrich on the commission of the Grand Duke Ernst Ludwig von Hesse. Behrens, though trained as a painter, built his own house there. This building established him as a highly competent architect. It is a three-dimensional counterpart of the Belgian linear style that he had used in his graphic work. His ability to unify the curving lines with structural vertical and horizontal forms is particularly evident on the exterior, especially in the design of the door.

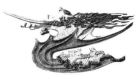

490-1—P. BEHRENS, the assembly room of the AEG turbine factory, Berlin, 1910-12; facades and flanks.

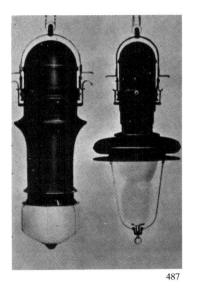

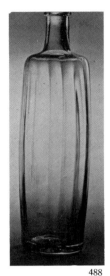

487 488

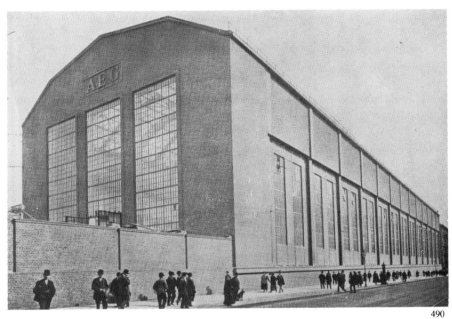

490

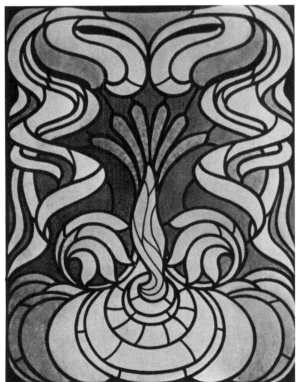

489

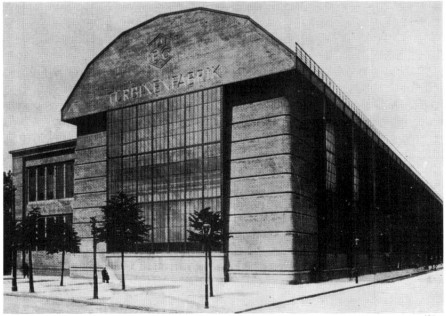

491

Simplicity, and an interest in the function of buildings, characterize Behrens' architecture, and these preoccupations made his work important for the architects of the Modern Movement. Behrens systematically studied the production methods of the AEG Co. in Berlin before producing a design for their turbine factory (1910-12), formulated to accommodate the company's production methods. The

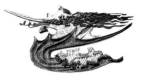

492

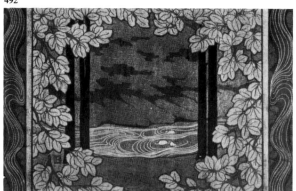

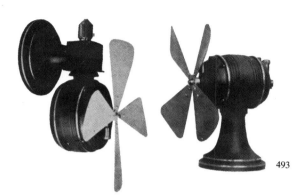

493

492—P. BEHRENS, *Brook*, c. 1901. Charlottenburg (Berlin),
Kunstbibliotek der Ehemals Staatlichen Museum.
493—PETER BEHRENS, two fans, 1912.
494—FRIEDRICH W. KLEUKENS, illustration from the *Book of
Esther*, 1908; the first book printed by the Ernst-Ludwig-Press,
Darmstadt.
495—P. BEHRENS, Behrens House, Darmstadt, 1901; exterior.
496—P. BEHRENS, door of Behrens House, Darmstadt.
497—P. BEHRENS, Behrens House, Darmstadt; interior.

factory is essentially a huge shed, but its form is dignified by the
allusion on the facade to a Greek temple. The surface of the facade is
modelled by projecting and receding planes and ornamented only by
the elegant lettering of the inscription in the pediment and the striated
corner treatment. In contrast, the sides and rear of the building are
very plain.

494

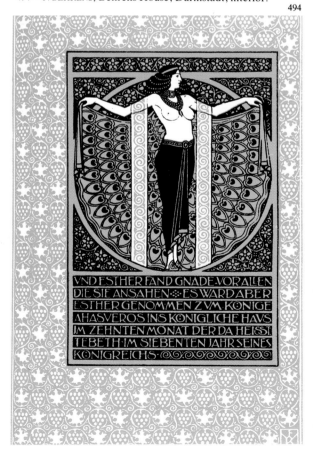

495

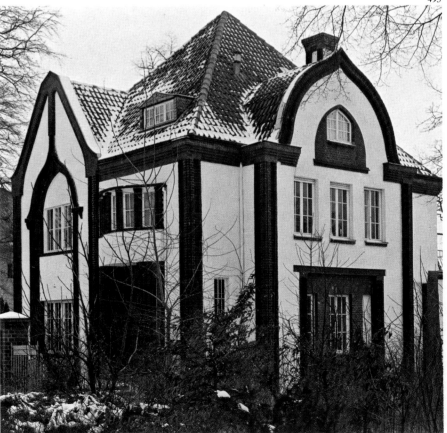

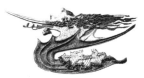

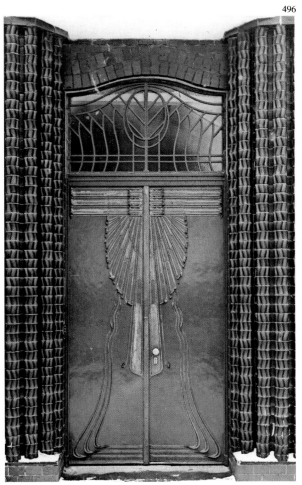

496

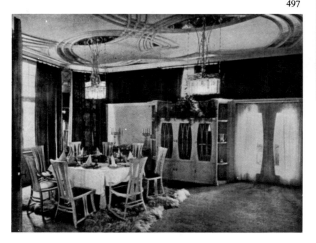

497

498—P. BEHRENS, Höchster Farbwerke, Frankfurt-am-Main, 1920-24; entrance to the offices.

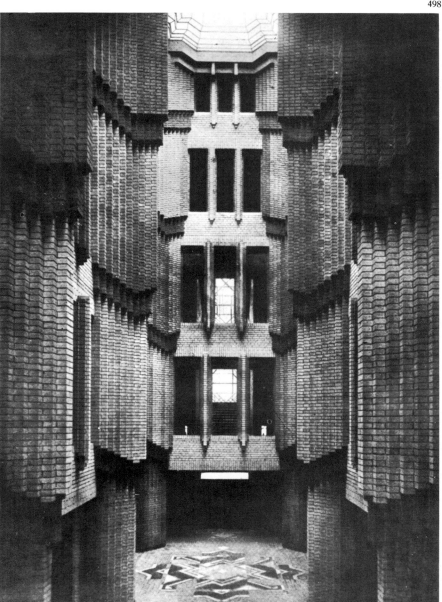

498

Functional design and sensitivity to composition control the design for Höchster Farbwerke (1920-24). Here again Behrens has adapted the effect of a repetitive structure, and the building achieves solidity and clarity of structure as well as a high level of surface articulation.

The last truly Art Nouveau building in Germany was van de Velde's Deutscher Werkbund Theater (1914) in Cologne. Here the curving line still dominates the plan and decorative elements.

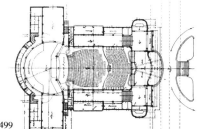

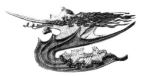

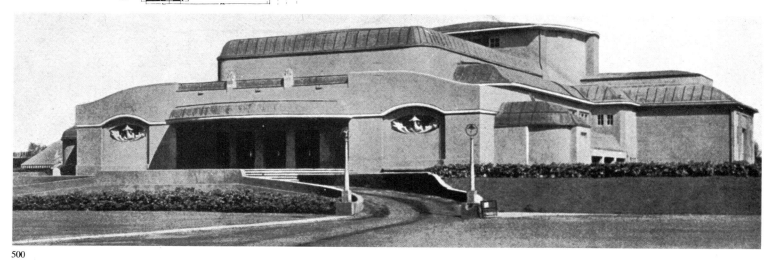

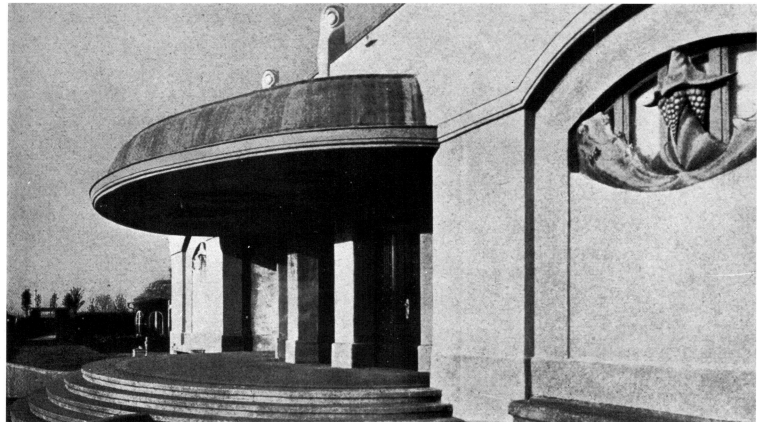

499—H. VAN DE VELDE, Werkbund Theater, Cologne, 1914 (demolished); plan.
500—H. VAN DE VELDE, Werkbund Theater, 1914.
501—H. VAN DE VELDE, Werkbund Theater, 1914; entrance.

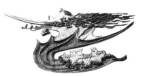

However, by this date the style of the building was anachronistic, and after the First World War the ascendancy of rationalist architecture began.

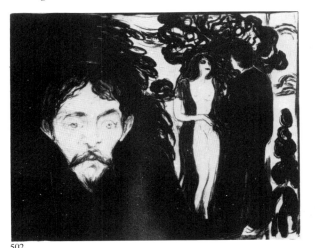

502—EDWARD MUNCH, *Jealousy*, 1896. Oslo, Kommunes Kunstsamlingen Munch Museum.
503—E. MUNCH, *The Kiss*, 1902; fourth version. Oslo, Kommunes Kunstsamlingen Munch Museum.
504—E. MUNCH, *The Madonna*, 1895. Oslo, Kommunes Kunstsamlingen Munch Museum.

In 1892 two important events occurred which stimulated the taste for Art Nouveau painting and graphics. The first was an exhibition of the work of the Norwegian artist, EDVARD MUNCH (1863-1944), in Berlin at the Verein Berliner Künstler. Munch's work created a

504

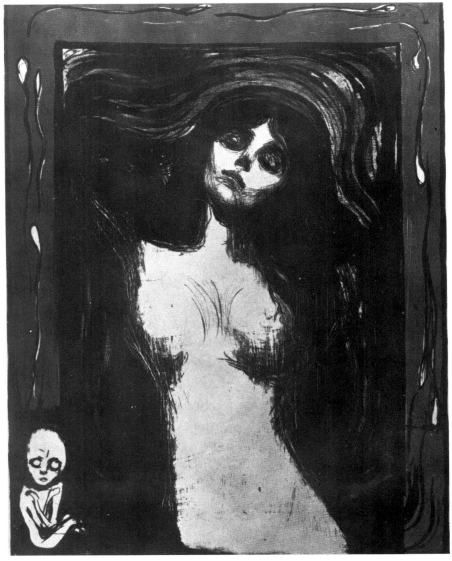

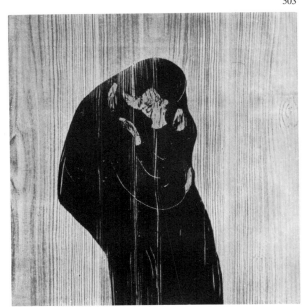

502

503

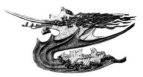

505

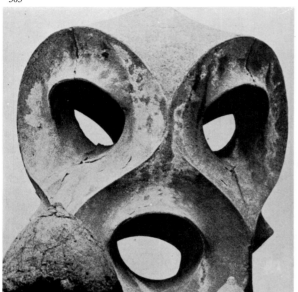

scandal and the exhibition quickly closed. It caused such turmoil and reaction against the avant-garde that in 1899 the Berliner Secession was formed, led by the Impressionist Max Liebermann. The second event was the formation of a group who based themselves on the Belgian Société des XX, the XI. Max Klinger (1857-1910) and Ludwig von Hofmann (1861-1945) were members of this group.

Although Munch was Norwegian, he worked in Berlin and his work was the major source for many German painters. The use of

507

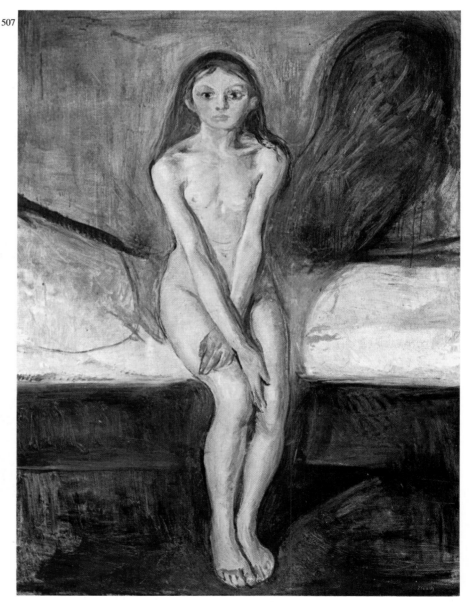

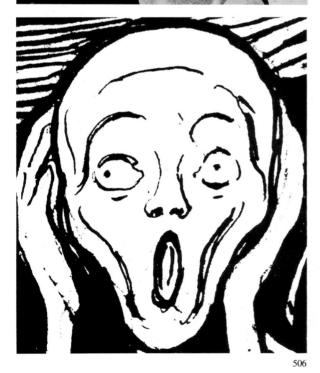

506

505—ANTONI GAUDÍ, the Casa Milà, Barcelona, 1905-10; chimney, detail.
506—E. MUNCH, *The Scream*, c. 1895.
507—E. MUNCH, *Puberty*, 1894.
508—E. MUNCH, *The Vampire*, c. 1893. Oslo, Kommunes Kunstsamlingen Munch Museum.

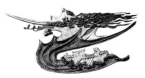

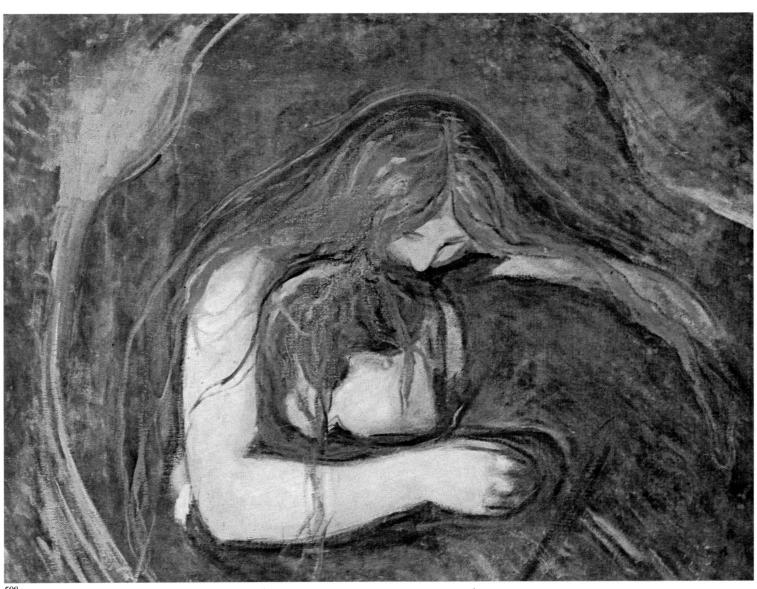

508

curvilinear line to suggest anxiety is notable in his work. This is most evident in the paintings executed by Munch in the years after the Berlin exhibition, which were readily appreciated by the German avant-garde. These include *The Scream* (1895) and *The Madonna* (1895). Here forms are reduced almost to calligraphic signs. Other works by Munch are less synthetic and seek to explore more complex psychological themes; typical of these are *The Vampire* (1893), *Puberty* (1894) and *Jealousy* (1896). These all express in various ways Munch's tortured fascination with the image of woman as a destructive creature, a theme in his life as much as in his work.

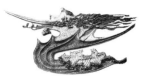

MAX KLINGER (1857-1920) was one of the first German artists to respond to the new decorative qualities in painting and the applied arts. There are also reminiscences of Munch's style and imagery in Klinger's work. His earlier work, for example *The Judgment of Paris* (1885-87), is in a calmer, more academic tradition. In the 1890s his paintings show a radical break with this tradition. In the etching

509

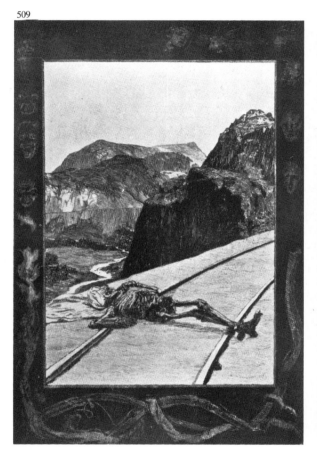

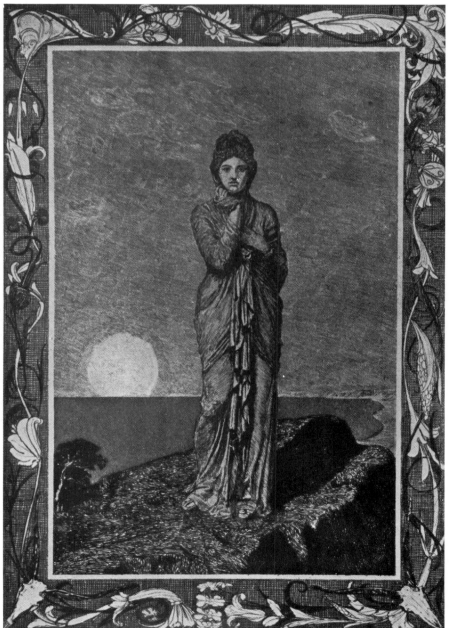

509—MAX KLINGER, *On the Rails*, 1889; engraving from the *Work of Death*. Munich, Staatliche Graphische Sammlung.
510—M. KLINGER, *Psyche on the Edge of the Sea*, 1890; engraving from the album *Love and Psyche*. Munich, Staatliche Graphische Sammlung.
511—M. KLINGER, *The Sleeper*, c. 1900. Munich, Staatliche Graphische Sammlung.

510

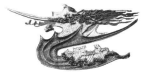

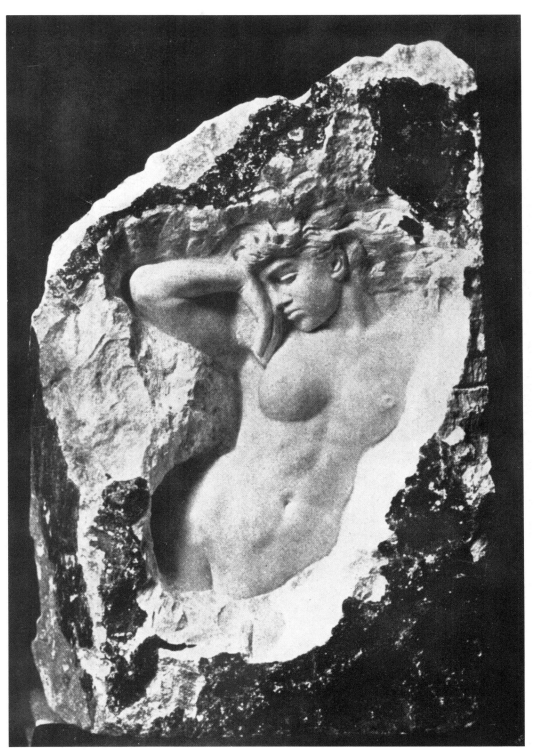

511

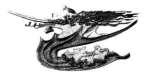

512

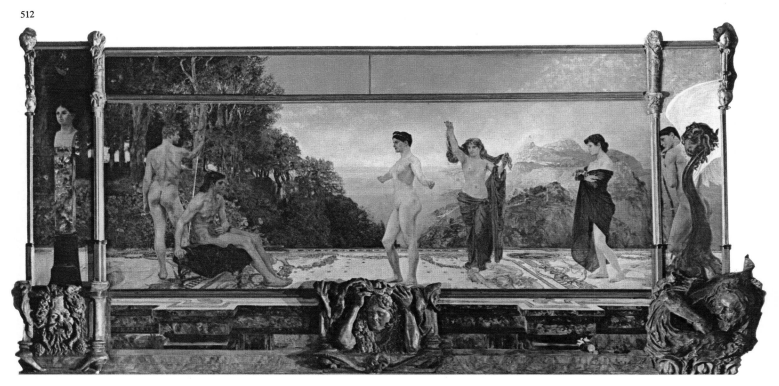

512—M. KLINGER, *The Judgment of Paris*, 1885-87. Vienna, Kunsthistorisches Museum.
513—LUDWIG VON HOFMANN, *Idyllic Landscape with Bathers*, c. 1900. Schweinfurt, coll. George Schäffer.
   *—page 190, CHARLES DOUDELET, illustration for a poem by Maeterlinck, from *Serres Chaudes*.
514—FRANZ VON STUCK, *Die Suende*, 1893. Munich, Bayerische Staatsgemäldesammlungen.

Psyche by the Sea Shore (from the suite of illustrations of *Cupid and Psyche*, 1890), the image of desolation is contrasted with the lush floral borders inspired by Rococo decoration. By 1899 his designs are more unified. In the etching *On The Railway Lines* (1899) the angular lines of the skeletal figure are echoed in the border. This gives the small work a compelling unity of effect.

513

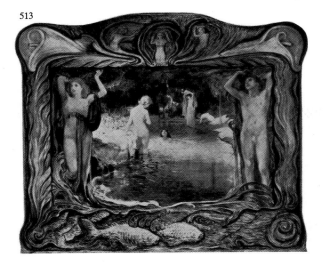

Another member of the Berlin Secession was FRANZ VON STUCK (1863-1928). Von Stuck worked initially in a style inspired by the ornate Symbolism of Arnold Böcklin (1827-1901). He soon developed his own style which combined softened contours, rich colouring and erotic subject matter. The figure in *Die Suende* (1893) closely resembles Khnopff's enigmatic sphinx figures, which stimulate emotions of pain and pleasure. In the following years this style became much harder. It exploited the contrast of colour and chiaroscuro with firm outline. In *Amazon and the Centaur* (c. 1912) this style is perfected, and the violence and eroticism of the subject heightened.

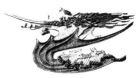

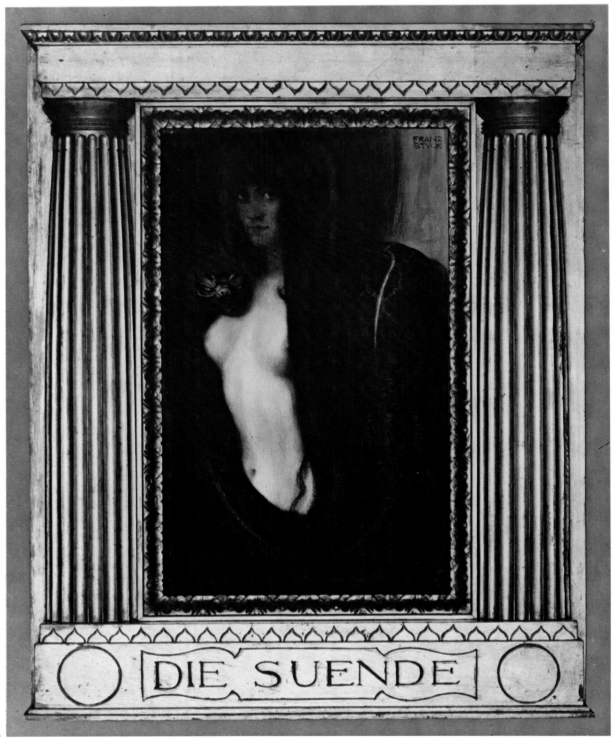

514

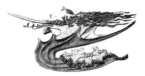

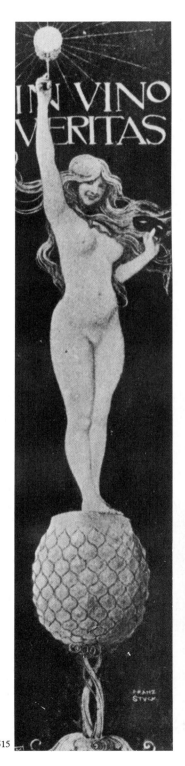

515

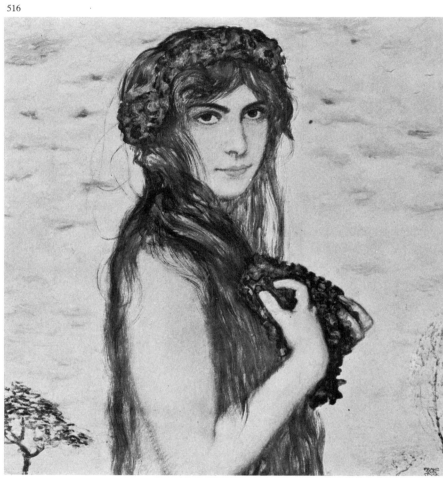

516

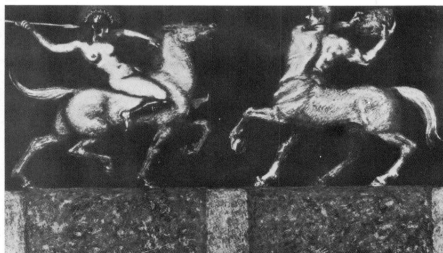

517

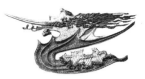

Von Stuck's work was important for the development of his contemporary LUDWIG VON HOFMANN (1861-1945). Hofmann's work is altogether more lyrical, and usually depicts figures in idyllic landscapes.

Apart from Obrist, ERNST BARLACH (1870-1938) is the most outstanding German Art Nouveau sculptor. Barlach had studied in Hanover, Dresden and Paris. The primitive shapes he found in Russia (he had visited Russia in 1905) were the decisive influence on his

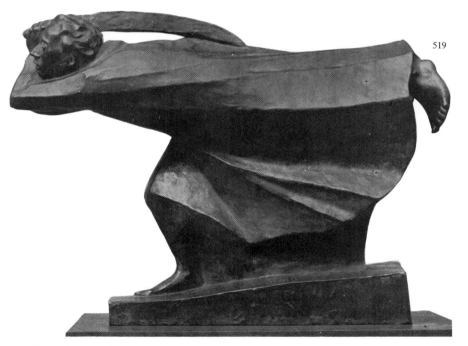

519

515—F. VON STUCK, *In Vino Veritas*, 1892. Berlin, National Gallery.
516—F. VON STUCK, *Spring*, c. 1912. Darmstadt, Hessisches Landesmuseum.
517—F. VON STUCK, *The Amazon and the Centaur*, c. 1912.
518—ERNST BARLACH, *The Poet Theodor Däubler*, 1909.
519—E. BARLACH, *The Avenger*, 1914. Ratzeburg, coll. Barlach.

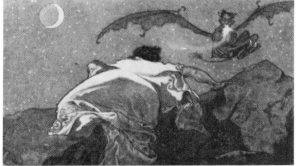

518

work. He used the same materials as his prototypes: wood and terracotta. Barlach's themes were drawn from the daily life of peasants and from popular legend. His work is strong and mobile. *The Avenger* is typical of his later work, where Art Nouveau influence gives way to Expressionism. It prefigures Boccioni's use of flattened volumes and straight lines to portray movement.

10-Austria

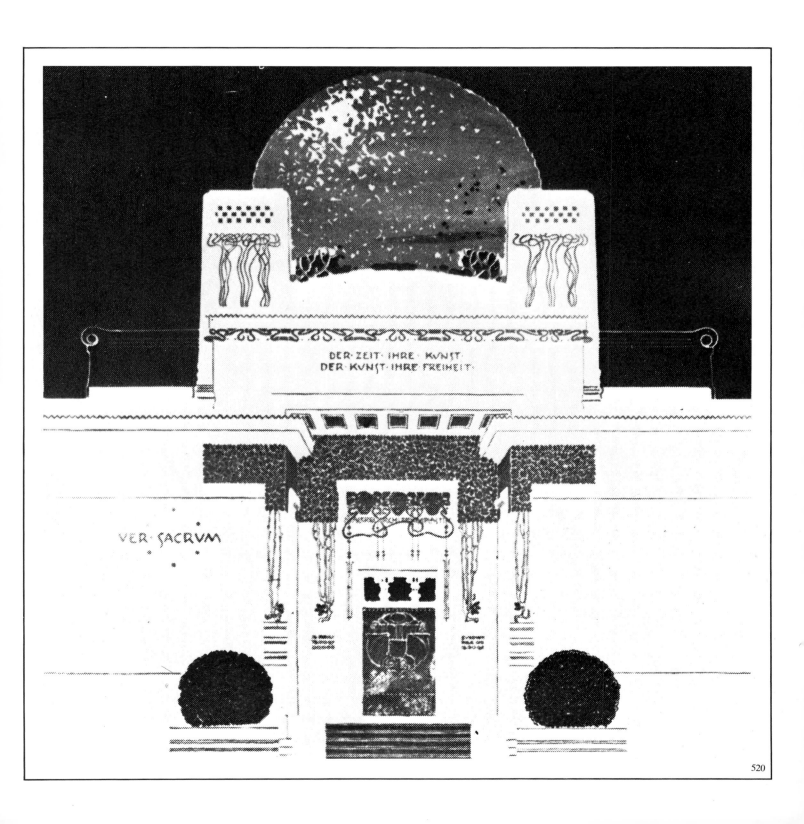

Art Nouveau arrived late in Austria and (with a few notable exceptions) its influence was almost entirely confined to Vienna. It first entered Viennese artistic life in 1897, when the Vienna Secession or Vereinigung bildender Künstler Österreichs Secession was set up. Gustav Klimt designed the poster for this exhibition which included works by Emile Bernard, Arnold Böcklin, Eugène Grasset, Max Klinger, Fernand Khnopff, Puvis de Chavannes, Auguste Rodin, Franz von Stuck and Henry van de Velde.

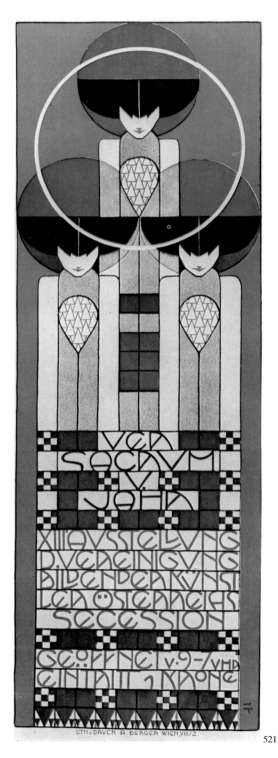

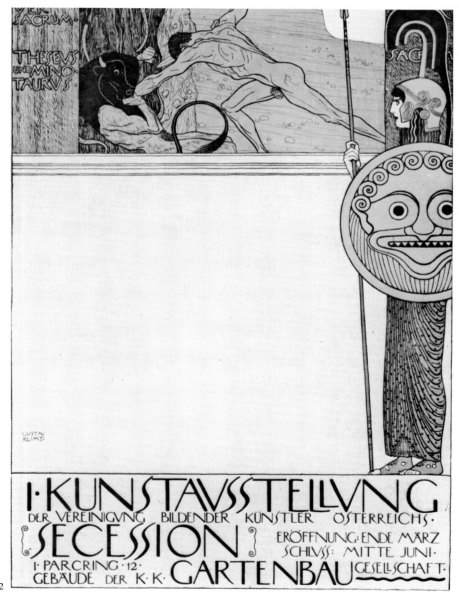

521   522

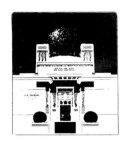

520—and symbol of Chapter 10, pp. 194-225 – JOSEPH MARIA OLBRICH, poster for the II exhibition of the Vienna Secession, 1898.
521—KOLOMAN MOSER, poster of the XIII exhibition of the Vienna Secession. Vienna, Albertina.
522—GUSTAV KLIMT, poster of the I exhibition of the Vienna Secession, 1897. Darmstadt, Hessisches Landesmuseum.

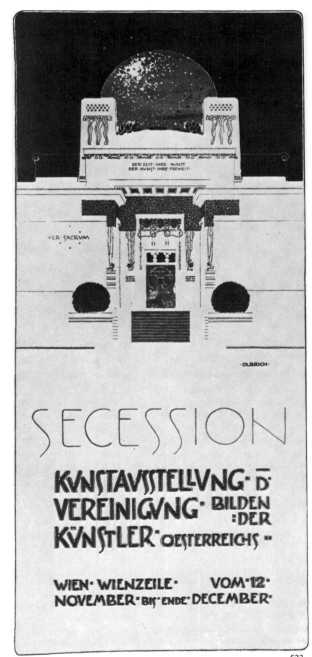

523

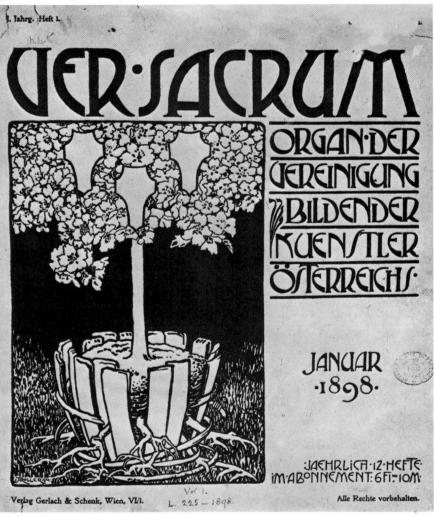

524

523—J. M. OLBRICH, poster for the II exhibition of the Vienna Secession, 1898.
524—ALFRED ROLLER, cover for the first issue of *Ver Sacrum*, January 1898.
525—JOSEF HOFFMANN, *Kleinstadt Idyll*, decorative border for the printed musical score of the poem *Small Town Idyll*, by Max Bruns, c. 1901.

This was followed by the publication of the Viennese Art Nouveau magazine *Ver Sacrum*. This periodical was important for the diffusion of the new style; in its first years it published illustrations by English Pre-Raphaelites and Puvis de Chavannes, as well as works by artists who were to be at the forefront of the Viennese Art Nouveau style: Joseph Olbrich, Josef Hoffmann and Koloman Moser.

Art history also had a role to play in the development of the new style. Alois Reigl's *Stilfragen* (Problems of Style) (1893), which outlined the history of the decorative arts in Egypt and the Byzantine

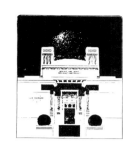

526—K. MOSER, poster for the V exhibition of the Vienna Secession, 1899.
527—OTTO WAGNER, Karlsplatz Underground Station, Vienna, 1898-99, project.
   *—page 196, A. ROLLER, *Day and Night*, 1900.

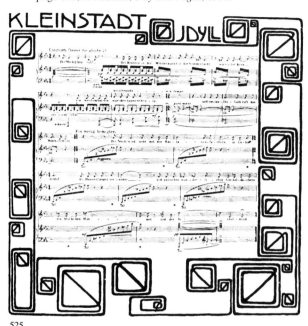

525

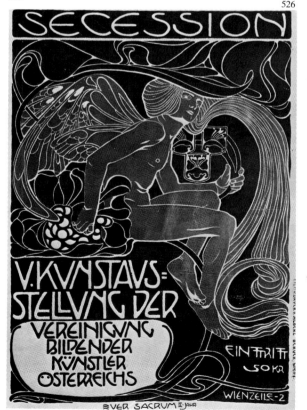

526

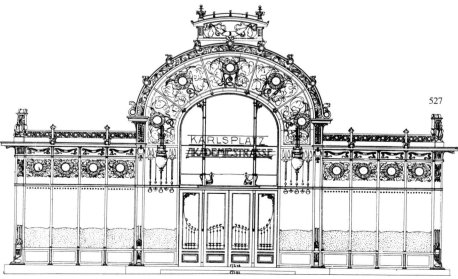

527

Empire, was a formative influence on Viennese artists. OTTO WAGNER (1841-1918) was the influential promoter of the movement in the field of architecture. Wagner had begun his career by building in an historicizing manner, drawing elements from Renaissance, Baroque, Rococo and even occasionally from the period of Louis XVI. However, as his style developed, Wagner tended towards simplicity and geometrical order. By 1895 Wagner had consolidated his principles in a book, *Moderne Architektur* (which was widely read and very influential with the younger generation). The book stated the case for an architectural style which is free from historicism.

Wagner's Karlsplatz Underground Station (1897-99) is one of his earliest works which approaches the Art Nouveau style. In this building he developed cubic space and the use of decorative black and white ornament which became a characteristic of the Viennese Art Nouveau movement after 1900. Similarly, richly coloured tiles contrast with a simple horizontal and vertical structural grid on the facade of The Majolikahaus (1898). In his design for an Academy of the Figurative Arts (1897-98) Wagner integrates the cubic format with the curving arabesque Art Nouveau line more fully. The building was originally crowned with an elaborate ironwork cupola which echoed the geometry of the supporting arches.

Wagner's own architecture, except for the Church at Nussdorf (1897), does not fulfil the promise of the simplicity called for in his book. This was accomplished by his pupils. JOSEPH MARIA OLBRICH (1867-1908) and Josef Hoffmann were prominent among them. They successfully pursued the architectural design experiments which they had begun while working for *Ver Sacrum*.

One of Olbrich's first buildings of interest was his Haus der Wiener Secession (1898-99), which was built to house the society's annual

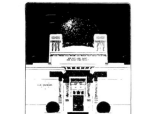

528—O. WAGNER, Underground Station, Vienna, 1898-99.
529—O. WAGNER, Karlsplatz Underground Station, Vienna, 1894-97.
530—O. WAGNER, the Nussdorf Lock, 1897; section.
531—O. WAGNER, Majolikahaus, Vienna, c. 1890.
532—O. WAGNER, Nussdorf Lock, 1897.
533—LEOPOLD BAUER, Valentino Jakubeckis House, Vienna, c. 1902; design of the facade.
534—O. WAGNER, project for an Academy of Figurative Arts, 1897-98.

531

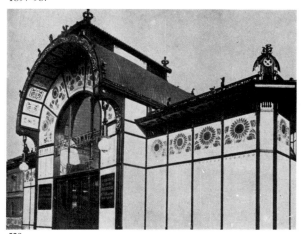

528

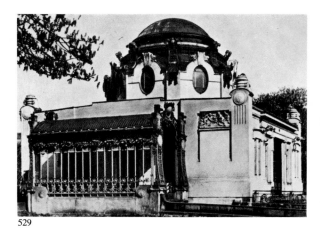

529

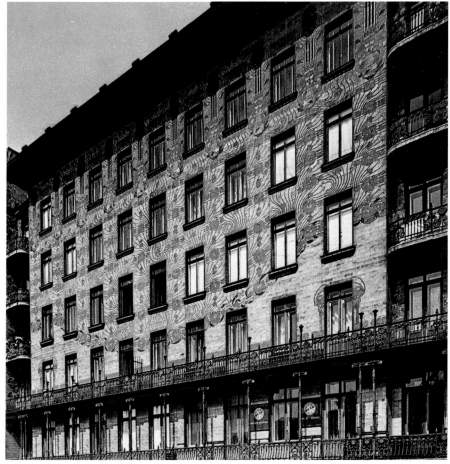

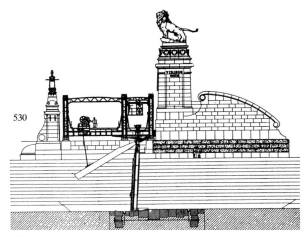

530

535—O. WAGNER, Majolikahaus, Vienna, c. 1890; detail.
536—O. WAGNER, Church, Nussdorf.

532

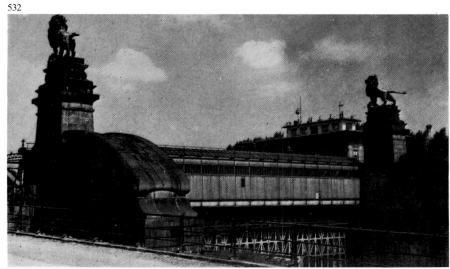

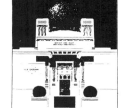

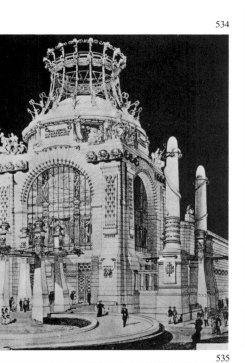

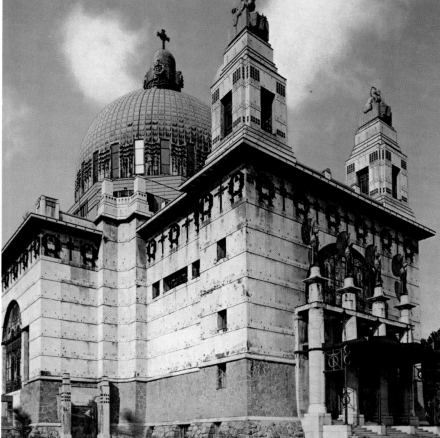

537—O. WAGNER, Wagner House, Vienna, Hüttelberstrasse 28; interior design 1900; stained-glass windows designed by Adolf Böhm.

536

533

534

535

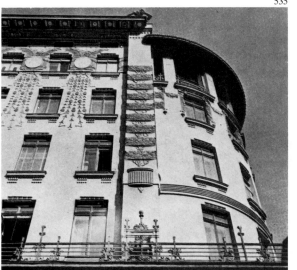

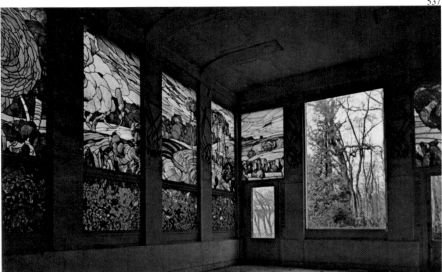

537

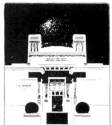

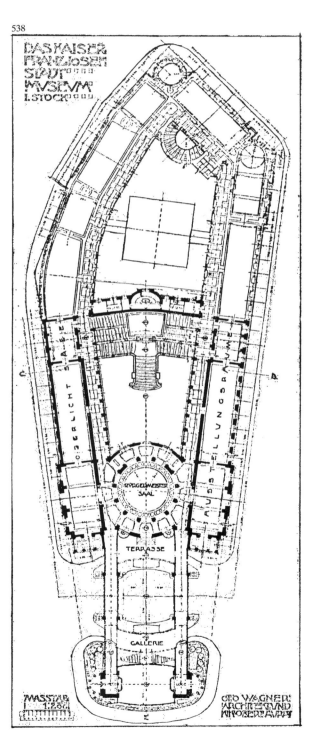

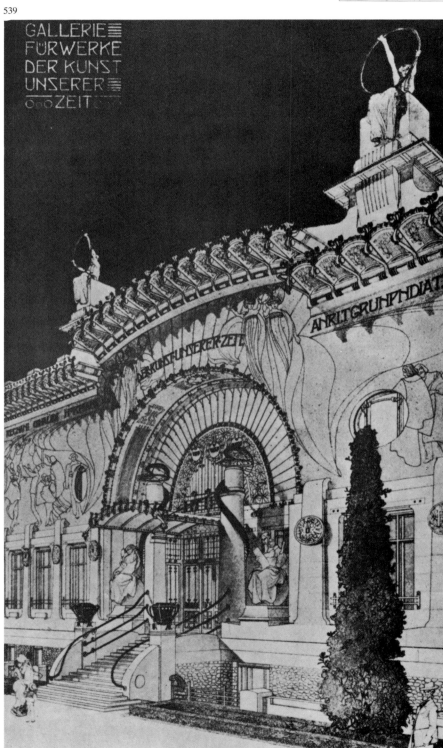

538—O. WAGNER, project for a Museum of Modern Art; plan.
539—O. WAGNER, project for a Gallery of Modern Art; elevation.

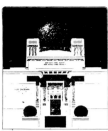

540

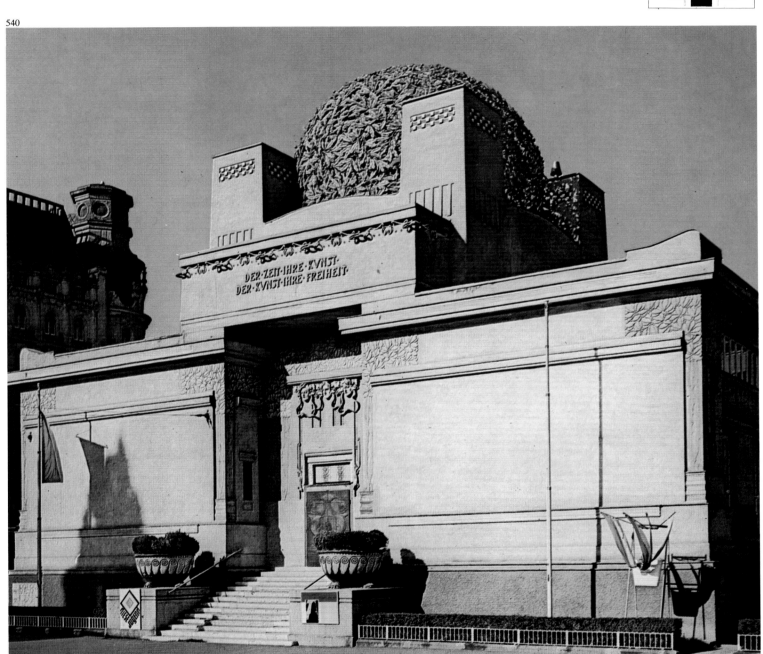

540—J. M. OLBRICH—The Secession House, Vienna, 1898-99.

exhibitions. The building is defined by the interplay of cubes and spheres, which give it a monumental simplicity. The flat planes of the building are enlivened in restricted zones like the frieze by a flat foliage decoration while the leaves decorating the dome are in high relief. The building is one of the earliest examples of the successful use of strong, simple volumes in Art Nouveau architecture, and it

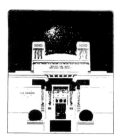

541
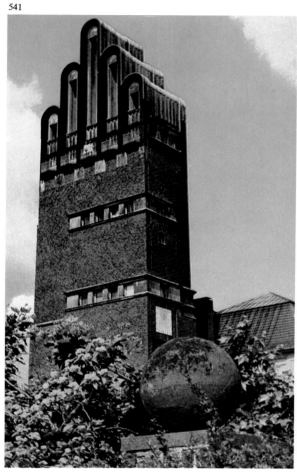

542
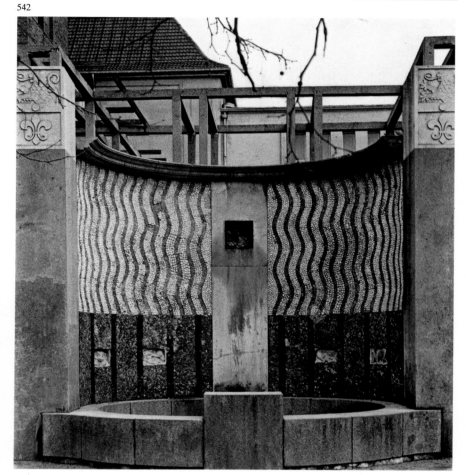

541—J. M. OLBRICH, The Wedding Tower, Mathildenhöhe, Darmstadt, 1907.
542—J. M. OBRICH, The Exhibition Palace and Wedding Tower, Darmstadt, 1907.
543—J. M. OLBRICH, The Exhibition Palace, Mathildenhöhe, Darmstadt; fountain.
544—J. M. OLBRICH, The Preacher's House, Darmstadt, 1903.
545—J. M. OLBRICH, project for the house of Dr Stöhr, c. 1899.
546—J. M. OLBRICH, silver teapot set with amethyst, 1901. Darmstadt, Hessisches Landesmuseum.
547—J. M. OLBRICH, silver candlestick set with amethyst, 1901. Darmstadt, Hessisches Landesmuseum.

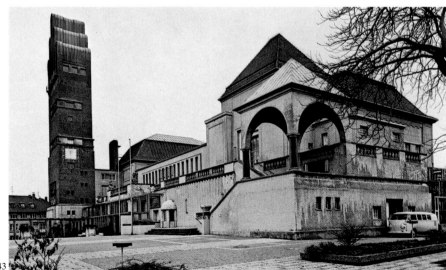
543

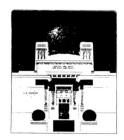

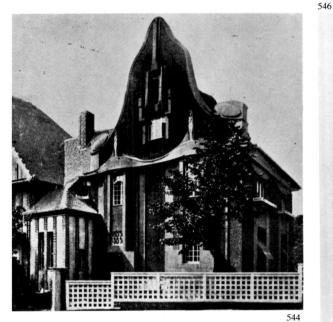

544

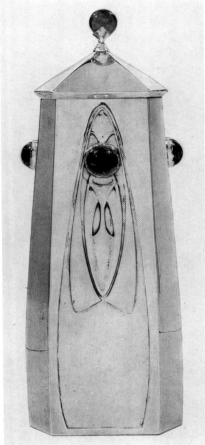

546

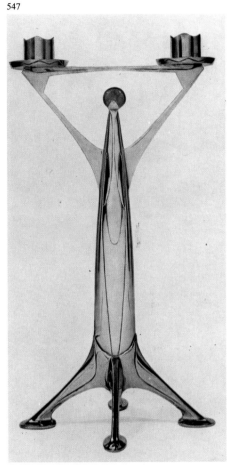

547

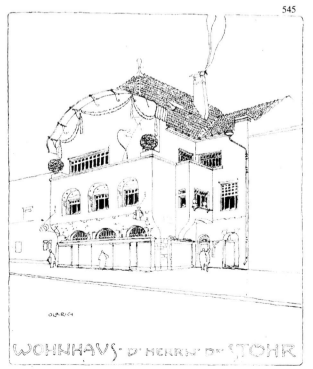

545

WOHNHAVS D' HERRN D' STOHR

marks the definitive point of departure for the Viennese architectural
style.

Reminiscences of Glasgow architecture, and even of van de Velde,
persist in Olbrich's designs – for example, his house for Dr Stohr
c. 1899. By 1900 his architecture had acquired its definitive form first
postulated by the Secession building. In his Exhibition Palace and
Marriage Tower (1905) there is barely any trace of the curving line
which dominated the Art Nouveau style in so many other countries at
this time. The work is again characterized by the organization of the
volumes. Curves play a structural role, in the arches of the portico,
the niche of the fountain and in the crown of the Marriage Tower.
Ornament is subordinated to flat surfaces and some of these receive
flat, rippling patterns. The fashion for flat surface decoration can be
seen in Olbrich's own studio house. The porch and dining room are
decorated with the flat linear and spiral patterns which Gustav Klimt
used to such advantage in his paintings.

In JOSEF HOFFMANN's work the simplification of ornament is even
more evident. The repetition of simple shapes like spirals or black and

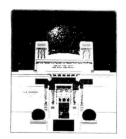

548

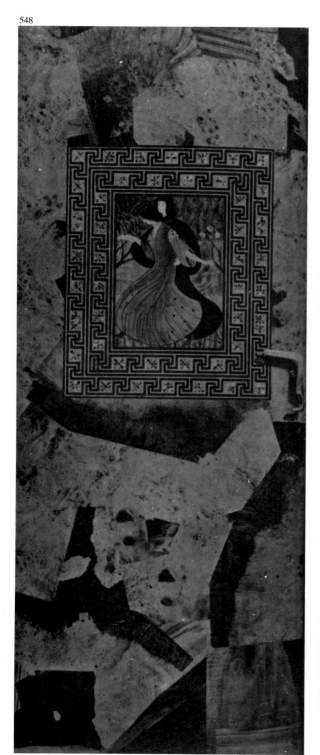

549

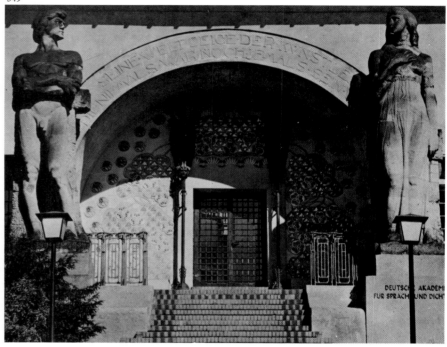

550

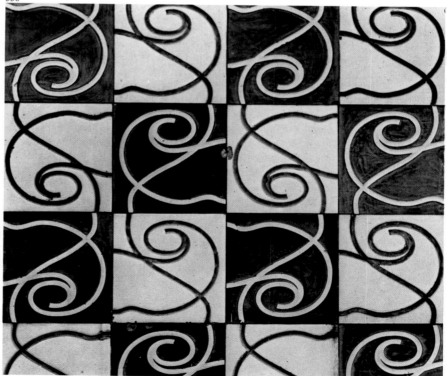

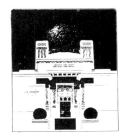

551

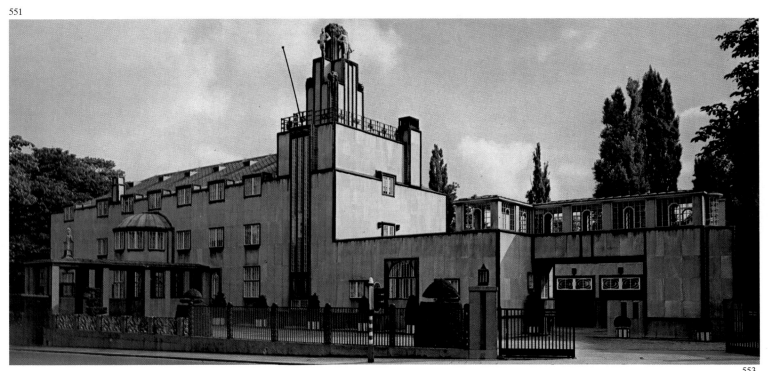

553

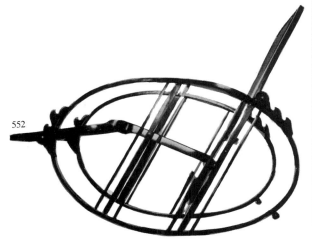

552

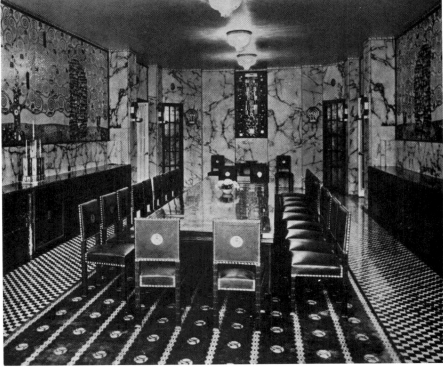

548—J. M. OLBRICH, wall decoration in the Olbrich House, 1901.
549—J. M. OLBRICH, Olbrich House, Mathildenhöhe, Darmstadt, 1901; entrance.
550—J. M. OLBRICH, decoration in ceramics on the facade of the Olbrich House, Darmstadt.
551—J. HOFFMANN, Palais Stoclet, Brussels, 1905-11; facade.
552—J. HOFFMANN, rocking chair in beechwood, designed for the Jacob and Josef Köhn company in Vienna, c. 1905.
553—J. HOFFMANN, Palais Stoclet, Brussels; dining room with mural mosaics by Gustav Klimt.

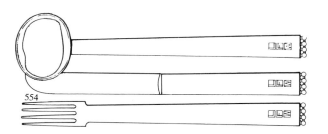

554

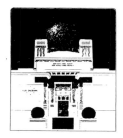

555

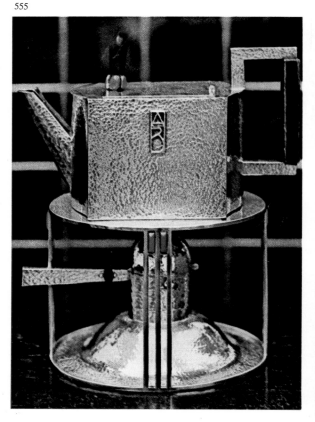

556

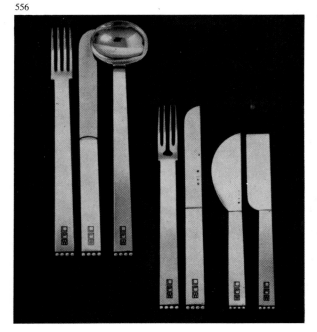

557

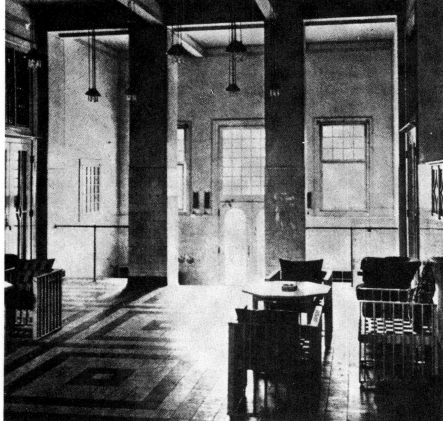

white squares is especially evident. It earned him the nickname 'Chequerboard' Hoffmann. This is particularly visible in the interior of the Palais Stoclet (1905-11).

The exterior of this building is important for several reasons. It was carefully planned and designed so that the different parts of the building would relate both to each other and to the site. The whole design, including the railings, is unified. It is entirely free from the curving arabesque line found in Art Nouveau buildings. For the sake of uncluttered clarity, Hoffmann dispensed with many traditional elements like the cornice, and his plan and elevation are based on the relationship between clearly legible volumes.

The prototypes for this sort of planning are English and Scottish. The interior of Hoffmann's earlier Purkesdorf Sanatorium, when compared to the Palais Stoclet, is obviously related to Mackintosh's work which he would have known through reading *The Studio*.

Similarly, outside influences, this time possibly from Belgium, seem to be operating on the metalwork designs of Olbrich and Hoffmann. But the delicate linearity of Belgian work is modified by the rational geometry appreciated by these Viennese artists.

554—J. HOFFMANN, design for cutlery (see n. 556).
555—J. HOFFMANN, samovar, 1904.
556—J. HOFFMANN, cutlery with the monogram LFW (Lily and
Fritz Wärndorfer), 1904 (see n. 554).
557—J. HOFFMANN, Purkesdorf Sanatorium, Vienna, 1903-04;
the entrance hall, c. 1906.
558—HOFFMANN SCHOOL, cigar cabinet. Vienna, Österreichisches Museum für Angewandte Kunst.

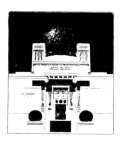

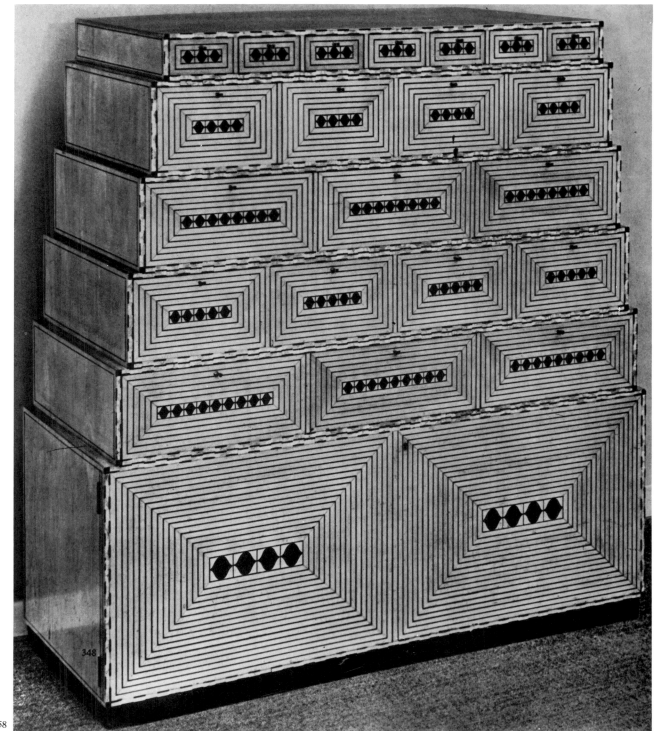

558

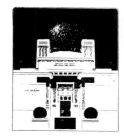

562

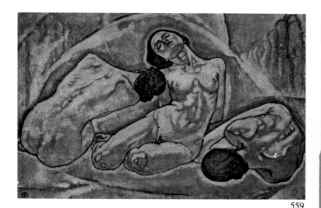

559

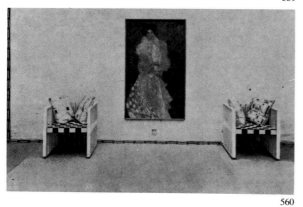

560

561

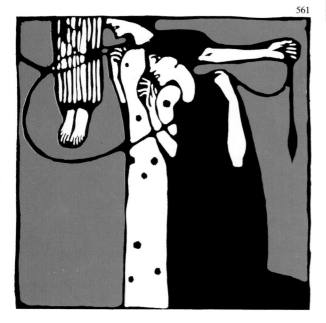

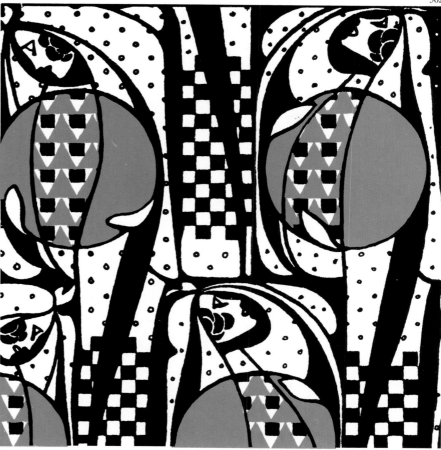

KOLOMAN MOSER (1868-1916) was the outstanding artist of the Viennese Secession in the applied arts. Between 1900 and 1915 Moser was involved in a variety of projects but prominent among them was his graphic work. Moser was very successful in the commercial field of graphics and he designed bank notes and stamps with the strong contrasting patterns characteristic of Viennese art. His feeling for bold design is also evident in his designs for *Ver Sacrum*. Here the interplay between the vertical straight lines and the curves suggests the influence of Klimt and Mackintosh. He also used the black and white chequerboard pattern taken from Hoffmann in his book illustration.

Moser worked in three dimensions. He treated metalwork objects in an especially novel way. Their shapes are basic geometric forms, the sphere, cube, cylinder, etc. Their surfaces are highly polished and any decoration is confined to the structural parts of the object. An example of this is the jewel casket. The vase and sugar bowl dispense almost entirely with decoration. They are highly sophisticated essays into the decorative potential of pure form.

559—K. MOSER, *The Fates*, 1902.
560—K. MOSER, the installation of Gustav Klimt's exhibition at the Secession House in Vienna, 1904.
561—K. MOSER, design for wallpaper.
562—K. MOSER, design for a book cover.
563—illustration for *Worfrühling* (Beginning of Spring) by R. M. Rilke, 1901.

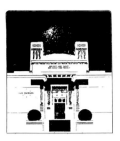

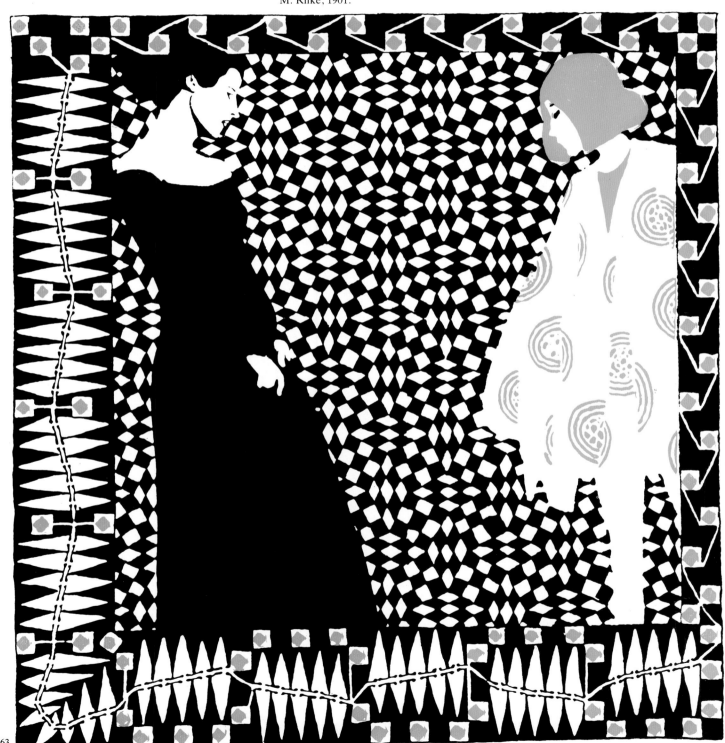

563

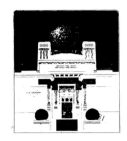

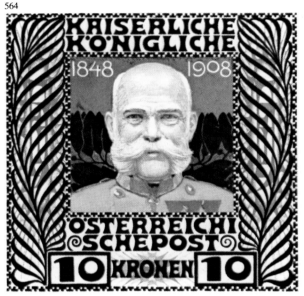

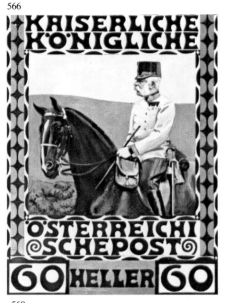

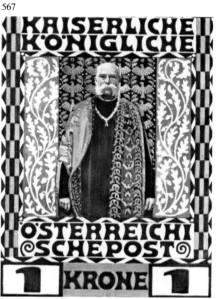

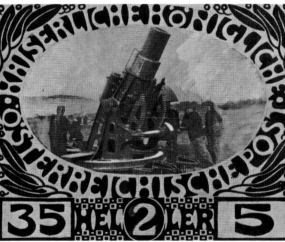

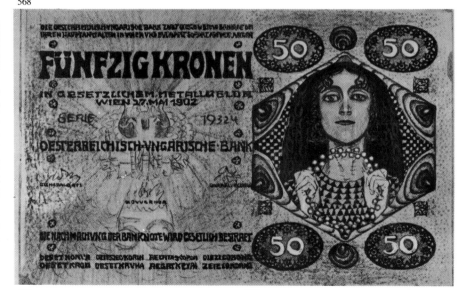

564—K. MOSER, 10 crown stamp with the portrait of the Kaiser, 1908.

565—K. MOSER, 60 cent stamp for the 1908 Jubilee.

566—K. MOSER, 1 crown stamp with a portrait of Franz Joseph, decorated in gold leaf, 1908.

567—K. MOSER, sketch for stamp with military subscription, 1915.

568—K. MOSER, 50 crown banknote, 1902.

569—K. MOSER, 5 crown stamp, *Schönbrun*.

570—K. MOSER, 2 crown stamp, *Hofburg*, 1908.

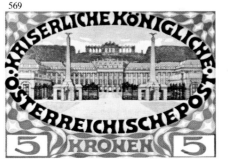

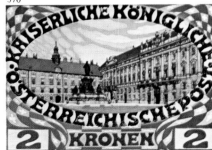

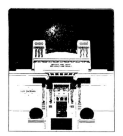

571—K. MOSER, vase and sugar-bowl. Vienna, Österreichisches Museum für Angewandte Kunst.
572—JOSEPH MARIA OLBRICH, Secession House, Vienna, 1898-99; hall with stained-glass window by Moser.

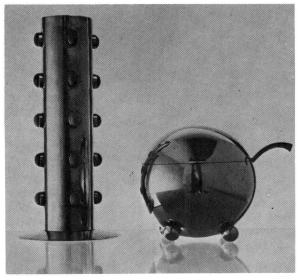

571

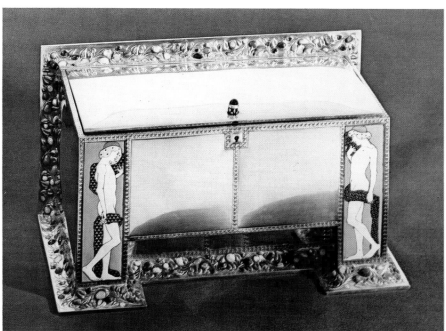

573

572

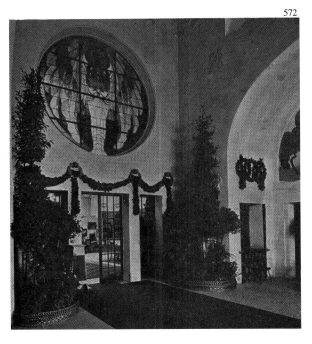

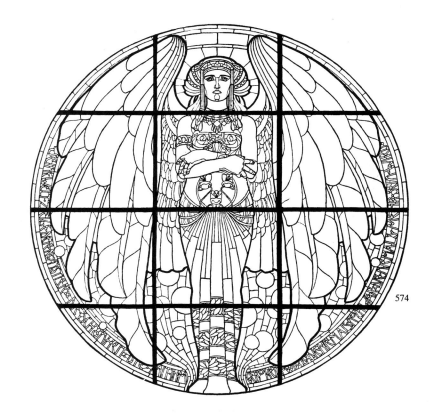

574

573—K. MOSER, jewel box.
574—K. MOSER, design for the circular window in the Secession House, Vienna, 1897-98.

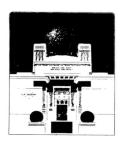

575

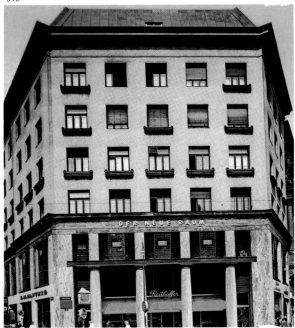

576

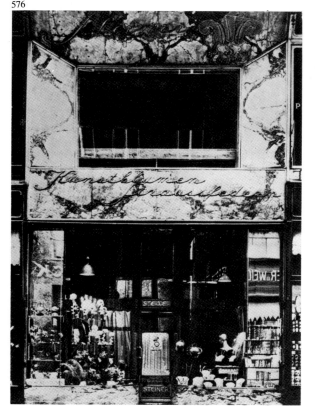

577

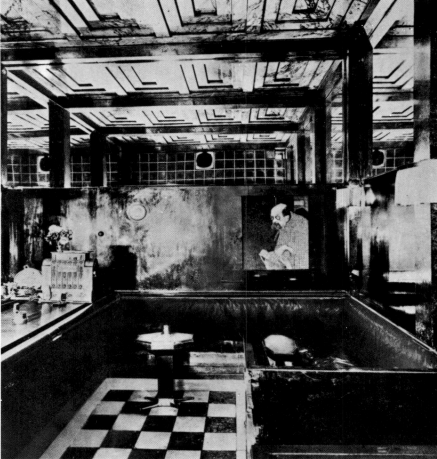

The work of ADOLF LOOS (1870-1933) was initially in the curving Secessionist style but it quickly progressed towards a more concentrated geometry, even barer and more orientated towards monumental effect than the architecture of either Olbrich or Hoffmann.

Loos exploited simple shapes in the interiors of the Café Américain in Vienna and the Villa Karma in Montreux in 1904. His insistence on contrasting black and white squares is influenced by Hoffmann. This is less evident in his later work. His facade for the apartment block on the Michaelplatz in Vienna (1910) is wholly unornamented and rational in the treatment of surfaces as is his house on the Nothartgasse (1913). The success of these buildings depends entirely on the lucid geometry of the volumes and the rhythm of the windows and the use of rich materials for their effect. His design for the house of Josephine Baker (1928) in Paris is entirely in the spirit of the Modern Movement. The building is based on a modular system. The surface is broken only by unarticulated windows. The hard contours of the windows are broken illusionistically by the black and white stripes.

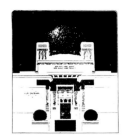

575—ADOLF LOOS, house on the Michaelplatz, Vienna, 1910.
576—A. LOOS, Steiner Store, Vienna, 1907.
577—A. LOOS, Café Américain, Vienna.

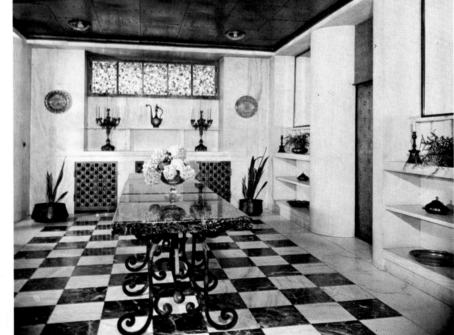
580

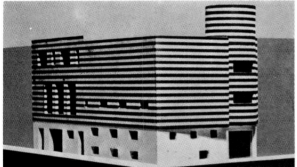
578

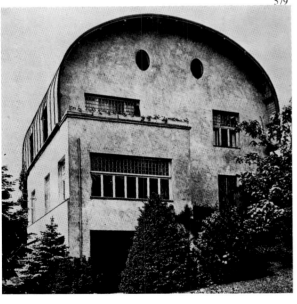
579

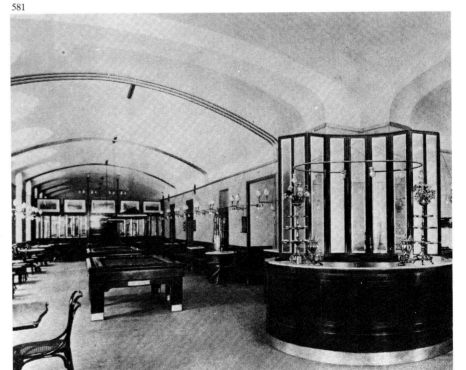
581

578—A. LOOS, model of the house of Josephine Baker in Paris, 1928.
579—A. LOOS, house in Nothartgasse, Vienna, 1913.
580—A. LOOS, dining room in the Villa Karma at Montreaux, 1904.
581—A. LOOS, Museum Café, Vienna, 1899.

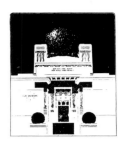

582

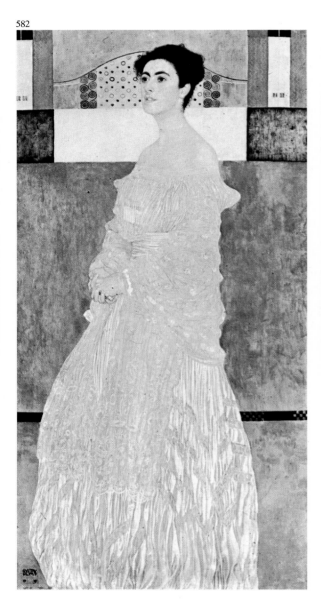

583

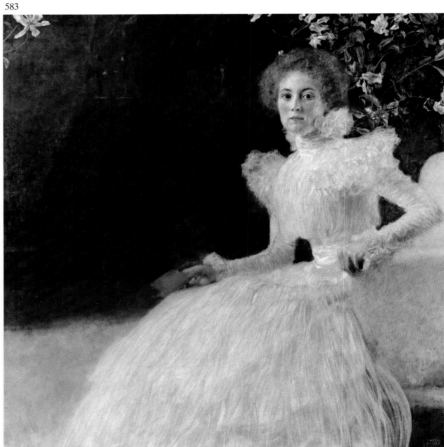

582—GUSTAV KLIMT, *Margaret Stonborough-Wittgenstein*. Munich, Bayerische Staatsgemäldesammlungen.
583—G. KLIMT, *Sonia Knips*, 1898. Vienna, Österreichisches Museum für Angewandte Kunst.
584—G. KLIMT, *Judith II (Salome)*, 1901. Venice, Museo d'Arte Moderna.
585—G. KLIMT, *Medicine*, Vienna, University, 1901-08 (destroyed).

GUSTAV KLIMT (1862-1918) was the most disturbing personality of the Viennese Secessionist movement, and he is arguably the most important Art Nouveau painter. Klimt's early style was a subtle classicizing variation of French and Belgian Post-Impressionism – this can be seen in his *Portrait of Sonia Knips* (1898). He quickly rejected this style in favour of a more linear style, evident in the portrait of Margaret Stonborough-Wittgenstein, where the elegant outline of his figure is contrasted with flat areas of colour. His highly individual mature style is already defined in the *Judith I* (1901), where the figure is shown against a rich golden background that resembles those found in Byzantine painting. Byzantium was a common metaphor at the time for the decadence of civilization, and Klimt seems to use the hint of it here as a means of conjuring hieratic and sensual association. Parts of the woman's body – her head, breast and arm – break forward, while her golden collar has the effect of drawing her back.

In the *Judith II* (1901) the spatial ambiguity is developed even further. Here the surface and depth of the painting are controlled by brilliantly coloured areas of pattern. Judith's body – her head,

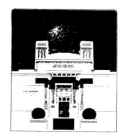

584

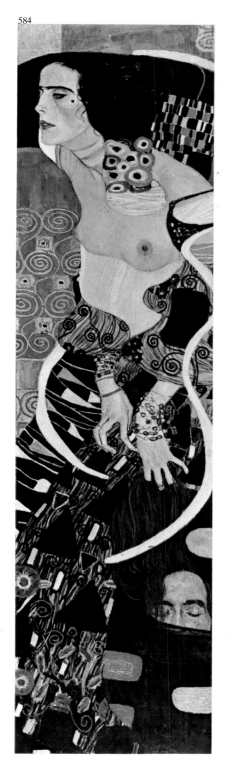

585

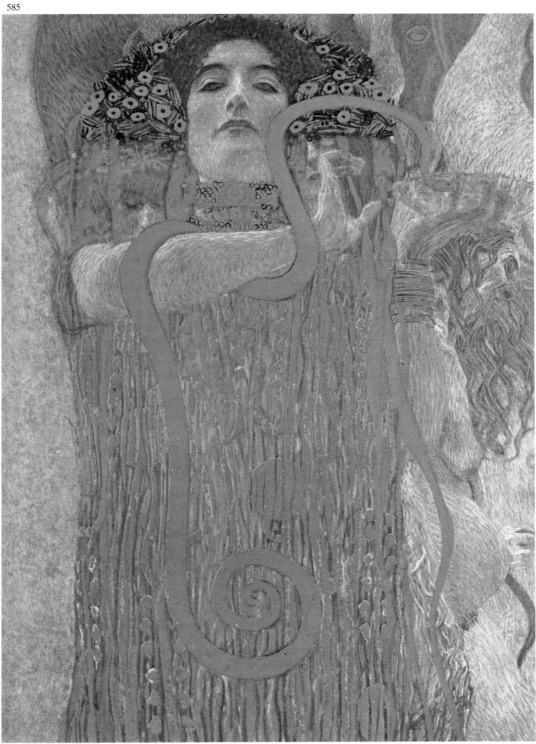

586—G. KLIMT, *Judith I (Salome)*, 1901, Vienna, Österreichisches Museum für Angewandte Kunst.
587—G. KLIMT, *Red Fish*, 1901-02. Soleure, private collection.
588—G. KLIMT, *The Virgin*, 1913. Prague, Narodni Galerie.
589—G. KLIMT, *The Sunflower Garden*, Graz, coll. Fritz Böck.
590—G. KLIMT, preparatory design for the Stoclet mosaic,
1911; *The Embrace*, detail. Vienna, Österreichisches Museum
für Angewandte Kunst.

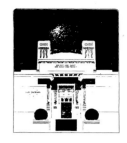

586

587

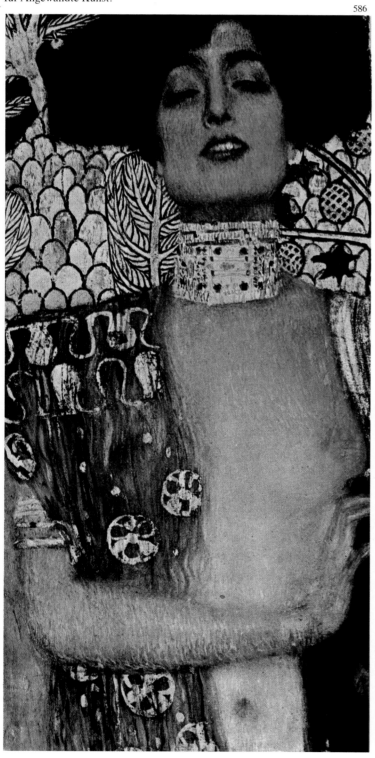

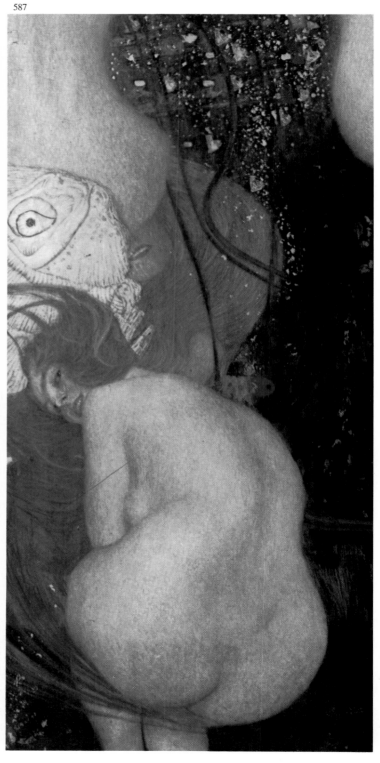

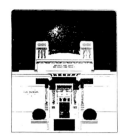

588   590

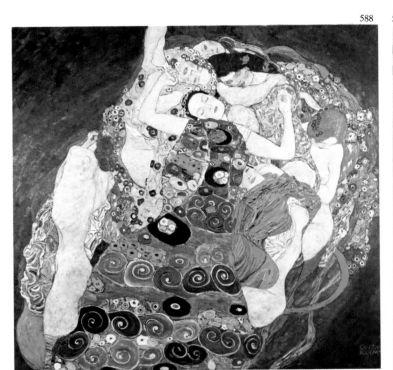

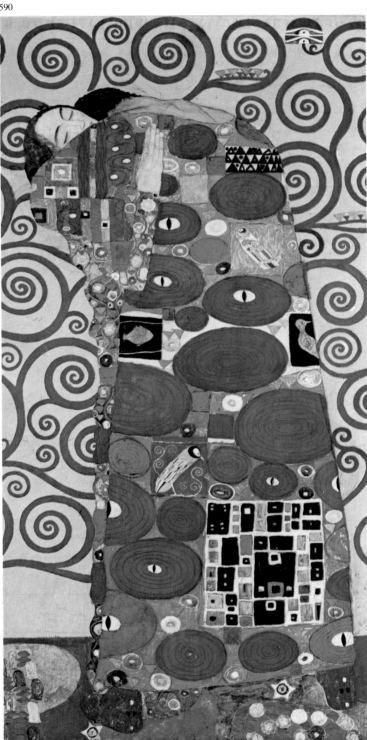

589

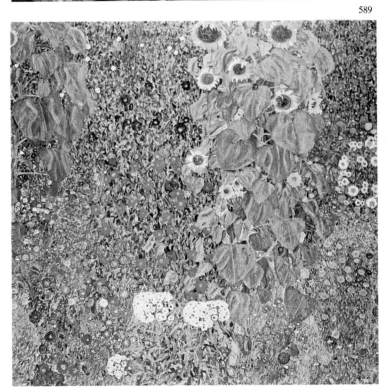

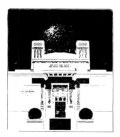

591

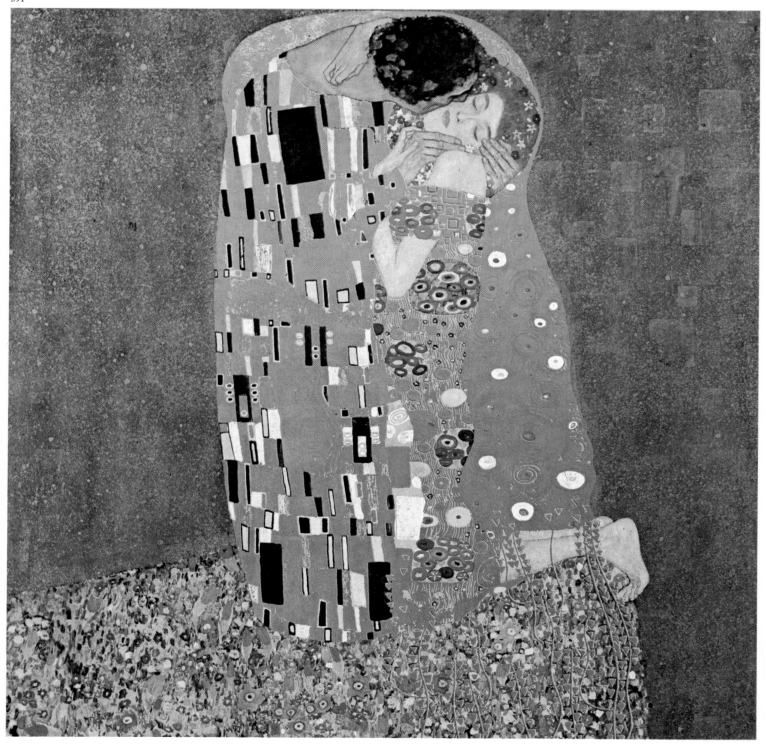

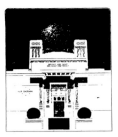

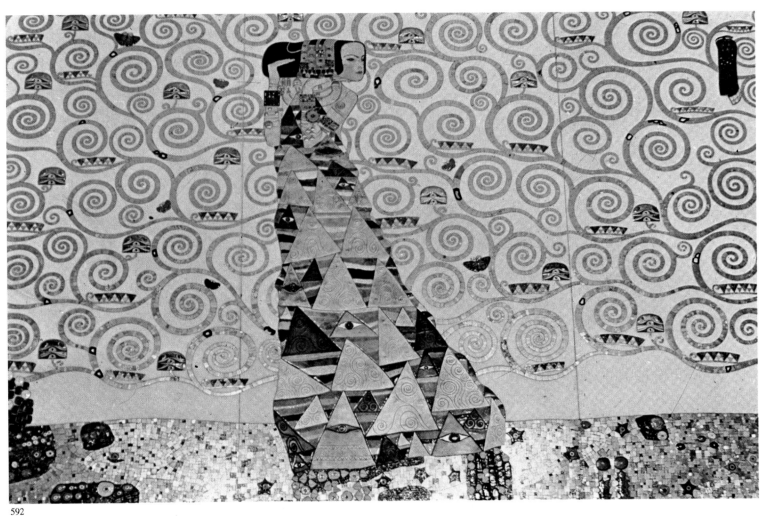

592

591—G. KLIMT, *The Kiss*, 1908. Vienna, Österreichisches Museum für Angewandte Kunst.
592—G. KLIMT, *The Wait*, detail of the Stoclet mosaic, Palais Stoclet, Brussels.

shoulders and breasts – break out from the planes of differently patterned surfaces.

Three of Klimt's most interesting works were destroyed by the Nazis, who thought that they were decadent. These were paintings for the ceiling decorations in the Great Hall of the University of Vienna (1899-1907) and they represented the Faculties. Two of them, *Medicine* and *Jurisprudence*, were acquired by Moser and the third, *Philosophy*, by August Lederer. They were all destroyed at Immendorf Castle. Large-scale work by Klimt does, however, survive; he provided mosaic designs for the dining room in the Palais Stoclet designed by Hoffmann. Like the *Judiths*, these show a desire to integrate the separate vibrant elements on the surface into an expressive whole. This tendency is particularly marked in *The*

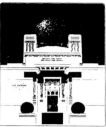

593

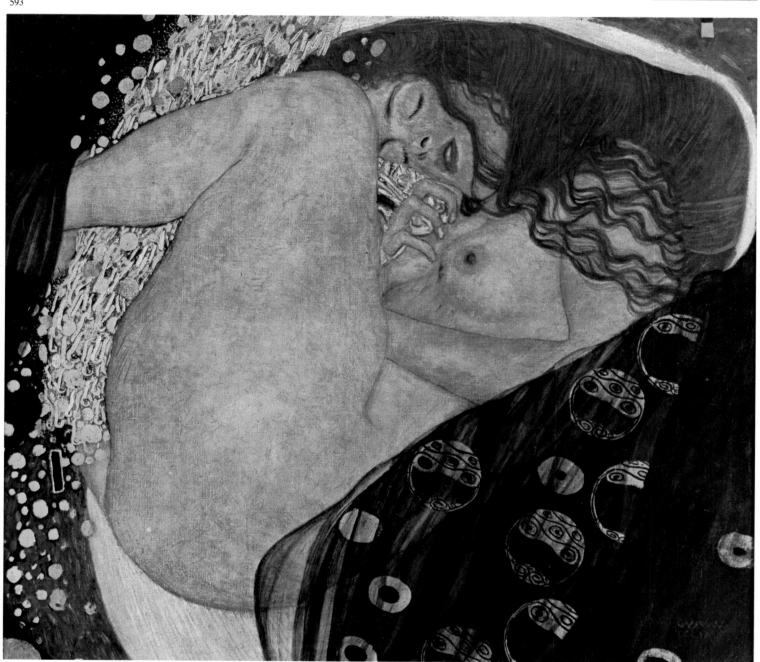

593—G. KLIMT, *Danäe*, 1902.

Sunflower Garden (1905-06). In *The Embrace* (1907), a preparatory design for the Stoclet scheme, the figures are subordinated to the decorative demands of the surface. The decorative elements – the spirals, simplified birds, and eyes – are quotations from Egyptian sources, appropriate for the design of mosaics, and they reappear in

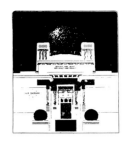

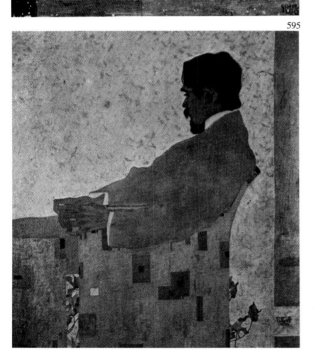

Klimt's mosaic *The Wait* (1905-11) in the Palais Stoclet.

The anxiety generated by the restless patterns in *The Embrace* is not present in Klimt's painting *The Kiss* (1908), where the lovers, wrapped in a patterned cloth of gold against a softened golden ground, reach a peak of lyrical expression. In Klimt's later works the planar composition of the paintings is abandoned in favour of spiral compositions. This is evident in *The Virgin* (1913) in which the figures are drawn into a whirlpool composition. This induces a sense of ambiguity and it marks a shift in Viennese painting towards the Expressionism of Schiele.

594—EGON SCHIELE, *Water Sprites I*, 1907.
595—E. SCHIELE, *Anton Peschka*, 1909.
596—E. SCHIELE, *The Dead Mother*, 1910. Vienna, coll. Rudolf Leopold.

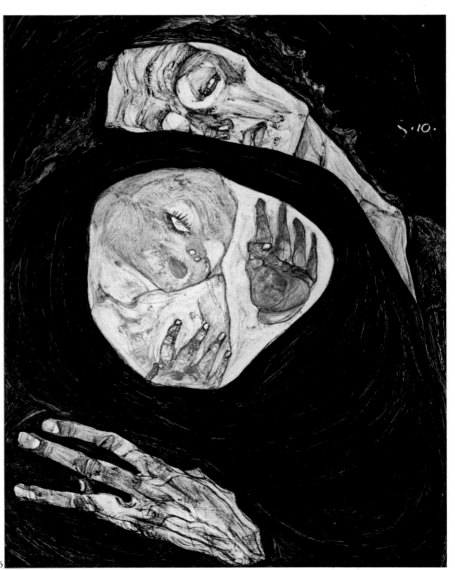

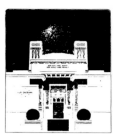

597

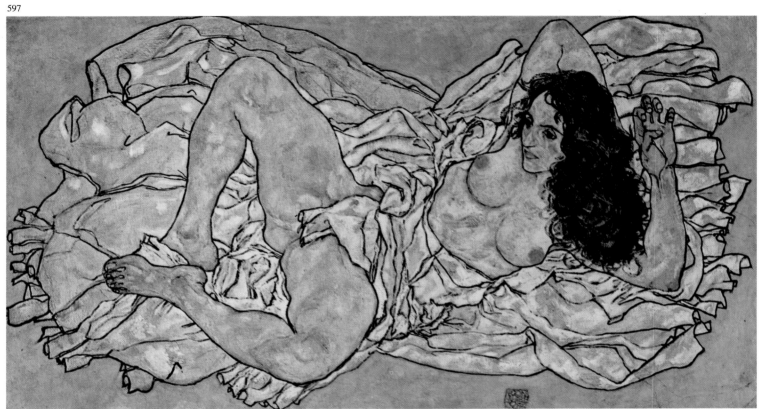

598

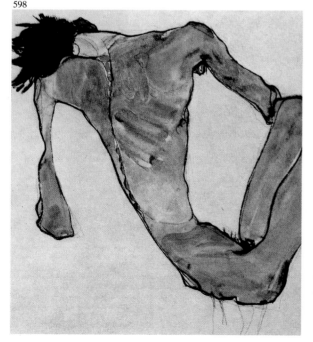

599

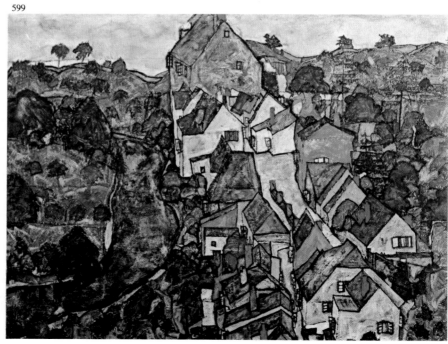

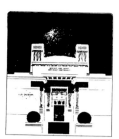

600

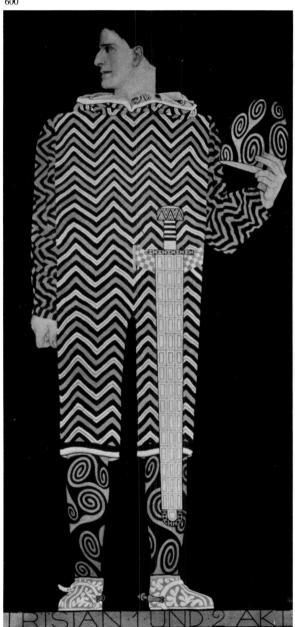

601

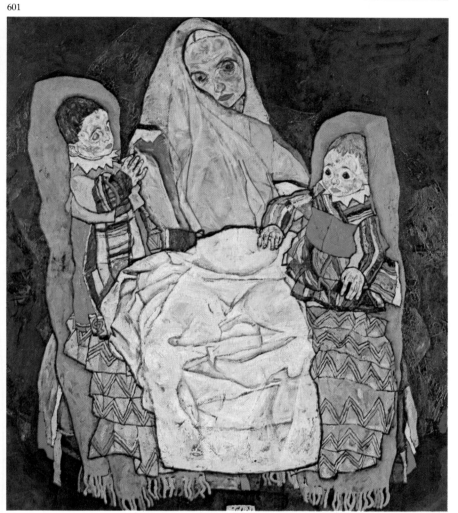

597—E. SCHIELE, *Reclining Woman*, 1917. Vienna, coll. Rudolf Leopold.
598—E. SCHIELE, *Male Torso*, c. 1911.
599—E. SCHIELE, *Landscape at Kremau*, 1916. Linz, Wolfgang Gaulitt Museum.
600—C. O. CZESCHKA, costume for *Tristan and Wotan*, 1908.
601—E. SCHIELE, *Mother with Two Children*, 1915-17. Vienna, Österreichisches Museum für Angewandte Kunst.

EGON SCHIELE (1890-1918) met Klimt in 1907 and his work was immediately influenced by the older man's work. His *Water Sprites I* (1907) shows Klimt's influence in the way that the figures are set against a flat ground composed of planes, and he too explores the erotic possibilities created by the ambiguous position of the figures and their relationship to the spectator. Klimt's decorative outline is also present in the painting, as well as in the *Portrait of Anton Peschka* (1909). By the following year Schiele was working in an altogether more personal idiom.

The *Dead Mother* of 1910 goes far beyond Klimt's suggestion of anxiety in the use of the spiral composition. Here the spiral is used to isolate the figures. By 1915 Schiele was working mainly on figure compositions which are only marginally relevant to Art Nouveau. He was preoccupied with the desire to paint his vision of female eroticism. He achieved this by painting them within dark animated contours reminiscent of Art Nouveau outlines.

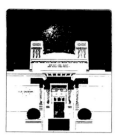

602

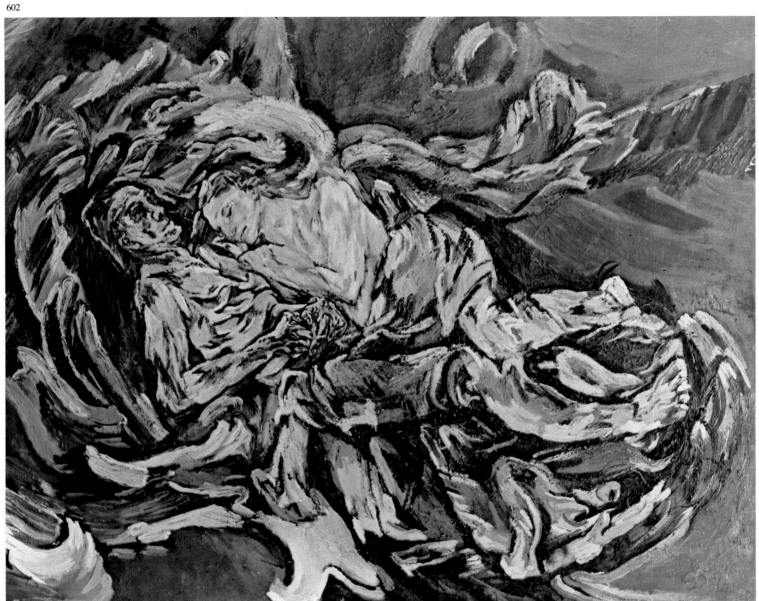

602—OSKAR KOKOSCHKA, *The Bride of the Wind*, 1914. Basle, Kunstmuseum.
603—O. KOKOSCHKA, *Marquise of Rohan-Montesquieu*, 1909-10. Rome, coll. Paul E. Geier.
604—O. KOKOSCHKA, illustration for his book *Träumenden Knaben* (Children's Dreams), 1908.
605—O. KOKOSCHKA, *Pietà*, poster for the theatre at the Secession House, Vienna, 1909.

OSKAR KOKOSCHKA's (1886-1980) development from Art Nouveau to Expressionism parallels Schiele's. In the illustrations for his book *Die Traumenden Knaben* (1908) the concentric lines and almost abstract shapes which define the image have an almost melodic quality. The colour is also warm and harmonious. By 1909 his mature style had evolved and it was unrelated to Art Nouveau. The poster *Pietà* (1909) is a vehicle for gruesome iconography. It inverts the promise of decorative harmony in the illustrations in order to express fear and horror.

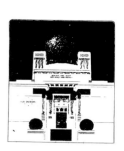

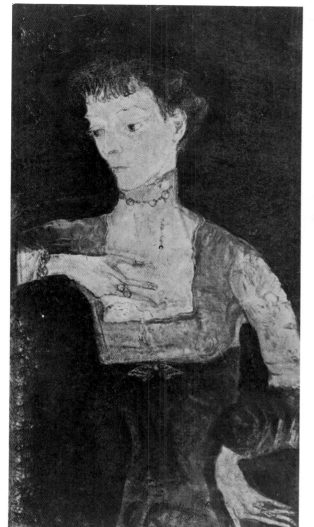

603

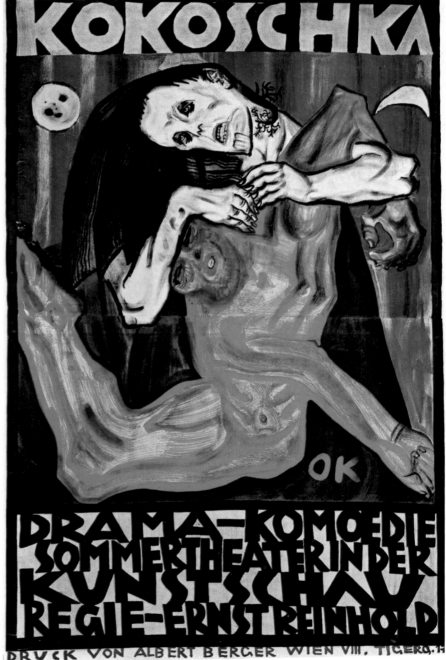

605

604

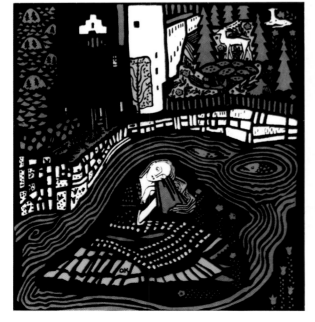

By 1914 Kokoschka had developed his late style, which lies wholly within the Expressionist tradition. *Bride of the Wind* (1914) is an elemental work which acts entirely through the suggestive properties of the brushwork.

11-Switzerland

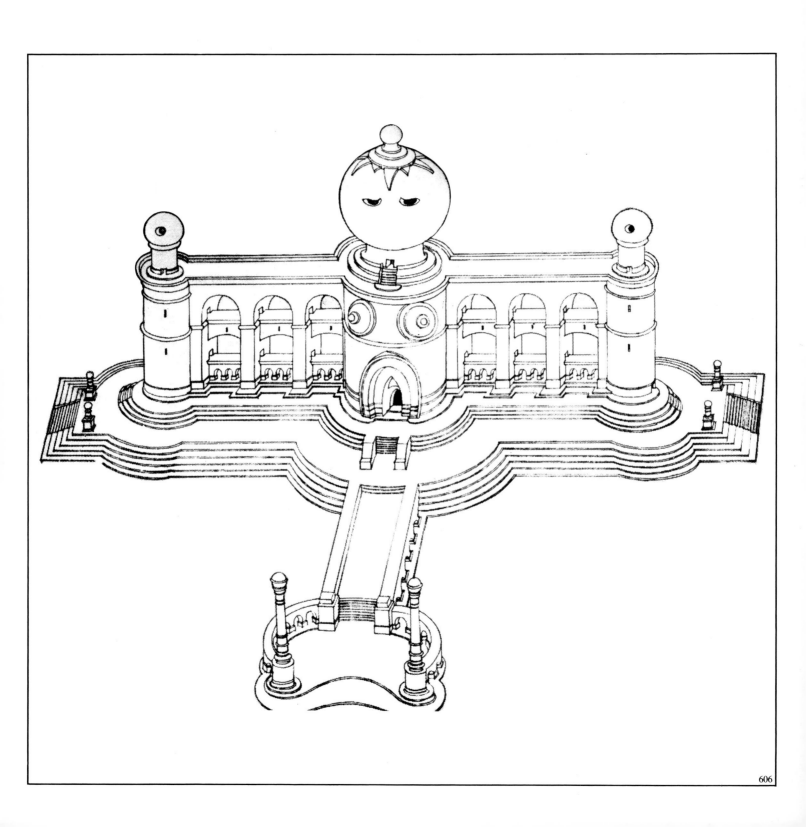

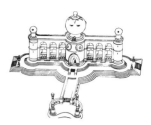

607

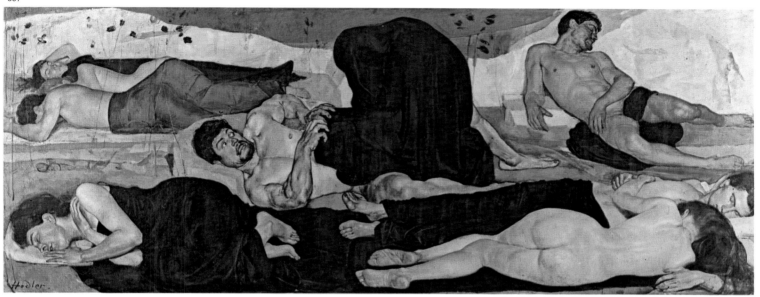

606—and symbol of Chapter 11, pp. 226-231—TRASCHEL, *Palace of Ecstasy*, design in the Swiss pavilion at the Paris Exhibition in 1900.
607—FERDINAND HODLER, *Night*, 1890. Berne, Kunstmuseum.
608—F. HODLER, *Truth*, 1902, Zurich, Kunsthaus.
  *—page 227, OTTO ECKMANN, illustration.

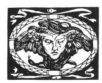

608

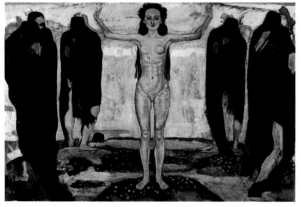

In Switzerland, Art Nouveau failed to achieve the widespread popularity which it enjoyed almost everywhere else in Europe, and its only representatives were the painters Ferdinand Hodler and Arnold Böcklin, who were only marginally affected by the style. The work of these artists in the 1890s and afterwards, was so involved with Symbolism that it can only be characterized by reference to it.

FERDINAND HODLER (1853-1918) studied in Geneva, visited Spain (where he discovered Velásquez) and eventually settled in Munich. In 1891 he exhibited in Paris where he met the Nabis who introduced him to Pre-Raphaelite painting. He also first saw paintings by Puvis de Chavannes in Paris. The influence of Puvis de Chavannes on Hodler is evident in the works he produced after this period. In his early paintings, for example *The Night* (1890), the allegorical subject matter is represented realistically in the manner of Velásquez. In his later works, his unearthly settings and figures are derived from Puvis. In *The Elect* (1893-94) the calm gravity and overall blondness of tone show the French painter's influence. The vibrant and occasionally brilliant colour and the hard contours are possibly indebted to Runge. However, the subtle and mysterious atmosphere which envelops his compositions is entirely personal. *The Day* (1890) is a similar work, although its decorative qualities indicate the influence of the Art Nouveau style. Here a sense of the timelessness of dawn is evoked by the naked figures who shield their eyes from the light of day. This painting is an allegory set as in Puvis's paintings in an indeterminate location. The broken contours and the decorative foreground, however, recall Art Nouveau.

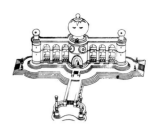

609

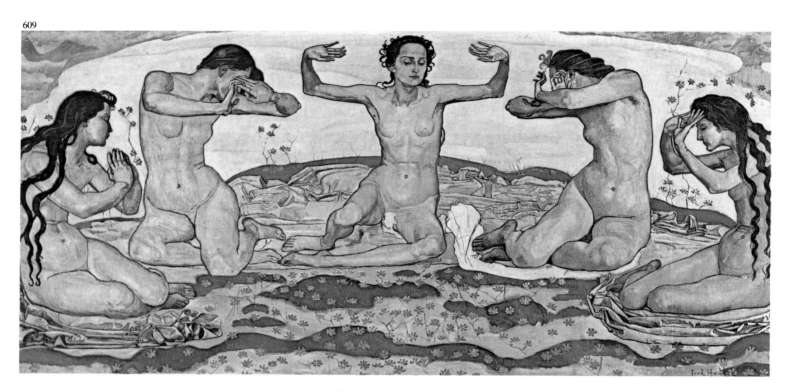

610

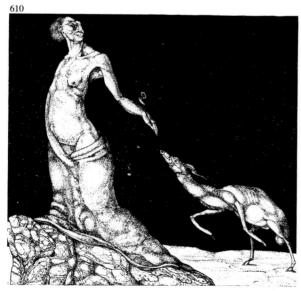

611

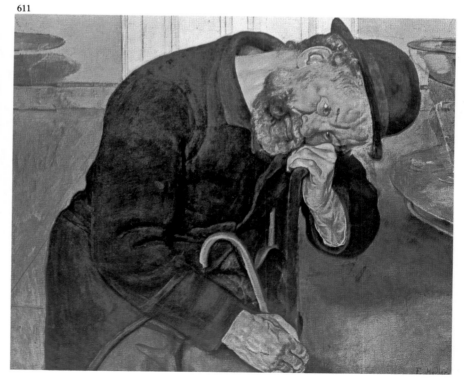

609—F. HODLER, *Day*, 1900. Berne, Kunstmuseum.
610—PAUL KLEE, *A Woman and a Beast*, 1904.
611—F. HODLER, *A Soul in Pain*, 1891-92.

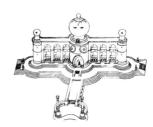

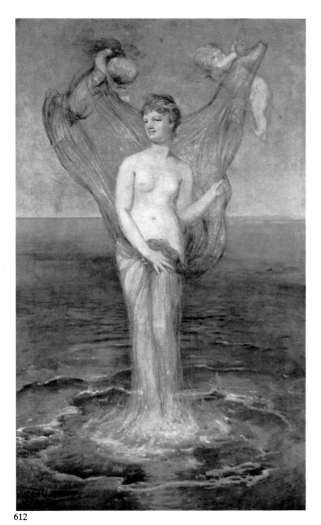

612

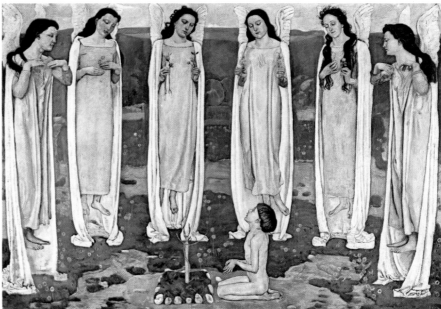

613

ARNOLD BÖCKLIN (1827-1901) was born in Switzerland, but he lived in Florence and later in Munich. His mature landscapes, like the very famous *Island of the Dead* (1880) are austere and contain draped figures who turn from the spectator. In his later work, he broke abruptly with this theme and became preoccupied with death and destruction. In *The War* (1896) and *The Plague* (1896) he adapted the

614

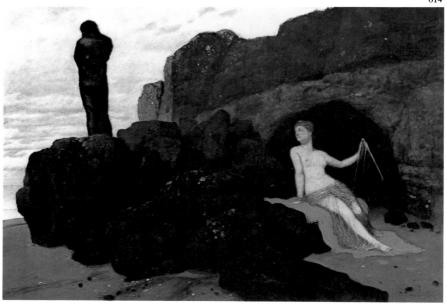

612—ARNOLD BÖCKLIN, *Blue Venus*. Basle, Kunstmuseum.
613—F. HODLER, *The Elect*, 1893-94; a fresco on the wall of the dining room in the house of van de Velde on the Hohenhof, Hagen (see n.315).
614—A. BÖCKLIN, *Odysseus and Calypso*, 1883. Basle, Kunstmuseum.

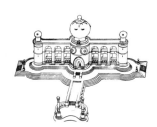

615

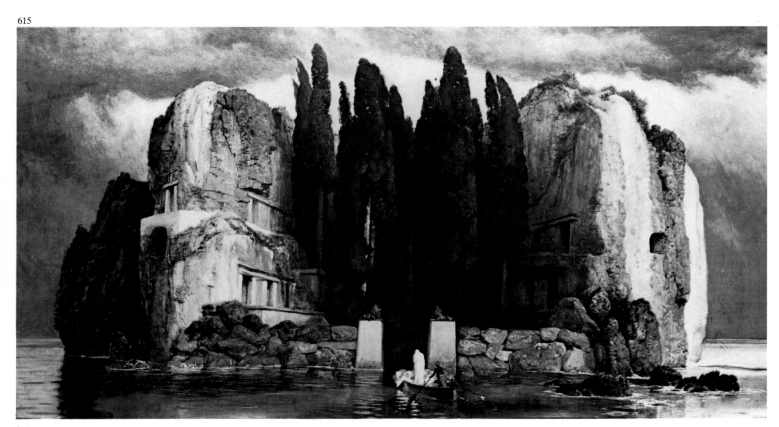

616

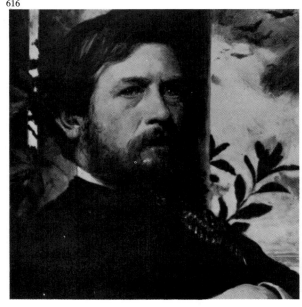

617

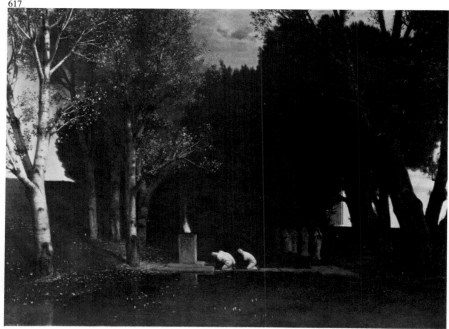

615—A. BÖCKLIN, *The Island of the Dead*, 1830. Leipzig Museum der Bildender Kunst.

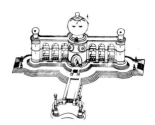

618

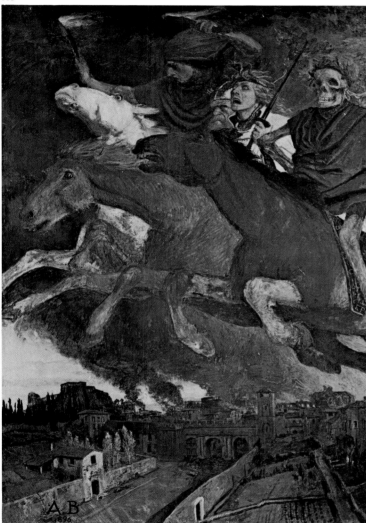

619

616—A. BÖCKLIN, *Self-Portrait* (n.d.). Berlin, Staatliche Muse-um Preussischer Kulturbesitz.
617—A. BÖCKLIN, *The Sacred Wood*, 1882. Basle, Kunstmuseum.
618—A. BÖCKLIN, *The Plague*, 1898. Basle, Kunstmuseum.
619—A. BÖCKLIN, *War, 1896*. Dresden, Staatliche Kunstsammlungen.
  *—page 231, ornamental inset from *The Studio*.

suggestion of the expressive use of line taken from Art Nouveau, but he rejected the notion of an overall decorative effect. These complex and anxious paintings come closer to the Symbolist painting of Puvis de Chavannes and later to those of James Ensor.

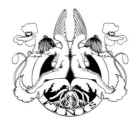

12-Scandinavia

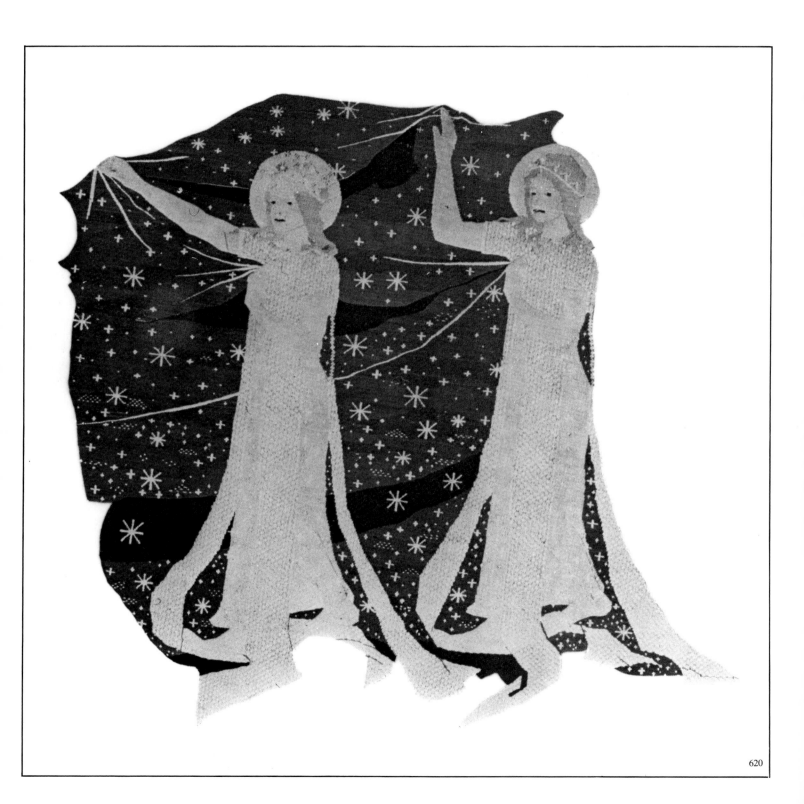

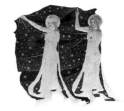

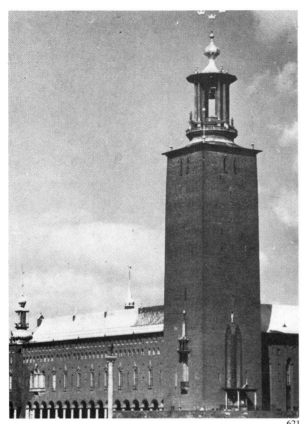

Art Nouveau arrived in Scandinavia at a time when national and folk traditions were being revived. The presence of the Art Nouveau influence during this revival resulted in a revitalization of many of the traditional forms.

In Denmark, these two tendencies operated simultaneously in the work of the architect MARTIN NYRUP (1849-1921). His Raadhus (1909-23) in Copenhagen is a traditional town hall, which is a rectangular block with crenellations on the top, and it has a clock tower. However, in the interior it shows a new feeling for decorative effect. This is particularly evident in the delicate quality of the metal structure. Another Danish architect who achieved startling effects with his use of Art Nouveau principles was P. V. Jensen Klint. In his church at Copenhagen, built in honour of N. F. S. Grundtvig, the fundamentalist preacher, he applied Art Nouveau geometry to create a daring facade in the pattern of a church organ.

Similarly, in Sweden Art Nouveau geometric elegance was used to transform traditional forms. This is well expressed in the work of Ragnar Oestberg; his City Hall, Stockholm (1923) successfully unites the traditional prototype with the elegant volumetric Viennese style.

621

620—and symbol of Chapter 12, pp. 232-241—FRIDA HANSEN, *The Milky Way*, carpet for the Norwegian hall at the Exhibition in Paris in 1900; detail.
621—RAGNAR OESTBERG, City Hall, Stockholm, 1909-23.
622—MARTIN NIJRUP. WENCK. VISCHER, Raadhus, Copenhagen; interior.
623—M. NIJRUP. WENCK. VISCHER, Raadhus, Copenhagen; exterior.

622

623

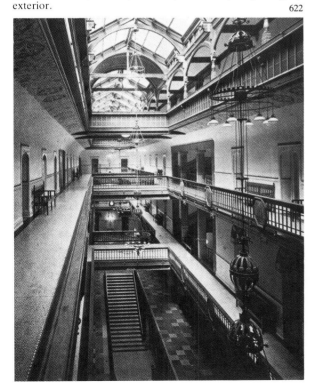

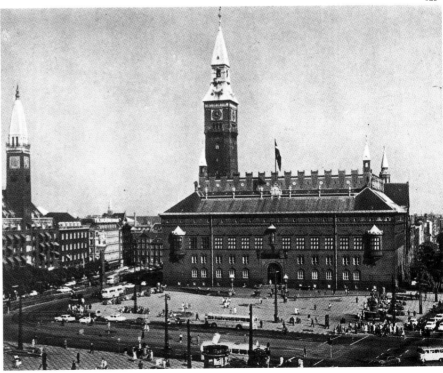

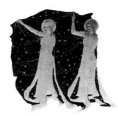

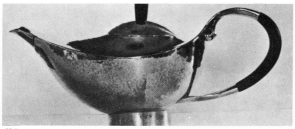

624

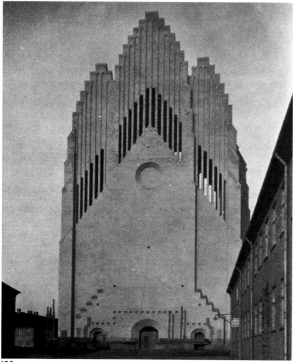

625

627

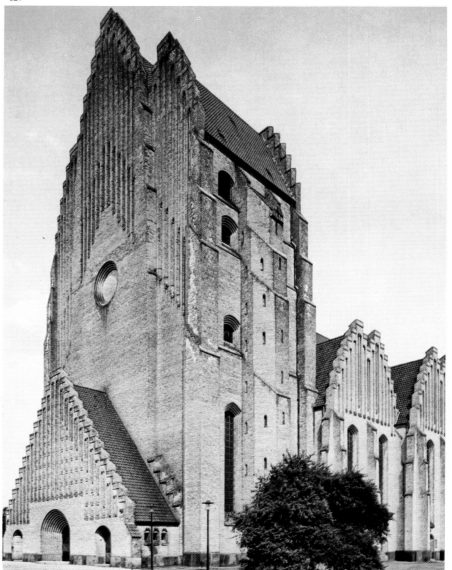

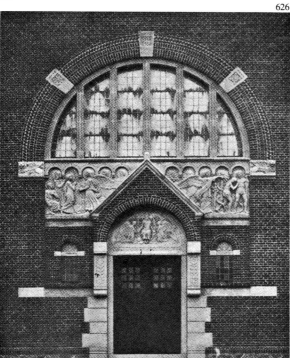

626

628

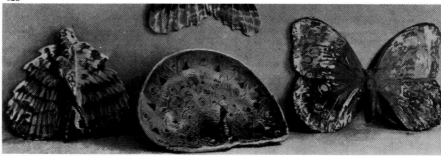

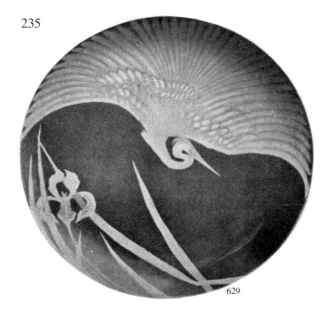

629

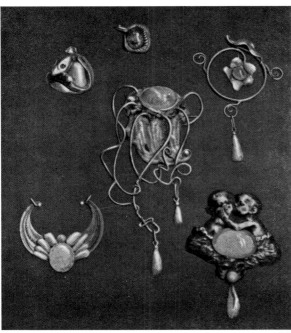

630

The most widespread acceptance of Art Nouveau in architecture was to take place in Finland, where it developed rapidly towards a style anticipating the Modern Movement. In his Central Station, Helsinki (1906-14) ELIEL SAARINEN (1873-1950) combined the decorative possibilities of repeated verticals and rhythmically recessed planes with clarity of proportion and utilitarian economy that makes this building an important model for later developments. However, Saarinen also enjoyed using freer curvilinear decoration and this can be seen in his project for an interior (1902). The vernacular Gothic idiom has been embellished with a sense of space and decorative ornament. The same characteristics are present in the Finnish Pavilion at the Paris International Exhibition (1900), which Saarinen designed in collaboration with HERMAN GESELLIUS (1874-1916) and Armas Lindgren (b. 1874). The three architects, who worked together, had very different attitudes. When Gesellius was given most scope, as in the Helsinki Federal Bank (1903), the decorative quality of his architecture is apparent. Gesellius's mixture of Art Nouveau with native traditions has a delicate feeling for fantasy and elaboration. In his staircase for a Helsinki insurance building (1901), the plan

631

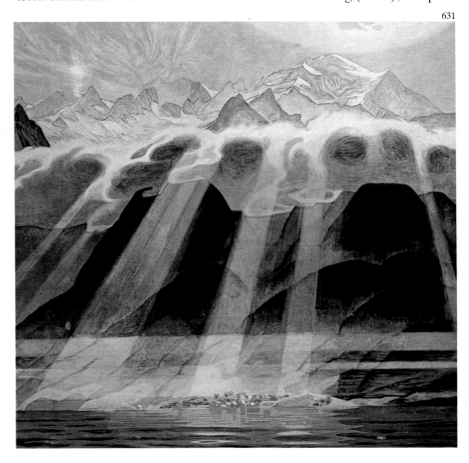

—page 233, ornamental inset from *The Studio.*
624—J. RHODE, teapot, 1906.
625,627—P. V. JENSEN KLINT, Grundtvig memorial church, Copenhagen 1913-26.
626—THOMAS BARENTZEN, Church of St Ausgarius, Odense, c. 1909.
628—S. LERCHE, butterfly and peacocks in polychrome ceramics exhibited at the Turin Exhibition, 1902.
629—plate in porcelain by Copenhagen, exhibited at the Turin Exhibition, 1902.
630—S. LERCHE, jewellery exhibited at the Turin Exhibition, 1902.
631—JENS FERDINAND WILLUMSEN, *Mountain Under the Sun*, 1902.

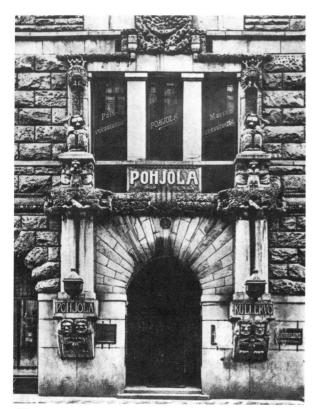

632

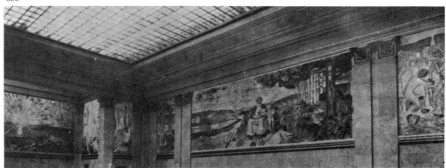

of the stair is a sweeping curve reminiscent of French taste, but the simple grid pattern of the balustrade is typically Finnish.

SELIM LINDQUIST (b. 1867) shares the Viennese Art Nouveau taste for combining simple cubic and spherical forms. This can be seen in the Villa Hensi (1910), where the regular tiling and railings are typically Finnish.

In painting, the name of EDVARD MUNCH (1863-1944) is most commonly associated with the period when Art Nouveau flourished. However, Munch's work, which uses an arabesque line not dissimilar in appearance to that of Art Nouveau, exhibits a tension and neurotic anxiety which separates it from the movement. These characteristics dominate his frescoes for the Great Hall of the University of Oslo. Even the peaceful subject of the *Alma Mater* (1909-11) seems disturbed by the artist's complex emotions.

633

632—The Pohjola Building, Helsingfors, 1901.
633—Great Hall of the University of Oslo, with frescoes by Edvard Munch.
634—EDVARD MUNCH, *Alma Mater*, 1909-11, fresco; University of Oslo.
635—HUGO SIMBERG, *Frost*, 1895.
636—ARMAS LINDGREN, cupboard, 1901.
637—GERHARD MUNTHE, tapestry, exhibited at the Paris Exhibition in 1900.
   *—page 237, ornamental inset from *The Studio*.

634

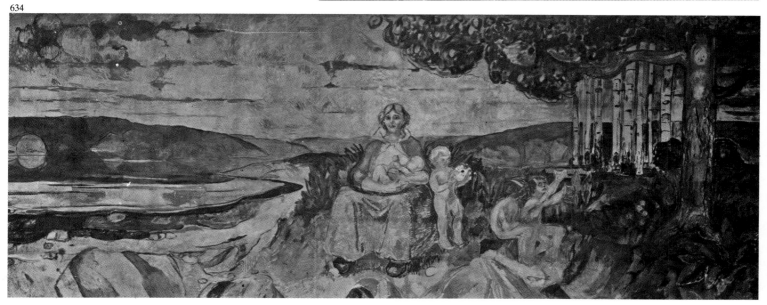

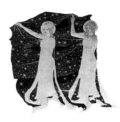

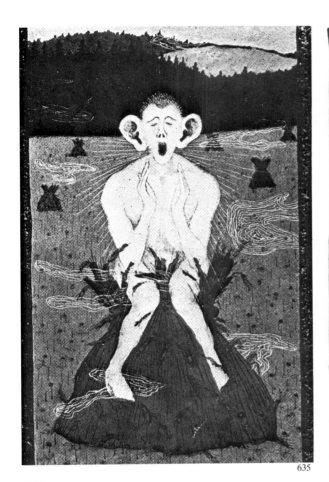

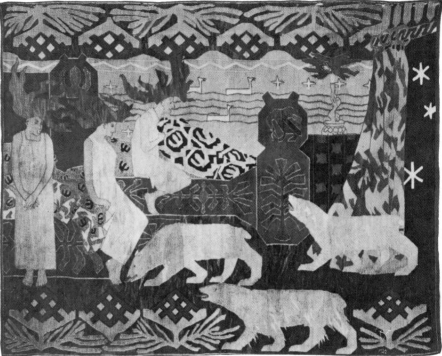

637

The work of the Finn HUGO SIMBERG (1873-1917) has similar tensions to those in Munch's painting. Although Simberg adopted a much flatter, hard-edged style than Munch, and a greater emphasis on curvilinear pattern, he still created images of great strength. His *Frost* (1895) can be compared to Munch's contemporary work in the paradoxical way that the decorative surface pattern increases the harshness of the image.

Simberg was a pupil of the leading Finnish exponent of the applied arts AKSELI GALLÉN KALLELA (1865-1931). The background of his *Portrait of Sibelius* (1894) exhibits a certain quality of decorative arabesque line derived from Art Nouveau and from van Gogh. However, the brooding intensity of the figure, and the vertical and horizontal borders, introduce a tension into the work which anticipates the Expressionism of Munch.

In the applied arts, textiles, which had a long tradition in Scandinavia, benefited most from the impact of the Art Nouveau style. Around the turn of the century a number of artists were active in this field, and they assimilated the new style while remaining faithful to existing forms.

635

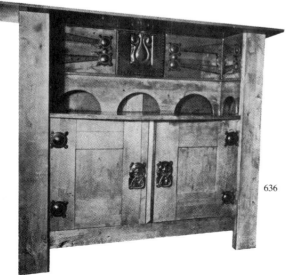

636

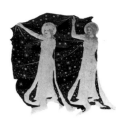

638

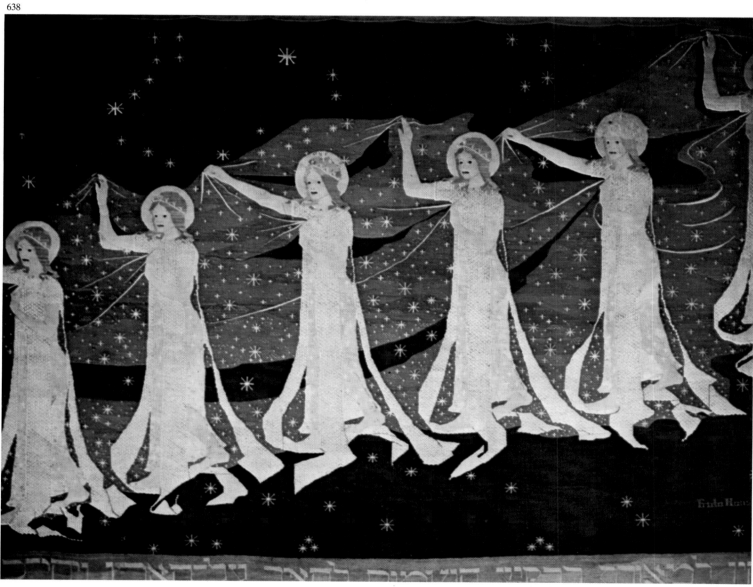

The Norwegian FRIDA HANSEN (b. 1855) based his work on
folklore. This was recast with the more elegant and decorative style of
Art Nouveau. Hansen's *The Milky Way* (1900) shows a certain
ingenuousness in the naive treatment of the figures, but the piece is
subject to a subtly orchestrated system of rhythmic arabesques which
place the work in the mainstream of continental Art Nouveau.

Refining the design of local forms controlled the development of
ceramics in Finland. In Sweden the Art Nouveau style was very
influential, especially in the work of A. WALLANDER (1862-1914),
which has floral ornament and a sense of the arabesque line,
suggestive of strong Belgian or French influences.

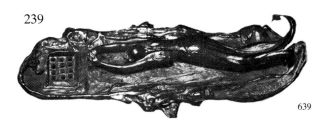

639

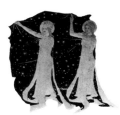

640

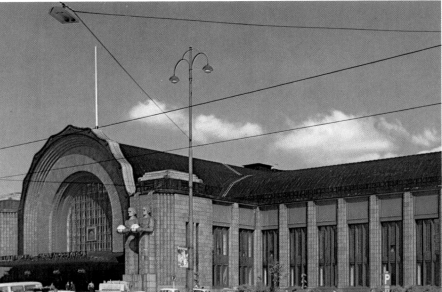

642

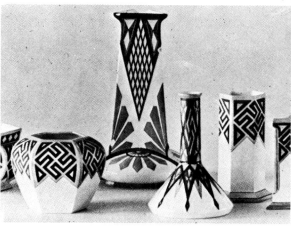

638—FRIDA HANSEN, *The Milky Way*, 1900 (see n.620).
639—V. VALLGRES, door handle.
640—Porcelain vases by the Finnish company 'Arabia', 1902-12.
641-2—ELIEL SAARINEN, Central Station, Helsinki, 1906-14.
643—E. SAARINEN, project for a dining room, 1902.

641

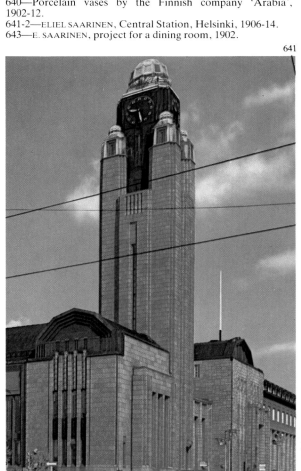

643

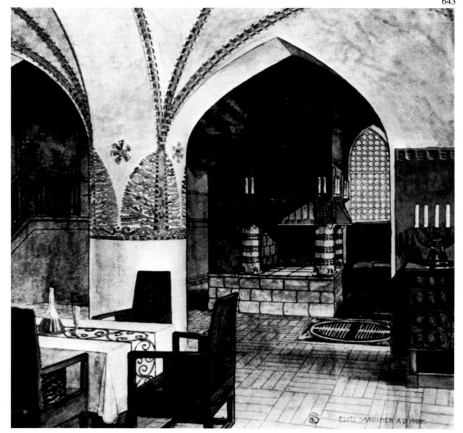

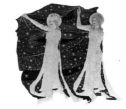

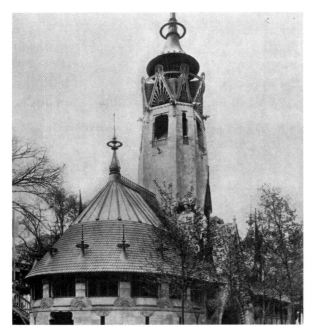

644

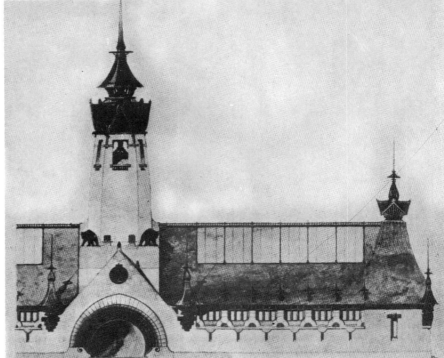

647

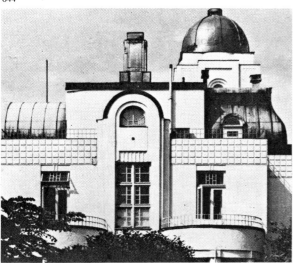

645

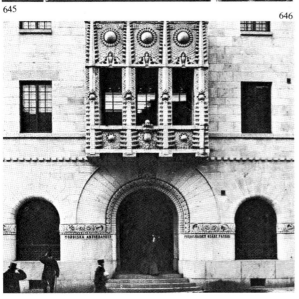

646

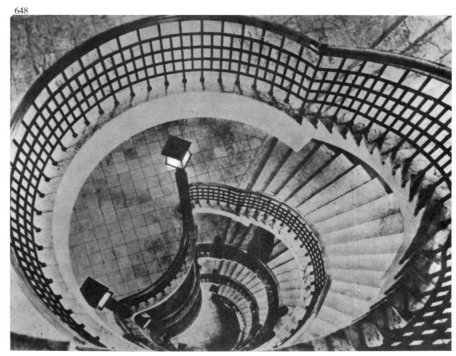

648

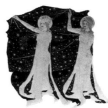

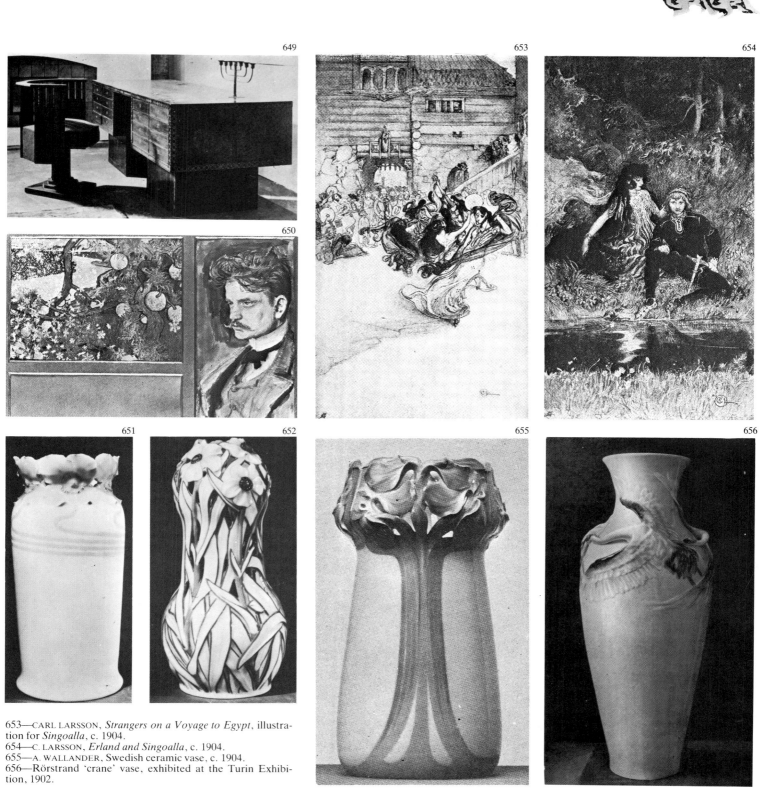

653—CARL LARSSON, *Strangers on a Voyage to Egypt*, illustration for *Singoalla*, c. 1904.
654—C. LARSSON, *Erland and Singoalla*, c. 1904.
655—A. WALLANDER, Swedish ceramic vase, c. 1904.
656—Rörstrand 'crane' vase, exhibited at the Turin Exhibition, 1902.

13-Eastern Europe

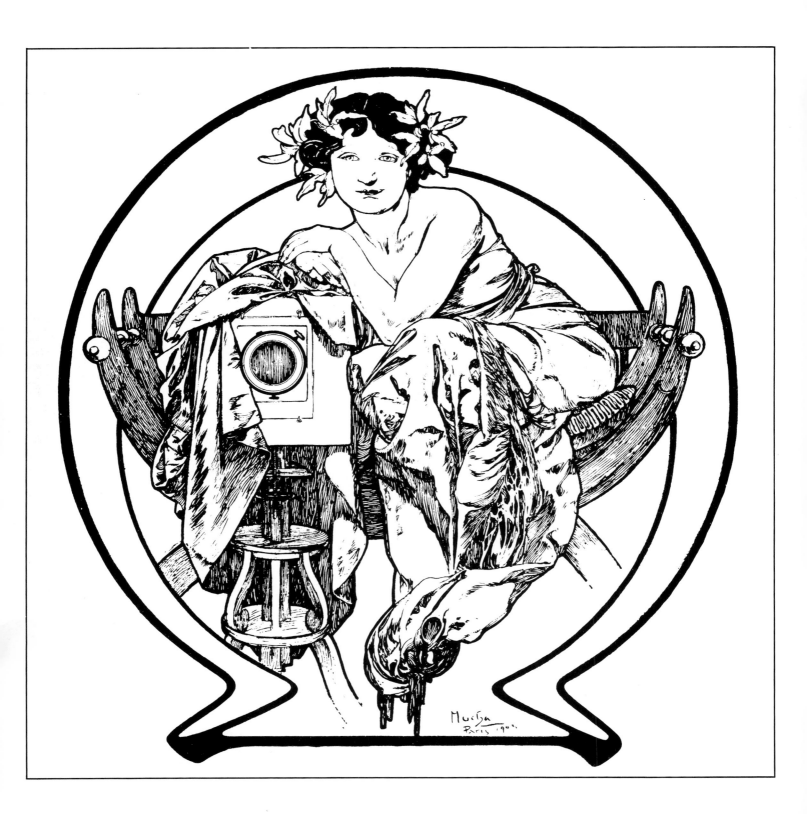

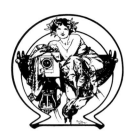

657—and symbol of Chapter 13, pp. 242-263—ALPHONSE
MUCHA, *Photographic Art*, 1904.
658—ODON LECHNER, Postal Savings Bank, Budapest, 1899-
1902.
659—EDOUARD WIGAND, classroom, c. 1907.
660—E. WIGAND, dining room in the 'Hungarian style',
c. 1907.
661—E. WIGAND, dining room in the 'modern style', c. 1907.

In Eastern Europe Art Nouveau was received under similar circumstances to those operating in Scandinavia. The new style was adapted
to already well established traditions, especially in architecture and in
the applied arts. In the other branches of the arts, the situation was
complicated by the desire in many of these countries to develop a
specifically nationalist style in opposition to the cultural domination
of Russia.

In architecture the influence of Art Nouveau was varied and took
different forms within the same country. In Hungary, Odon Lechner
(1845-1914) adapted the floral curves of the style to his decoration of
the attic of the Post Office Savings Bank in Budapest (1899-1902).

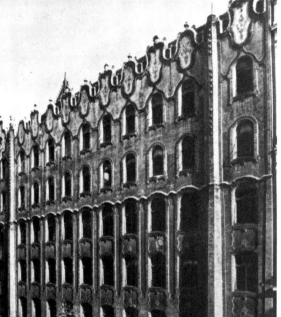

658

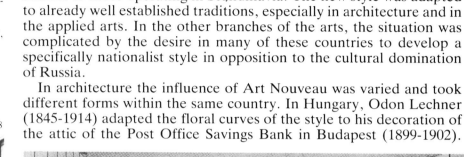

660

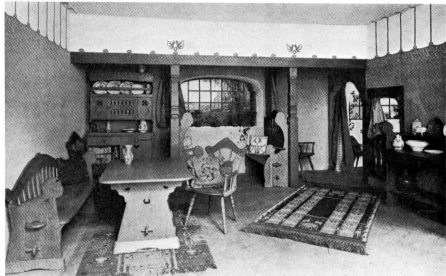

661

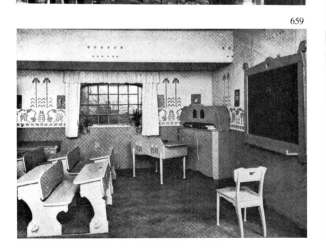

659

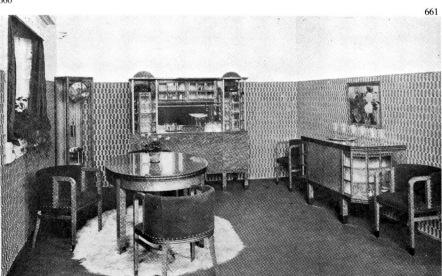

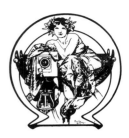

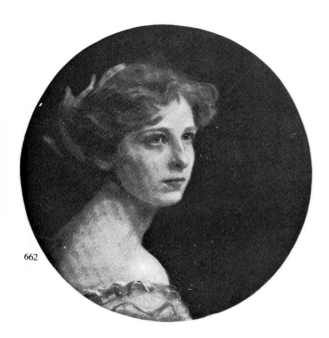

662

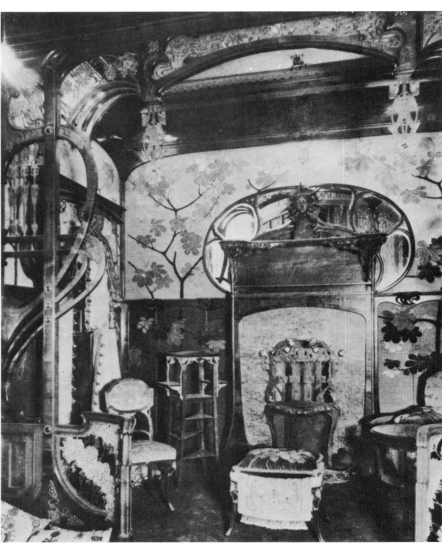

663

Just over a decade later, in the Theatre of Wood (1913), Joseph (b. 1877) and Lazló (1875-1933) Vagó used the stronger and more elegant idiom of Viennese architecture. In both cases, Art Nouveau was used to revitalize established building types and to create a new style of

662—P. A. LASZLÓ, study for a portrait, c. 1907.
663—FORK, studio in the Hungarian pavilion at the Paris Exhibition, 1900.
664—ELEK FALUS, typographic decoration, c. 1907.

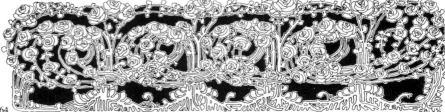

664

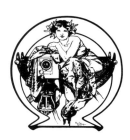

667

665—EDMUND KAEZIANG, *Vision of Good Friday*, c. 1899.
666—PAUL HORTI, entrance arch to the Hungarian section at
the Turin Exhibition in 1902.

665

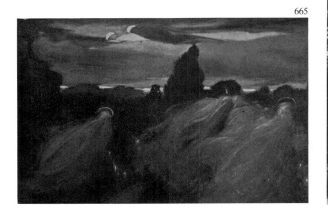

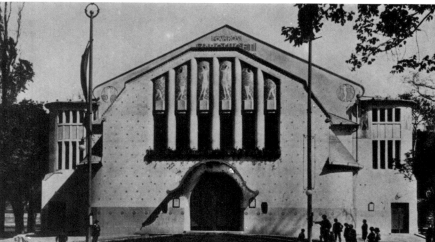

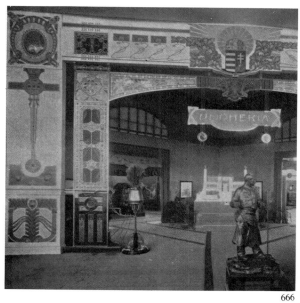

666

668

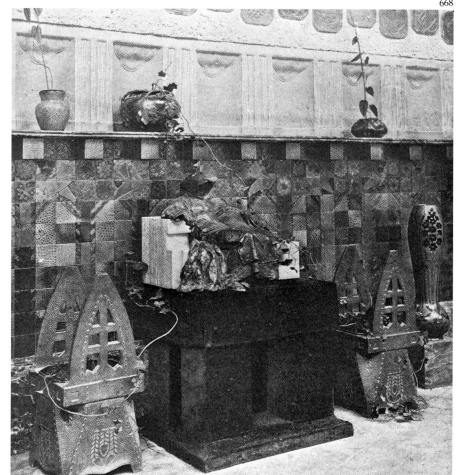

667—JOSEF AND LAZLÓ VAGÓ, The Theatre of Wood, Budapest, 1913; facade.
668—GEZA MARÓTHI, Hungarian section of the Milan Exhibition 1906; the sculpture gallery.

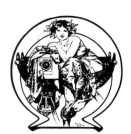

669

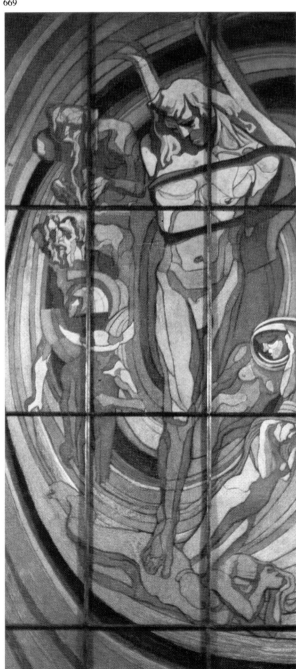

670

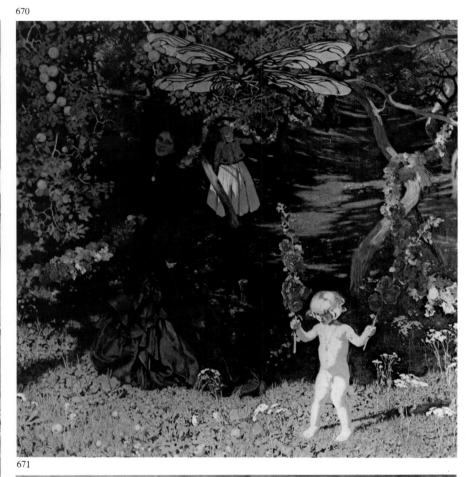

671

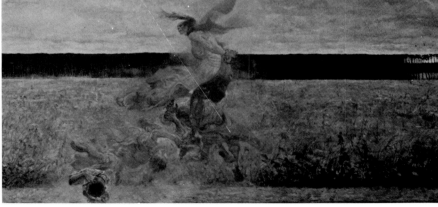

669—STANISLAW WYSPIANSKI, *Apollo-Copernican System of Astrology*, 1904. Cracow, Muzeum Narodowe.
670—JOSEF MEHOFFER, *The Strange Garden*, 1903. Warsaw, Museum Narodowe.
671—JACEK MALKZEWSKI, *The Hurricane*, 1893-94.

architecture which was orientated towards the West rather than Russia.

In Yugoslavia, Art Nouveau was used as a means of enriching the highly ornamental local architectural style which was rooted in the

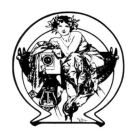

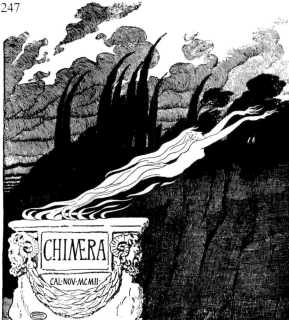

672

672—EDWARD OKUN, cover for the magazine *Chimera*, Warsaw, 1902.
673—JAN BUKOVSKY, cover for *Dialogues on Art* by Oscar
Wilde, 1906.
674—J. MALKZEWSKI, *Eloe'z çialem Ellenai*, 1908-09.

673

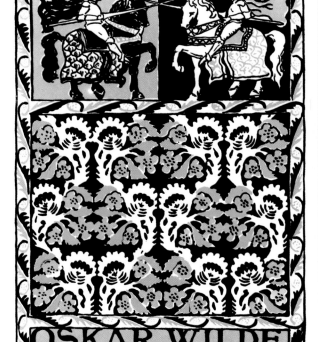

674

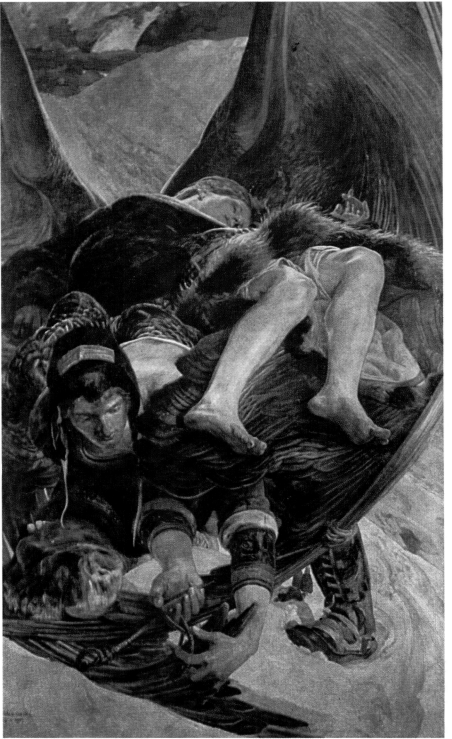

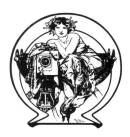

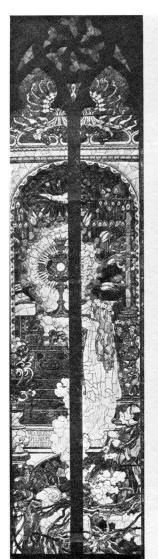

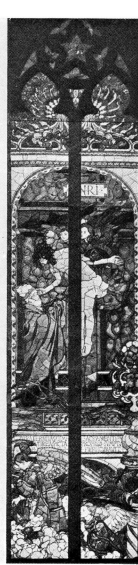

675

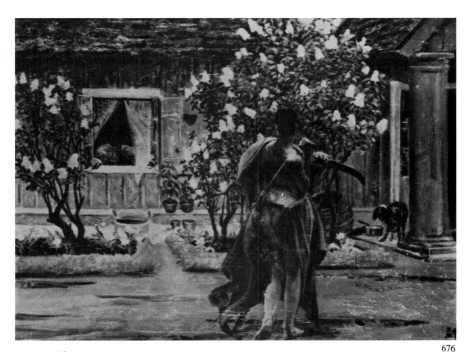

676

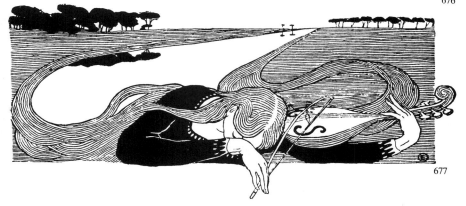

677

675—JOSEF MEHOFFER, stained-glass window in Freiburg cathedral, c. 1907.

676—J. MALKZEWSKI, *Thanatos*, c. 1908-9. Warsaw, Muzeum Narodowe.

677—E. OKUN, vignette for *Salve Regina* by Jan Kasprowicz, in *Chimera*, 1901.

late Byzantine tradition. In response to the rise of nationalism and the desire to escape foreign stylistic influences perpetuated by the Academy, Art Nouveau was rapidly accepted by the new generation of architects.

The earliest examples of the new style are the row of houses in Belgrade designed by M. ANTONOVIĆ (1901), where abstract variations on floral motifs govern the design of the iron balustrade. This was harmoniously integrated with the rhythm of the building, which derives from local traditions. A similar example of the way Art Nouveau was successfully grafted on to local style is KUĆA KALLINA's tile decoration on an apartment block in Zagreb. Here the floral motifs of the new style are perfectly integrated with the exuberance of the building's decorative articulation. The model for the decoration

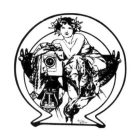

678

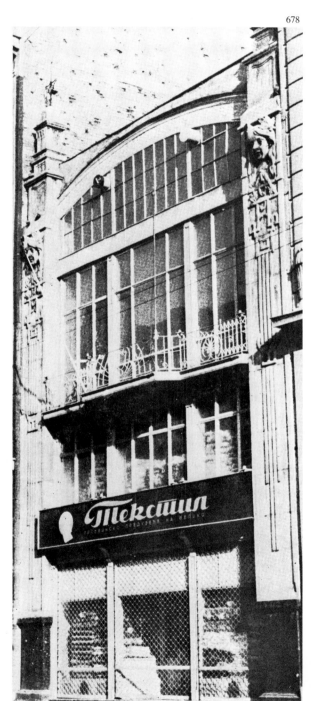

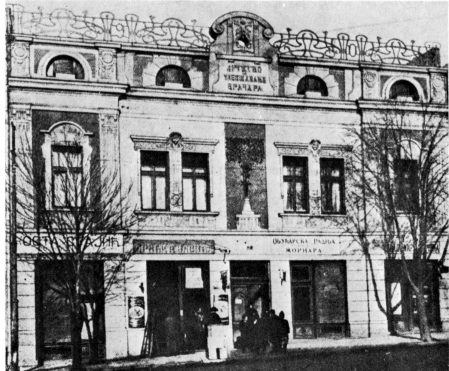

was probably Wagner's Majolikahaus in Vienna.

Other Yugoslavian architects who were influenced by Art Nouveau include BRANKO TANAZEVIĆ (b. 1876), ANDREA STEPANOVIĆ, NIKOLA NESTOROVIĆ and M. RUVIDIĆ. However, in the work of these architects, the floral and abstract lines of Art Nouveau are contained within the Baroque style of local architecture. Nevertheless, the decoration on a house designed by Tanazević in Belgrade (1912) is reminiscent of the flat decorated surfaces of Viennese Art Nouveau building. Details of the facade of a residential building, designed by Stepanović and Nestorović in Belgrade (1907), show an awareness not only of the decorative possibilities of Art Nouveau, but also how the spatial qualities of the style had been assimilated into the Baroque-influenced facade. This is evident in the Beogradska Zagruda (1905-07) in Belgrade, built by the same architects.

In Czechoslovakia the influence of Art Nouveau architecture led to the wholesale adoption of the style as the official architectural style. Whole quarters of Prague (like Brussels) were developed on the principles of the Art Nouveau movement. In painting, Art Nouveau style was assimilated together with other influences, notably those of

679

678—V. AZRIJEL, Robni Department Store, Belgrade, 1907.
679—M. ANTONOVIĆ, house in Belgrade, 1901.

Naturalism and Symbolism. In Poland features of all three movements found their way into the work of JACEK MALCZEWSKI (1854-1929). His allegorical paintings use natural elements such as wind and

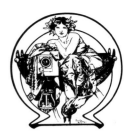

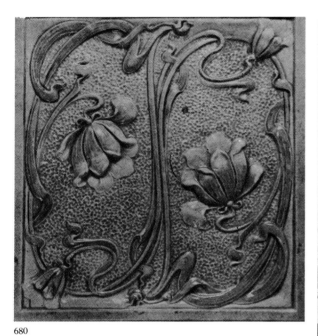

680

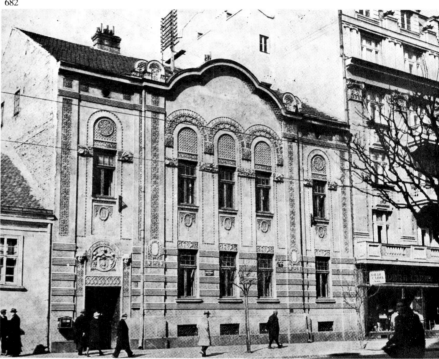

682

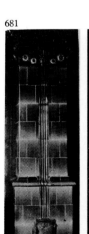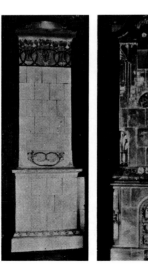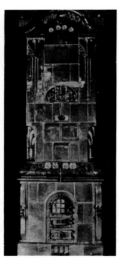

681

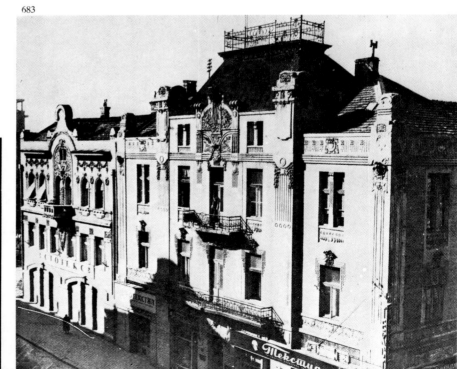

683

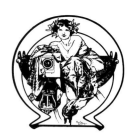

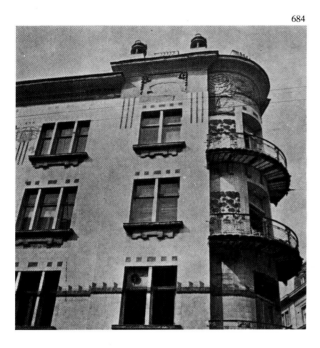

684

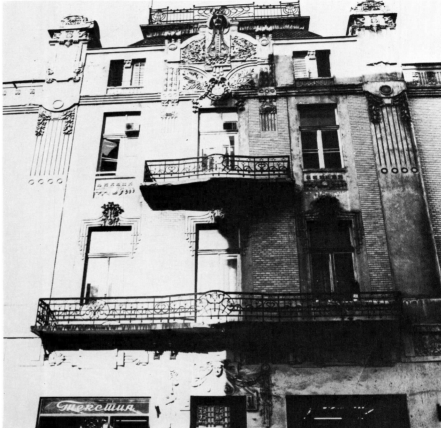

686

680—KUĆA J. KALLINA, tile.
681—K. J. KALLINA, stoves.
682—BRANCO TANAZEVIĆ, facade, Belgrade, 1912.
683—ANDREA STEPANOVIĆ. NIKOLA NESTOROVIĆ, apartments, Belgrade, June 7th Street, 1907.
684—K. J. KALLINA, ceramic decoration on a building in Zagabria, 1903.
685—LEON KOEN, *Spring*, c. 1906. Belgrade, National Gallery.
686, 687—details of n. 683.

685

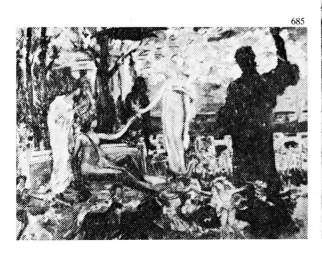

687

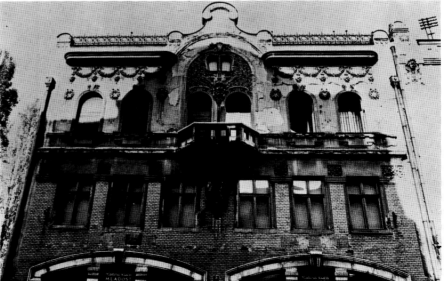

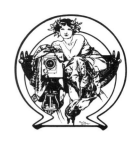

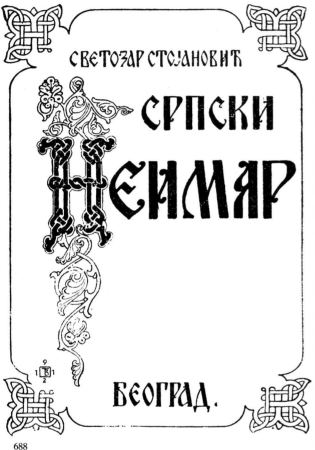

688

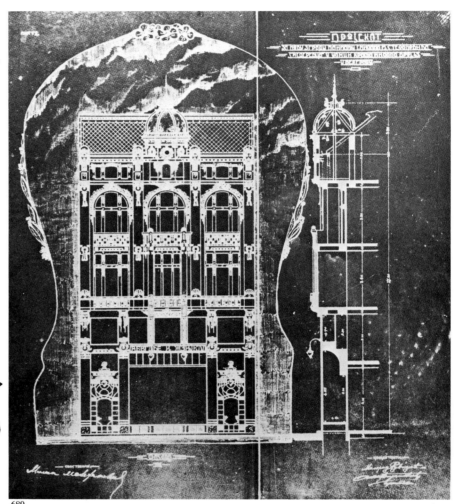

689

690

688—Title page, 1912.
689—M. RUVIDIĆ, project for the Zgrada Smederevske Bank,
Belgrade, 1905-07.
690—B. TANAZEVIĆ, project, c. 1901-04.
691—ARNOST HOFBAUER, programme for a recital by Hana
Kvapilova, 1899.
692—ANDREA STEPANOVIĆ NIKOLA NESTOROVIĆ, The Beogradska Zadruga, Belgrade, 1905-07.
693—ELEK FALUS, typographical decoration, c. 1907.

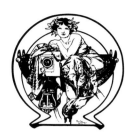

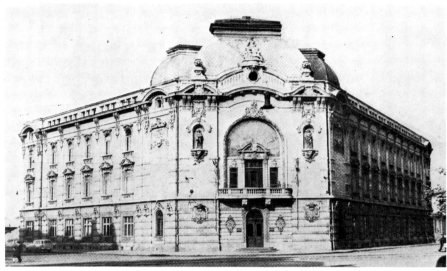

692

691

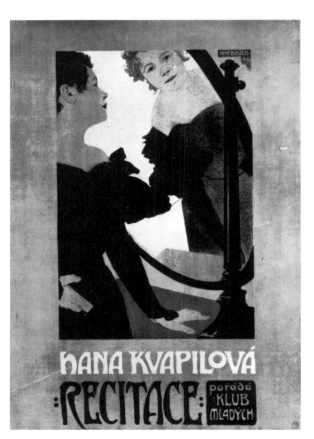

sunlight for expressive purposes. In *Hurricane* (1893-94) and *Thanatos* (1898-99), these elements have a decorative arabesque vitality that relates them to the aesthetics of the Art Nouveau movement.

JOSEPH VON MEHOFFER's (1869-1946) work can be characterized by a similar blend of Naturalism and Symbolism. His *The Strange Garden* (1903) seems to be a precise rendering of nature, but on closer inspection the figures and their ambiguous setting carry allegorical meaning.

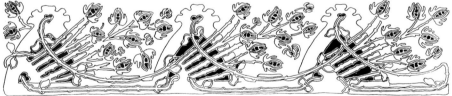

693

In Yugoslavia, painting also drew on elements from a wide range of styles. In the works of LEON KOEN the influence of the plein-airists co-exists with an evocative treatment of symbolic figures. Koen's *Spring* (c. 1906) shows strong affinities with the work of the Polish painters.

The sources of Czechoslovakian painting in the period are less disparate. In the paintings of VITEZLAV KAREL MASEK (1865-1927), decorative Symbolism dominates. His *The Prophetess* (c. 1893) is a shadowy, evocative figure, clad in Byzantine costume and evoking the mysterious splendour of a classical age.

Preoccupations with the occult and astrology dominate the work of FRANTISEK KUPKA (1871-1957), whose paintings are probably the

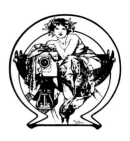

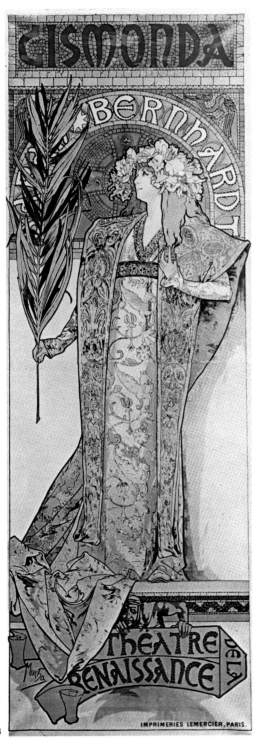

most powerful of the Eastern European painters. In *Resistance—The Black Idol* (1900-03), a huge brooding silhouette is set against a bare snowscape lit by the evening sun. *The Beginning of Life* (1900-03) is another mystical painting. Here an embryo accompanied by a flower floats over an imaginary lake. The atmosphere is mysterious and heavily indebted to Redon's similar juxtaposition of objects floating in ambiguous settings. Kupka's work also expresses the erotic, sado-masochistic tendencies of Symbolism and Art Nouveau, which had been developed by Beardsley. His *The Conquering Worm* combines the images of death with the nude in a symbolic context—the figure is

695

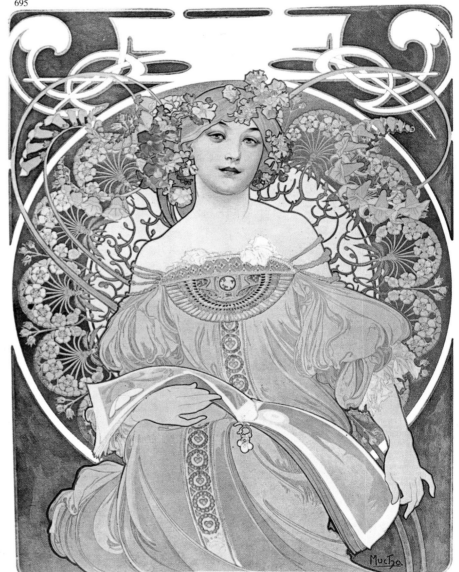

694

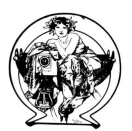

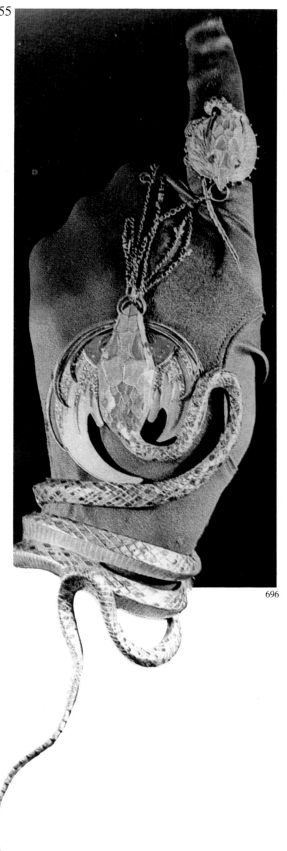

696

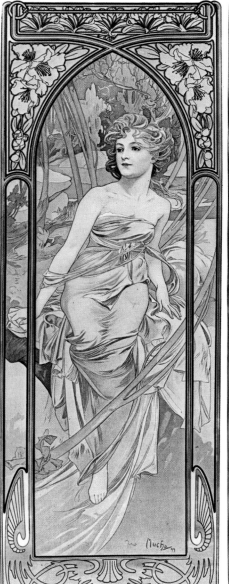

697

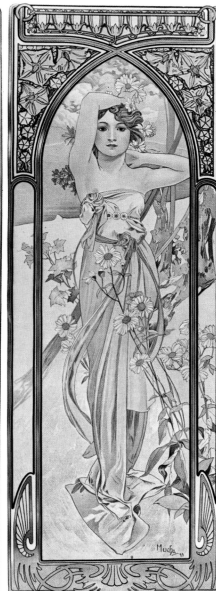

half woman, half griffin. Although the precise meaning of this image is unclear, it exudes an atmosphere of feminine power and cruelty.

In later years, Kupka developed a more abstract style based on the free use of strong contrasting colours and tones, which anticipates Orphism. His *The Lake* (1909), although strongly reminiscent of Paul Serusier's *Talisman* (1889), is nevertheless highly original in the way the subject is subordinated to the desire to create a decorative surface.

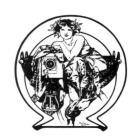

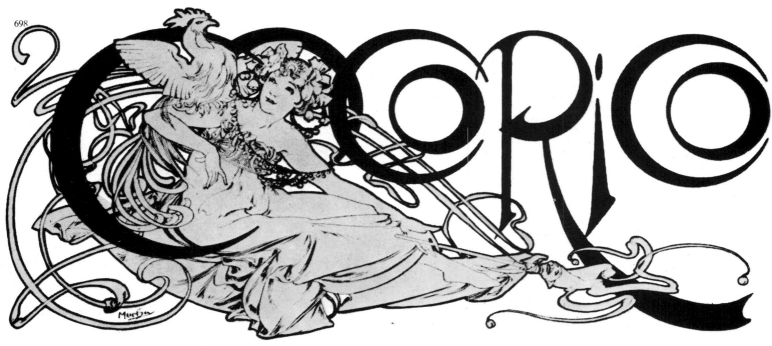

698

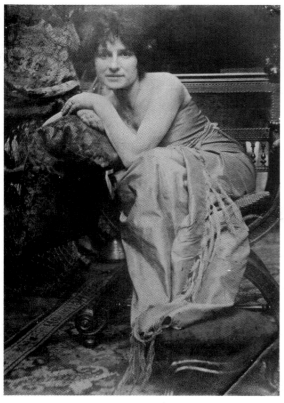

699

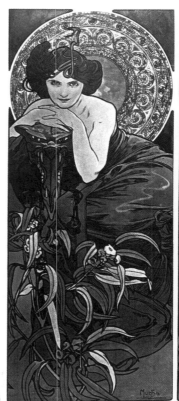
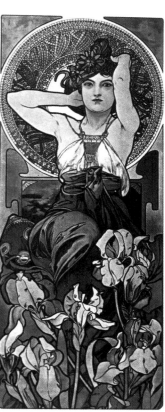

700

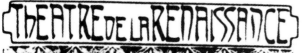

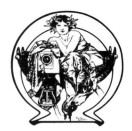

701

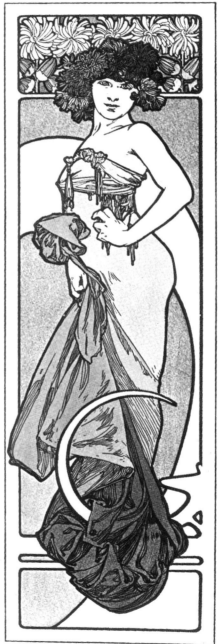

702

703

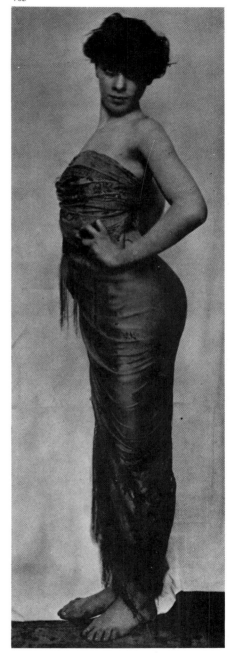

In Eastern Europe Art Nouveau style was most successful in the field of applied arts. The strong linear forms of the movement are found in the elegant interiors of the Hungarian Edouard Wigand (b. 1870), which are indebted to the work of van de Velde. In Poland, very decorative posters and illustrations for magazines like the

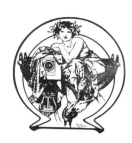

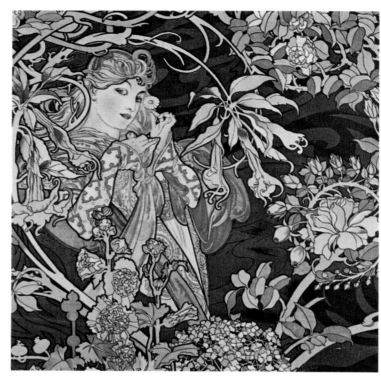

704

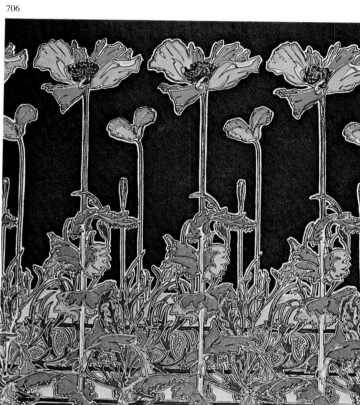

706

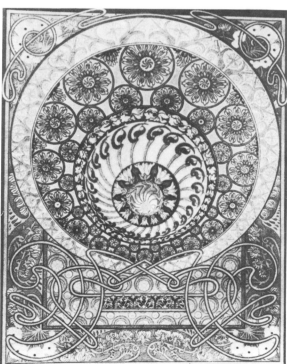

705

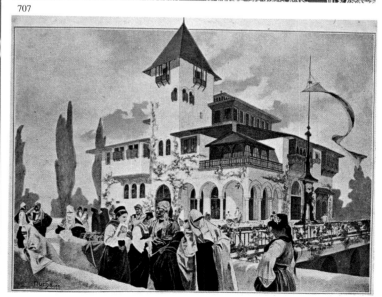

707

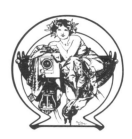

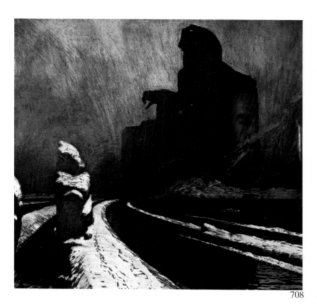

708

710

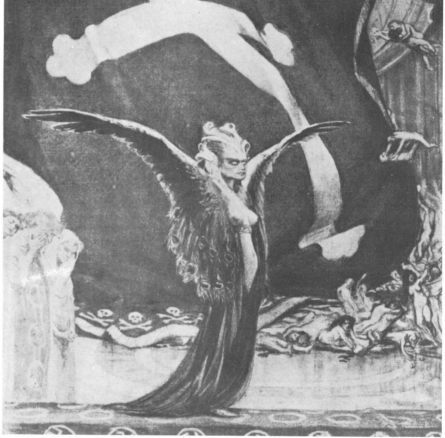

704—A. MUCHA, *Woman with a Daisy*, c. 1897-98.
705—A. MUCHA, carpet in the Austrian pavilion at the Paris Exhibition, 1900.
706—A. MUCHA, design for wallpaper, 1902.
707—A. MUCHA, pavilion of the Bosnia Erzegovina at the Paris Exhibition, 1900.
708—FRANTISEK KUPKA, *Resistance – The Black Idol*, 1900-03. Prague, Narodni Galerie.
709—F. KUPKA, *The Beginning of Life*, 1900-03.
710—F. KUPKA, *The Conquering Worm*. Oslo, National Gallery.

709

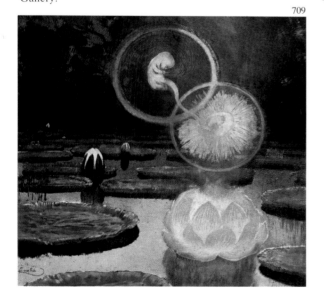

important *Chimera* were made by graphic artists. However, the field is dominated by the success of one figure above all, that of ALPHONSE MUCHA (1860-1939).

Mucha owed his success to the patronage of Sarah Bernhardt, who had similarly promoted the career of Lalique. Mucha designed the poster for Bernhardt's performance as *Gismonda* in 1894 at the Théâtre de la Renaissance in Paris. It was an immediate success because of the Byzantinizing style and the clarity of the strong decorative line. Soon after the completion of the poster, Mucha was commissioned to design some jewellery for Bernhardt which was executed by the famous Parisian jeweller Fouquet. This commission was for a bracelet and ring in the form of a snake which coiled around the wrist and finger. They were attached by gold chains and the gold was set with turquoise and red enamel (for the snake's eyes). This beautiful object, with its associations with luxury, death and eroticism, was worn by Bernhardt for her performance as Medea in 1898.

Over the next few years, Mucha enjoyed considerable popularity as a poster designer and illustrator. His work is a personal expression of

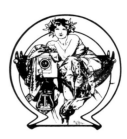

711

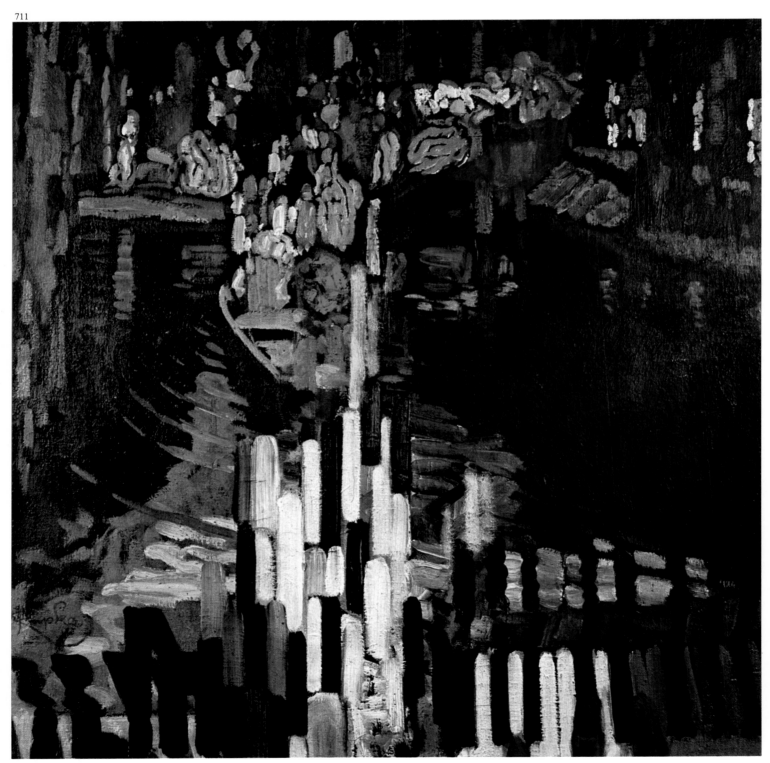

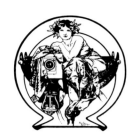

712

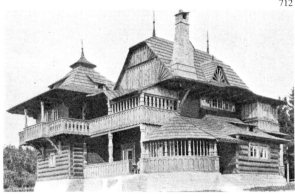

714

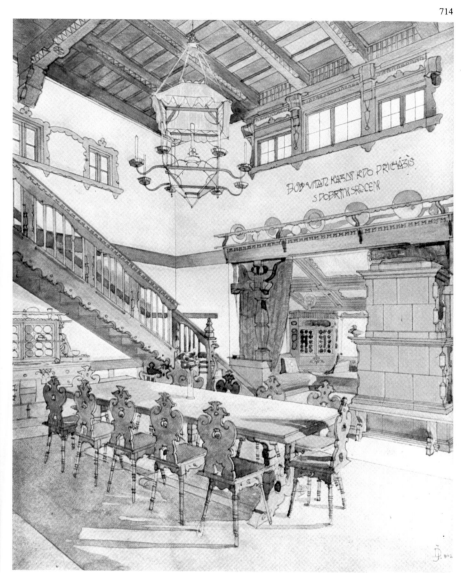

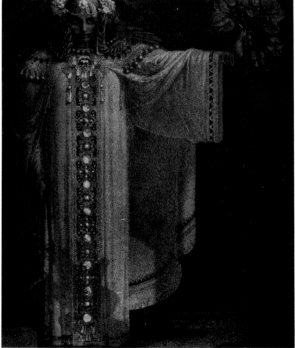

713

711—F. KUPKA, *Piano Keys – The Lake*, 1909, Prague, Narodni Galerie.
712—DUSAN JURKOVIĆ, Resek Villa.
713—VITEZLAV KAREL MASEK, *The Prophetess*, c. 1893. Paris, Musée du Louvre.
714—D. JURKOVIĆ, dining room in the Resek Villa; watercolour.

a wide range of influences. The elegant contours of Japanese woodcuts containing areas of brilliant colour are combined with geometric-decoration drawn from Byzantine and Moorish art. His panels, *The Four Times of Day* (1900), which were intended as decorative panels for an interior, show a sensitivity to the more fluid, gentle curves of the arabesque line which supplanted the earlier insistence on more solid geometric forms. However, Mucha continued to use geometric contour in more subtle ways. While the poster for Bernhardt in the play *La Samaritaine* (1897) is a little stiff, this stiffness had disappeared by 1900. Although both were based on photographs, the composition of *Amethyst*, from the series *Four*

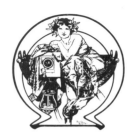

715

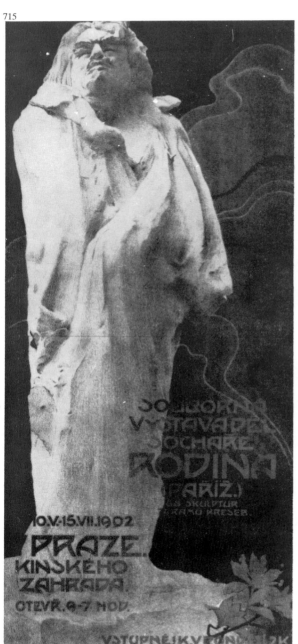

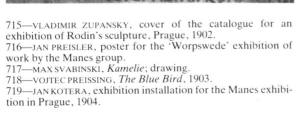

716

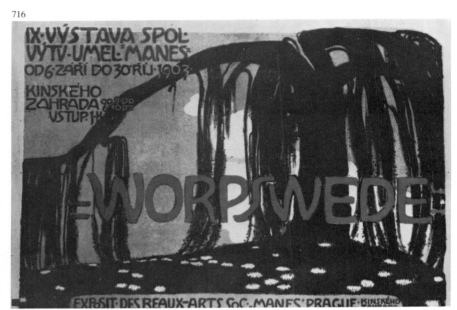

717

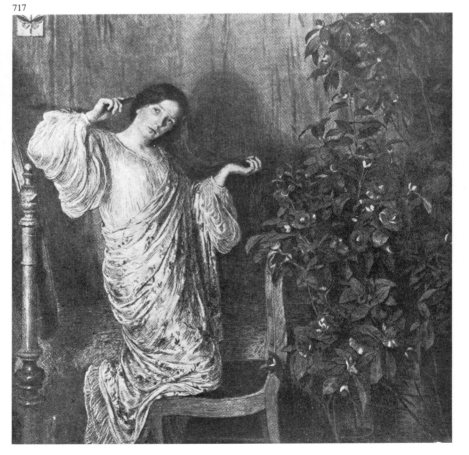

715—VLADIMIR ZUPANSKY, cover of the catalogue for an exhibition of Rodin's sculpture, Prague, 1902.
716—JAN PREISLER, poster for the 'Worpswede' exhibition of work by the Manes group.
717—MAX SVABINSKI, *Kamelie*; drawing.
718—VOJTEC PREISSING, *The Blue Bird*, 1903.
719—JAN KOTERA, exhibition installation for the Manes exhibition in Prague, 1904.

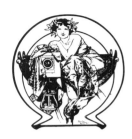

718

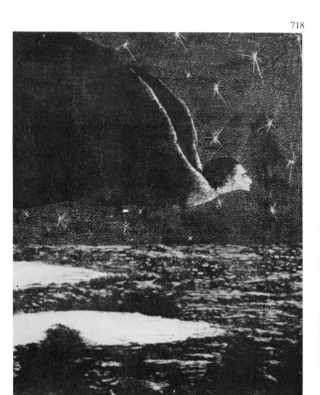

720

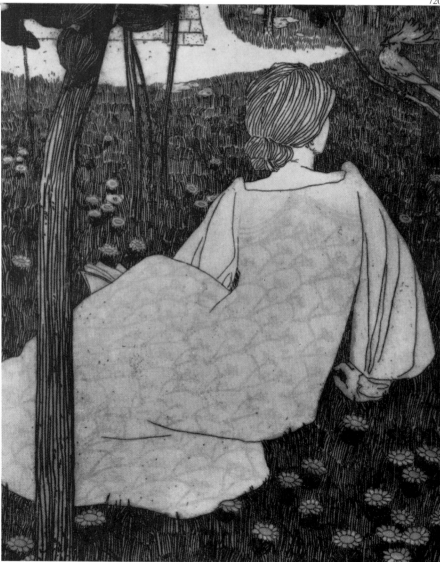

719

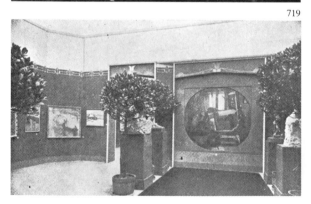

721

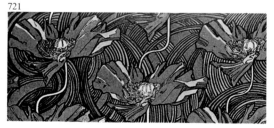

Precious Stones (1900), displays a more overall rhythm and freedom than the *Samaritaine* poster, while it loses none of the latter's firmness of design.

Mucha also designed book illustrations, carpets and wallpapers. In these media Mucha's visually stimulating floral arabesque lines enclose jewel-like colours.

720—FRANTISEC KOBLIHA, illustration of the poem *Vampire* by Karel Hlavacek, in *Late in the Morning*, 1909.
721—A. MUCHA, wallpaper, 1902.

14-Russia

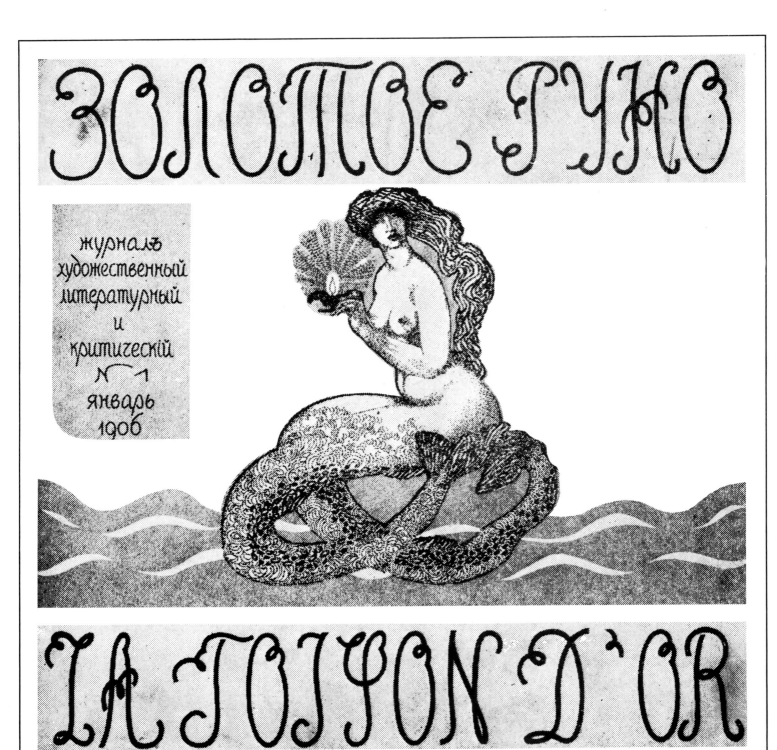

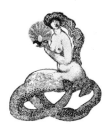

As in Scandinavia and in the countries of Eastern Europe, the Art Nouveau style came to Russia at a time when the arts were seeking to revive folk tradition. The immediate background for the arts of the period was in the work of The Wanderers, a group of artists who had chosen to start a movement that was socially orientated rather than to follow academic traditions. This became the model for the later movements which operated outside official circles.

723

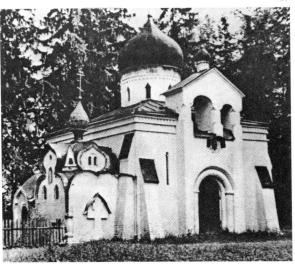

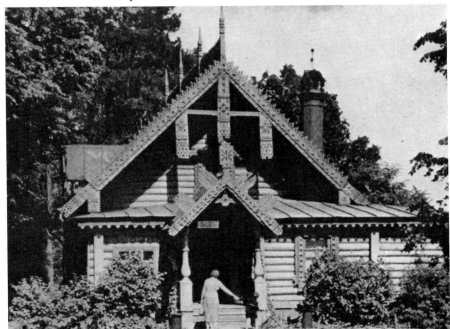

722—and symbol of Chapter 14, pp. 264-277 – EUGENI LANCERAY, cover of the first issue of *The Golden Veil*, 1906.
723—Church at Abramtsevo, 1880-82.
724—SAVVA MAMONTOV, washstand, exhibited at the Paris Exhibition, 1900. Abramtsevo Museum.
725—Abramtsevo Museum.

725

724

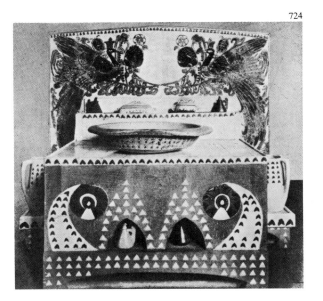

One of the first of these independent movements was established by SAVVA MAMONTOV (1841-1918) and his wife ELISABETH (1847-1909). Mamontov was a wealthy merchant who set up a community of artists and artisans at his farm at Abramtsevo on the outskirts of Moscow. Here he established the School of Arts and Trades for his workers, and later he built a small church for the community and then a private opera theatre. The first opera performed at this theatre was Rimsky Korsakoff's *The Maiden of the Snows* with sets designed by Victor Vasnetsov. The Church at Abramtsevo (1880-82) followed the traditions of orthodox architecture and ignored the influence of western styles which had characterized Russian ecclesiastical building. Similarly, the community's museum was a traditional wooden construction.

Mamontov's initiative was followed by the Princess MARIA TENI-SHEVA (1867-1928), who founded the Institute of Decorative Arts at Talashkino in collaboration with the painters Vassily Miliuti and Nikolai Roerich (1874-1947). The Talashkino style in the decorative arts, with its simple rustic forms and bold colours and which

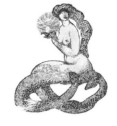

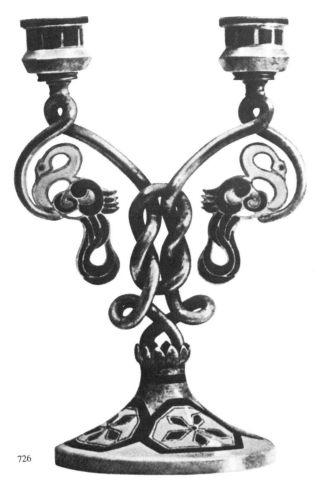

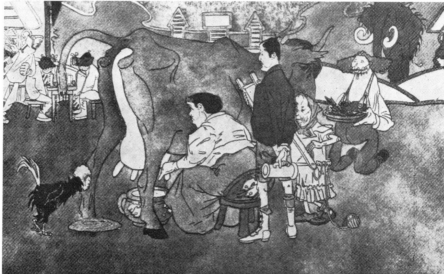
728

occasionally reached a high level of decorative effect, is based on folk art. However, the painting executed by the Talashkino Group was far more sophisticated and tended towards a synthesis of Art Nouveau and Symbolist prototypes. Vassily Miliuti's *Legend* (1905) exhibits something of Klimt's ability to evoke a feeling of mystical intensity in the way the figure emerges from the decorative background. Folk art was the starting point for MIKHAIL VRUBEL's (1856-1910) work, for example his decoration of a balalaika (c. 1900), but he quickly

726—Talashkino workshop, candelabra in bronze decorated in enamel 'champlevé' style, after a design by Princess Tenicheva; 1900. Talashkino.
727—House in Talashkino, c. 1900.
728—PAVEL SHCHERBOV, *Idyll*; caricature which appeared in the newspaper *Shut* (Fool) in 1890, depicting the Princess Tenicheva (the cow), Diaghilev, Filosov, Nesterov, Repin and Mamontov (the mammoth).

727

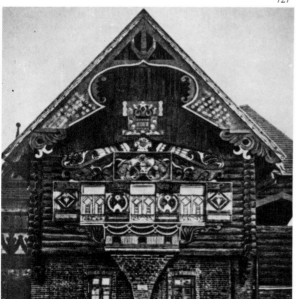

729

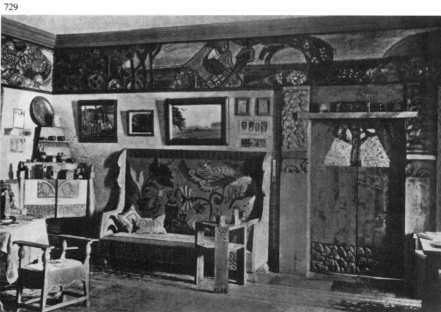

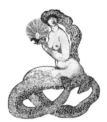

730

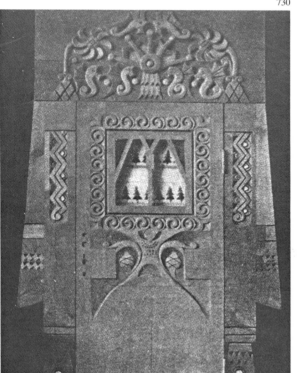

732

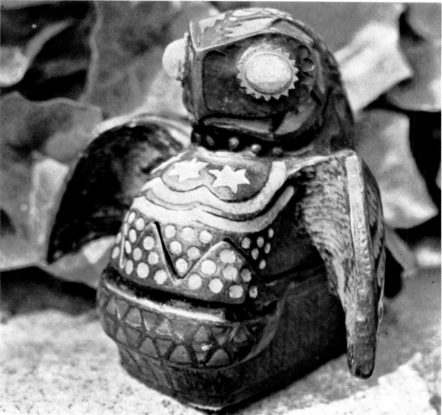

731

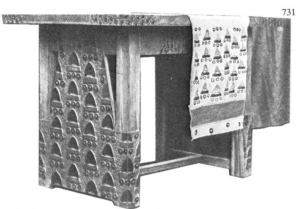

733

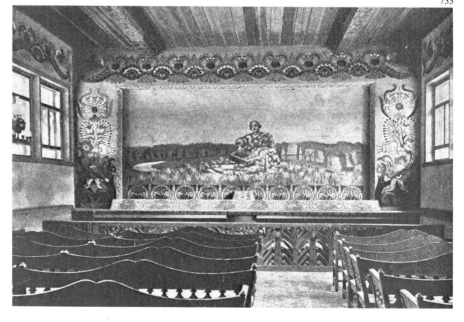

729—Princess Tenicheva's drawing room at Talashkino; lacquered settle designed by the Princess, frieze by Nikolai Roerikh.
730—Carved door and surround in the Talashkino theatre.
731—A. ZINOVIEV, Talashkino workshop table. Talashkino.
732—PRINCESS TENICHEVA, *Barn Owl*, Talashkino, 1908. New York, coll. Rothschild.
733—A. MALIUTIN, Talashkino theatre; auditorium.

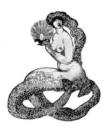

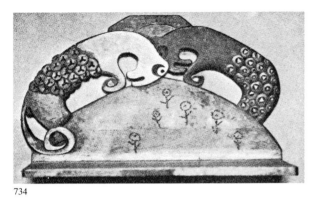

734

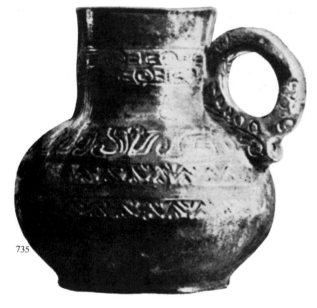

735

737

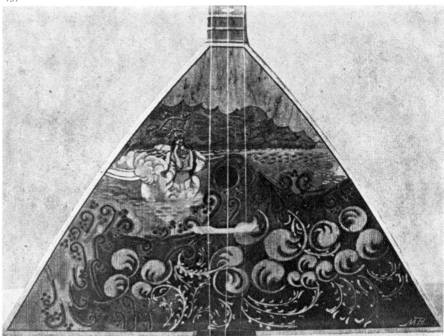

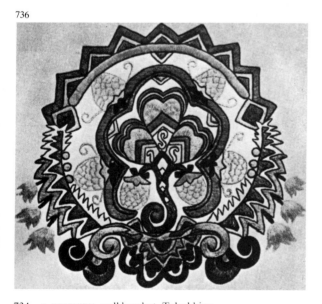

736

developed towards a more elegant style. His *The Demon* of the same period already shows a familiarity with contemporary decorative painting, particularly that of the Nabis. However, he rapidly turned towards a style based on the combination of forms taken from folk art and the curvilinear forms of Art Nouveau and Symbolism. He produced works of great decorative complexity which often contained symbolic motifs. Paintings like *The Siren* (1899), with its concern for overall structural rhythms relate his painting to the Belgian Art

738

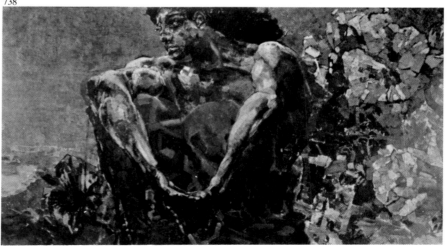

734—A. ZINOVIEV, wall bracket. Talashkino.
735—Talashkino workshop, ceramic jug, c. 1900.
736—Talashkino workshop, embroidered textile designed by Princess Tenicheva, c. 1900. Talashkino.
737—MICHAEL ALEXANDROVIC VRUBEL, balalaika, c. 1900; Talashkino workshop.
738—M. A. VRUBEL, *The Demon*, c. 1890.

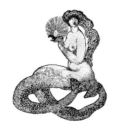

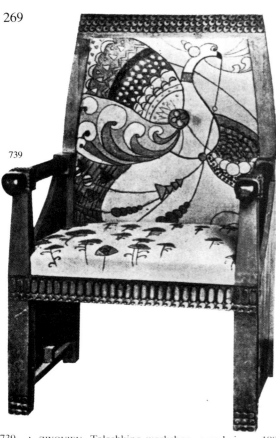

739

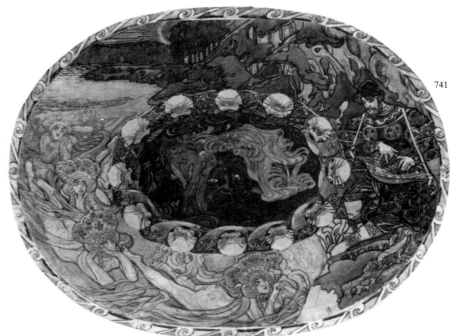

741

Nouveau style, while the mysterious iconography and an expressive treatment of paintings like *The Fallen Angel* (1910) suggest the influence of painters like Khnopff, Delville and Redon.

In the cultured court at St Petersburg, a modernist vitality invaded the world of the theatre and the performing arts. After the World of

739—A. ZINOVIEV, Talashkino workshop, armchair, c. 1900. Talashkino.
740—Talashkino workshop, table. Talashkino.
On pages 270, 271
741—M. A. VRUBEL, *Siren*, 1899. Leningrad, State Museum.
742—M. A. VRUBEL, *The Fallen Angel*, 1901; detail. Moscow, Pushkin Museum.
743—LÉON BAKST, *The Beautiful Princess* (from *The Firebird*), 1910. Milan, Galeria del Levante.
744—L. BAKST, *Sadko*, 1910. Milan, Galeria del Levante.
745—L. BAKST, cover of a programme for the ballet *L'Après-midi d'un faune*, with music by Claude Debussy.
746—M. A. VRUBEL, *Siren*, 1899. Leningrad, State Museum.
747—M. A. VRUBEL, *The Pearl*, 1904. Moscow, State Tretyakov Gallery.
748—L. BAKST, costume for *The Firebird* by Stravinsky, c. 1910 (Ballets Russes).
749—L. BAKST, set design (detail) for the ballet *Shéhérazade*, 1909. Paris, Musées des Arts Decoratifs.
750—VASSILY MILIUTI, *Legend*, 1905.

740

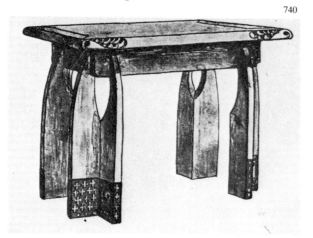

742

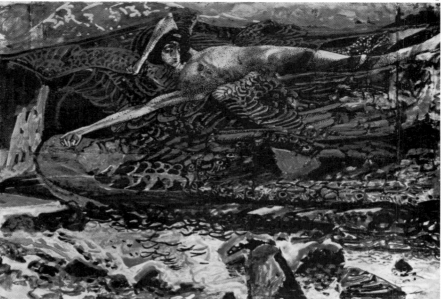

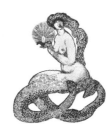

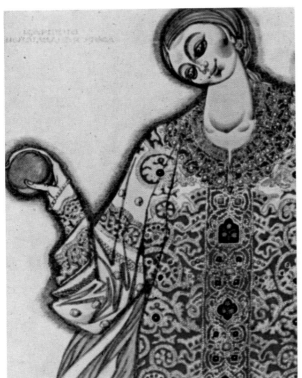

743

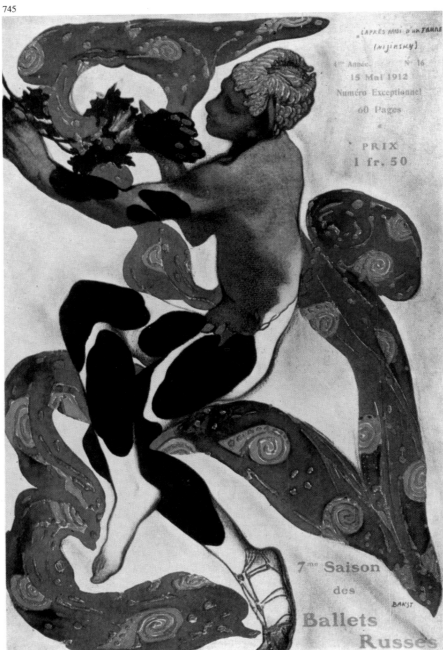

745

744

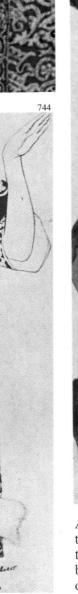

Art Group had been founded by ALEXANDER BENOIS (1870-1960), the scene was set for the innovations of the Ballets Russes. They made their debut in Paris in 1909 with *La Pavillon d'Armide* and *Prince Igor* by Borodin; the decor and the costumes were exotic combinations of oriental and folk motifs designed by LÉON BAKST (1867-1924).

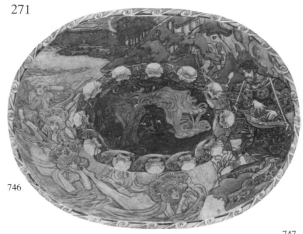

746

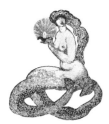

749

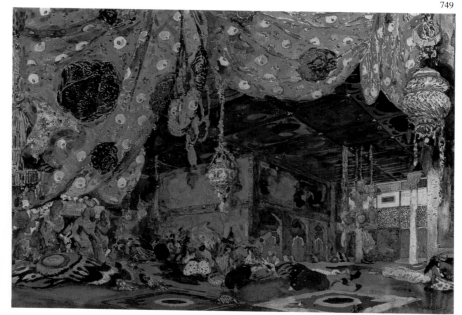

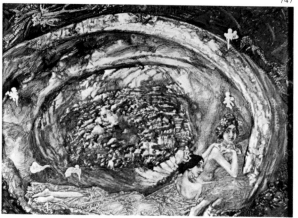

747

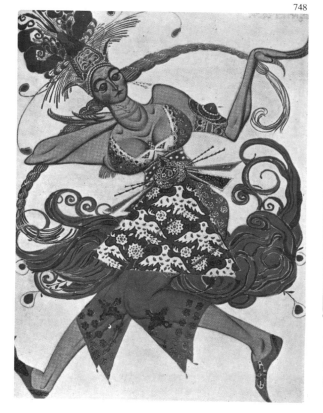

748

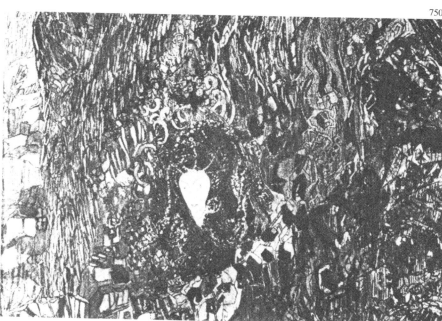

750

Bakst's jewel-encrusted designs were highly original developments of the Art Nouveau style in the way they maintained the freshness and strength of traditional and primitive art, while providing for the sophisticated stylized performances which Sergei Diaghilev's direction demanded. A generation of artists followed Miliuti and Vrubel

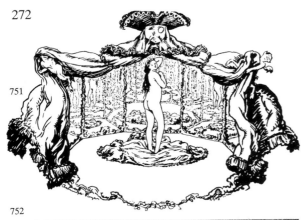

751

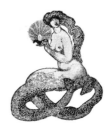

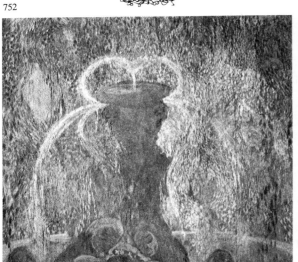

752

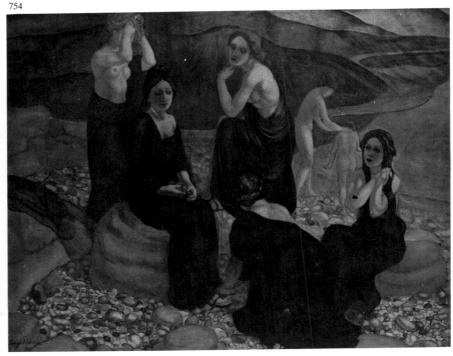

754

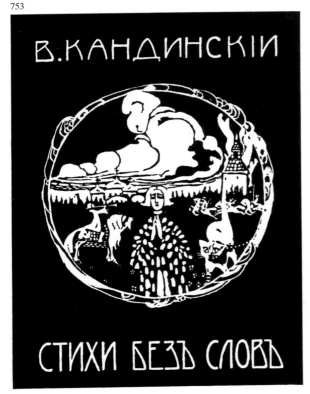

753

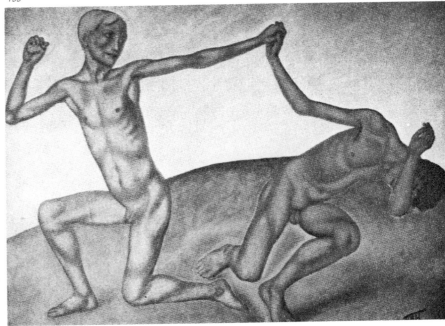

755

who had started their careers as decorative artists, but who later experimented in the Cubist, Futurist and Expressionist movements. MIKHAIL LARIONOV (1881-1964) and NATALIA GONCHAROVA

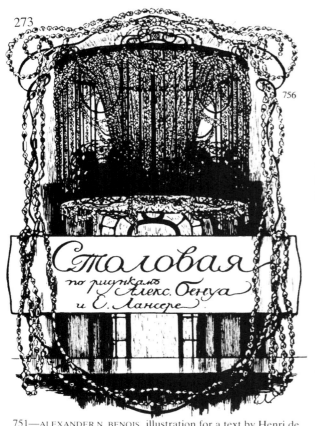

756

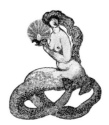

758

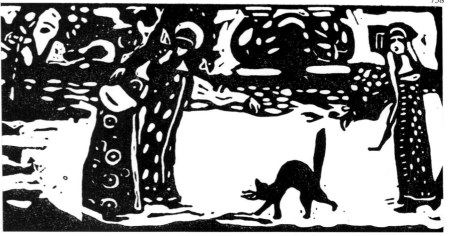

759

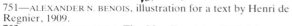

751—ALEXANDER N. BENOIS, illustration for a text by Henri de Regnier, 1909.

752—PAVEL KUZNETSOV, *The Blue Fountain*, 1905. Moscow, State Tretyakov Museum.

753—WASSILY KANDINSKY, title page for *Poems Without Words*.

754—KUZMA SERGEIVITCH PETROV-VODKIN, *The Shore*, 1908.

755—K. S. PETROV-VODKIN, *Boys at Play*, 1911.

756—EUGENE E. LANCERAY, illustration for the magazine *Mir Iskusstva*, 1903.

757—FJODOR SHEKHTEL, Russian pavilion at the Glasgow Exhibition, 1906.

758—V. KANDINSKY, *The Black Cat*, 1907; detail.

759—F. SHEKHTEL, project for Yarislav Station, 1903-04; elevation.

760—Siberian Pavilion at the Paris Exhibition, 1900.

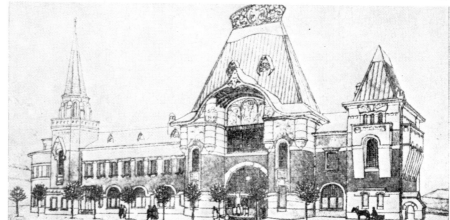

757

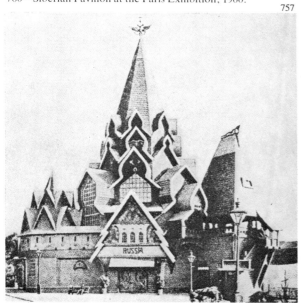

760

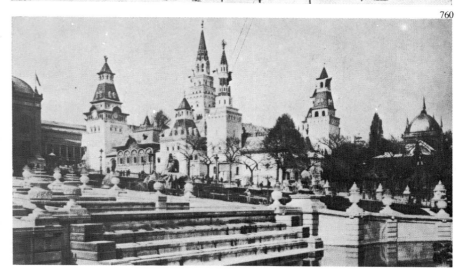

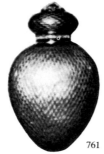

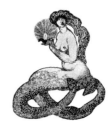

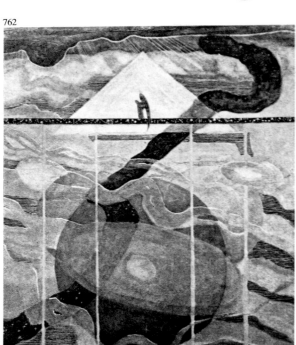

762

761

764

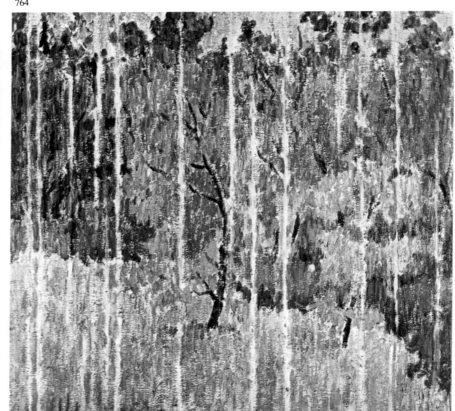

763

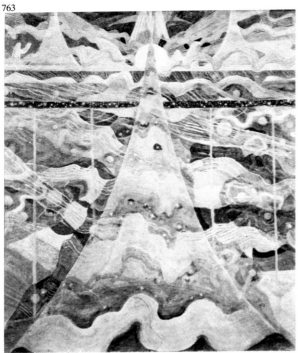

765

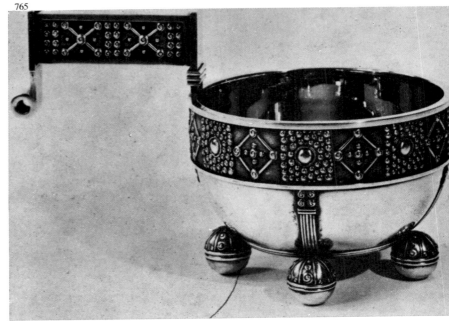

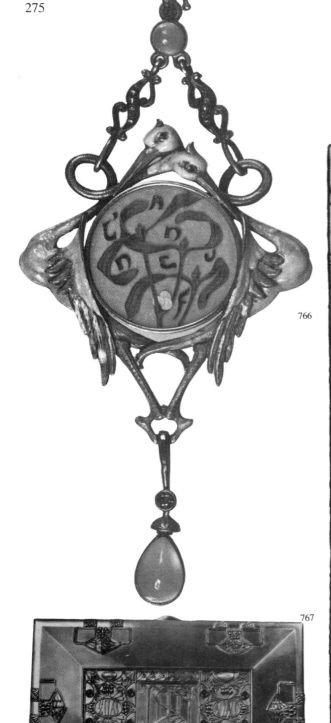

766

767

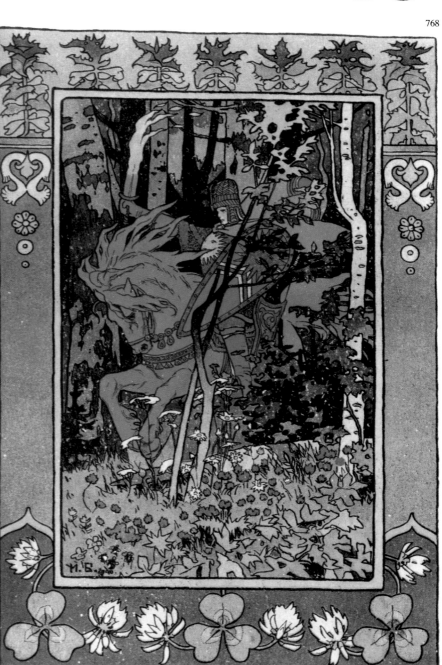

768

(1881-1962), and Pavel Kuznetsov (b. 1874) all worked in c. 1905 in a style which exploited surface effects in imitation of Miliuti. MYKOLAS KONSTANTAS CIURLIONIS (1875-1911) was also successful in surpassing Russian Symbolist prototypes with works of great decorative clarity. His series *Music of the Stars* (1908) uses pattern and

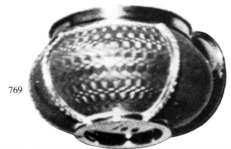

769

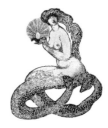

770

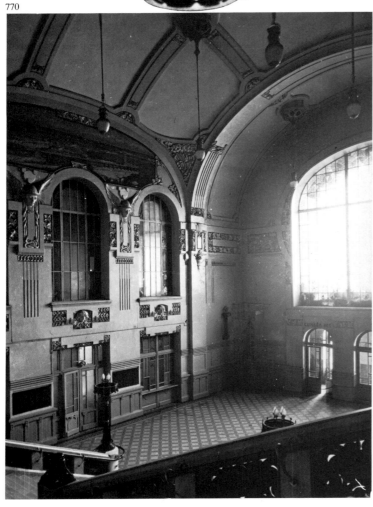

771

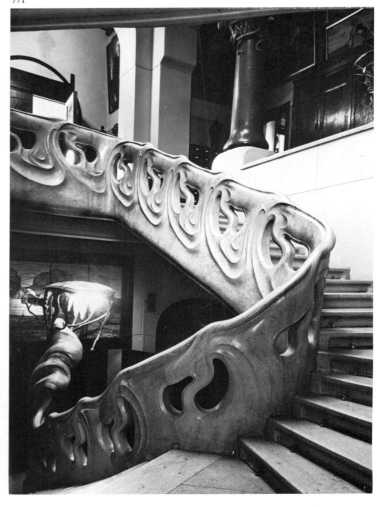

geometrical forms which are almost entirely emancipated from any representational role to suggest an abstract, harmonic, ethereal world.

The best remembered Russian painter of the period is WASSILY KANDINSKY (1866-1944) who, after his involvement with the Blaue Reiter Group, is considered to have made the first abstract painting. In the first decade of the century, Kandinsky was influenced by the Secessionist style and he produced a series of magnificently compact illustrations which have strong areas of black and white and tense curves recalling Munich illustration as well as woodcuts of his native Russia. A comparison between the church at Abramtsevo (1880-82), designed by VICTOR VASNETSOV (1840-1926), with the work of FEODOR SHEKHTEL (1856-1926) shows how architecture in Russia transcended the influence of folk and academic traditions. Although Shekhtel's Russian Pavilion for the Glasgow Exhibition of 1906

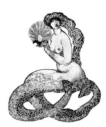

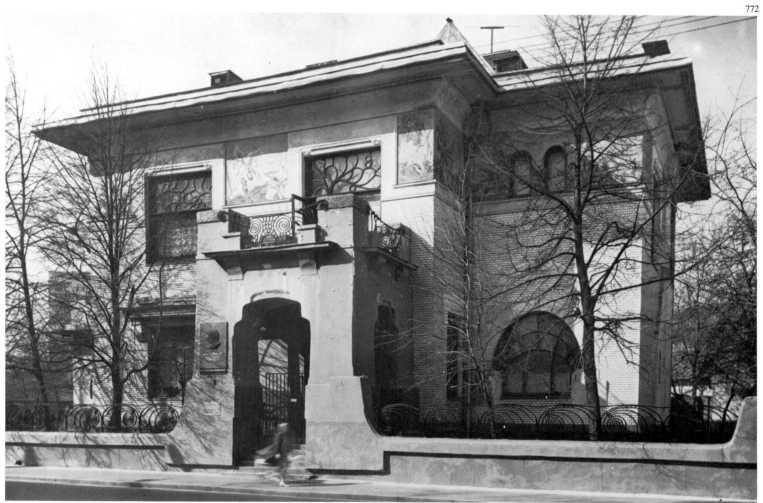

772

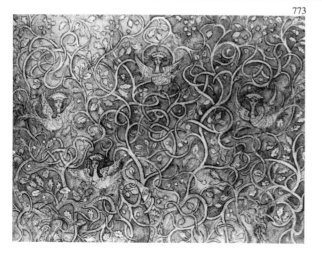

773

contains many quotations from traditional forms, his earlier work on his Ryabuchinsky House (1900-02) shows that he had a complete command of the Art Nouveau style. The facade is a crisp and elegant exercise in Viennese Secessionist architecture. The planes are strong and well defined, with spare and subtle areas of floral decoration. The interior contains a staircase which is a fluid mass of floral, mobile forms worthy of Horta or of van de Velde.

The most famous Art Nouveau artist in Russia was the jeweller and goldsmith CARL FABERGÉ (1846-1920). Fabergé inherited a Russian sensibility for geometric and linear decoration which emerges most strongly in his metalwork. Fabergé's mature style was influenced by the French Art Nouveau style, especially by the work of Lalique, and his designs became more fluid and curvilinear. The jewellery he made under the influence of French models integrates the Russian pleasure in colour and pattern with Lalique's refined floral line.

15-The United States

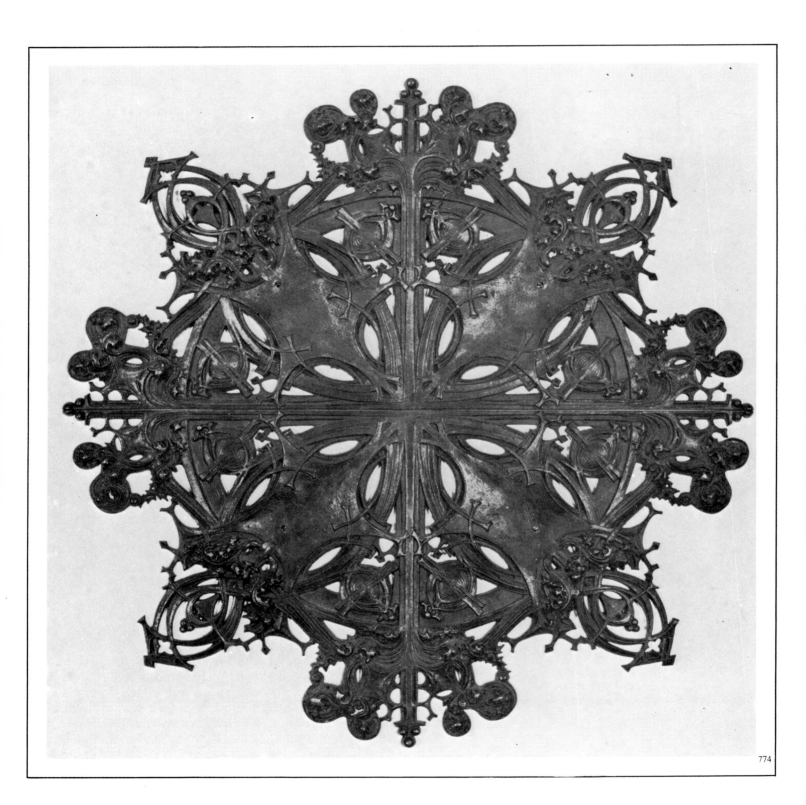

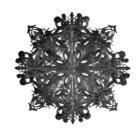

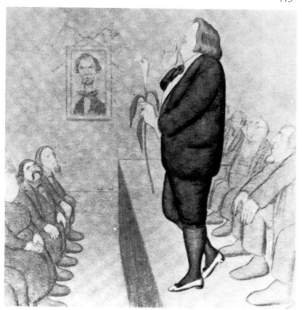

775

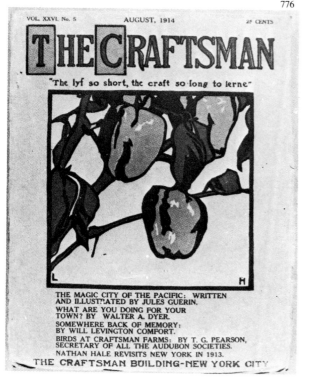

774—and symbol of Chapter 15, pp. 278-307 – studio of Louis Comfort Tiffany, medallion for the elevator door in the Carson, Pirie, Scott & Co. building, Chicago, 1899; designed by George Grant Emslie.

776

In America, where the Art Nouveau movement dominated the field of architecture and the applied arts, there were distinct phases in its development. The character of the style was also affected by strong regional influences. In addition, any account of the diffusion of the style in America must take into account uniquely American forms (for example, the skyscraper). Thus the background to American Art Nouveau is one of the most complex in the history of the movement.

While on a lecture tour of America in the winter of 1882-83, Oscar Wilde included the following advice in one of his lectures:

'I find that what your people need is not so much high, imaginative art, but that which hallows the vessels of everyday use. . .'

This statement prophesied the ascent of the applied arts in the following two decades, when new ideas were rapidly assimilated because of the growth in the demand for printed information. One of the major events which promoted the development of the applied arts was the Philadelphia Centennial Exhibition (1876) commemorating American Independence. This was followed by the Chicago World Fair of 1893. In 1901 the 'Craftsman' Movement was founded and its journal *The Craftsman* began a sixteen-year run. In the same year other East Coast periodicals began publication, including *The Ladies Home Journal* and *House and Garden*. Journals had begun to appear earlier in Chicago: *House Beautiful* first appeared in 1896, in 1899 the *Fine Arts Journal* was published, and *Western Architect* started its thirty-year run in 1902. The Chicago Arts and Crafts Society had been founded in 1897, as a result of the already considerable popularity of craft goods.

The development in American furniture design between the years 1880 and 1910 is illustrative of the many factors which helped to formulate American Art Nouveau. The work of ISAAC SCOTT marks the starting point of American acceptance of European modernism. His furniture of the late 1870s bears all the hallmarks of late colonial workmanship; solidity, simplicity and clear but unostentatious decoration. However, the influence of the contemporary English Arts and Crafts Movement is also noticeable in the Gothic shapes and the conscious historicism present in the pieces. By the beginning of the 1880s, more wholly decorative pieces were made by, among others, Duncan Phyle. In these, flat surfaces are pierced by scroll-work, or replaced by wickerwork arabesques. Art Nouveau decorative motifs

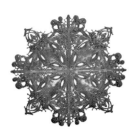

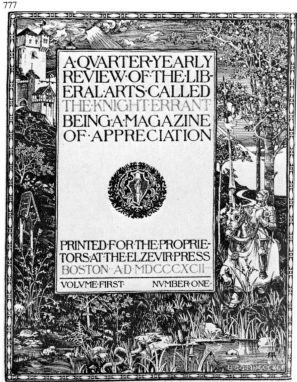

777

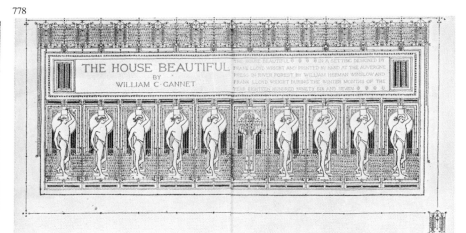

778

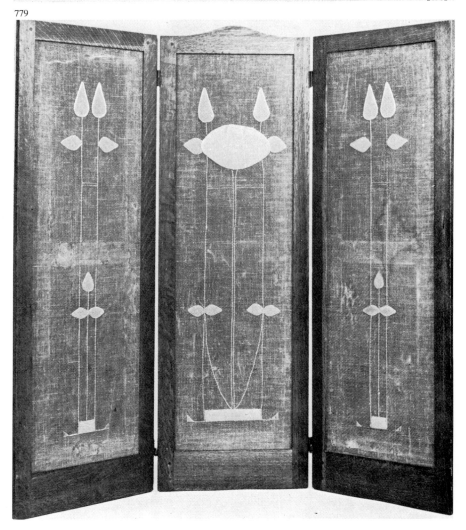

779

775—MAX BEERBOHM, 'The name of Dante Gabriel Rossetti was pronounced for the first time in the Western United States. Year: 1882; reporter: Mr. Oscar Wilde`, 1916. London, Tate Gallery.

776—Cover of *The Craftsman*, August, 1914.

   *—page 279, WILLIAM BRADLEY, ornamental inset.

777—BERTRAM GROSVENOR GOODHUE, cover of the *Knight Errant*, April, 1892.

778—Cover of *The House Beautiful*, 1897.

779—GUSTAV STICKLEY, screen, 1905.

780—ISAAC E. SCOTT, bookcase, 1875. Chicago, School of Architecture.

781—I. E. SCOTT, desk, 1879. Chicago, School of Architecture.

782—W. H. BRADLEY, cover of *The Inland Printer*, 1894.

783—W. H. BRADLEY, cover of *The Inland Printer*, 1894.

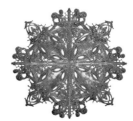

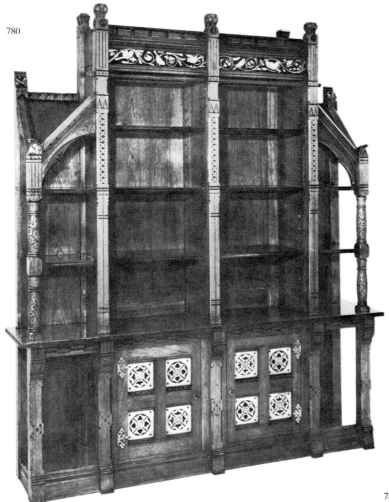

780

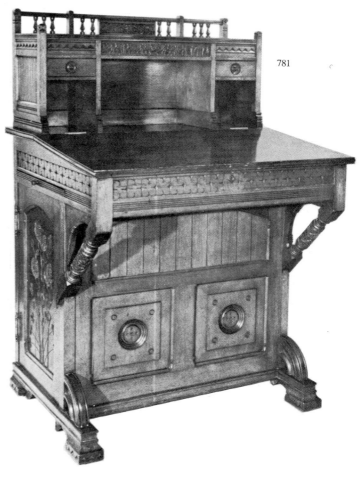

781

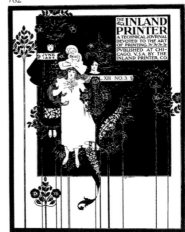

782

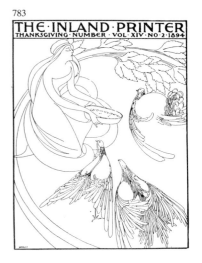

783

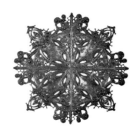

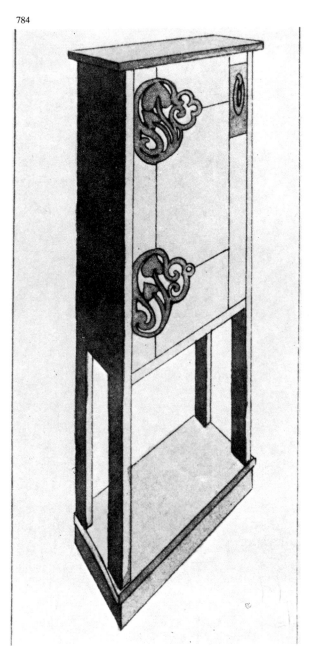

784

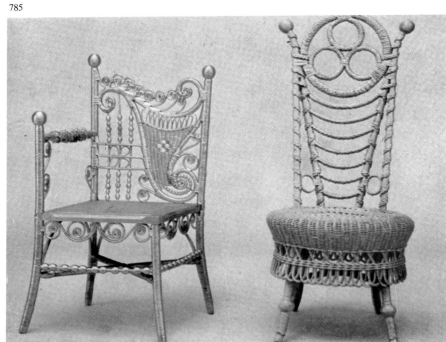

785

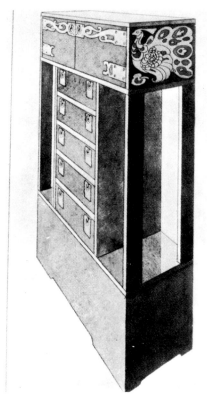

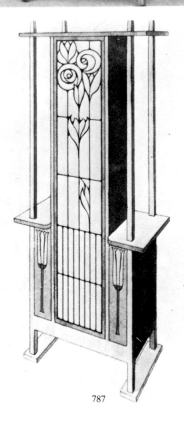

784—W. H. BRADLEY, project for a cabinet for a living room or entrance hall, 1901. New York, The Metropolitan Museum of Art.

785—Gilded wicker chair with a lyre back, designed by Duncan Phyle; and a high-back colonial chair, c. 1880.

786, 787—W. H. BRADLEY, design for a chest of drawers for a living room or entrance hall, 1901. New York, The Metropolitan Museum of Art.

786   787

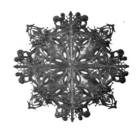

788

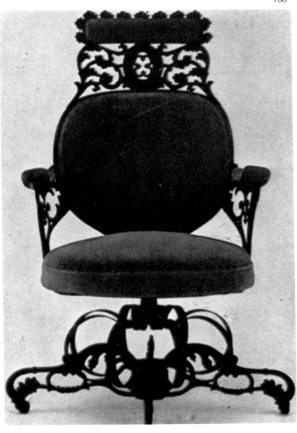

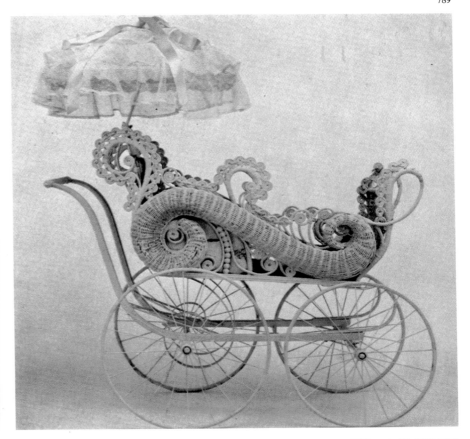

788—Revolving chair, c. 1880.
789—Indian wicker baby carriage, c. 1880.
790—W. H. BRADLEY, design for a cupboard, 1901. New York, The Metropolitan Museum of Art.
791—W. H. BRADLEY, design for a cupboard. New York, The Metropolitan Museum of Art.

On pages 284, 285
792—CHARLES ROHLFS, detail of n. 793.
793—C. ROHLFS, chest of drawers, c. 1900.
794—C. ROHLFS, chair, 1898.
795—Roycroft Group, dish.
796, 798—Roycroft Group, bookends, the first designed by Karl Kipp; the second c. 1909.
797—Roycroft Group, photograph frame designed by Frederick Kanz, c. 1910.

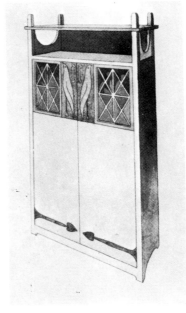

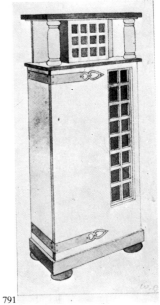

790

791

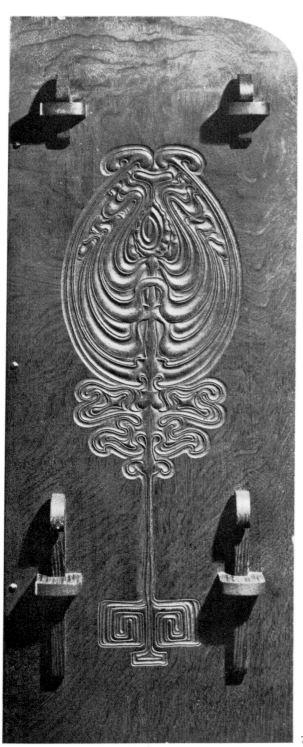

792

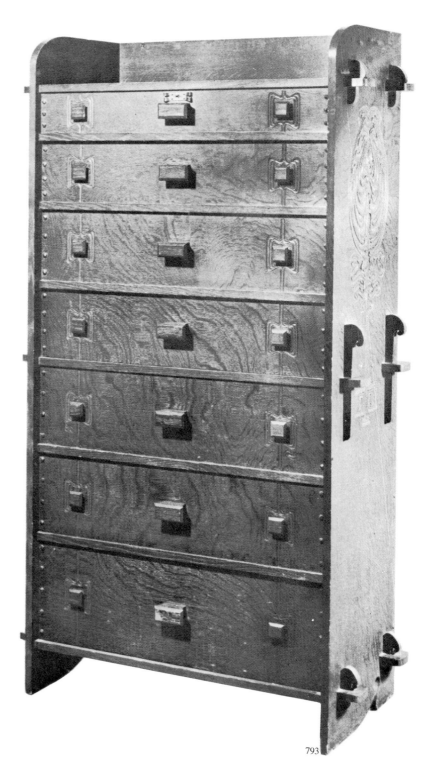

793

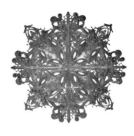

are carved on to the Arts and Crafts inspired pieces by CHARLES ROHLFS. In the work of WILLIAM BRADLEY (1868-1962), American furniture takes on a definite Art Nouveau appearance. His work is characterized by the elegant vertical lines which dominate his designs, suggesting the influence of early Mackintosh furniture or possibly a common source from within the English Arts and Crafts Movement. These pieces gain visually from the discrete areas of arabesque decoration which are often inspired by bird motifs.

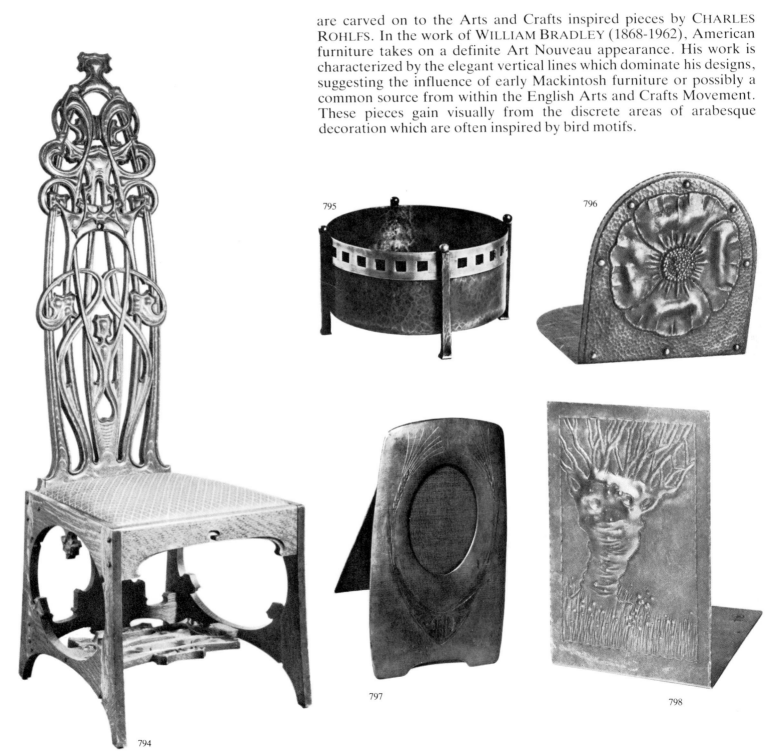

794

795

796

797

798

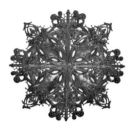

799

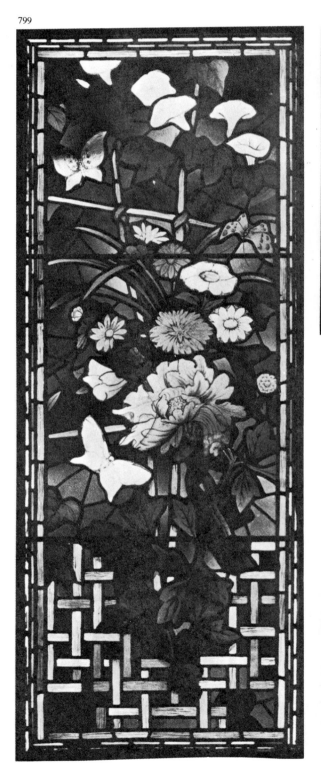

800

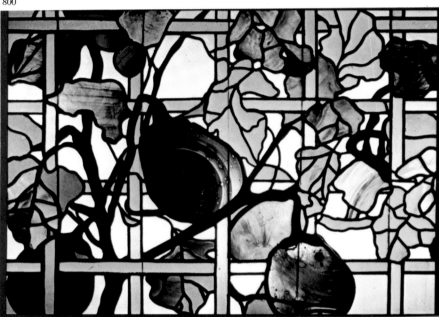

In Chicago, FRANK LLOYD WRIGHT (1869-1959) had incorporated
elegant vertical and curvilinear forms into designs for ironwork made
by him for use in his architectural practice as early as 1895. By 1904
these decorative works assumed an almost Viennese character in the
use of bold verticals and patterned surfaces. The same sensitivity to
ornamental values embellished his furniture designs. The dining table

801

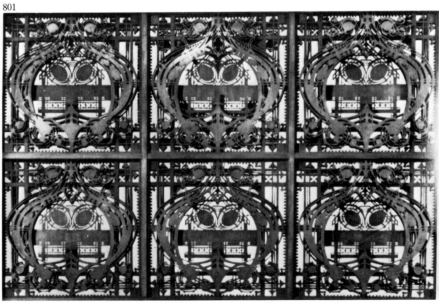

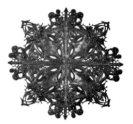

799—JOHN LA FARGE, stained-glass window, c. 1877.
800—LOUIS COMFORT TIFFANY, stained-glass window, 1879-81.
801—Louis H. Sullivan studio, a frieze designed in collaboration with Louis G. Millet, 1894; detail. Chicago, The Art Institute.
802—GEORGE GRANT ELNISLIE, chair, 1909.
803—FRANK LLOYD WRIGHT, gate, 1895. Chicago, The Art Institute.

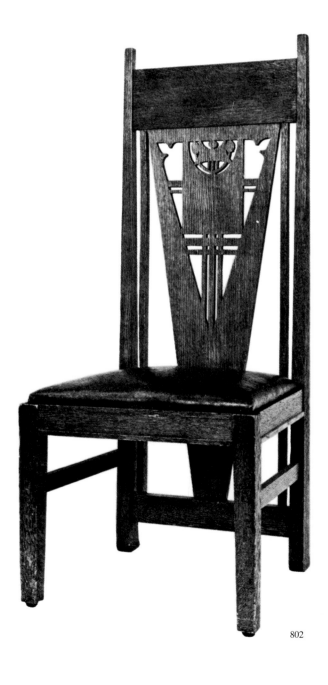

802

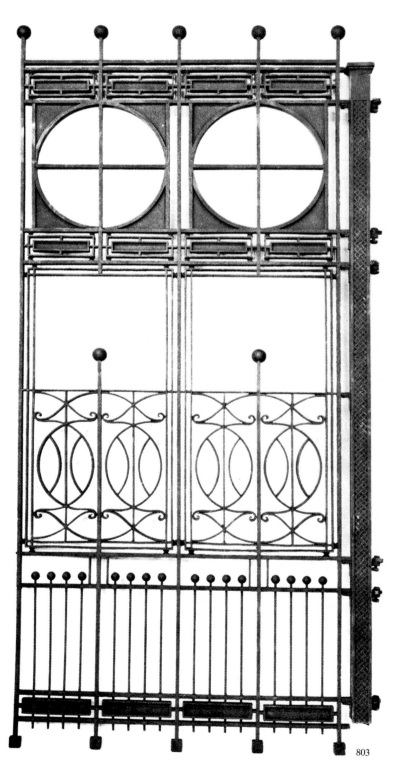

803

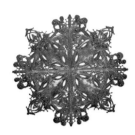

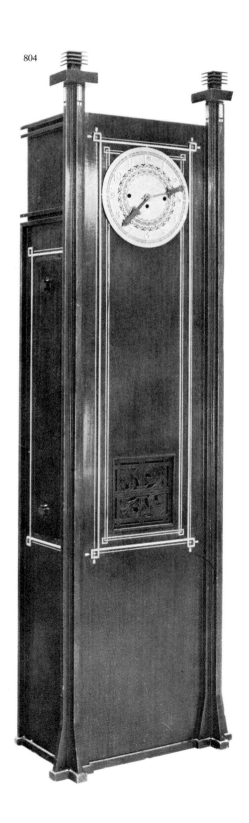
804

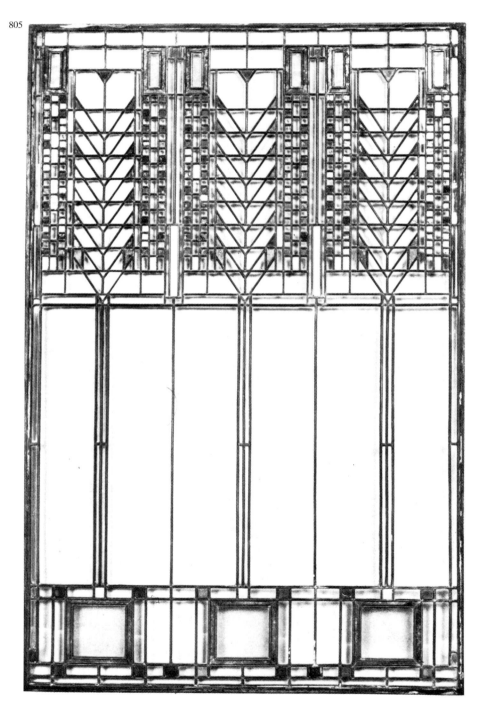
805

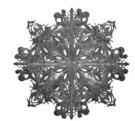

804—G. G. ELNISLIE, grandfather clock, 1912. Chicago, The Art Institute.
805—F. LLOYD WRIGHT, window, 1904. Chicago, The Art Institute.
806—F. LLOYD WRIGHT, dining table and six chairs, 1908. Chicago, The University Collection.
807—ADELAIDE ALSOP ROBINEAU, porcelain vase, 1905.
808—ARTUS VAN BRIGGLE, vase, 1902.
809—HANNA TUTT, vase, 1908.
810—L. A. MATHEUS, desk.

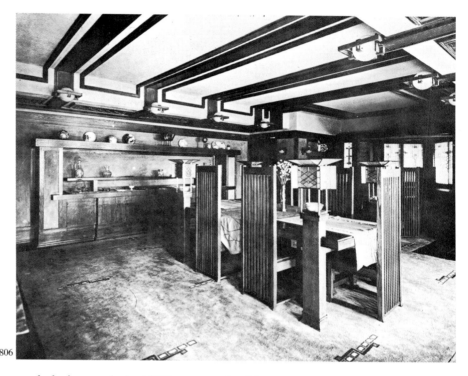

806

and chairs made in 1908 seem poised between Art Nouveau elegance and the rationalism that was to become Wright's hallmark in later years.

On the East coast, the definitive formulation of the Art Nouveau style in furniture design was produced by the ROYCROFT GROUP,

807

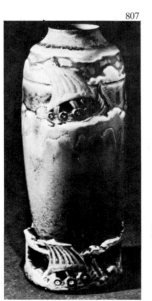

808

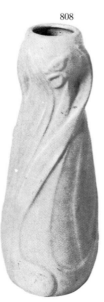

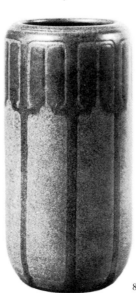

809

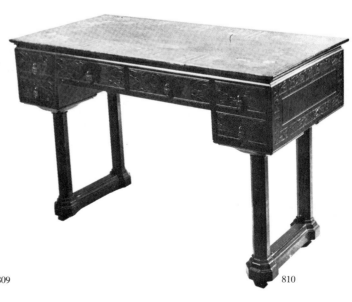

810

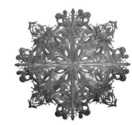

811—CHARLES SUMNER GREENE, chest of drawers, 1908.
812—Newcomb College Pottery, vase, c. 1898. Cincinnati, Art Museum.
813—GEORGE F. KENDRICK, vase, 1898-1902.
814—F. H. RHEAD, plate, 1902-04.

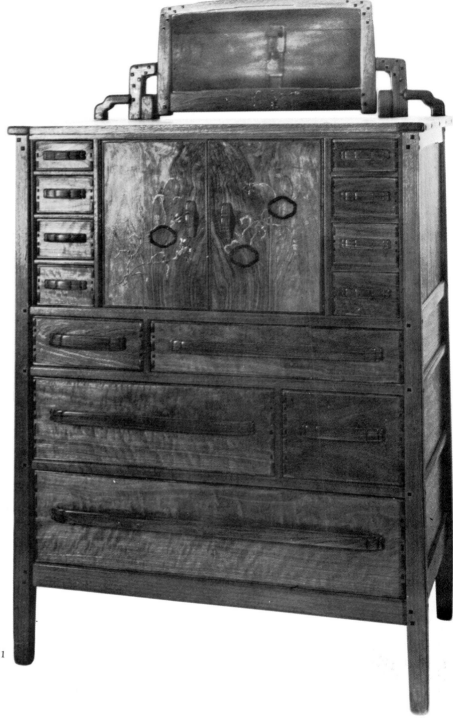

811

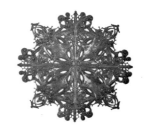

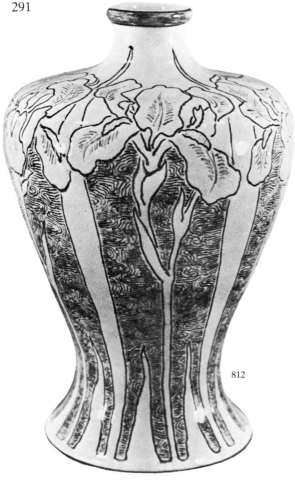

812

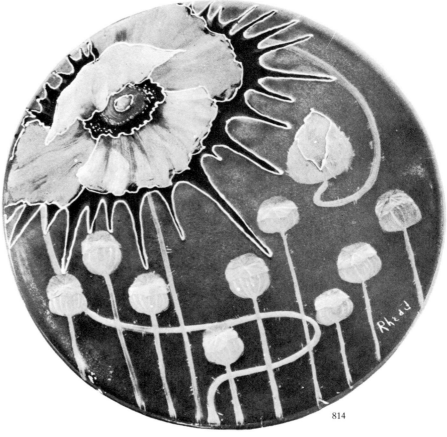

814

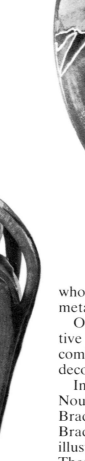

813

who were brought together by Elbert Hubbard. Their furniture and metalwork have strong shapes and heavy floral decoration.

On the West coast, furniture design's most successful representative is Charles Sumner Greene. His work of c. 1908 is essentially a combination of shapes derived from colonial furniture, with the spare decoration acquired from the later Art Nouveau style.

In graphics Bradley found the most expressive possibilities in Art Nouveau. Initially working in the linear style developed by Beardsley, Bradley quickly exploited his personal feeling for the whiplash line. Bradley's designs burst on the American public with his cover illustrations for the *Chap-book* (1893) and *The Inland Printer* (1894). These are distinguished by their elegant use of black as a foil to colour and decorative line. In other works for *The Inland Printer* (1894) and the later poster for Victor Bicycles (c. 1905) he continued to exploit the contrast of black and white in combination with the decorative value of repeated lines. In 1904 Bradley conceived the elegant covers for the *Chap-book* based on popular and children's illustration, but he endowed them with his own immaculately graceful decorative sense.

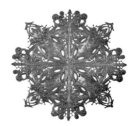

815

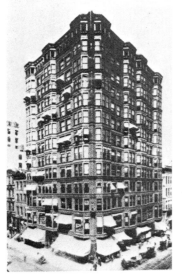

816

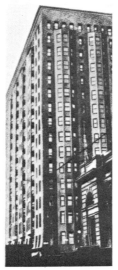

George Wharton Edwards (b. 1859) was another graphic artist whose Art Nouveau work relies on the relationship between lines and tonal areas characteristic of English illustration, but which here shows an American simplicity and economy.

America had many competent artists who worked in ceramics and glass: JOHN LA FARGE (1835-1910) is one worthy of note for his stained glass windows. However, this field is dominated by the refinement and the technical virtuosity present in the glass of LOUIS COMFORT TIFFANY (1848-1933), whose early works recall those of La Farge.

Although Tiffany's art originated in European prototypes, it became the principal model for European glassware in the last decade of the nineteenth century. Tiffany went to Europe to study painting and interior decoration. There he acquired a taste for the exotic and oriental, fashionable at the time, and which can be seen in his frequent use of motifs drawn from Japanese and Moorish art. Two examples of these influences are his interior decorations in the Bella Apartments (1880) and in the Tiffany House (1884).

817

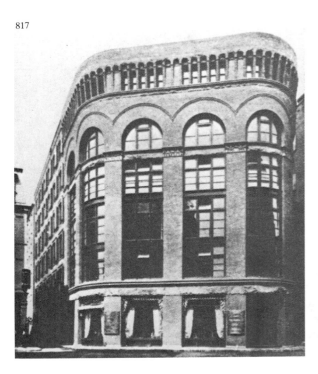

818

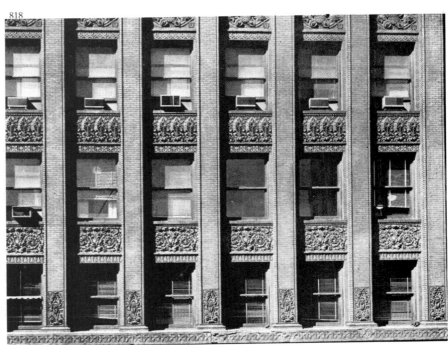

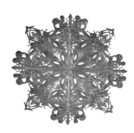

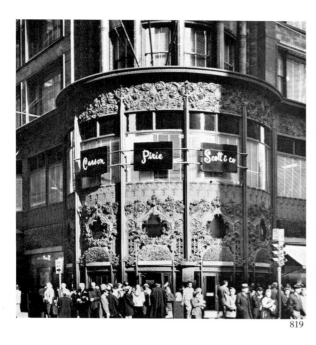

819

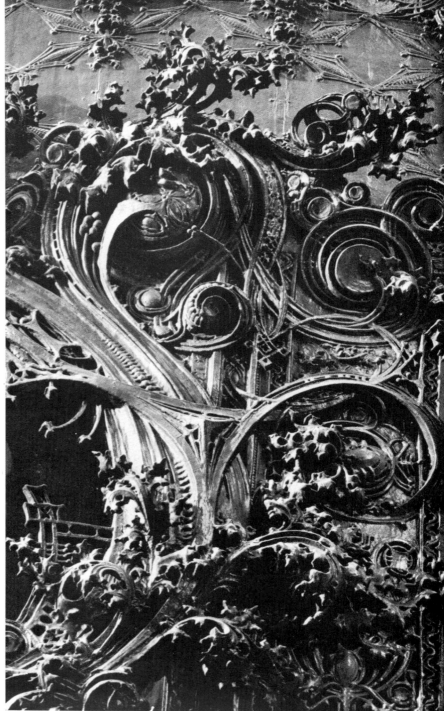

820

815—HOLABIRD & ROCHE, Tocoma Building, Chicago, 1886-87.

816—JOHN WELBORN ROOT. BURNHAM, Monadnock building, Chicago, 1883.

817—HENRY H. RICHARDSON, Harnes Pray Building, Boston.

818—LOUIS H. SULLIVAN, Wainwright Building, St Louis, 1890-91; detail of the facade.

   *—page 292, L. H. SULLIVAN, *The Germ as the Seat of Power*, ornamental inset.

819—L. H. SULLIVAN, Carson, Pirie, Scott & Co. building (now Schlesinger & Mayer), Chicago, 1899-1904; detail of the entrance.

820—L. H. SULLIVAN, Carson, Pirie, Scott & Co. building, Chicago; detail of the decoration on the entrance.

On page 394

821—L. H. SULLIVAN, medallion (see n. 774 and 819).

822—L. H. SULLIVAN, Guaranty Building, Chicago, 1894-95; detail of the elevator shaft.

823—L. H. SULLIVAN, Auditorium, Chicago, 1886-90.

824—L. H. SULLIVAN, Auditorium, Chicago; interior.

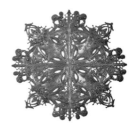

821

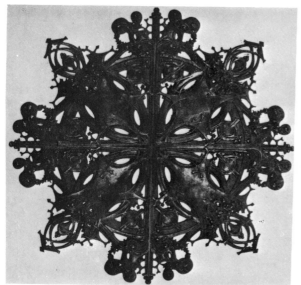

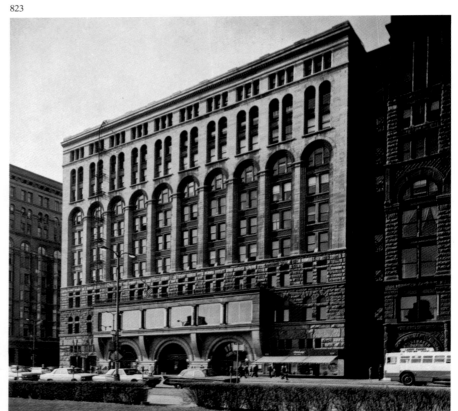
823

822

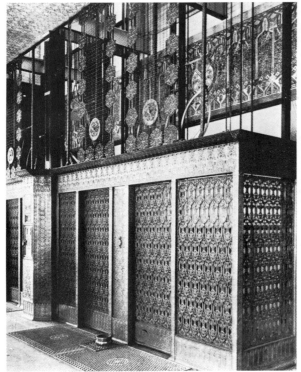

824

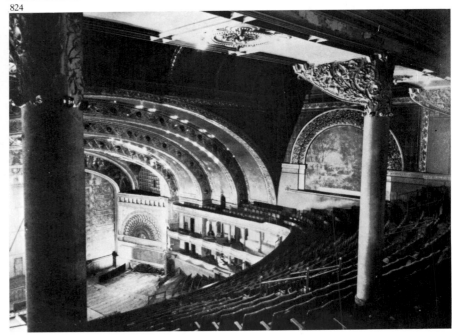

825—L. H. SULLIVAN, Bayard Building, New York, 1897-98; detail of the facade.
826—L. H. SULLIVAN, Guaranty Building, Chicago, 1894-95; detail of the facade.

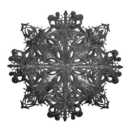

825

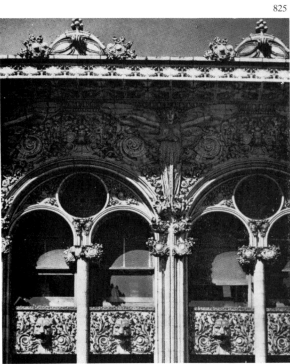

827—L. H. SULLIVAN, Plate XVI from *A System of Architectural Ornament According with a Philosophy of Man's Powers*, Chicago, 1924.

826

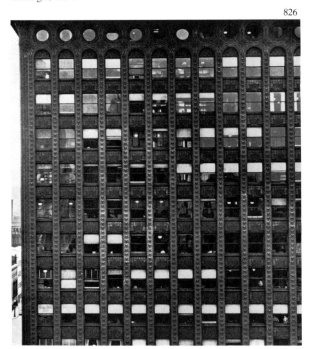

827

IMPROMPTU

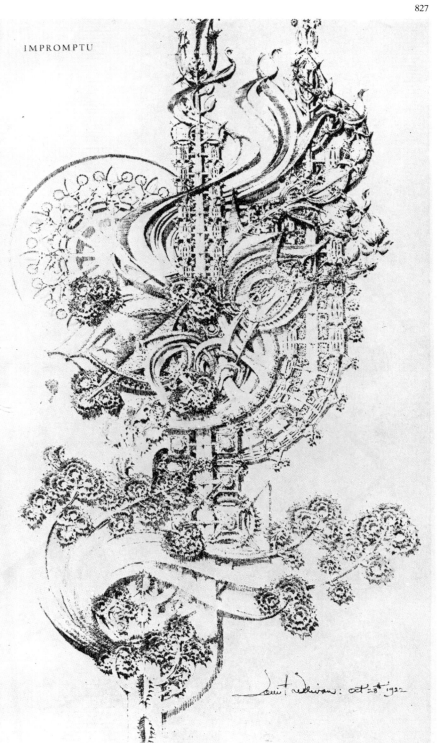

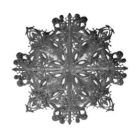

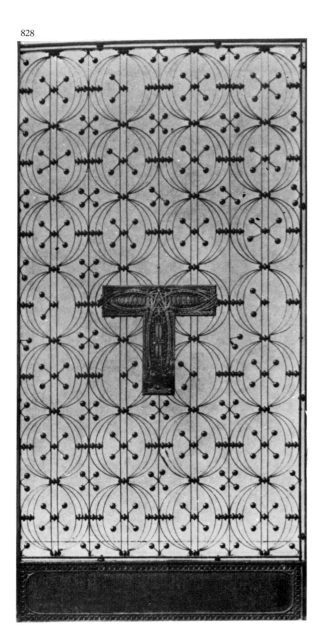

828

Tiffany's achievements in glassware have been compared to Loïe Fuller's dancing. Both are characterized by their swirling rhythmic vitality and opalescence. In 1880 Tiffany patented what he called *Favrile* glass, or feverish, animated glass, which gives the glass a mobility of colour. This illusion of surface movement is achieved by coloured patterns whose lines increase the sense of curvature and give the objects a wonderful sheen.

Tiffany's slightly later work concentrated on combining enamelled glass or glass of different transparencies with decorative metal supports. One of the finest examples of his work in this medium is his famous Dragonfly table lamp (c. 1900). Later in his career Tiffany also designed jewels which he saw as personalized works of art. Although they lack the arabesque rhythm of Lalique's jewellery, their geometrical settings often carry beautiful areas of iridescent enamels, arranged in intricate mosaic patterns.

829

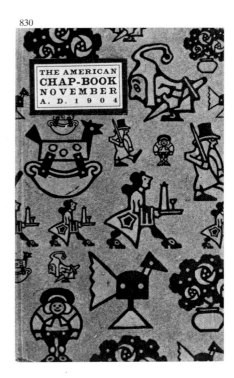

830

828—L. H. SULLIVAN, linear decoration on terracotta.
829, 830—W. H. BRADLEY, covers for *The American Chap Book*, October, November, 1904.
  *—page 296, THEO VAN RYSSELBERGHE, ornamental inset from *Histoires souveraines*, by V. de l'Isle Adam, 1899, Brussels.
831—SCOTSON CLARK, poster for *The New York Recorder*, 1895.
832—W. H. BRADLEY, poster for Victor Bicycles, c. 1905.
833—GEORGE WHARTON EDWARDS, illustration from *Epithalamion* by Edmund Spencer, New York, 1896.

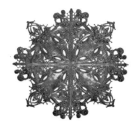

831

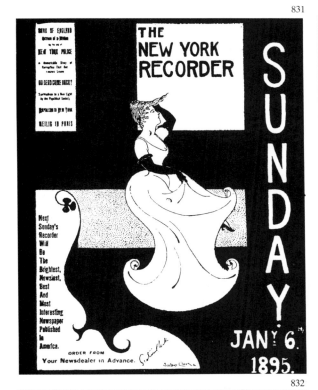

832

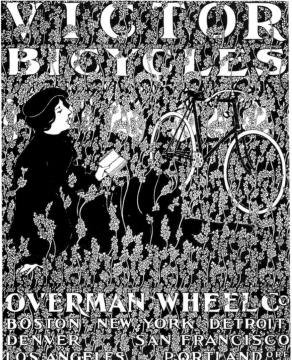

833

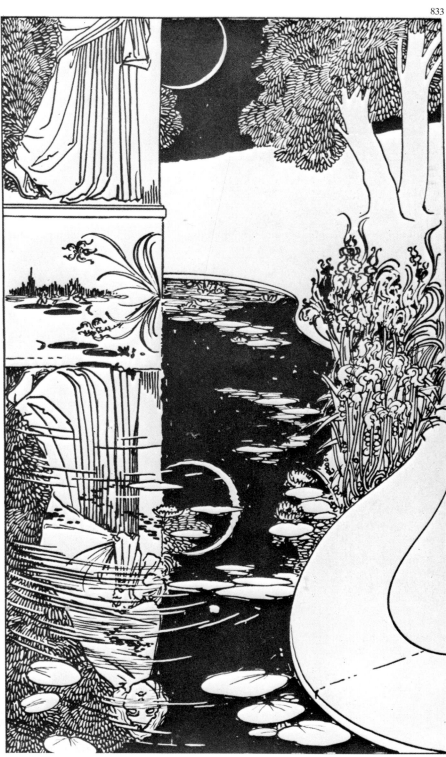

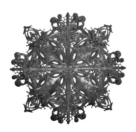

Of painting and architecture, the two major arts, architecture received the most beneficial stimulus from the Art Nouveau Movement. The most noteworthy representative of decorative painting in the period is ALBERT PINKHAM RYDER (1847-1917). Between 1890 and 1910, Ryder produced works which portrayed an imaginative allegorical world, which depended on the work of Redon and the

834
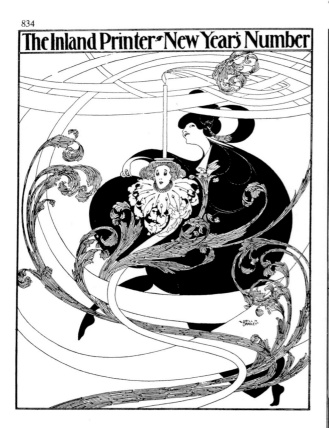

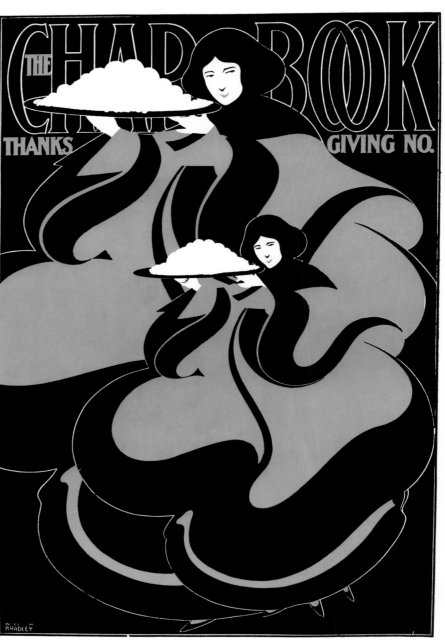

834—W. H. BRADLEY, cover for *The Inland Printer*, 1895.
835—W. H. BRADLEY, cover for *The Chap Book*, c. 1893.
836—F. LLOYD WRIGHT, Unity Church, Oak Park, Chicago, 1906-07; interior.

835

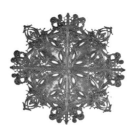

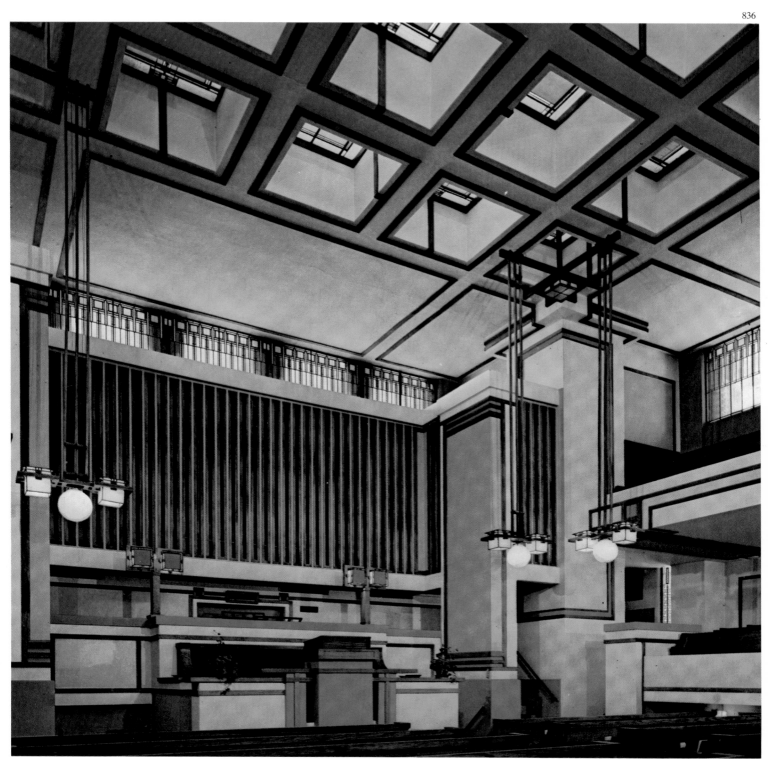

837—F. LLOYD WRIGHT, The Imperial Hotel, Tokyo, 1916-22 (demolished); view from the courtyard.
838—Original design of 1889 for the Mozart Gardens, Chicago.
839—F. LLOYD WRIGHT, Wolf Lake Resort, Illinois; design of 1895.
840—F. LLOYD WRIGHT, McAfee House, Chicago, Lake Michigan; design of 1894.

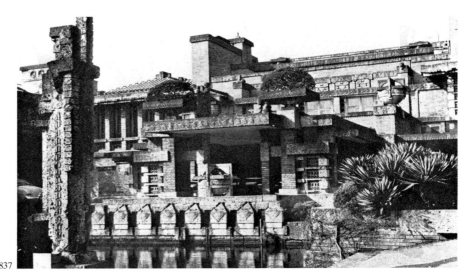

837

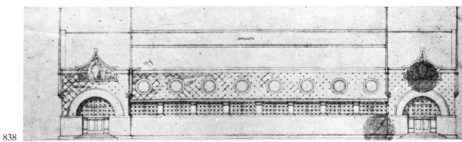

838

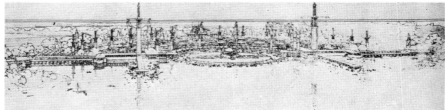

839

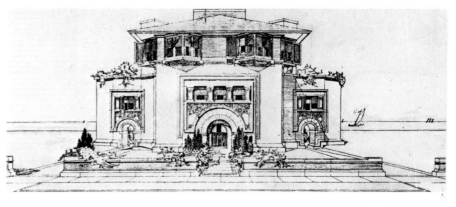

840

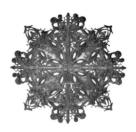

Symbolists. His major painting is possibly *The Horse and Death* (1895-1910), which depicts Death riding through a barren landscape while a snake slithers in the foreground.

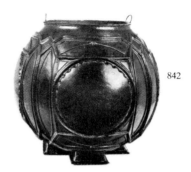

842

In architecture two figures dominate the period and both were Chicago architects. They are LOUIS H. SULLIVAN (1856-1924) and FRANK LLOYD WRIGHT (1869-1959). Although other architects were experimenting with the skyscraper and its decorative potential in the 1880s, it was Sullivan who produced the most definitive version of the new building type.

Sullivan's early buildings show a desire to impose a Renaissance architectural language onto modern forms. His auditoria (1886-90) have tall arcades enclosing windows above rusticated lower storeys, a

841

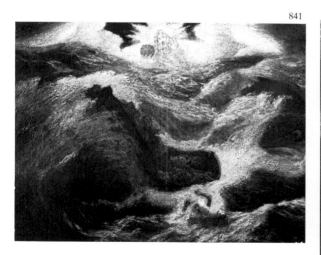

841—ALBERT PINKHAM RYDER, *Jonah*, 1890. Washington, Smithsonian Institution.
842—F. LLOYD WRIGHT, urn, c. 1898-99. Chicago, coll. M. & W. R. Hesbrouck.
843—A. PINKHAM RYDER , *The Horse and Death*, 1895-1910. Cleveland, Museum of Art.

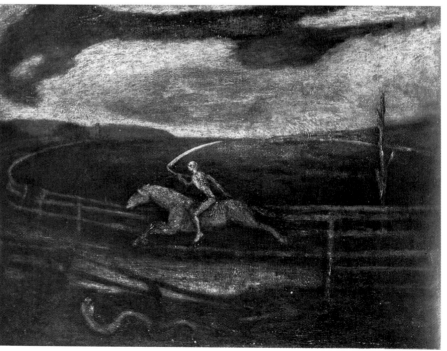

843

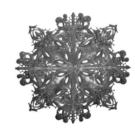

844

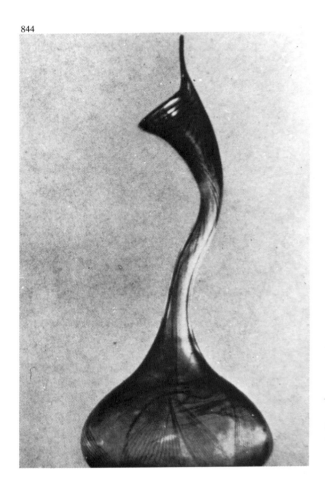

845

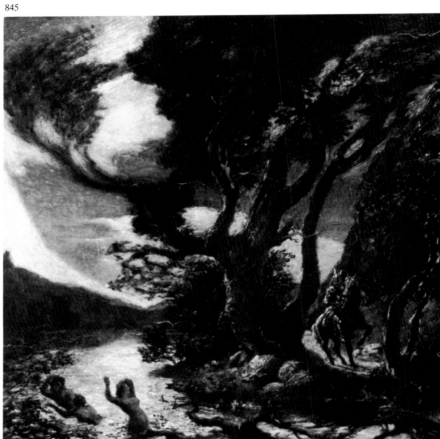

844—L. C. TIFFANY, vase in *Favrile* glass, c. 1900. Paris, Musée des Arts Décoratifs.
845—A. PINKHAM RYDER, *Siegfried and the Daughters of the Rhine* c. 1910. Washington, National Gallery of Art.
846—L. C. TIFFANY, *Spring*, 1898.
847—L. C. TIFFANY, vase in *Favrile* glass, c. 1900.
848—L. C. TIFFANY, plate in enamelled copper.
849—L. C. TIFFANY, vase, c. 1900.

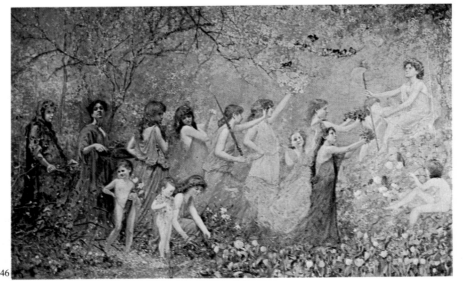

846

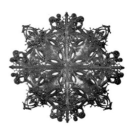

847

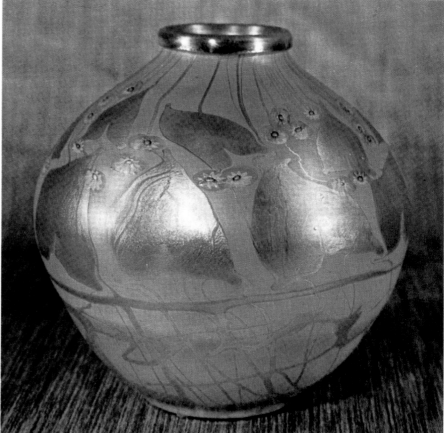

849

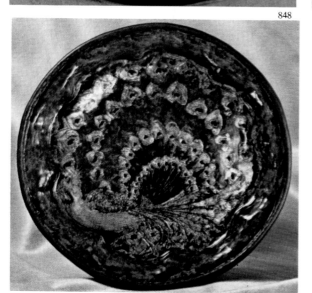

848

scheme which derives from the Roman palaces of Raphael and Giulio Romano (16th c.). On the interior however, he was already using floral ornament. These details found their way onto the exterior in his next important work, the Wainwright Building (1890-91), where he used the same structural scheme. When he built the Bayard Building (1897-98) his taste for highly ornamented facades had increased. In this building the cornice and windows are surrounded by an exuberance of floral and curvilinear carving that recalls the Venetian Rococo architecture in its fine details and rhythmic patterning. Sullivan derived his preference for this type of ornament from his teacher, Frank Furness, and from his admiration for the nineteenth-century decorative theorist, Owen Jones. Like Jones, whose *Grammar of Ornament* (1856) was a very successful pattern book for architectural decoration, Sullivan published his own decorative inventions in *A System of Architectural Ornament* (1924).

Sullivan's most advanced exercise in architectural ornamentation was the entrance he designed for the Carson, Pirie and Scott Co. store (1899-1904). Here the Rococo model is entirely absorbed in a more

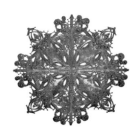

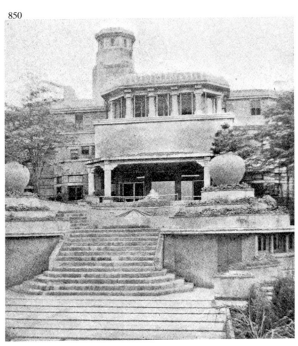

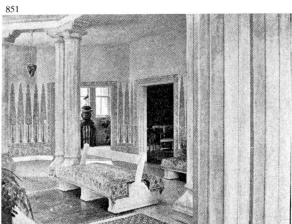

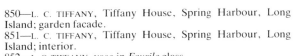

850—L. C. TIFFANY, Tiffany House, Spring Harbour, Long Island; garden facade.
851—L. C. TIFFANY, Tiffany House, Spring Harbour, Long Island; interior.
852—L. C. TIFFANY, vase in *Favrile* glass.
853—L. C. TIFFANY, series of vases in *Favrile* glass, 1895-1905.

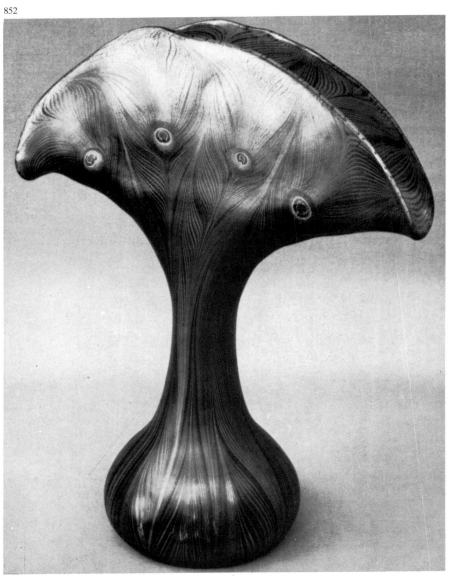

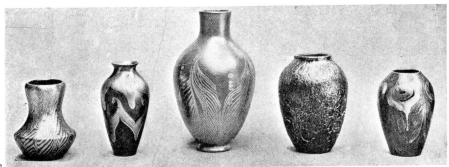

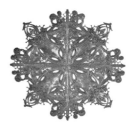

854

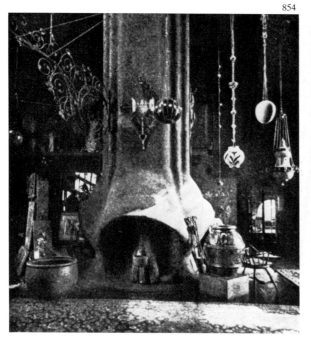

854—L. C. TIFFANY, fireplace in the Bella Apartments in New York.
855—L. C. TIFFANY, window in 'American' opaline glass. New York, The Museum of Modern Art.
856—L. C. TIFFANY, fireplace in the Tiffany apartment, 72nd Street, New York, 1883.

855

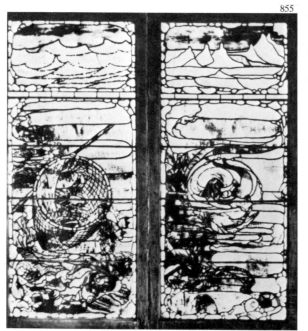

856

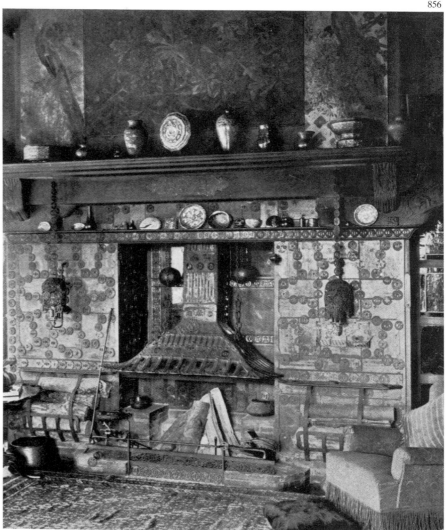

modern taste for the arabesque line, but the ornament remains historicist in its complexity and detail.

Frank Lloyd Wright was trained in the Sullivan office, but his work is more emancipated from both Art Nouveau and historicism. However, in a series of designs which he made in the 1890s, a very strong feeling for decorative surfaces emerges, although this is accompanied by an already highly developed sense of clearly expressed volume and space. A good example of this is his project for the McAfee House of 1894. His early maturity is exemplified by the Unity Church at Oak Park (1906-07). The design is not totally rationalist because here the rectangular planes are organized to give a unified decorative scheme reminiscent of the best Viennese and Glasgow architecture.

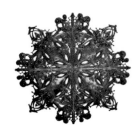

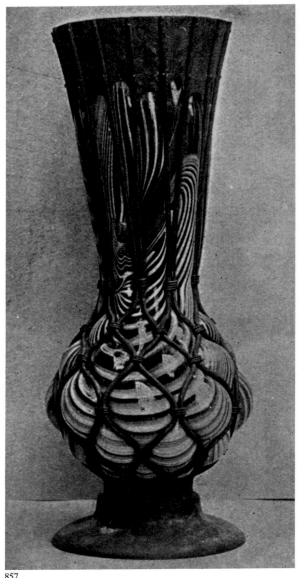

857

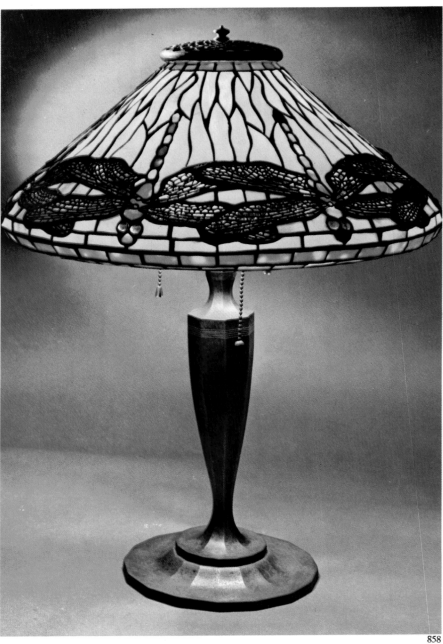

858

857—L. C. TIFFANY, vase in metal and *Favrile* glass.
858—TIFFANY STUDIOS, table lamp with a 'dragonfly' design in
Favrile glass and bronze. Chicago, coll. Mr & Mrs Sidney
Lewis.
859—L. C. TIFFANY, table lamp in *Favrile* glass, mounted on
copper.
860—L. C. TIFFANY, necklace made of gold, enamel and gems.
861—L. C. TIFFANY, 'Oyster Boy' stained-glass window, 1905.
862—L. C. TIFFANY, *Favrile* glass trademark.

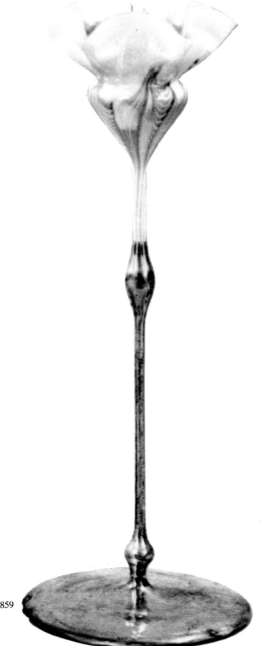

859

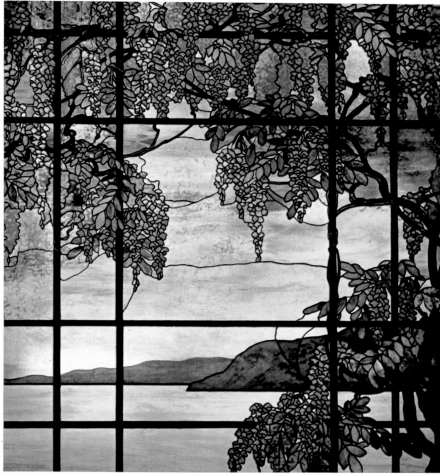

861

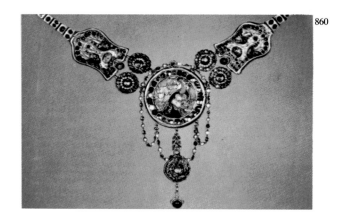

860

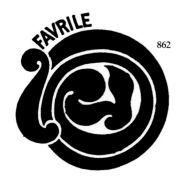

862

16-Italy

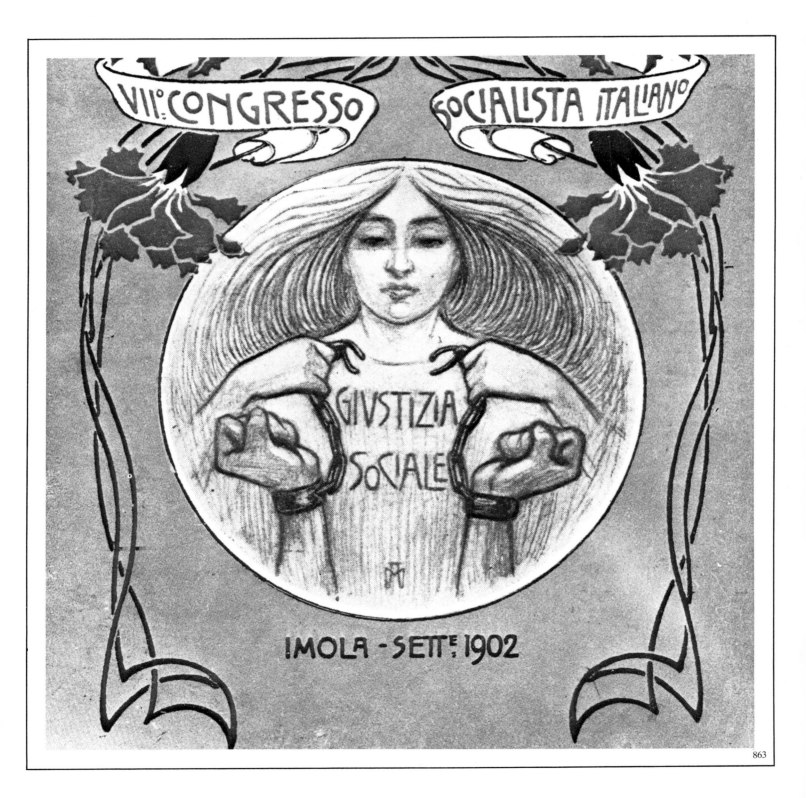

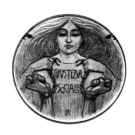

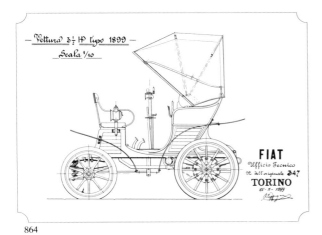

864

In Italy, Art Nouveau came to be known as Stile Liberty, which took its name from the famous London department store which sold oriental and Art Nouveau goods. The name also linked it with ideological overtones consistent with the rise of nationalism in the country during the last quarter of the nineteenth century. The resonances behind the name itself reflect the ambiguous background to the rise of the style in Italy. Art Nouveau never became a truly popular or democratic style, and far from being an essentially nationalistic movement, its various manifestations were associated strongly with the regional centres producing them. In fact, it was identified by the general public in Italy as bourgeois taste.

In Italy, the plastic arts belonged to a wider cultural background not entirely sympathetic to Art Nouveau taste. In literature there was a growing interest in socially relevant or didactic works which were fundamentally hostile to the aestheticism of Art Nouveau. The musical scene was dominated by the late Romantic sentimentality of Puccini, whose interest in the Orient was at least sympathetic to Art Nouveau. Against this very fluid situation in the arts the Italians began to look to Continental Art Nouveau for inspiration in the 1890s. The immediate background to the rise of the Stile Liberty was the influx of German and Austrian capital and influence into Italy after the Triple Alliance in 1882. This set the scene for the Secessionist style to become an important element of Italian Art Nouveau in later years. Another imported influence was the founding in Rome in 1885 of the group In Arte Libertas, whose artistic and ideological models were Morris and the Pre-Raphaelites.

863—and symbol of Chapter 16, pp. 308-343 – A. MAJANI, poster for the VII Congress of the Italian Socialist Party, Imola, 1902.
864—Fiat 3, 1/2 HP, 1899, drawing.
865—EDOARDO GIOIA, *Spring*, illustration for *The Studio*, 1901.

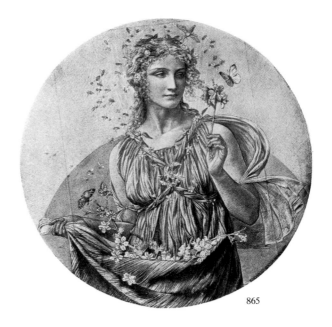

865

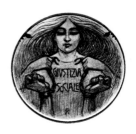

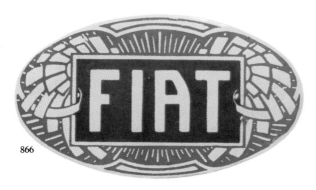

866

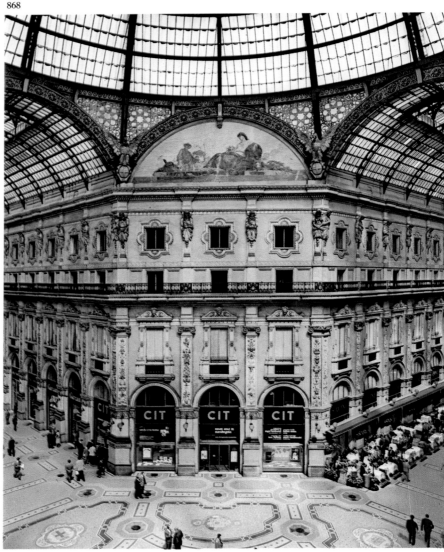

868

866—FIAT trademark.
867—FIAT licence plate.
868—GIUSEPPE MENGONI, Vittorio Emmanuele II Gallery, Milan, 1863-67.

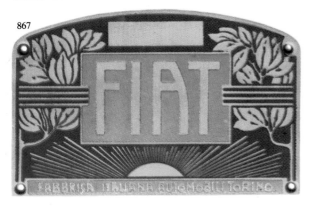

867

Giulio Aristide Sartorio, Edoardo Gioia and the other members of the In Arte Libertas group were unable to give Art Nouveau a proper theoretical basis, and this often led to a lack of clarity in their objectives. This was exemplified in the work of D'Annunzio. Other members, Fogazzaro and Gozzano, were less preoccupied by its aestheticism and more by moralistic or 'spiritualistic' concerns, while Giacosa was primarily absorbed with the social injustices then prevailing.

The most tenuous cultural links with the Art Nouveau movement were those of a group of writers and poets, including De Bosis, Onofri, Corazzini and Giaconi. Their lack of ideological commitment to and concern with the expression of intimate feelings and experi-

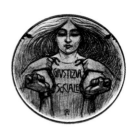

ences gave them more in common with the French Parnassians and the international Symbolist movement than with their Italian contemporaries.

The widely divergent tastes of society at that time were also reflected in the theatre: the social realism of Giacosa, Sem Benelli and Niccodemi contrasting with the melodrama in the work of Puccini, whose achievements were tempered by the influence of Post-Romanticism and 'orientalist' aesthetic ideals.

The highly complex situation surrounding this particular period of Italian artistic achievement has not been given serious critical appraisal until recent years. Most of this research has been done by Italian scholars, as foreign publications have rarely attempted to examine the Italian Art Nouveau movement in either a serious or systematic way. In October 1974 an International Conference devoted to the Italian Art Nouveau movement indicated the number of

869—G. ROSTER, glasshouse in the gardens of the Tuscan Horticultural Society, Florence, 1879.
*—page 311, RAIMONDO D'ARONCO, sketch for the pavilion at the Turin Exhibition, 1902.

On pages 312, 313
870—ALBERTO MARTINI, cover for *Poesia* by Benelli, Marinetti and Ponti.
871—D. CAMBELLOTTI, poster for *Il divenire Sociale*, 1907.
   *—page 312 – design for *Novissima*, 1901.
872—R. D'ARONCO, central pavilion at the Turin Exhibition, 1902.
873—R. D'ARONCO, tomb and library at Yldiz, project, 1905.
874—R. D'ARONCO, mosque in Karakeny Square, Galata, 1903.
875—R. D'ARONCO, design for an entrance to the Turin Exhibition, 1902.

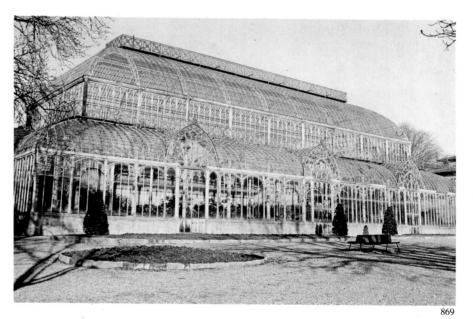

869

scholars involved in this area, and resulted in the creation of the *Archivi del Liberty Italiano*. Relevant documentation is being gathered and collated in a constructive attempt to make up for past neglect. This volume does not allow for a comprehensive discussion

on the total current knowledge available and will summarize the main aspects of the overall scene, concentrating on the important centres of influence and the main personalities.

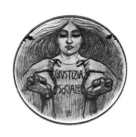

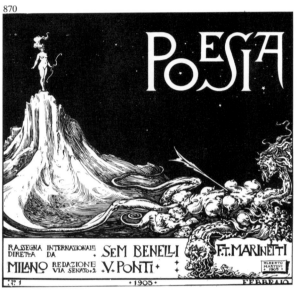

870

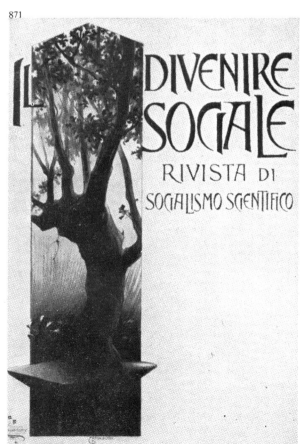

871

The art magazines of the 1890s reflect the impact of the new taste. The important *Arte Italiana Decorativa e Industriale* (1890-1914) which appeared early in the decade, was a traditionalist magazine and it set the tone for similar periodicals. However, several new magazines began to appear which sought to promote modernist tendencies. Among these were *Emporium*, produced by the Bergamo Institute of Graphic Arts from 1895; *L'Arte decorativa moderna*, published in Turin from 1902 and *L'Architettura Italiana*, which began publication in 1905. One magazine, *L'Italia che ride*, published in Bologna in 1900, varied from the others by way of its socialist tendencies, and it contained in its short life some of the most important graphic work produced by the movement. With its ideology based on secularism and international socialism, it was completely opposed to the more decadent aspects of the Pre-Raphaelite influence.

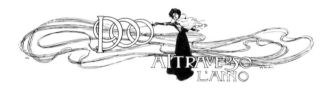

Novissima, under the editorship of Edoardo De Fonseca, was published in both Milan and Rome and underlined the expansionist decentralizing nature of Art Nouveau in Italy. Turin, Milan, Rome and the area of Emilia-Romagna all became major centres in their own right.

Among the first centres to foster the new style was Turin, which had a long tradition of innovative architecture. In 1902 the International Exhibition was held there and it was a showcase for many fine buildings designed by RAIMONDO D'ARONCO (1857-1932). These included not only some of the less important structures, but also the main pavilion. These structures show D'Aronco to be completely free from any trace of romantic medievalism (e.g. the Porta Terraglia in Milan which he restored in 1882), or eclecticism (evident in his sketches for the Ponte Maria Teresa and the facade for the main pavilion of the first Turin International Exhibition of 1890, and later for the exhibition at Udine in 1903). These buildings, for the large part, are conceived in a style that is close to Secessionist architecture, and they emphasize the volume of buildings by massing simple

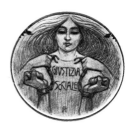

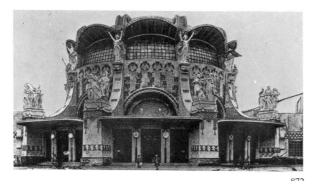

872

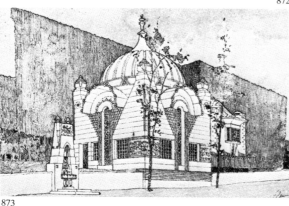

873

geometric shapes. However, D'Aronco adds rhythm to the structure by applying rich decoration. Sometimes his preference for large, open curves gives his work an almost Expressionist character. In his later work, D'Aronco developed certain motifs drawn from Islamic architecture (he worked for a time in Istanbul) to create the delicate and refined decorative architecture which can be seen in his design for a mosque in the Karakeuy Square in Galata (1903).

Another Turin architect associated with Art Nouveau was PIETRO FENOGLIO (1865-1927). His most definitive statement of the style is his own house (1902). Here the characteristic floral line of French and

874

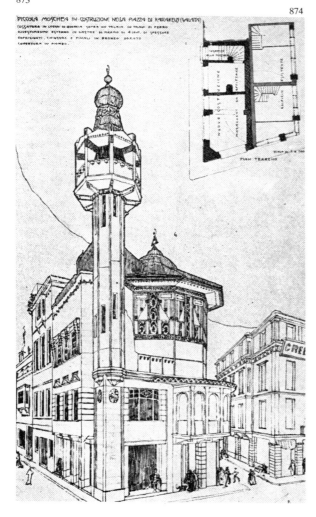

875

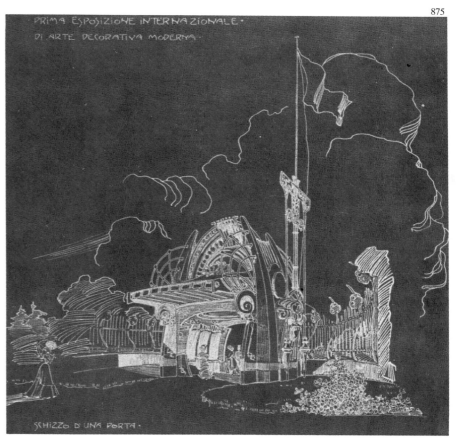

Belgian Art Nouveau architecture is expressed on the surface. The same interest in the decorative properties of the floral line is evident in the work of E. Velati-Bellini, whose work also contains references to the geometry of later Secessionist architecture. A similar combination of an ordered, planar structure with rich and elaborate ornament operates in the buildings of Antonio Vandone, whose Maffei House was decorated with ironwork designed by ALESSANDRO MAZZUCO-

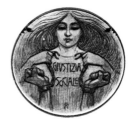

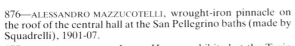

876

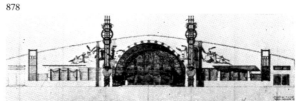

878

879

876—ALESSANDRO MAZZUCOTELLI, wrought-iron pinnacle on the roof of the central hall at the San Pellegrino baths (made by Squadrelli), 1901-07.

877—E. VELATI-BELLINI, Lauro House, exhibited at the Turin Exhibition, 1902.

878—R. D'ARONCO, The Art Pavilion, National Exhibition in Udine, 1903.

879—PIETRO FENOGLIO, Fenoglio House, Turin, 1902; detail.

877

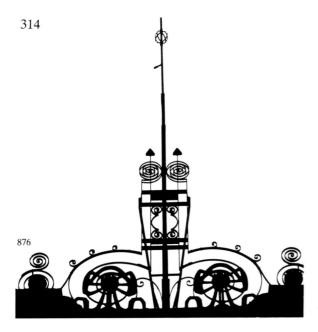

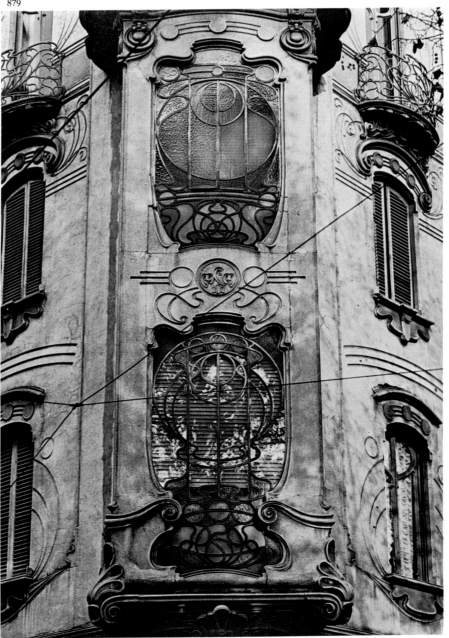

878

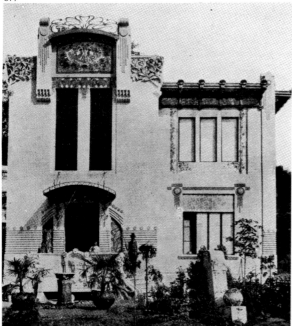

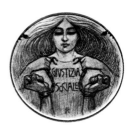

TELLI (1865-1938). Mazzucotelli provided ironwork for many buildings throughout Italy, after he had acquired Defendente Oriani's factory in Milan in 1891. His taut and elegant productions are the finest examples of Italian architectural decorative ironwork of the period, reflecting a uniquely expressive energy that gives an added dimension to the buildings with which he was involved.

Also working in Turin was the architect Alfredo Premoli, who designed the headquarters building for FIAT in Corso Dante, and

880—GIUSEPPE SOMMARUGA, Castiglioni Palace, Milan, 1903.

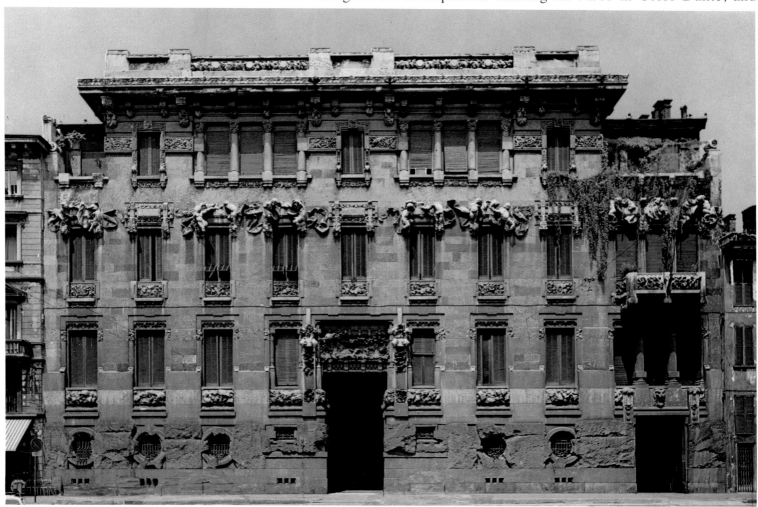

880

On pages 316, 317
881, 882—G. SOMMARUGA, details of the windows in the Castiglioni Palace, Milan, 1903.
883—ANTONIO VANDONE, Maffei House, Turin; details (reliefs by Alloati and wrought iron by Mazzucotelli).
884—ULISSE STACCHINI, project for Milan central station, 1902.
885—G. SOMMARUGA, detail of the railings of the Villa Faccanini-Romeo (Columbus Clinic), Milan, 1912-13.

Annibale Rigotti who worked in Cagliari on the *Palazzo Comunale* (1914), and in Bangkok on the *Palazzo del Trono* (The Throne Palace) on which he collaborated with the ceramics specialist Galileo Chini.

Another Lombard architect of considerable talent was GIUSEPPE SOMMARUGA (1867-1917). His Palazzo Castiglioni (1903) in Milan,

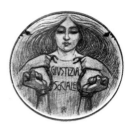

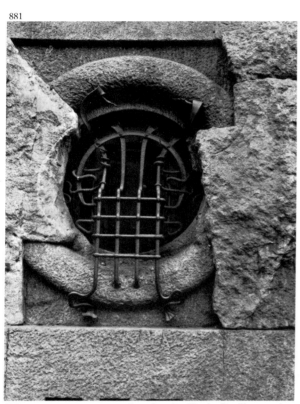

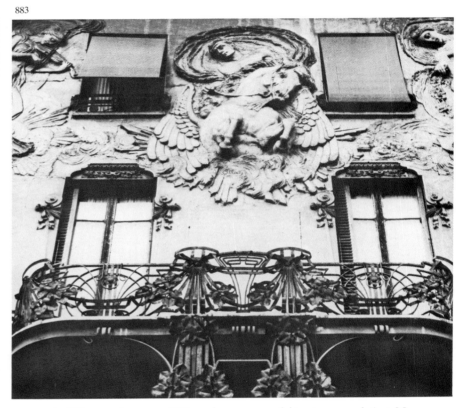

886—ERNESTO BASILE, project for the Florio Pavilion at the Milan Exhibition, 1906.
887—CALLIGARI'S WORKSHOP, railings in Udine, illustrated in *Per l'Arte*, n.II, 1909.
*—page 317, R. D'ARONCO, project for a pavilion at the Turin Exhibition, 1902.

was a brilliant mixture of Renaissance architecture and Art Nouveau decorative elements. The floral ornament and the putti above the windows add vitality to the dignity of the whole structure.

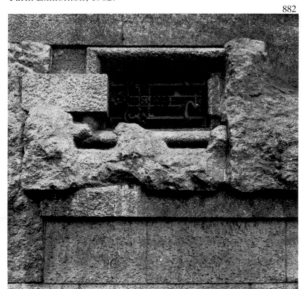

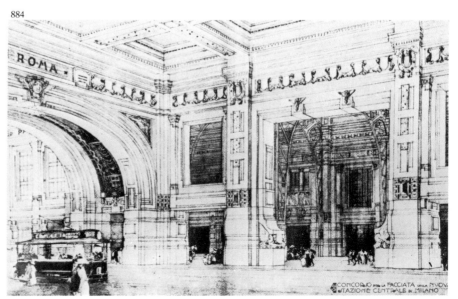

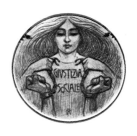

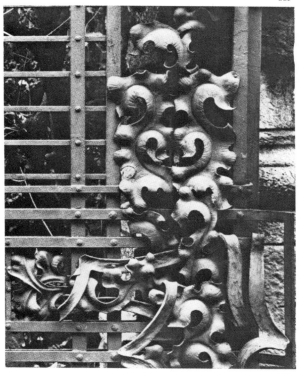
885

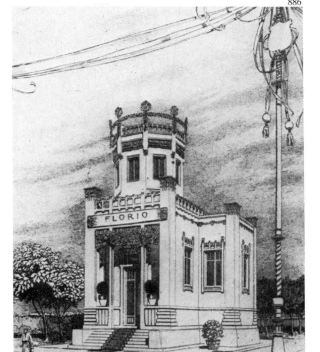
886

Sommaruga's other works include the beautiful Villa Romeo (1908), which is now the *Clinica Columbus*. Among his contemporaries working in Milan at the same time were the architects Alfredo Campanini and Luigi Broggi. Many of their buildings are enhanced by the use of ironwork from the studio of Mazzucotelli. Sebastiano Locati and Gino Coppedè were also in Milan, the latter involved with the International Exhibition of 1906, which was to coincide with the opening of the Sempione Tunnel. Their work was distributed throughout Lombardy, but sadly much of it, in Varese for example, was destroyed during the Second World War.

A competition for the design of a new main railway terminus was held in 1911-12, but it was a Florentine architect, Ulisse Stacchini, and not a Milanese who won the commission. As well as the terminus, which was eventually erected between 1925 and 1931, Stacchini was also responsible for the design of the Monumental Cemetery in Monza.

A more overtly Secessionist style pervades the work of the Milanese architect Giovanni Battista Bossi, whose Galimberti House (1905) is decorated with tiles manufactured by the Ceramica Lombarda. The vertical emphasis of the building and its delicate ironwork combine with the visually compelling tiling to produce a building close to Otto Wagner's work in Vienna. GINO COPPEDÈ (1886-1927) also worked in Genoa, alongside Guzzoni, who designed the Casa Zanelli (1908); Dario Carbone, who produced designs for the new Palazzo della Borsa (1912); and Giuseppe Bregante. Here, Coppedè designed the Mackensie Castle (Castello Mac Kensie, 1890). However, Coppedè's most memorable work was done in Rome were he built the eclectic Coppedè Village. This complex of buildings, whose ornaments incorporate motifs from medieval, Renaissance and Baroque styles, creates an occasionally bewildering but always exciting impact.

Bologna was a city whose cultural atmosphere was very susceptible

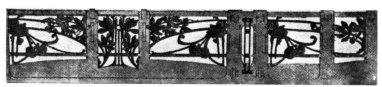
887

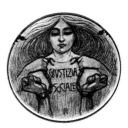

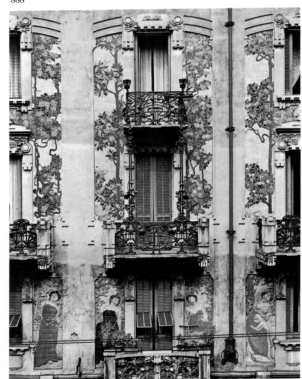

888

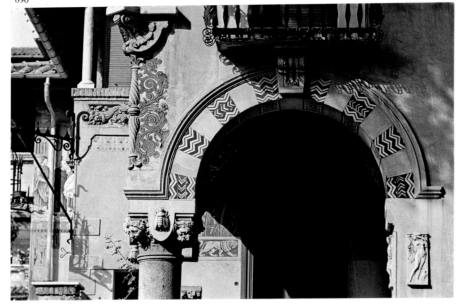

889

890

888—GIOVAN BATTISTA BOSSI, Galimberti House, Via Malpighi, Milan, 1905.
889-891—GINO COPPEDÈ, buildings in the Coppedè Village, Rome; details.
892—GIAMBATTISTA COMENCINI, hall of the Piscitelli-Taeggi House, Naples, c. 1901.
893—ADOLFO DE CAROLIS, illustration for *Francesca da Rimini*, by Gabriele D'Annunzio, 1902.

to other European influences. It was strongly ideological and 'anti-decadent' in character and this was reflected in the magazine already discussed, *L'Italia che ride*. PAOLO SIRONI (1858-1927), a Milanese architect, spent some time in Bologna. He acquired agricultural land where he built a series of small villas in the Art Nouveau style. Further expansion of the style within Bologna was blocked by the city fathers, who frowned upon its apparent indulgence. The work of De

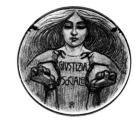

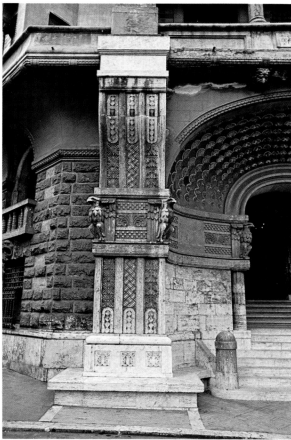

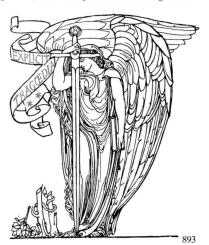

891

Atto V.
Scena ultima.

tenuto per la falda della sopravvesta a un ferro della cateratta. Francesca, a quella vista inattesa, getta un grido acutissimo, mentre lo Sciancato si fa sopra all'adultero e lo afferra per i capelli forzandolo a risalire.

GIANCIOTTO.

Sei preso nella trappola,

ah traditore! Bene ti s'acciuffa

per queste chiome!

La donna gli s'avventa al viso minacciosa.

FRANCESCA.

Lascialo!

Lascialo! Me, me prendi! Eccomi!

Il marito lascia la presa. Paolo balza dall'altra parte della cateratta e snuda il pugnale. Lo Sciancato indietreggia, sguaina lo stocco e gli si avventa addosso con impeto terribile. Francesca in un baleno si getta tra mezzo ai due; ma, come il marito tutto si grava sopra il colpo e non può ritenerlo, ella ha il petto trapassato dal ferro, barcolla, gira su sé stessa volgendosi a Paolo che lascia cadere il pugnale e la riceve tra le braccia.

FRANCESCA morente.

Ah Paolo!

Lo Sciancato per un attimo s'arresta. Vede la donna stretta al cuore dell'amante che con le sue labbra le suggella le labbra spiranti. Folle di do-

lore e di furore, vibra al fianco del fratello un altro colpo mortale. I due corpi allacciati vacillano accennando di cadere; non danno un gemito; senza sciogliersi, piombano sul pavimento. Lo Sciancato si curva in silenzio, piega con pena un de' ginocchi; su l'altro spezza lo stocco sanguinoso.

891

892

*—page 319, R. D'ARONCO, sketch of the door for the Turin Exhibition, 1902.

893

Carolis on the Palazzo del Podesta (1911-28) was unpopular and his frescoes, painted in a heavily mannered imitation of Michelangelo, were not a success with the establishment. Later, however, the city was visited by Bistolfi who, during his stay, created the monument to Carducci.

In Naples there was a lively cultural life and, as an international seaport, the city was open to considerable outside influences. Both Vittorio Pica and Giovanni Teserone were active participants in the dissemination of the new ideas, especially in the field of the applied arts, that constantly flowed into the city. Their efforts resulted in the Museo Industriale (The Industrial Museum), in 1882 which provided a comprehensive collection of major works in the Art Nouveau style, both from Italy and elsewhere.

The Venetian, G. B. COMENCINI, exhibited a special skill in creating refined and harmonious interiors, as exemplified by the Hotel Londra (1899) and the Hotel Santa Lucia (1906). Others who demonstrated a fine sense of curvilinear asymmetry in their designs were Francesco De Simone (Palazzina Velardi); Leonardo Paterno Baldizzi (Casa Marotta); Michelle Capo (Villa Cuomo) and Gregorio Botta (Villa Pappone).

In addition to these, and probably the best known, was GIULIO U. ARATA (1881-1962) from Piacenza, who designed the Palazzo Mannajuolo (1909) and also worked on the Terme di Agnano (1919). The style of his exteriors was always distinguished by a lively exuberance.

There was ample scope for the propagation of the Art Nouveau style throughout Tuscany, but especially within the coastal resorts where keeping in step with international fashion carried a level of

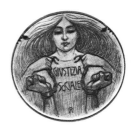

894—ERNESTO BASILE, divan for the Ducrot Co., Palermo, illustrated in *L'Art Décoratif*, 1903.

895—TOMMASO MALERBA, cloister built by the Inserra Reinforced Concrete Co. at the second agricultural exhibition in Catania, 1907.

896—E. BASILE, bedroom designed for the Ducrot Co., Palermo, illustrated in *L'Art Décoratif*, January, 1903.

896

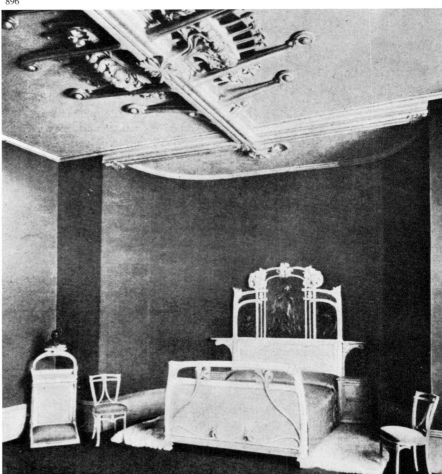

894

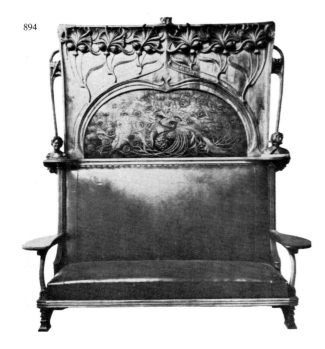

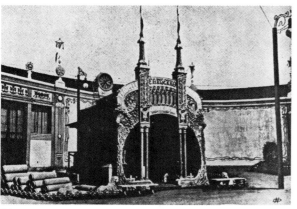

895

prestige comparable to that of the main cities. Viareggio, Forte dei Marmi and the whole Versilia region contain numerous, and in some instances outstanding, examples of Art Nouveau style.

ERNESTO BASILE (1857-1932) worked for a time in Rome where he designed a project for the Florio Building in Milan in 1906, but he is famous for his work in Palermo. Basile produced objects in a wide range of fine and applied arts, and in Italy he came closest to the Art Nouveau ideal of the complete craftsman. In 1899 he began his murals at the Villa Igea in a flat curvilinear style, in which flowers are used as the setting for the figures which are painted in the same flat curvilinear style. The curving rhythms of the murals are echoed in the decoration of the whole villa; a screen in wood and glass he executed for the villa exemplifies this consistency. Basile's other projects, like the bedroom he designed for the Ducrot Company (1903), show a sophisticated understanding of the relationship of objects to the space they inhabit.

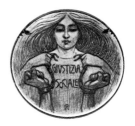

897—E. BASILE. E. DE MARIA BERGLER, the hall of the Hotel
Villa Igea, Palermo, 1899-1900; fresco decorations.
898—E. BASILE, screen in wood and glass from the Hotel Villa
Igea, 1900. Palermo, Hotel Villa Igea.

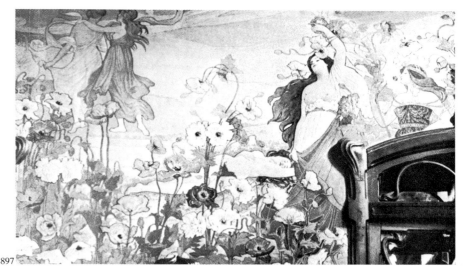

897

898

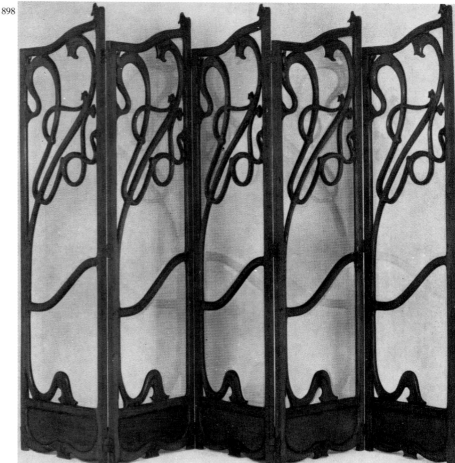

On page 322
899—GIOVANNI MICHELAZZI, villa in Viale Michelangelo, Florence, 1904; detail (ceramic decorations by Galileo Chini).
900—G. MICHELAZZI, Villa Ravazzini in Via Scipione Ammirato, Florence, 1907-08; detail.
901—GAETANO ORZIALI, Villa Dandia, Lucca, 1914.
902— G. MICHELAZZI, Villa Lampredi in Via Giano della Bella,
Florence.

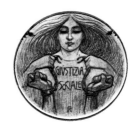

899

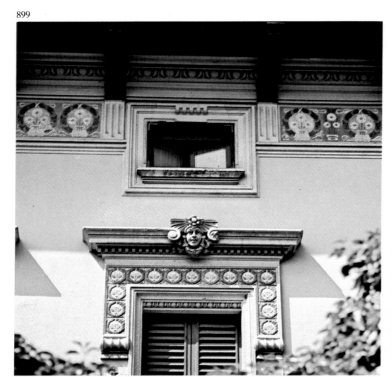

901

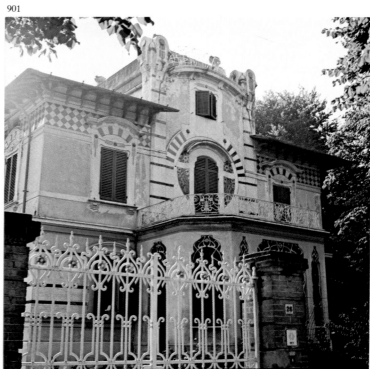

900

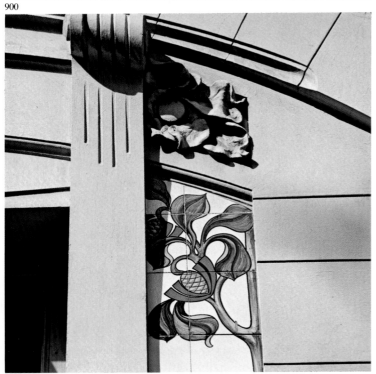

902

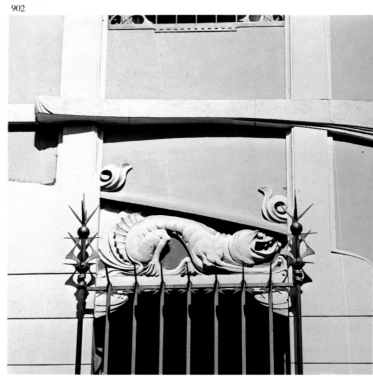

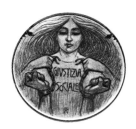

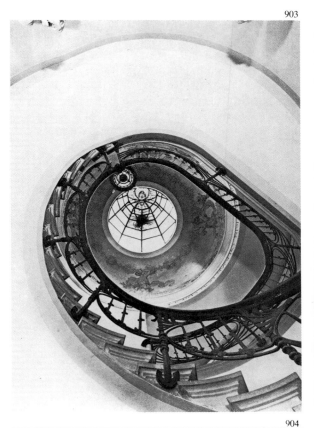

903

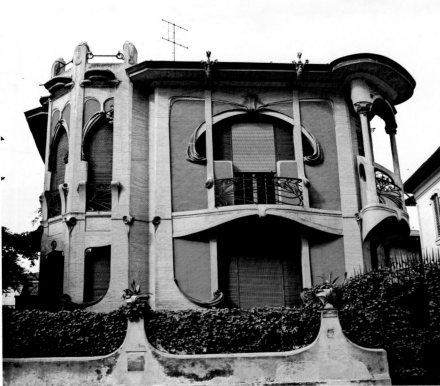

905

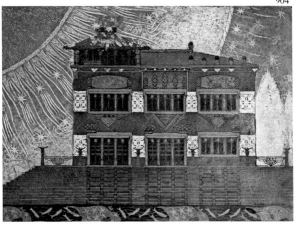

904

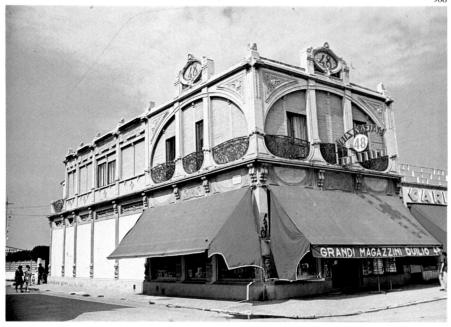

906

903, 905—G. MICHELAZZI, Villa Broggi-Caraceni in Via Scipione Ammirato, Florence, 1911; staircase and the facade.
904—BENVENUTO BENVENUTI, *Villa at the Seaside*, c. 1911.
906—G. MICHELAZZI, Diulio Stores '48', Viareggio, c. 1910.

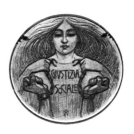

In Florence there were two reasons for resistance to the new Liberty style: firstly it was not a leading urban centre, and secondly it was still encumbered with the status of its Renaissance past, which was kept alive by periodicals like *Leonardo* and *Hermes*. GIOVANNI MICHELAZZI (1879-1920) came out of this tradition and he first updated Florentine tradition and then he surpassed it.

In his early buildings, like the small villa in the Viale Michelangelo (1904) and the Villa Ravazzini (1907-08), he uses a Renaissance vocabulary in a contemporary idiom. However, even at this stage of his career, his work shows a considerable refinement of ornament and pattern. This emerges strongly in the Art Nouveau buildings which he executed after 1910. His Villa Broggi-Caraceni (1911) is a fully integrated design based on a fluid curvilinear movement on the facade. This is carried through the detailing of windows, balconies and the cornice, which are articulated in expansive curves, independent of the wall plane, and complemented by Galileo Chini's ceramics and Angielo Vannetti's stucco reliefs. In the interior the elegant and airy staircase echoes the design of the exterior.

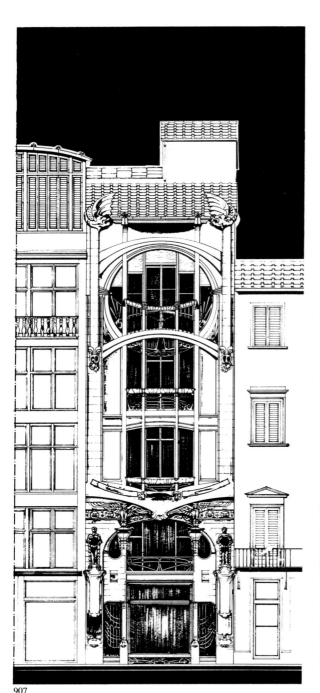

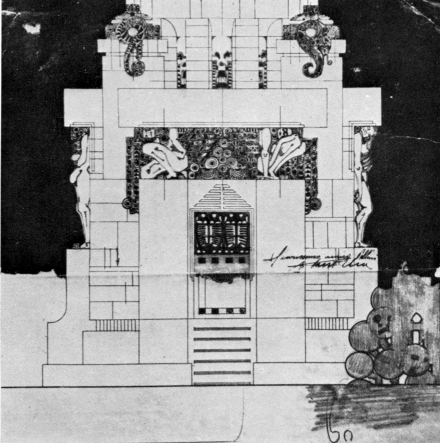

907—G. MICHELAZZI, Studio House in Borgo Ognissanti, Florence, 1912-13 (drawing by Paolo Bambi).
908—ANTONIO SANT'ELIA, study for a mausoleum, 1911-12, Milan, coll. Pellini.

908

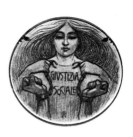

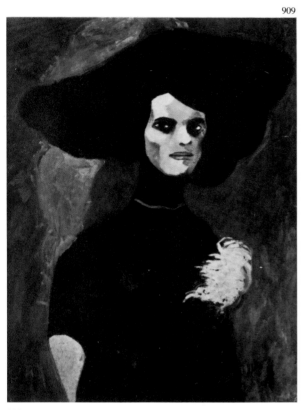

The Casa-galleria in Borgo Ognissanti, only recently attributed to Michelazzi, is one of the few examples of Art Nouveau style within the old city centre (most are to be found in the more recently built suburbs). It is squeezed between two existing buildings, its facade reflecting a violent tension as if it were trying to burst out from the constraints of its location.

Returning after the First World War, Michelazzi found that the Art Nouveau style he loved so deeply had been adopted by academia and officialdom who had debased it, turning it into a medium depicting only the power of the state. This so depressed him that it took only an insignificant domestic crisis to overpower his sanity and drive him to suicide.

Other architects working in Florence included Adolpho Coppedè, Enrico Dante Fantappie, Paolo Emilio Andre and Ugo Giusti. All were part of the artistic community that revolved round Michelazzi. In his constant battles against the existing orthodoxies, he maintained a simple clarity of vision that seemed to elude his companions.

909—LORENZO VIANI, *The Pearl*, 1911. Prato Galleria Falsetti.
910—GAETANO MORETTI, street-lamp on the Electricity Centre, 1906, Trezzo d'Adda.
*—page 325, R. D'ARONCO, sketch of a pavilion for the Turin Exhibition, 1902.

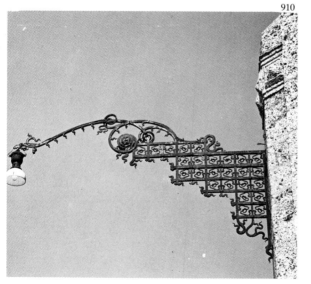

ANTONIO SANT'ELIA (1888-1916) became famous as a Futurist and he is best remembered for his development of 'al gradiente' (axionometric) design so favoured by modern architects. Sant'Elia's first architectural works were entirely within the Secessionist style of Art Nouveau that became popular in Italy. In 1922 he designed a mausoleum which shows this influence very strongly in the use of elegant cubic forms and sculptural decoration which enhances the surface without disturbing the volume of the building. There is even a suggestion of Klimt in the way the ornamental panels decorated with spiral patterns are the background for the figures.

Another important architect who worked in a Secessionist style is GAETANO MORETTI (1886-1938). Moretti built the Electricity Centre in Trezzo d'Adda. Here a Secessionist taste for embellishment is combined with a distinctly oriental-looking openwork decoration. Even the design of details like the street lamps on the exterior, which have great vitality of effect, conforms to this preference.

The commission given to Giuseppe Brega for the Villa Ruggeri (1902-07) in his home town of Pesaro, was exceptionally specific. His patron asked him to recreate symbolically the fanciful memories the patron had gathered during his travels (he had been searching for ideas for use in his ceramics factory). The result is a fascinating creation of expressive vitality.

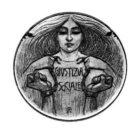

911

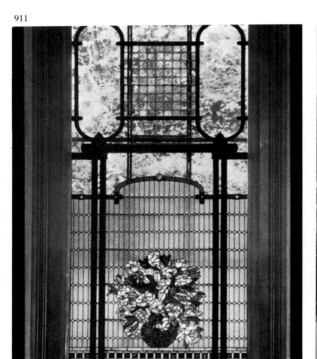

913

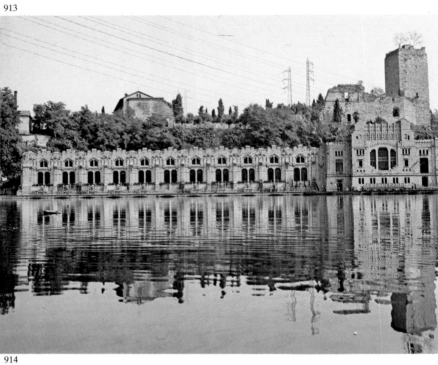

912

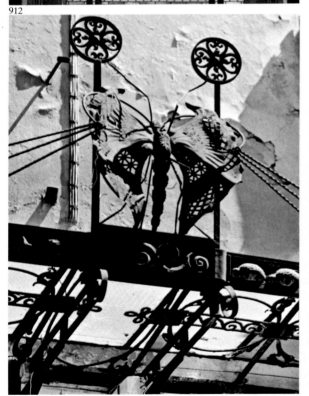

914

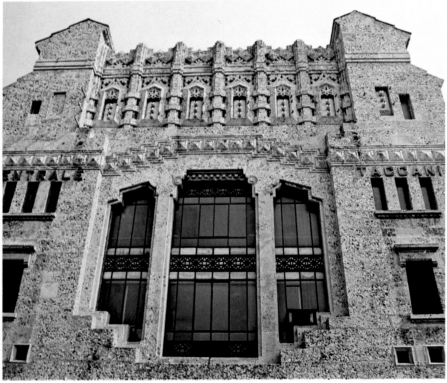

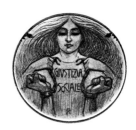

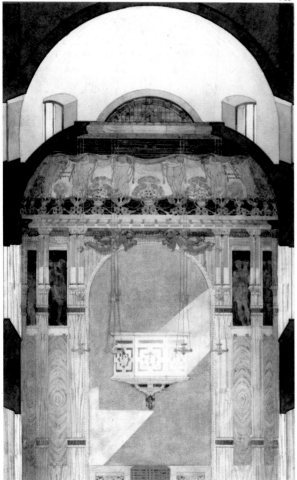

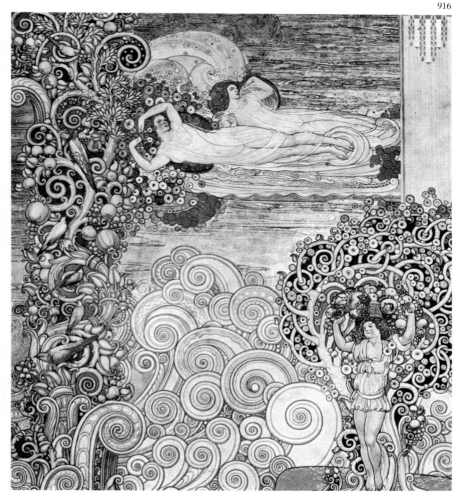

915

916

911—G. BUFFA. G. BELTRAMI, window of the Casino at San Pellegrino Baths, 1904-07. Leghorn, Museo Fattori.
912—Detail of the wrought iron on the cinema at Pietrasanta.
913, 914—GAETANO MORETTI, Electricity Centre, Trezzo d'Adda, 1906.
915—GIUSEPPE LUNARDI, project for the chapel of San Leonardo, Lucca, 1912; watercolour. Florence, coll. Lunardi-Gheradini.
916—GALILEO CHINI, fresco in the Berzieri Baths at Salsomaggiore, 1922.

In Trieste the architect Zaninovic worked alone, developing his own individual style. This happened to be constantly at odds with the repetitive nature of the accepted official style of the region and consequently, in addition to many local problems, he was faced with persistent obstruction in his efforts.

At the Villa on Venice's Lido, Guido Costante Sullam was able to benefit from Scottish and Austrian influences when revitalizing the decorative motifs used in the paintings and drawings of the Symbolist and Art Nouveau movements. The floral and peacock designs on the staircase, as well as in the beautiful decorative ceramics and ironwork, exemplify this.

The wide range of styles which characterize Italian Art Nouveau architecture are also present in painting and sculpture. In the Lombard region, GAETANO PREVIATI (1852-1920) and GIOVANNI SEGANTINI (1858-1899) both developed a Symbolist style based on

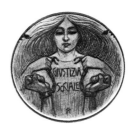

917-919—GIUSEPPE BREGA, Villa Ruggeri, Pesaro, 1902-07; drawing of the eastern facade; view of the villa; detail of the stucco decoration.
920, 922—GUIDO COSTANTE SULLAM, villa on the Lido in Venice; staircase and a view from above.
921—ADOLFO WILDT, *Self-portrait*, 1906-08.
  *—page 329 R. D'ARONCO, design of a pavilion for the Turin Exhibition, 1902.

On pages 330, 331
923—A. DE CAROLIS, illustration for the *Divine Comedy* (*Hell*, Canto XXII), c. 1904.
924—GAETANO PREVIATI, *Day Wakens Night*, 1905. Trieste, Museo Revoltella.
925—GIOVANNI SEGANTINI, *The Chastisement of Lust*, 1897. Zurich, Kunsthaus.
926—G. SEGANTINI, *The Wicked Mothers*, 1897. Zurich, Kunsthaus.

918

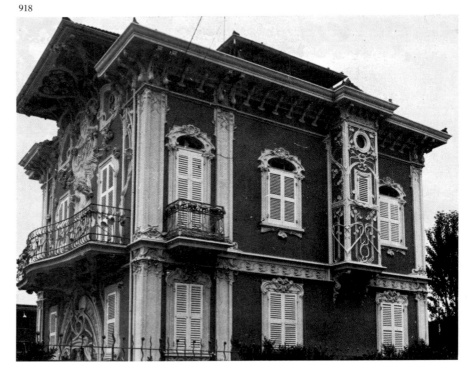

917

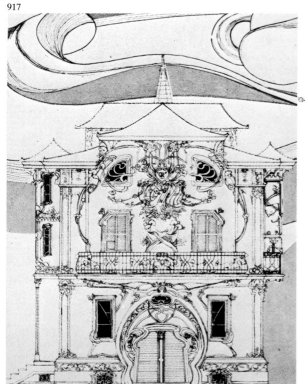

919

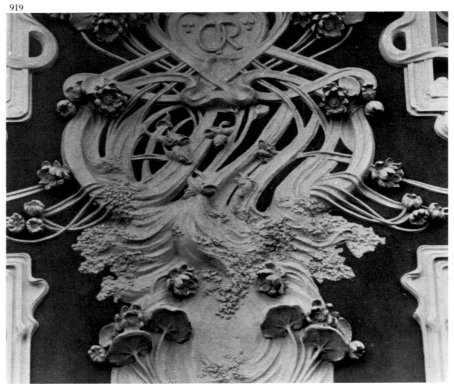

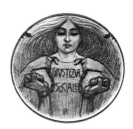

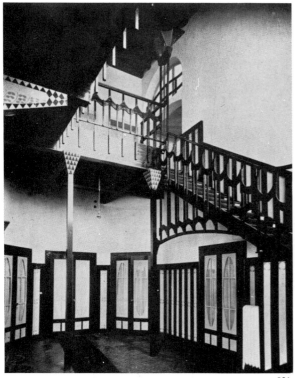

920

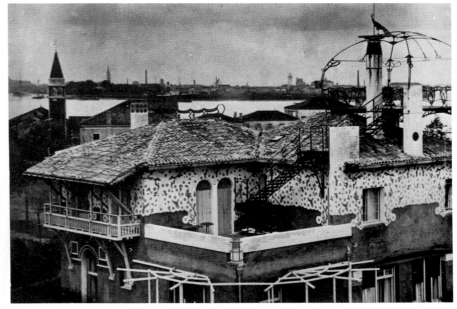

922

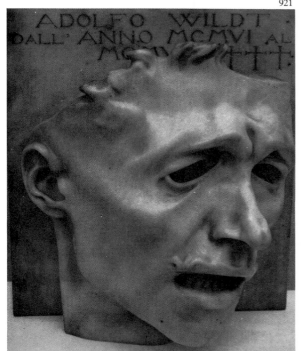

921

that of the French and the Belgians. Both painters organized the surface of their paintings in a highly decorative way, but both expressed a fantasy and desolation which removes their work from the realm of Art Nouveau.

ADOLFO WILDT (1868-1931) was also active in Milan during the period. His work, while very decorative, often conveys a deep sense of anxiety. Like Previati and Segantini, references to Art Nouveau were peripheral elements in his work, but he occasionally used the arabesque line. This can be seen in the linear organization of his *Self-Portrait* bust (1906-08).

The organization of sculpture with a rhythmic composition characterizes the work of the Turin sculptor LEONARDO BISTOLFI (1859-1933). His *Dream*, which is part of a funerary monument, shows how successfully he achieved this.

In Treviso, ALBERTO MARTINI (1876-1954) produced graphic works in the wake of Art Nouveau. These have a strong erotic content and often contain bizarre juxtapositions. For this reason they were enthusiastically admired by the Surrealists in the 1920s and 1930s.

Among Roman artists, ADOLFO DE CAROLIS (1874-1928) and DUILIO CAMBELLOTTI (1876-1960) came close to a truly Art Nouveau style. In the latter's illustrations for Dante's *Divine Comedy*

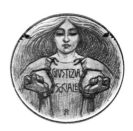

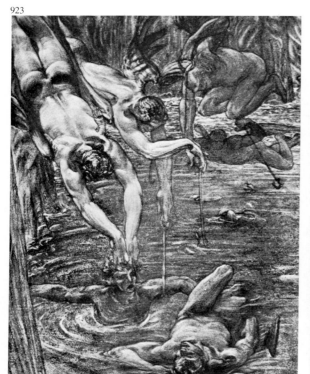

923

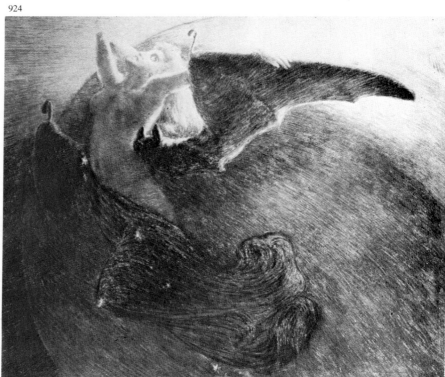

924

925

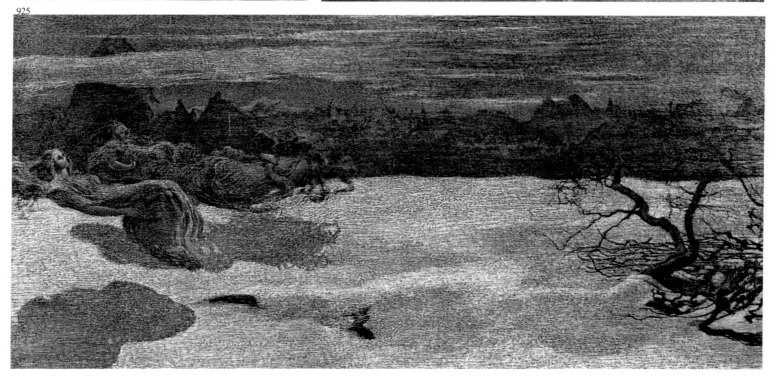

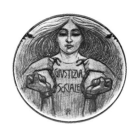

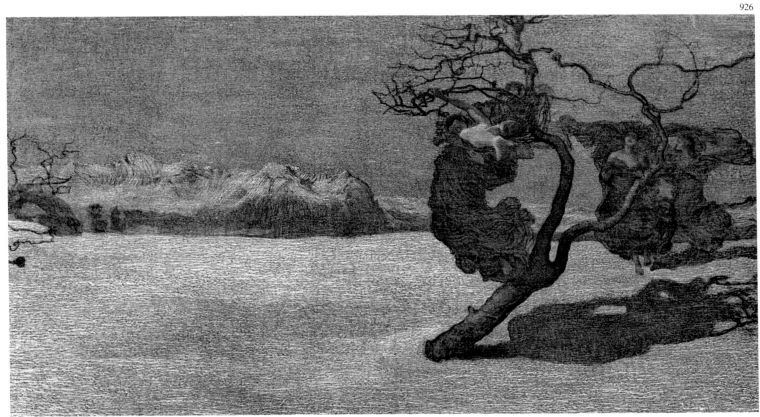

926

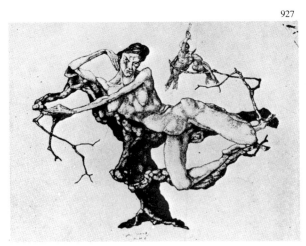

927

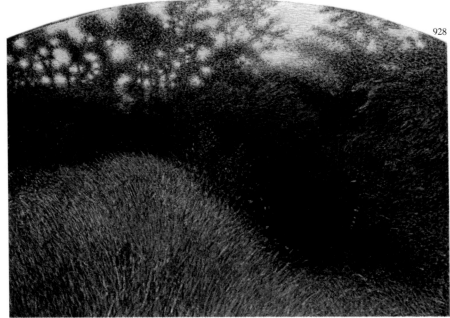

928

927—PAUL KLEE, *The Virgin in the Tree* (Invention 3), 1903.
Berne, Kunstmuseum.
928—GIUSEPPE PELLIZZA DA VOLPEDO, *The Bramble Bush*.
Piacenza, Galleria d'Arte Moderna.

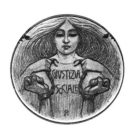

929
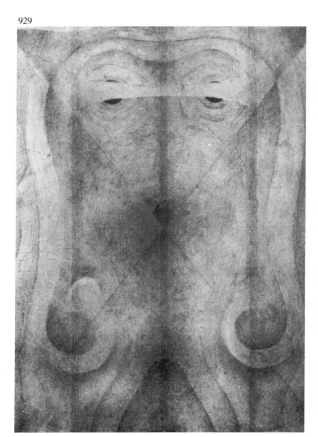

930
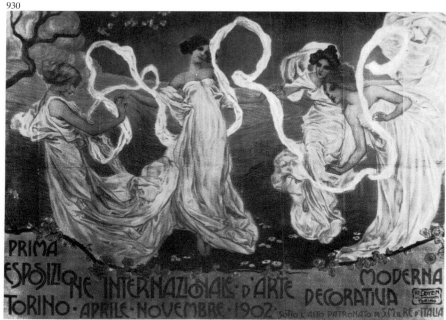

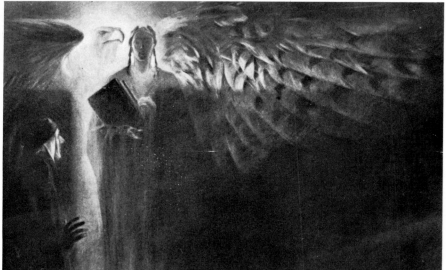
931

929—ROMOLO ROMANI, *Lust*, 1904-05. Brescia, Museo Civico.
930—LEONARDO BISTOLFI, poster for the Turin Exhibition, 1902.
931—D. CAMBELLOTTI, illustration for the *Divine Comedy*, (*Paradise*, VI), c. 1904.
932—L. BISTOLFI, *The Dream*, tomb of Erminia Cairati Vogt, Milan; detail.
933—L. BISTOLFI, monument to Segantini. Turin, Galleria Civica d'Arte Moderna.

(1904), the scroll-like draperies and the rhythmically organized surface suggest the artist's adherence to the style. In Tuscany GALILEO CHINI (1873-1954) exploited Art Nouveau motifs in the tiling he designed for architectural decoration and in his painting. The fresco he painted in the Berzieri Baths at Salsomaggiore (1922) is an outstanding example of late Art Nouveau. Here the figures are set against spiral patterns and flattened, schematized foliage and vegetation.

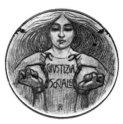

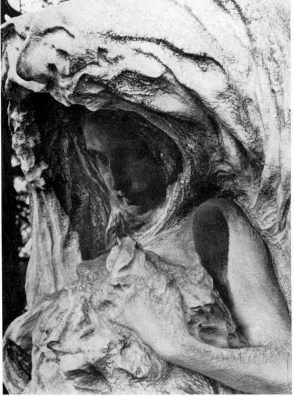

932

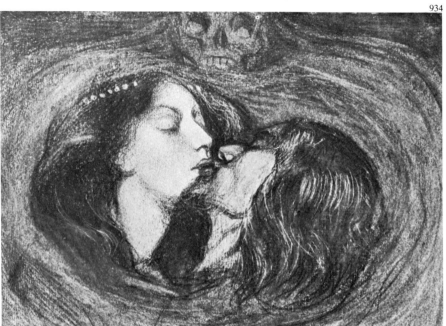

934

934—G. COSTETTI, illustration for the *Divine Comedy* (*Inferno*, Canto V), c. 1904.
935—FELICE CASORATI, *The Dream of the Pomegranate*, 1913. Turin, coll. Forti.

933

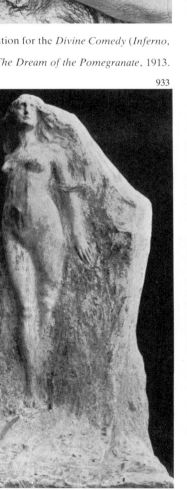

935

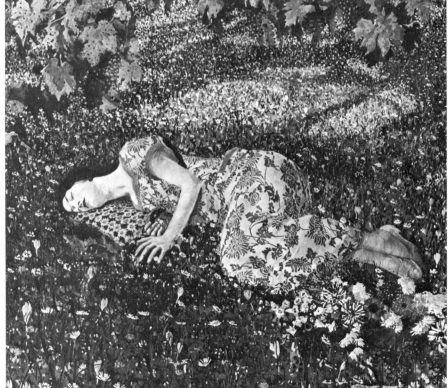

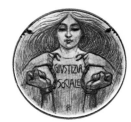

936

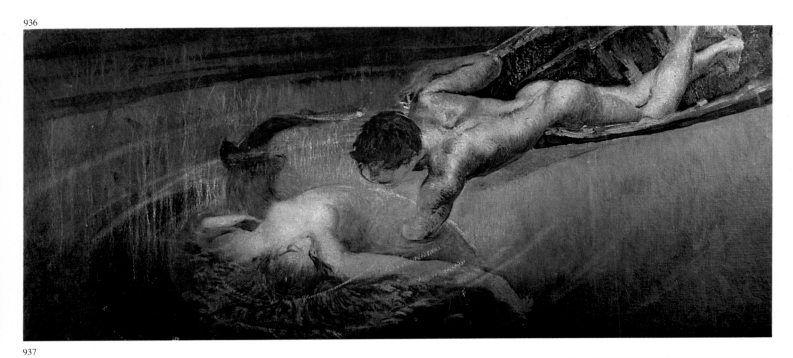

937

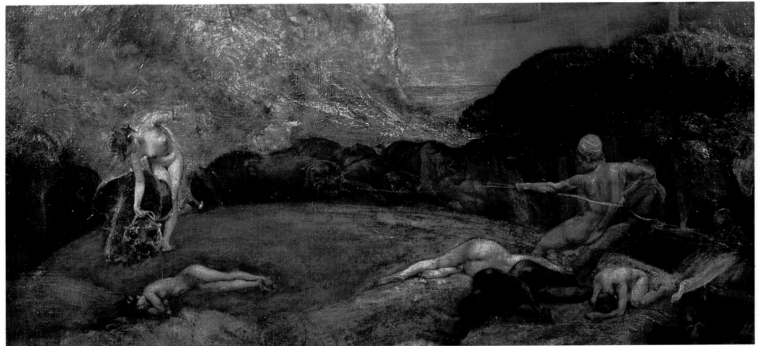

After returning from Thailand, Chini's painting style changed; he was drawn towards a more Post-Impressionist style. His most important work from this period, however, marked a brief return to

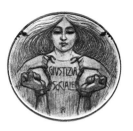

936—GIULIO ARISTIDE SARTORIO, *Green Abyss*, 1900. Piacenza, Galleria Ricci-Oddi.
937—G. A. SARTORIO, *Bacchanal*, c. 1894. Velletri, coll. Sartorio.
938—GALILEO CHINI, ceramic vase. Florence, coll. Crestini.
939—A. DE CAROLIS, illustration from *Francesca da Rimini*, by G. D'Annunzio, 1902.
940—Florentine Ceramic Society, decorative panel; detail. Florence, coll. Gherardini.

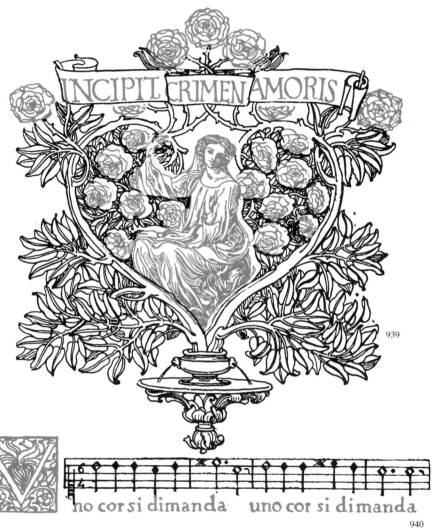

939

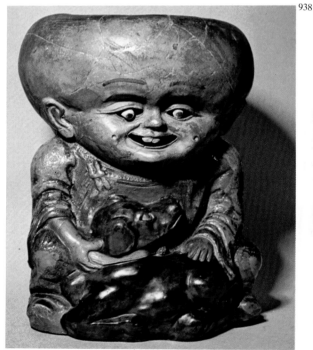

938

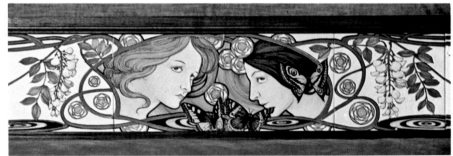

940

the style of Klimt, when it was used to decorate one of the rooms used for the 1914 Venice Biennale.

Chini will, however, be remembered primarily for his ceramics,

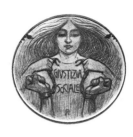

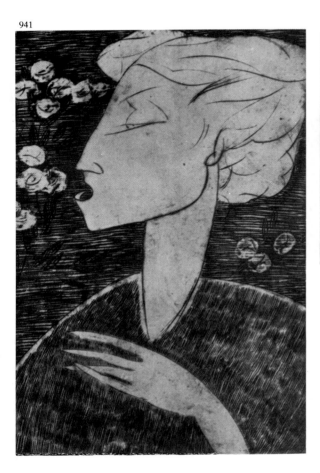

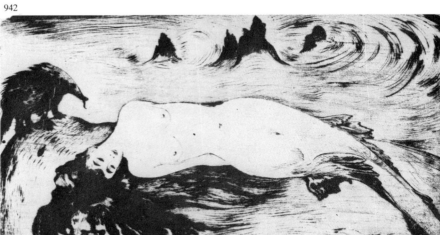

especially for his vases. They are among the finest examples of the Art Nouveau style in any medium. They are outstanding, both technically and artistically, in their use of fantasy decoration and the incorporation of oriental motifs.

VITTORIO ZECCHIN (1878-1947) designed and made Venetian glass in the Art Nouveau style. He worked at Ca'Pesaro, and he designed the decorative panels *One Thousand and One Nights* (1914) where a Klimtian sensitivity to the effects of contrasting areas of strongly coloured pattern is very evident.

More peripheral figures to the movement were FELICE CASORATI (1883-1963) and UMBERTO BOCCIONI (1882-1916) whose early work

941—ARTURO MARTINI, *Young Girl Adoring a Cluster of Roses*, c. 1913.
942—A. MARTINI, *The Sleeping Siren*, 1911. Milan, Civica Raccolta Bertorelli.
943—CARLO BUGATTI, living room furniture; Turin Exhibition, 1902.

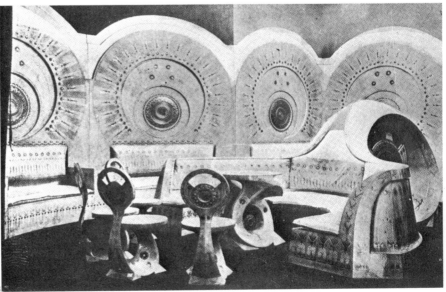

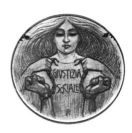

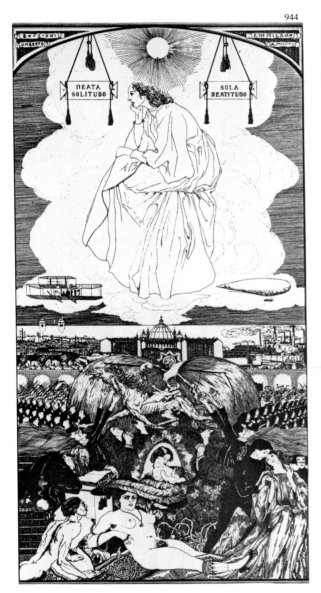

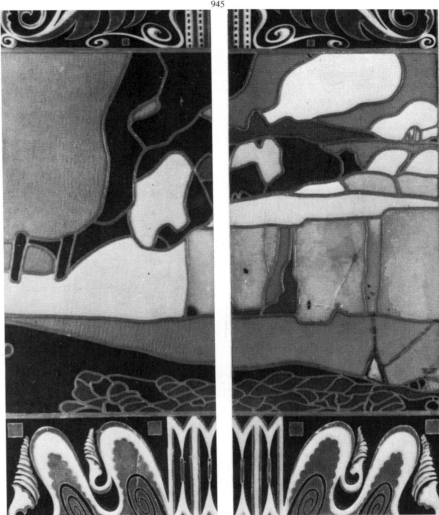

944—UMBERTO BOCCIONI, *Blessed Solitude*, 1908. Milan, Private collection.
945—TEODORO WOLF FERRARI, stained-glass window, c. 1912. Mestre, coll. Aristide Coin.

shows the influence of the decorative emphasis common to Art Nouveau painting and drawing. These two masters, however, went on to develop their own styles, Casorati towards a scrupulous realism and Boccioni towards Futurism.

In the applied arts, Liberty is again difficult to define stylistically. It is strongly felt in the early works of the designer CARLO BUGATTI (1855-1940). Bugatti's furniture designs around 1900 have a peculiarly crisp and massive quality, which in part stem from Secessionist influences, but which are also a personal response to more primitive Italian decorative styles.

Apart from the well-known names like Chini, Zecchin, Basile and Mazzocotelli in the field of the applied arts, there were also others involved in furthering the style of Art Nouveau. Umberto Bellotto, a Venetian noted for his wrought-iron work; and Benvenuto Benvenuti

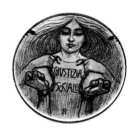

946

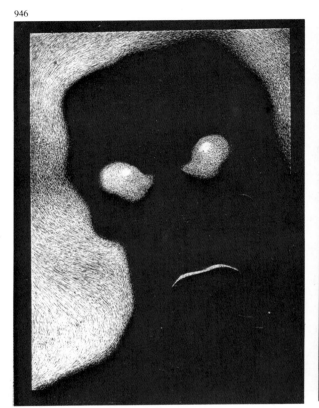

948

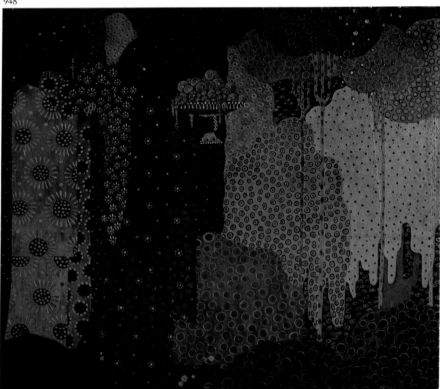

947

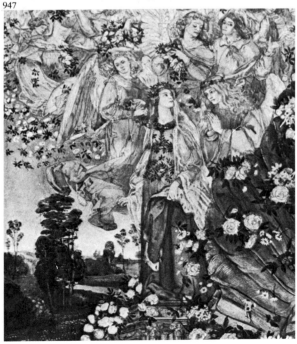

from Livorno, a painter who studied under Segantini and was also known for his interiors. In Milan, EUGENIO QUARTI (1867-1931) established a workshop from which emanated fantastic furniture and furnishings, all highly ornamented with asymmetrical motifs.

The period was particularly rich in ceramics, and several societies were formed to promote the craft. These included the Ceramic Society of Laveno, whose products are distinguished by their very Belgian floral decorations and slender proportions. The insistence on the arabesque organization of their designs characterized their work even when their products were figurative. In Palermo, Golia & Co. (subsequently Ducrot) produced Basile's work; Richard Ginori worked at Doccia near Florence, and the Società Fiorentina dell'Arte della Ceramica was founded by Galileo Chini. There was also Beltrami in Milan, specializing in stained glass; Calderoni, also in Milan, who were noted for their jewellery; and the furniture factory of Girard & Cutter in Florence. Similar societies existed for the other branches of the applied arts. Among these, two in particular deserve mention—the furniture factory of Carlo Zen and the association Amelia Ars. Both produced many very exotic and beautiful embroidery designs which rely on a tightly integrated interpretation of the floral line. Amelia Ars was set up by a group of local artists and

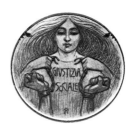

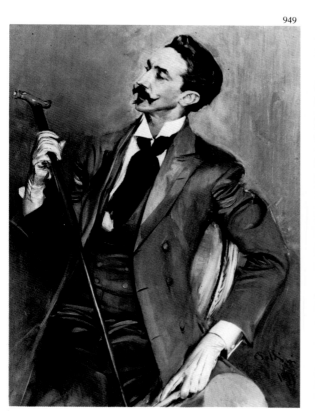

949

946—A. MARTINI, *Shadow*, illustration for the *Short Stories* by Poe. Milan, coll. Martini.
947—ARMANDO SPADINI, illustration for the *Divine Comedy* (*Purgatory*, Canto XXX), c. 1904.
948—VITTORIO ZECCHIN, *A Thousand and One Nights*. Turin, coll. Martano.
949—GIOVANNI BOLDIN, *Portrait of Robert de Montesquieu*, 1897. Paris, Musée Nationale d'Art Moderne.
950—V. ZECCHIN, *A Thousand and One Nights*, 1914. Venice, private collection.

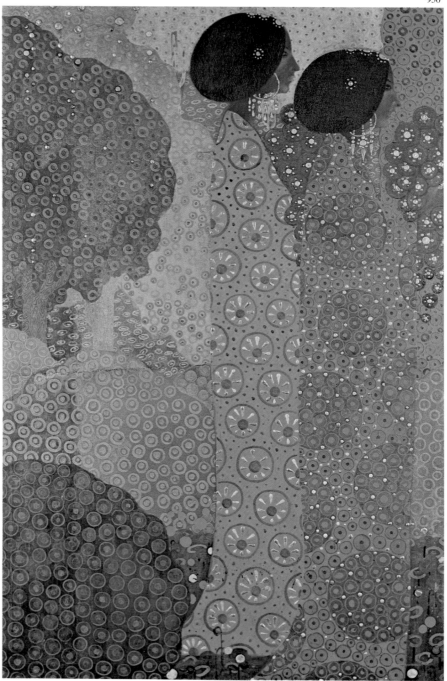

950

aristocrats. It was conceived to encourage and promote the applied arts. Apart from embroidery they created works of stained glass, wrought iron and leather binding; each work reflected an imaginative

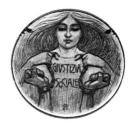

951—LEOPOLDO M. METLICOVICH, *Cabiria*, 1912. Milan, coll.
Ricordi.
952—CARLO ZEN COMPANY, divan with mirror, 1902 (textile by
Haas Co.), Turin exhibition, 1902. Parma, coll. Ranza.
953—AEMILIA ARS, lace designed by Tubbiani and Casanova;
detail.
954—ITALIAN CERAMIC COMPANY OF LAVENO, vase, c. 1903.
955—RICHARD-GINORI ITALIAN CERAMIC COMPANY, flower
vase, exhibited in Turin, 1902.

952

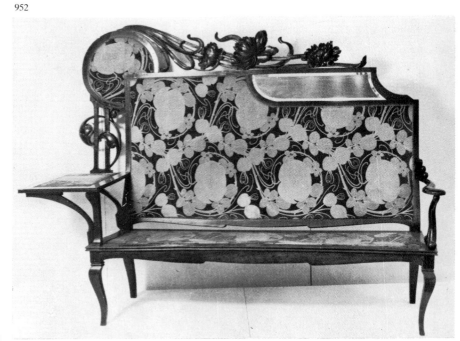

951

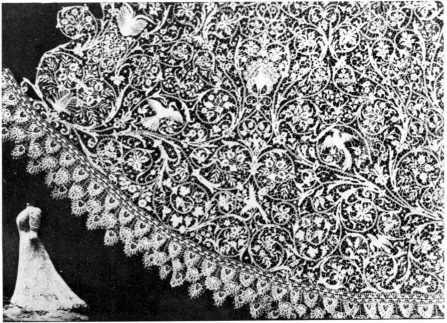

eclectic taste that was unfailingly combined with a high standard of
workmanship.
   Another important area of creativity was found within the printing
and publishing professions. At this time, magazine publishing and

953

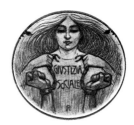

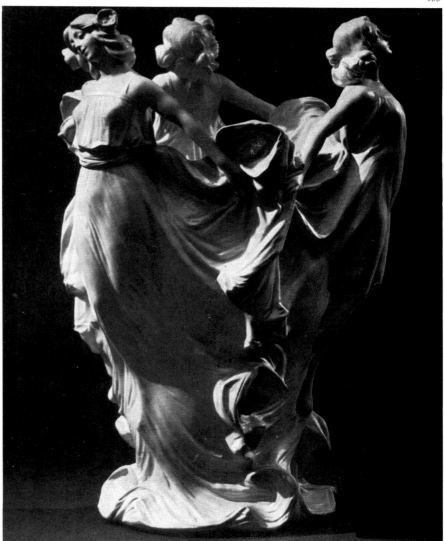

955

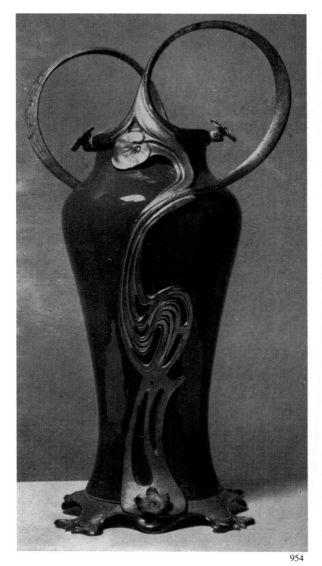

954

advertising were expanding. Much of what was created during this period not only shows considerable vitality and originality, but also little sign of a plagiarized outside influence.

In graphics and illustration, the names of Cambellotti and de Carolis have already been mentioned. To these should be added that of LEONELLO CAPPIELLO (1875-1942) and LEOPOLDO METLICO-VICH (1869-1944). In the latter's poster for Gabriele d'Annunzio's *Cabiria* (1912), the arabesque derived from Art Nouveau is already giving way to more solid, flat surfaces and contours that were to introduce later developments in the medium. However, the treatment of the flame and of the child's hair still betray the lingering expressive potential that could be found in the Art Nouveau line.

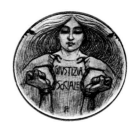

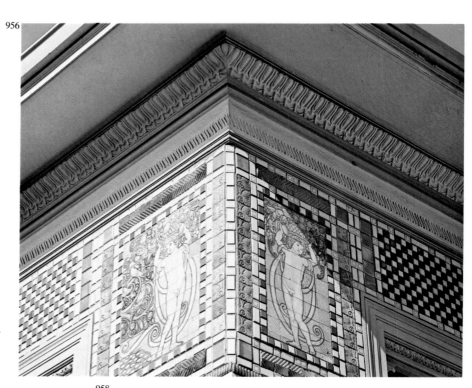

956—GALLILEO CHINI, ceramic decoration on the Villa Argentina, Viareggio, c. 1910.
957—G. LUNARDI, decorative design on paper; detail c. 1910.
958—G. LUNARDI, *Effect of the Moon*, c. 1907.
959—Calendar for the Nebiolo Company, 1900.

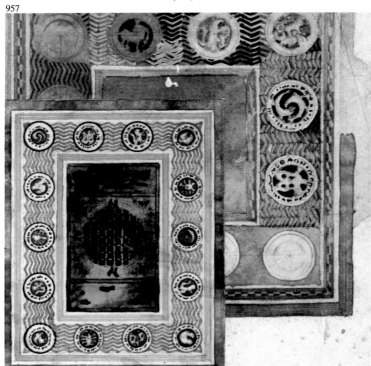

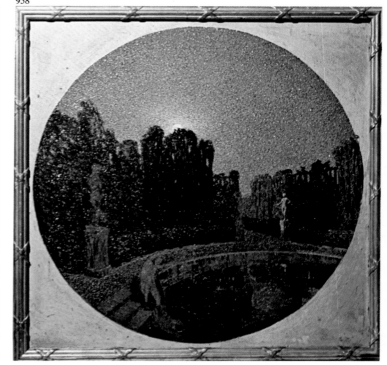

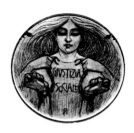

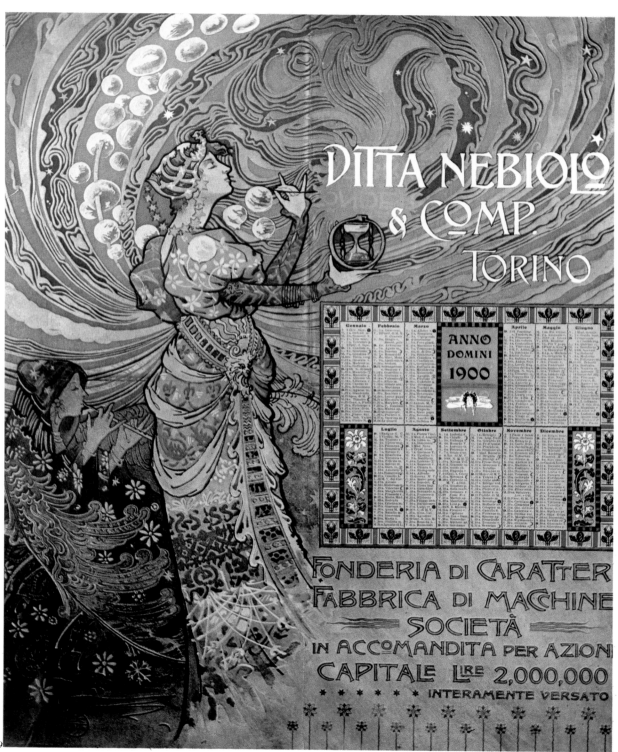

959

17–The Legacy of Art Nouveau

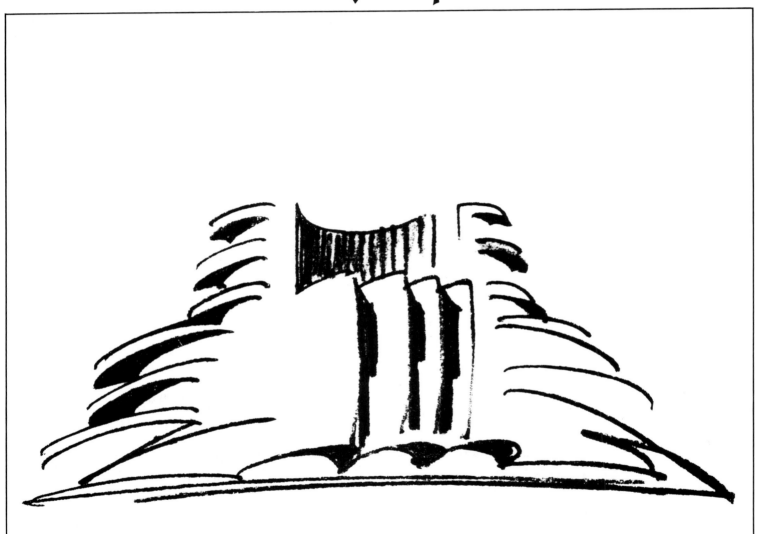

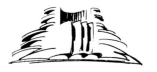

961

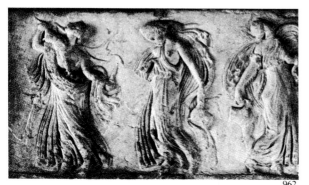

962

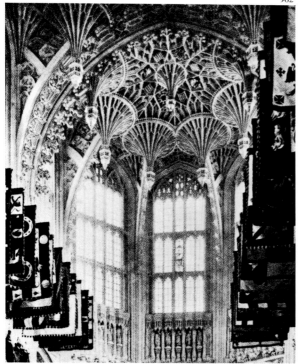

Great decorative art, from Roman sculpture to Gothic architecture and Piranesi, has been accepted into an orthodox system of historical classification. However, this has eluded Art Nouveau, which has not yet been accepted as an historically important style.

It may have been excluded from the mainstream of art history because it *was* a decorative art, and did not conform to the late nineteenth-century view that art should play an ideological or political role in society. Early in its development it aspired to a political role, but eventually the Art Nouveau style was rejected by the avant-garde and it never achieved the status of an official style worthy of imitation. Nevertheless, this brief chapter will show that, despite its critical misfortune, elements of Art Nouveau continued to exert an influence which can still be detected in the evolution of the art of our century.

In architecture, the line which grew out of floral motifs and which then became more abstract, is the immediate predecessor to Expressionism. Erik Mendelsohn's Einstein Tower (1919-21) has obvious precedents in Horta, van de Velde and Gaudí. This underlied a new style geared to emotional, rather than purely decorative, effects. The same use of Art Nouveau prototypes can be seen in the work of Rudolph Steiner, Hans Luckhardt and Hans Poeltzig. In more recent times a reassessment of the potential of decorative architecture has emerged in the work of the BBPR group, Pier Luigi Nervi, Luciano Baldessari and Enrico Castiglioni.

The tighter combination of elegant verticals and geometrical forms, which is the hallmark of Viennese and Glasgow Art Nouveau style, was the precedent for the rationalism of our century. In the development of Sant'Elia's work, the transition from Art Nouveau to Futurist and modernist forms was effected. Moreover, the insistence on the clarity of intersection between horizontal and vertical planes, first evident in Mackintosh's Glasgow Art School Library, later became characteristic of Constructivist and Neo-Plasticist painting. One of the earliest twentieth-century works which shows this principle is El Lissitsky's *Proun* (1924).

963

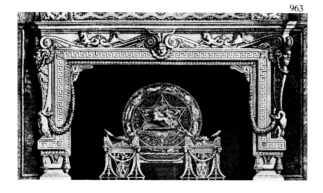

In the sphere of painting, however, it was the curvilinear line and the arabesque, which Art Nouveau had liberated from its representational context, that was taken over by modernism. This way of

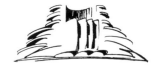

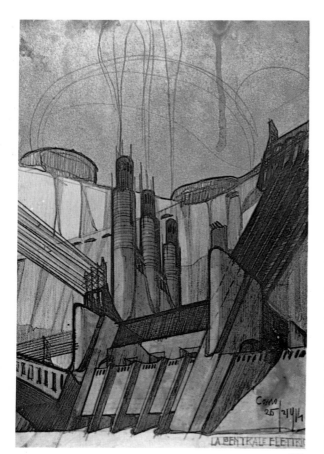

964

965

treating the surface organization of a painting played a vital role in the early work of Kandinsky and Piet Mondrian and it found its way into recent developments in painting exemplified by the work of the Americans Mark Tobey and Jackson Pollock. The more typically Symbolist line, softer in rhythm than that of Art Nouveau, and which was often used in a more expressive context, re-emerged in the shapes and patterns in Joan Miró's and Friedrich Hundertwasser's paintings.

The more purely decorative and sophisticated rhythms, textures and patterns employed by Klimt also underlie many recent works. Direct analogies may be drawn between the Austrian painter and the optical effects of Bridget Riley and Franco Grignani.

Perhaps the most directly discernible influence of Art Nouveau is in sculpture. Here the scale of the objects is similar and the range of materials used to make them is often the same. The repeated, floral curves characteristic of so much Art Nouveau sculpture find a wholly personal and modern feeling in the dynamic treatment Umberto Boccioni gives them. Constantin Brancusi's stress on the value of repeated rhythmic curves is indebted to the earlier style. Even the decorative quality of the Constructivists, who relied on simple forms only to achieve an effect, are reminiscent of the spatial rhythms and decorative silhouettes of Art Nouveau. In modern times, details of Henry Moore's work and the sculptures of Max Bill and Quinto Ghermandi, are indebted to the way Art Nouveau taught artists to look afresh at the decorative value of the floral line and its ability to trace elegant and subtle arabesque line and form in space.

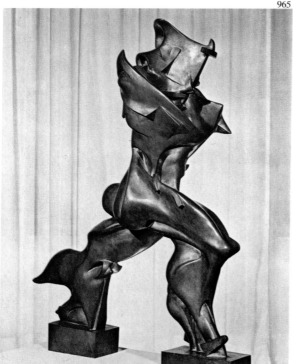

On pages 344, 345
960—and symbol of chapter 17, pp.344-358 – ERIK MENDEL-SOHN. *Bach's Toccata in D Major*, 1920; drawing.
961—Relief of dancing maenads; Roman copy of an original by Callimachus, V century BC. Rome, Museo Barracco di Scultura Antica.
962—Interior of Westminster Cathedral, XIII century.
963—GIOVANNI BATTISTA PIRANESI, engraving from *Diverse maniere di adornare i camini*, c. 1769.

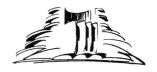

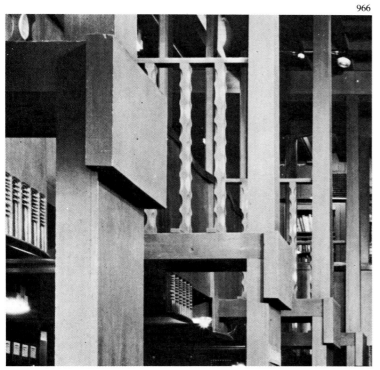

966

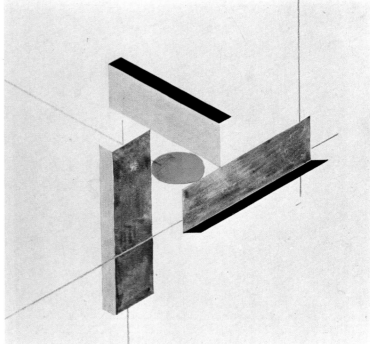

967

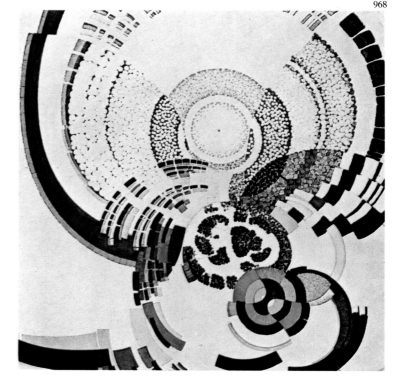

968

964—ANTONIO SANT'ELIA, *Electricity Centre*, 1914, Como, Museo di Villa Olmo.
965—UMBERTO BOCCIONI, *Forms in the Continuity of Space*, 1913. Milan, Galleria Civica d'Arte Moderna.
966—CHARLES RENNIE MACKINTOSH, interior, the Library of the Art School in Glasgow, 1907; structural detail.
967—EL LISSITSKY, *Proun*, c. 1924, detail.
968—FRANTISEK KUPKA, *Around a Point*, 1911-30; detail. Paris, Musée National d'Art Moderne.

On page 348
969—ERIK MENDELSOHN, Einstein Tower, Potsdam, 1919-21.
970—HANS POELTZIG, Felstpielhaus, project for Salzburg, 1920.
971—HANS LUCKHARDT, project for a theatre, 1922. Milan, coll. Accetti.
972, 973—RUDOLF STEINER, Goetheanum, Dornach, 1925-28; facade and staircase.

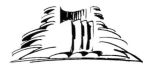

969

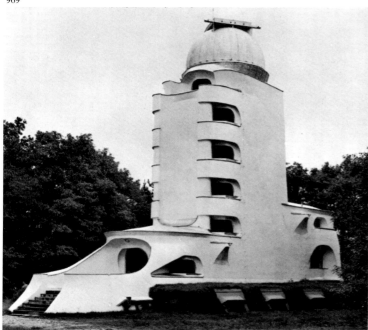

974, 977—LUCIANO BALDESSARI, Breda Pavilion, at the International Fair in Milan, 1952; plan and aerial view.
975—PIER LUIGI NERVI, Gatti Woollen Mill, Rome, 1951-53.
976—FREDERICK J. KIESLER, Endless House, 1960; detail of the interior.
978—B.B.P.R. GROUP, *Labyrinth,* X Triennale in Milan, 1954.
979—ENRICO CASTIGLIONI. project for a church, 1957; section.

970

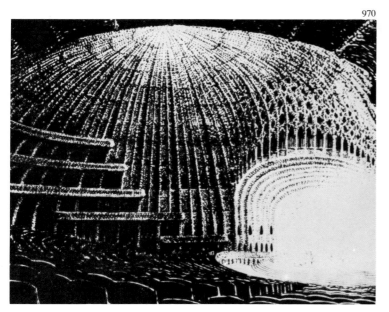

971

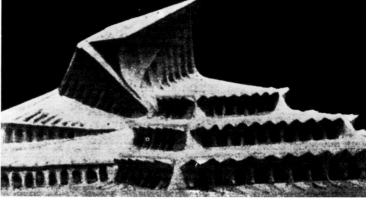

972

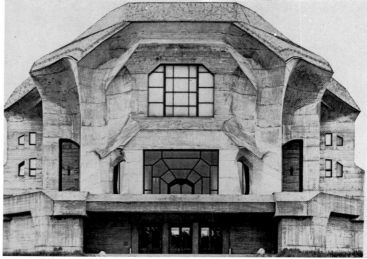

973

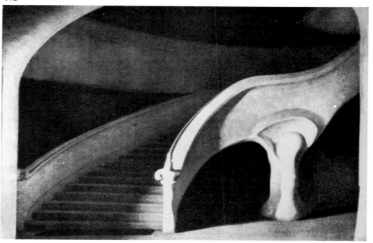

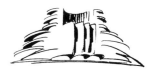

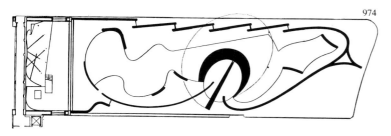

974

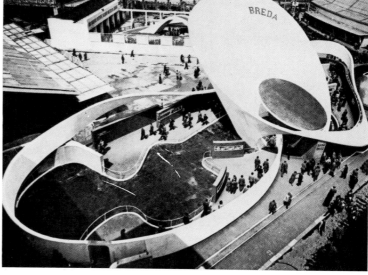

977

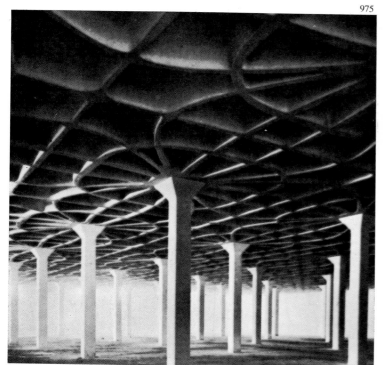

975

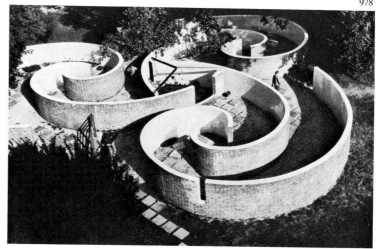

978

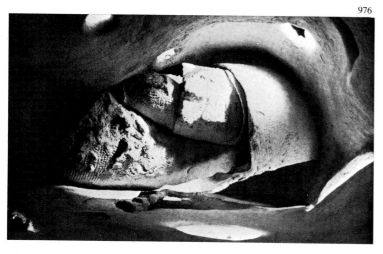

976

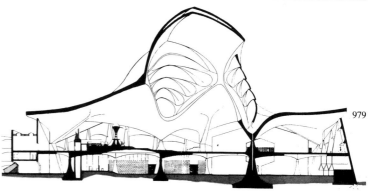

979

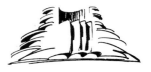

980

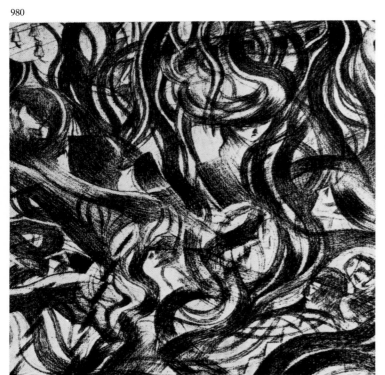

982

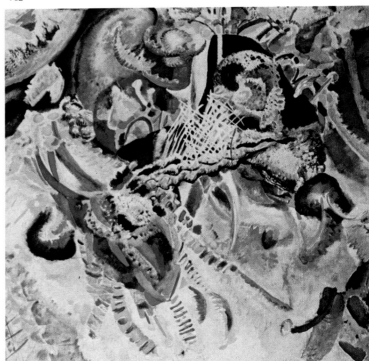

981

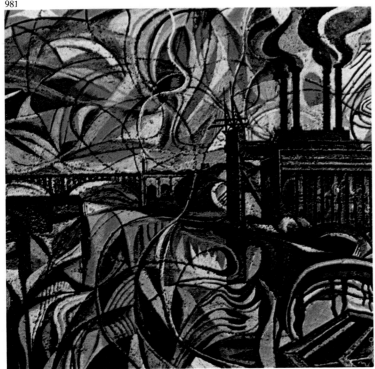

983

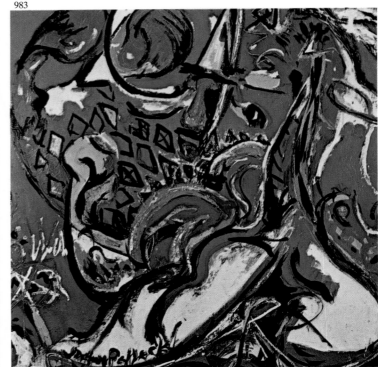

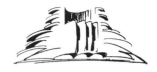

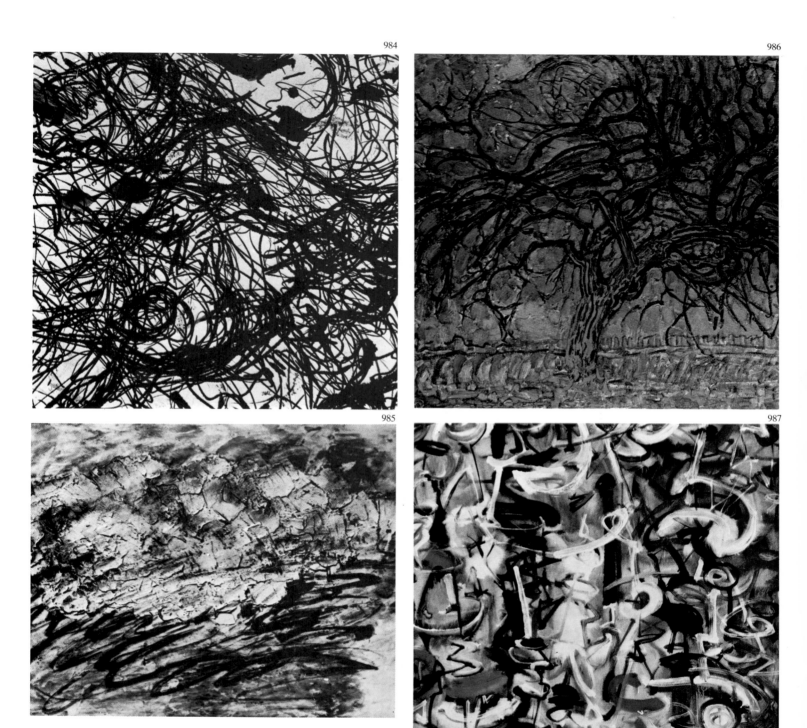

980—UMBERTO BOCCIONI, study for *States of the Soul*, 1911; detail. New York, The Museum of Modern Art.
981—DAVID BURLIUK, *Electricity Station*, 1924.
982—WASSILY KANDINSKY, *Escape*, 1913; detail. New York, Guggenheim Museum.

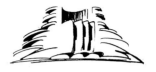

988

990

989

991

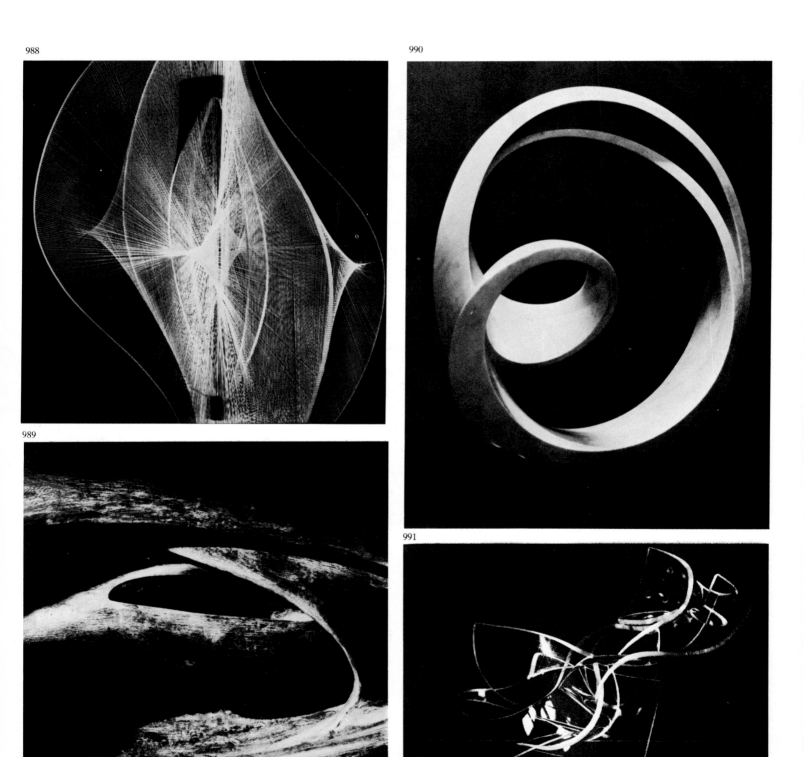

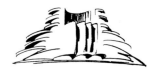

992

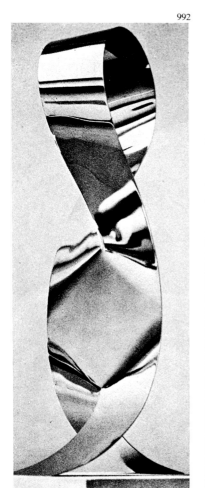

993

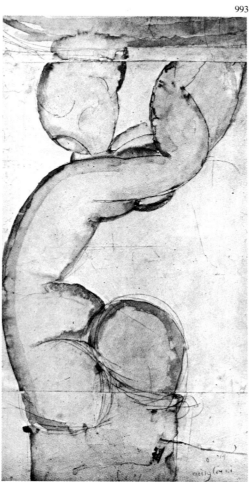

994

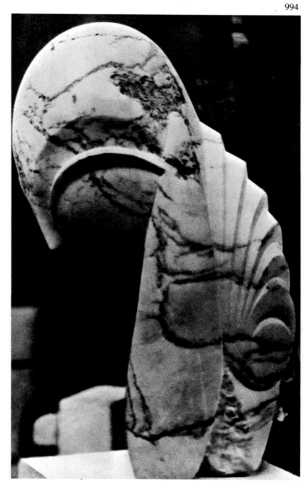

995

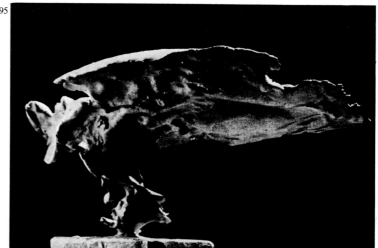

On pages 350, 351

983—JACKSON POLLOCK, *Masculine and Feminine*, 1942; detail. Pennsylvania, coll. H. Gates Lloyd.
984—EMILIO VEDOVA, drawing, 1937.
985—JEAN FAUTRIER, *The Frog Pond*, 1958; detail. Milan, coll. Panza di Biumo.
986—PIET MONDRIAN, *The Red Tree*, 1909-10; detail, The Hague, Gemeentemuseum.
987—MARK TOBEY, *Tropicalism*, 1948; detail. New York, Willard Gallery.

988—NAUM GABO, *Linear Construction*, n.2, 1949; detail. London, Tate Gallery.
989—HENRY MOORE, sculpture, 1952-53; detail.
990—CARMELO CAPPELLO, *Involution in a Circle*, 1960-71.
991—LAZLO MOHOLY-NAGY, *Spatial Modulator*, plexiglass sculpture. Detroit, Institute of Art.
992—MAX BILL, continuous sculpture.
993—AMEDEO MODIGLIANI, *Caryatid*, 1913-14; detail. London, Marlborough Collection.
994—CONSTANTIN BRANCUSI, *Mademoiselle Pogany*, 1919. New Canaan (Connecticut), coll. A. Ault.
995—QUINTO GHERMANDI, *Study for the Great Flight*, 1961.

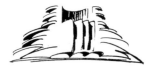

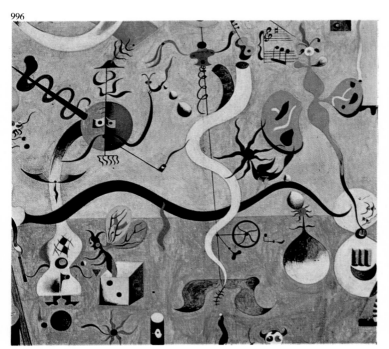

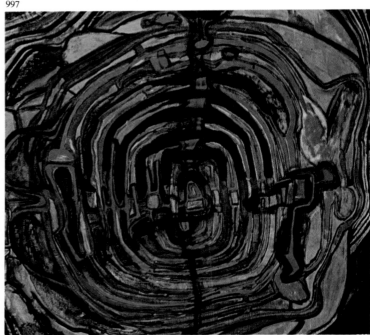

996—JOAN MIRÓ, *The Carnival of Harlequin*, 1924-25; detail. Buffalo, Albright-Knox Art Gallery.
997—FRIEDRICH HUNDERTWASSER, *Sun over Tibet*, 1959, detail. Milan, Private collection.
998—ERNST FUCHS, *Head of a Cherub*, 1961-65.

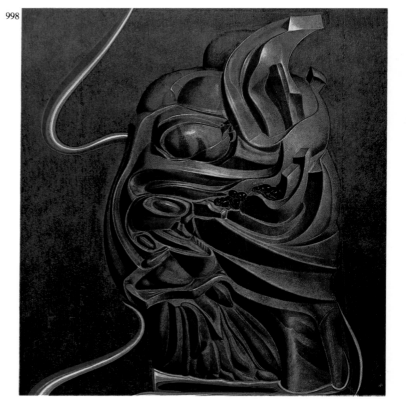

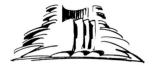

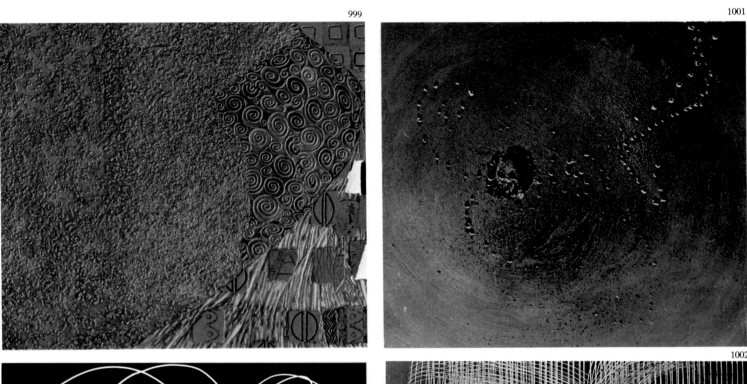

999

1001

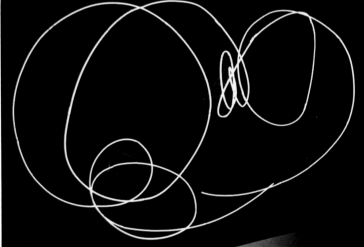

1000

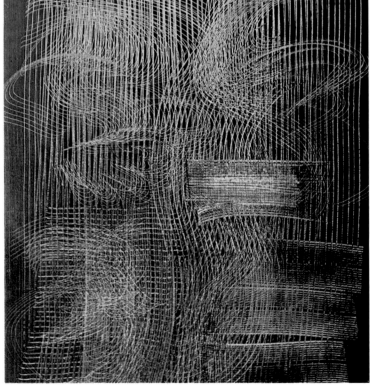

1002

999—GUSTAV KLIMT, the *Portait of Adèle Bloch-Bauer*, 1907. Vienna. Österreichisches Museum für Angewandte Kunst.
1000—LUCIO FONTANA, *Spatial Ambience*, Milan Triennale, 1951.
1001—L. FONTANA, *Spatial Concept*, 1952; detail. Milan, private collection.
1002—HANS HARTUNG, *T.1962-L.33*, 1962.

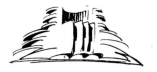

1003—BRIDGET RILEY, *Current*, 1964.
1004—FRANCO GRIGNANI, *Experimental Tension*, c. 1953. New
York, The Museum of Modern Art.

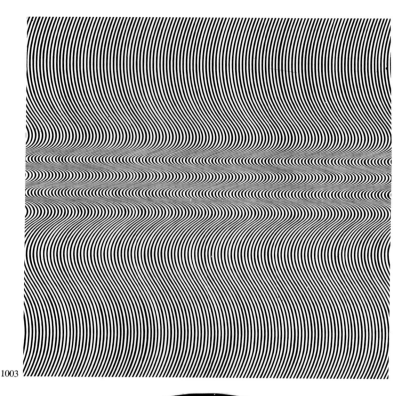

1003

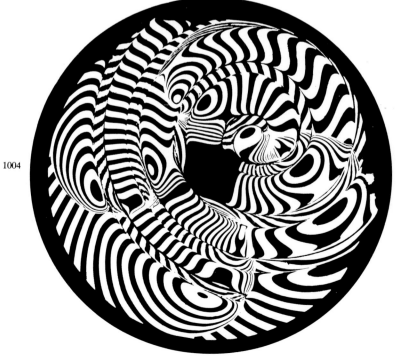

1004

Biographies of the Artists

1005—Austrian clock, Paris Exhibition, 1900. Florence, coll.
Cesaroni-Venanzi.

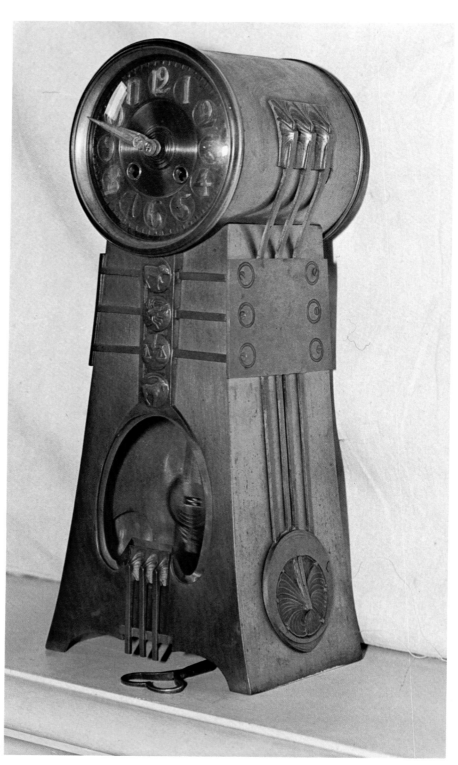

1005

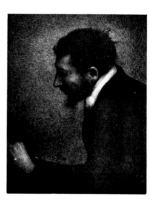

Georges Seurat, *Portrait of Aman-Jean*, 1883.

AMAN-JEAN, EDMOND
(Chevry-Cossigny, Seine et Marne, 1860 – Paris, 1935) French painter

He studied at the Ecole des Beaux Arts in Paris under the direction of Lehmann, together with Ernest Laurent. He exhibited first at the official Salon (1886), then in the first two Salons of the 'Rose et Croix' (1892 and 1893). He also exhibited regularly at the Salon de la Société Nationale. In 1924 he was co-founder with Besnard of the Salon des Tuileries.

Aman-Jean was a critic as well as a painter and lithographer. His style reflects his admiration for Rossetti and Burne-Jones, as well as his involvement with French Symbolist artists and writers.

APPIA, ADOLPHE
(Geneva, 1862 – Nyon, 1928) Swiss set designer and theatrical theorist

Appia is important for his theoretical writing (*La mise en scène du drame Wagnérien*, 1895; *La musique et la mise en scène*, 1899). He aimed at providing a visual equivalent to the music in his stage sets by using a moving light, which fluctuated in direction, intensity and colour according to the needs of the drama.

ASHBEE, CHARLES ROBERT
(Isleworth, 1863 – London, 1942) English architect and designer

He studied history at Cambridge, then decided to become an architect and went into the office of G. F. Bradley. He came under the influence of Ruskin and Morris. In 1888 he founded the Guild of Handicrafts, set up in Essex House in 1891, which specialized in furniture, metalwork, jewellery, printing and bookbinding. In 1897 he was elected a member of the Workers' Guild. In 1902 he moved the Guild to Chipping Camden, a village which he considerably rebuilt, but the group of craftsmen was dissolved in 1907.

On a lecture tour in America he met Frank Lloyd Wright and became the first English architect to recognize his importance, when he wrote the introduction to the 1911 Wasmuth edition which first published Wright's work in Europe.

In 1917 he went to Egypt and he later became civic adviser to the city of Jerusalem. As an architect he is best known for his group of houses in Cheyne Walk, London (No. 37, for his mother [1894] and Nos 38 and 39 [1904]).

BAKST, LÉON
(St Petersburg, 1867 – Paris, 1924) Russian painter and stage designer

Bakst studied at the Art Academy in Moscow and from 1893 in Paris. In 1890 he met Alexander Benois and Sergei Diaghilev. In 1898 he was one of the founder members of the Mir Iskusstva, 'World of Art', association and he organized exhibitions and published a magazine with the group. In 1902 he designed his first stage sets and costumes for the pantomime *Le coeur de la Marquise*. In 1906 he opened a school, attended by Chagall. In the same year he took part in the first exhibition of Russian art organized by Diaghilev at the Salon d'Automne in Paris. In 1908 he moved permanently to Paris and there he worked with Diaghilev and the Ballets Russes. He designed the sets and costumes for *Cleopatra, Schéhérazade, L'Après-midi d'un Faune*, etc.

In Paris, Bakst also made fashion drawings for the designer, Paul Poiret, which anticipated Art Deco. After his break with Diaghilev he designed the scenery and costumes for D'Annunzio's *Fedra*. His first biographer was André Levinson, who wrote *The Story of Léon Bakst's Life* in 1923.

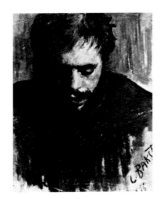

Amedeo Modigliani, *Portrait of Léon Bakst*, 1917.

BASILE, ERNESTO
(Palermo, 1857 – 1932) Italian architect

Son of the architect Giovanni Battista Basile, the architect of the Massimo Theatre in Palermo, Ernesto won the competitions for the Palace of Justice (1884) and the Parliament House (1889) in Rome. He was an expert in medieval architecture and Sicilian art and architecture. From 1877 he taught in Palermo and from 1880 at the School of Applied Arts in Rome, where he remained until 1890. He was well known for his 'villini' or little villas in Palermo and Rome; his most noted being the Hôtel Villa Igea and the Utveggio Palace in Palermo (1890s).

Eclectic and fairly historicist in his works before 1900, especially in those in Rome, his most original buildings date from the beginning of the century. The Basile House (1904) and the Frassini House (1906), both in Palermo, can be considered as two of the finest examples of Art Nouveau architecture in Italy. Later his style changed to classical revivalism in reaction against the functionalist architecture of the 1920s.

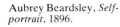

Aubrey Beardsley, *Self-portrait*, 1896.

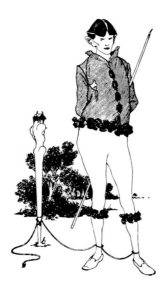

BEARDSLEY, AUBREY VINCENT
(Brighton, 1872 – Menton, 1898) English illustrator and graphic designer

He was educated in Brighton and then worked as a clerk in London. He admired Burne-Jones and Whistler and these influences can be seen in his drawings of 1890 and 1891. In 1892-93 he illustrated Malory's *Morte D'Arthur* for the publisher John Dent. The first number of *The Studio* (1893), which had a cover designed by Beardsley, contained an article on Beardsley by Joseph Pennell. Beardsley illustrated *Salomé* by Oscar

Wilde (published in 1894) and *The Yellow Book* was founded by Wilde, who made Beardsley art editor in 1894. This publication ceased with Wilde's arrest in 1895, but *The Savoy* magazine, founded by Leonard Smithers as a showcase for Beardsley's talents, began publication shortly after the demise of *The Yellow Book*. It published Beardsley's illustrations for the *Rape of the Lock* (1896), *Lysistrata* (1896), *Pierrot of the Minute* (1897) and Beardsley's own erotic novel *Under the Hill* (1896).

He suffered from tuberculosis and after 1895 his health declined. He died in 1898. The linearity and decorative qualities of his design had an important influence on Art Nouveau designers in Germany, Austria and Belgium.

BEHRENS, PETER
(Hamburg, 1868 – Vienna, 1940) German architect and designer

He studied at the Art School in Karlsruhe, and stylistically his early work is Jugendstil. He gradually rejected this decorative style in favour of a cubic, rationalist style. This is evident in his house in the artists' colony in Darmstadt (1901) and in the Pavilion of Decorative Arts at the Turin Exhibition (1902). In 1903 he left Darmstadt to live in Düsseldorf (1903-07) where he became director of the Kunstgewerbeschule. In 1907 he became a consultant to the electrical factory AEG and he designed several buildings for them, notably the turbine factory in Berlin (1908-09), where the demands of function determined the architecture.

Behrens's factories are among the earliest to be taken seriously as architecture. In 1925 he designed a house, New Ways, 508 Wellingborough Rd, Northampton. The house incorporated a room designed by Mackintosh in 1907.

After the First World War, Behrens was part of the Expressionist movement and in the late 1920s his architecture was more rational and uniform.

Thomas Phillips, *Portrait of William Blake*.

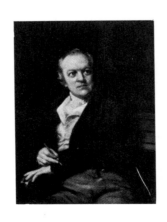

BLAKE, WILLIAM
(London, 1757 – 1827) English painter and poet

Blake earned a meagre living as a publisher's engraver, usually of other men's designs, but between this work he produced his own poems in books which he made and published himself, engraving the text and surrounding it with illustrations which he coloured by hand. In this way he published *Songs of Innocence* (1789), *Songs of Experience* (1794) and his *Prophetic Books* (1783-1804). In 1799 he moved to Sussex, to Felpham (where Beardsley later came to live); here he wrote *Milton* and *Prophetic Books*. In 1803 he returned to London, where he continued to work as an illustrator.

The painter, John Linnell, helped him to overcome his difficult financial situation, and he was able to dedicate himself to his best works, *Spiritual Portraits*, and illustrations for *The Book of Job* (1820-

26). He started the designs for the *Divine Comedy* (1827) which he did not finish because of bad health. His early work is within the Neo-Classical style although his verse and philosophy are more visionary. Blake's rejection of a logical arrangement of space and his subjective use of colour, light and form was influenced by both medieval and Mannerist examples. Ignored and rejected by his contemporaries, he was rediscovered by Dante Gabriel Rossetti and the Pre-Raphaelites.

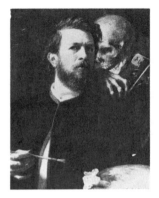

Arnold Böcklin, *Self-portrait with Death playing the Violin,* 1872.

BÖCKLIN, ARNOLD
(Basle, 1827 – Fiesole, 1901) Swiss painter

Böcklin lived most of his life in Italy. His early Roman landscapes are close to those of Corot, although he developed this style by introducing figures into his painting. His study of Pompeian frescoes led him towards a more monumental art (the frescoes for the Basle Museum, 1868-70), and the human figure began to dominate his composition (*Triton and Nereids*, 1873). His later work was more dramatic. He achieved this by his use of strident colour contrasts. Böcklin was a great influence on the German Symbolist painters, especially Thoma, Stuck and Klinger.

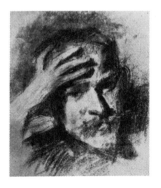

V. E. Borissov-Moussatov, *Self-portrait.*

BORISSOV – MOUSSATOV, VICTOR ELPIDIFOROVITCH
(Saratov, 1870 – Taroussa, 1905) Russian painter

After studying with Konowatov, he attended the School of Painting, Sculpture and Architecture in Moscow from 1890 to 1895, and the Academy of Art in St. Petersburg from 1892 to 1893. He went to Paris and worked in the studio of Cormon. In 1903 he went to live in Podolsk, near Moscow. He was a friend of the Symbolist poets Brjussov and Andrei Bely. In 1904 he had a series of exhibitions in Germany, organized by Cassierer. He also exhibited in Paris, where he lived for a while. He was influenced in Paris by Puvis de Chavannes and the Nabis.

BRADLEY, WILLIAM
(Boston, 1868 – Short Hill, New Jersey, 1962) American decorator, poster designer, publisher

In 1893 he opened a graphics studio in Chicago which quickly made him famous. In the same year he founded his own publishing and printing office, the 'Wayside Press' in Springfield, Massachusetts. He began to publish a magazine, *Bradley – His Book*, which contained articles and designs for paintings, books, wallpapers, upholstery and wall decorations. He intended to open a school of design for the decorative arts, but did not succeed in realizing the project. His work was shown in the first exhibition of American 'Arts and Crafts' in Boston in 1897. He also worked on a series of furniture designs published in the *Ladies*

Home Journal, which are close to the work of Voysey and Baillie-Scott, as well as the American, Wright. Bradley was also interested in architecture. He designed three houses for his family: one in Concord, Mass. (1902) and the other two in Short Hill, New Jersey (1910-20).

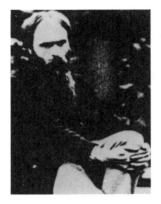

Edward Burne-Jones.

BURNE-JONES, EDWARD
(Birmingham, 1833 – London, 1898) English painter and poet

He was a close friend of Dante Gabriel Rossetti and William Morris, who greatly influenced him. He was a member of the Pre-Raphaelite Brotherhood, sharing with them an admiration for Blake and medieval art. Burne-Jones travelled in Italy in 1859, and in 1862 was in Milan and Venice with Ruskin. He made designs for the applied arts and, with Morris, was one of the founders of Morris, Marshall & Co. and of the Arts and Crafts Exhibition Society (1888). He became a baronet in 1894.

The subject matter of his paintings is usually allegorical, inspired by myths and legends like King Arthur and the Knights of the Round Table. His long-limbed knights and delicate young girls resemble those of Botticelli and Mantegna, whose works he had seen in Italy.

CASORATI, FELICE
(Novara, 1883 – Turin, 1963) Italian painter

After graduating in law in 1907, Casorati attended the Academies in Padua, Naples (1908-11) and Verona (1911-14). In 1915 he moved to Turin where he taught at the Academy. His early influences are Pre-Raphaelitism and Jugendstil, although in the early 1920s his contact with metaphysical painting and his interest in the painting of the Italian fifteenth century, make him seek an 'order' which is one of the dominant characteristics of Italian art at this period.

Galileo Chini, *Self-portrait*, 1901.

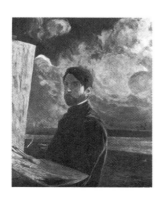

CHINI, GALILEO
(Florence, 1873 – 1954) Italian decorator, ceramist and painter

He moved from restoration into the field of ceramics when he opened a small factory in 1896. He had learned a variety of techniques and exhibited his beautiful vases at International Exhibitions in London (1898), Paris (1900) and Turin (1902). In the meantime he collaborated with architects (particularly Michelazzi) in the design of the decorative facades and interiors of houses. His cartoons of 1909 for the dome of the main building of the Venice Biennale are inspired by Klimt.

In 1911 he went to live in Persia, after being asked by the Shah to design the decorations for the Palace of the Throne, which had been designed by the architect Rigotti. He belonged to the Secessionist movement until 1925, when he turned, in painting, towards greater naturalism.

COPPEDÈ, GINO
(Florence, 1866 – Rome, 1927) Italian architect and decorator

He moved from sculpture to architecture, and his work, which was always Secessionist in style, is highly decorative, revealing a variety of influences particularly from medieval and fifteenth-century architecture. He worked in Genoa (Mackensie Castle), at Capo Santa Chiara (Bruzzo Castle and Pastorino Palace) and in Rome, where he created the Coppedè Village, near Via Po, which is remarkable for its eclectic style and an excess of decoration.

CRAIG, EDWARD GORDON
(Harpenden, England, 1872 – 1966) English theatre director, designer and theorist

Son of the actress Ellen Terry and of the architect Edward Godwin, he is considered one of the major innovators of the modern theatre because of his conviction that it is the director and not the actor who determines a production. He was also important for his use of stylized sets and special effects.

Among his productions are *Rosmersholm* by Ibsen and *Hamlet* by Shakespeare. He wrote *The Art of the Theatre* (1905); 'The Actor and the Über-Marionette' in the magazine *The Mask* (1908); *On Art and the Theatre* (1911) and *Towards a New Theatre* (1913). His graphic work and watercolours drew him close to the ornamental linearity of Art Nouveau, although his work has been seen as a precursor of geometric abstraction and kinetic art.

CRANE, WALTER
(Liverpool, 1845 – London, 1915) English painter and illustrator

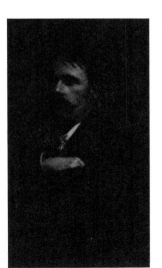

Pupil first of his father, the miniaturist Thomas Crane, then for three years of the engraver William Linton, he had the opportunity to study the works of the Pre-Raphaelites, who greatly influenced him, as well as Japanese woodcuts. With Morris and Burne-Jones, he started the Arts and Crafts Movement and he designed textiles and wallpapers, as well as working as a printer and book illustrator.

In 1873 he illustrated *The Frog Prince*, which was very much influenced by Japanese woodcuts. He also illustrated Grimm's *Fairy Tales* (1882), and one of the illustrations, the 'Goose Girl', was used by Morris for a tapestry. He was one of the founders of the Arts and Crafts Exhibition Society, which he directed. His graphic language, which can be characterized by his winding, sinuous line, is central to the development of the Art Nouveau movement.

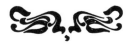

Walter Crane.

Among his writings are: *The Claim of the Decorative Arts* (1892); *Ideals in Art*; *Papers of the Arts and Crafts Movement* (1905); and *William Morris to Whistler* (1911).

D'ARONCO, RAIMONDO
(Gerona, 1857 – San Remo, 1932) Italian architect

From 1871 to 1874 he lived in Austria, where he worked as a bricklayer. After his return to Italy, he graduated in architecture at Venice University. His adherence to the Vienna Secession is demonstrated in the Palace of the International Exhibition in Turin in 1902. D'Aronco's style changed in Turkey, where he was state architect from 1896.

DAUM BROTHERS
(Auguste, 1853-1909; Antonin, 1864-1930) French industrial glass workers

They worked for their father, who had acquired a glass factory in Nancy. The Daum brothers were on good terms with Gallé and they contributed to the reputation of the School of Nancy in the art of glass making, in which they (especially Antonin) distinguished themselves. They were very successful at the 1893 Exhibition in Chicago.

DE CAROLIS, ADOLFO
(Montefiore dell'Aso, 1874 – Rome, 1928) Italian painter and engraver

He studied in Bologna and at the School of Industrial Design in Rome. He belonged to the group 'In Arte Libertas' founded in Rome by Claudio Costa, which was inspired by the ideals of a return to the tradition of the Pre-Raphaelites. He oscillated between a very decorative, floral style and the realism of Macchiaioli and Post-Impressionist painters. His best works are the illustrations for *La figlia di Jorio* and *Le Laudi* by D'Annunzio. The series of large frescoes in Pisa, Arezzo and Bologna (1908-28) have a dry, academic quality.

DE NUNQUES, WILLIAM DEGOUVE
(Monthermé, 1867 – Stavelot, 1935) Belgian painter

He belonged to an aristocratic and cultured family. After studying music he taught himself to paint. He was friendly with scholars and poets, and in 1894 he married Verhaeren's sister-in-law. He travelled a great deal to the Balearic Islands and his stay in Blaricum (1915-19) gave him the rich, oriental sources for *Bramante* and *Ardenne*.

Jean Delville.

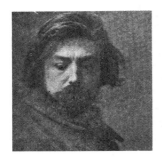

DELVILLE, JEAN
(Louvain, 1867 – Forest-les-Bruxelles, 1953) Belgian painter and writer

A follower of Sâr Péladan, both in his literary and pictorial works, he was greatly involved in Symbolism. He was four years in Rome and he painted *The School of Plato* there. In Paris, from 1892 to 1895, he was influenced by Villiers de l'Isle-Adam and by Barbey D'Aubreville, and he was a member of the Rosicrucians. Later he fell under the influence of Scriabin and then joined the followers of Krishna Murti. In 1892 he was among the founders of the Belgian group Pour l'Art, for which he designed the symbol, a sphinx. He also started an artistic and literary magazine, *L'Art et l'Idée*. In Belgium in 1906 he created Le Salon d'Art Idéaliste, in which French artists also participated. Among his literary works are: *Dialogue entre nous* (1895); *Le frisson du Sphinx* (1897); *Mission de l'Art* (1900). He was a professor at the Academy in Brussels and he taught at the Glasgow School of Art, between 1900 and 1905.

Maurice Denis, *Self-portrait*, 1899.

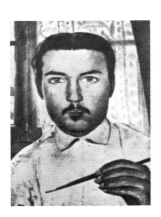

DENIS, MAURICE
(Granville, 1870 – Saint Germain-en-Laye, 1943) French painter

He attended the Lycée in Paris where he was friends with Vuillard and Roussel. At the Académie Julien he knew Bonnard, Ranson and Sérusier. In 1888, after Sérusier's visit to Pont-Aven, where Gauguin had started the Pont-Aven School, the Nabis group was founded, with Denis as a founder member.

Between 1905 and 1907 he was a Fauve; like Matisse, he treated colour as an independent decorative element. In this period he painted many portraits, landscapes and street scenes, in which strong, bright colours are contrasted. He designed and executed the wall decorations in the theatre of the Champs Elysées (1913) and in the Petit Palais, and he decorated many private villas. He taught at the Académie Ranson and in 1919 he founded, with Desvallières, the Ateliers d'Art Sacré. Among his theoretical texts on Symbolism are: *La défense du néo-traditionalisme* (1890), *Théorie* (1912), and *Nouvelles Théories* (1922).

Sergei Diaghilev.

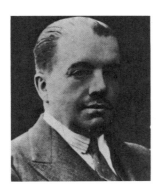

DIAGHILEV, SERGEI PAVLOVICH
(Novgorod, 1872 – Venice, 1929) Russian scholar and theatrical impresario

He studied music with Sokolov and Liadov, and began his career in the promotion of the arts by presenting exhibitions of contemporary Russian art in Paris. He met Benois and Bakst, who played a role in the realization of his Ballets Russes, in a circle of artists involved in the Russian magazine *Mir Iskusstva*, 'The World of Art'.

Diaghilev's ballet was very successful in Paris, and made Russian artists famous abroad. He heralded a period of fervent collaboration between choreographers, dancers, scenographers and avant-garde European painters. Artists involved with them included Picasso, who designed the sets for *Il cappello a tricorno* by De Falla, and Derain, who designed sets for *La boutique fantastique* by Respighi. *Parade* by J. Cocteau, with music by Satie, scenery by Picasso and choreography by Masin, was presented by Diaghilev. The most consistent collaborator c Diaghilev was the dancer Nijinsky.

DRESSER, CHRISTOPHER
(Glasgow, 1834 – 1904) English designer and writer

He studied at the School of Design in London from 1847 to 1854. His great interest was botany; he was especially fascinated by the structural laws which govern the forms of plants. He was a professor of botany and he wrote many books and papers on the subject.

In 1862 he published *The Art of Decorative Design* and also *The Development of Ornamental Art*, a critical guide to the International Exhibition of that year. After this exhibition he became an enthusiastic admirer of Japanese art. He visited Japan in 1876-77 and wrote *Japan: its Architecture, Art and Art Manufactures* (1882), which contributed to the interest in Japanese art generated by Whistler and Edward Godwin, and the goods on sale at Liberty's. In 1879 he formed a partnership with Charles Holmes of Bradford to import Japanese and other oriental goods into England. In 1879 he established a pottery (with Henry Tooth) at Linthorpe, near Middlesborough, which closed in 1882.

ECKMANN, OTTO
(Hamburg, 1865 – Badenweiler, 1902) German printer, painter and designer

He studied in Hamburg, Nuremburg and at the Academy in Munich. Initially a painter, he worked for some time in the circle of the Post-Impressionists. In 1894, he abandoned painting in favour of the decorative arts, working in the Munich Jugendstil. He was a designer and printer on the magazines *Pan* and *Jugend* and published *Dekorative Entwürfe* (1907), which was very influential for German graphics at the time. One of Eckmann's achievements was to create the semi-italic Art Nouveau typeface.

He was Professor of Graphics at the Kunstgewerbeschule in Berlin from 1897.

ENDELL, AUGUST
(Berlin, 1871 – 1925) German architect and designer

He was a student of philosophy, psychology and aesthetics at Tübingen and later at Munich under Theodore Lipps, where he was in contact with the leading artists of Jugendstil: Obrist, Riemerschmid, Pankok, etc. In 1898 he completed the decoration of the Elvira Studio in Munich (destroyed by the Nazis in 1944). It had a large, abstract motif derived from Chinese and Japanese sources running over the whole of the facade.

Endell returned to Berlin in 1901, where he designed the Buntes Theater. After the war in 1918, he became the Director of the Breslau Academy and remained there until the year of his death in 1925.

Endell designed textiles, jewellery and furniture. From 1898 he wrote a series of essays on aesthetics in the *Deutsche Kunst und Dekoration* (Darmstadt) and *Dekorative Kunst* (Munich), beginning the essay 'Um die Schönheit'.

FABERGÉ, CARL
(St Petersburg, 1846 – Lausanne, 1920) Russian goldsmith and jeweller

He worked in St.Petersburg, where his father, Gustav, had opened a silver and jewellery shop in 1842, which he took over in 1870. The family business soon became the leading firm of jewellers in the city and it received an Imperial appointment in 1881. Branches were opened in Moscow (1887), Kiev (1905) and London (1911-15). The speciality of the Fabergé workshop (which employed up to 500 specially trained craftsmen) was the infinite range of coloured enamels they produced. Their most ingenious objects were the little adult toys (like the elaborately decorated Easter eggs) which Russian and European royalty gave each other as presents. The business was nationalized after the 1918 Revolution, the staff disbanded and the stock sold. Fabergé went into exile to Riga and later Lausanne.

FEURE, GEORGES DE
(Paris, 1868 – 1943) Dutch decorator and graphic artist

Born Georges Joseph van Sluiters, de Feure adopted a French name on his return to Paris in 1890 after a long visit to his parents in Holland. De Feure trained with Chéret and worked on the interior decoration of the cabaret run by Rudolph Salis, *Le Chat Noir*. He painted and designed prints and posters in a highly individual floral and hard-edged style. These include a poster for *Paris Almanach* and prints for the prestigious periodical *L'Estampe Originale*. De Feure exhibited at the Barque de Bouteville (1892), the Salon de la Rose et Croix (1893 and 1894) and at the Société Nationale des Beaux Arts (from 1894). He decorated the Art Nouveau Pavilion at the International Exhibition of 1900 with Gaillard and Colonna.

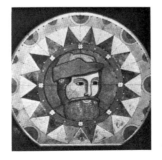

Charles Filiger, *Self-portrait*, c. 1903.

FILIGER, CHARLES
(Thann, Alto Reno, 1863 – Brest, 1928) Belgian painter

In Paris he worked in Colorassi's studio, and in 1869 he went to live in Brittany. A friend of Gauguin, Sérusier and La Rochefoucauld, he was influenced for some time by the aesthetics of the Pont-Aven School. After 1903 he elaborated a geometric style, partly inspired by Byzantine icons and by medieval stained glass windows. In 1891 with the Belgian group Les XX in Brussels and in 1892 at the Salon de la Rose et Croix in Paris, he exhibited a series of religious and mystical works.

GALLÉ, EMILE
(Nancy, 1846 – 1904) French designer and glassmaker

Gallé began working in ceramics (1864) in the factory of his father who was a glass and ceramic manufacturer in Nancy and Saint Clément. He was apprenticed to the Meisenthal glass factory (1866-67) and then he studied oriental glass in London (1871) and went to Paris and Italy. In 1874 he ran his father's ceramics factory in Saint Clément, which he united with the Nancy glass factory. In 1883 he began to manufacture cabinets as well as ceramics and glass, and a large team of artists, designers and technicians of many crafts worked for him. His Art Nouveau objects quickly became popular in Europe and America, and many of his glass vessels were sold at Bing's shop L'Art Nouveau in Paris and Nancy.

He participated in all the great International Exhibitions and in 1900 he became a member of the Stanislas Academy in Nancy. In 1901 he founded the School of Nancy of which he was president. He was also involved in the foundation of the People's University with Victor Prouvé and others, and he was one of the founders of the newspaper *L'Etoile de l'Est*.

His opalescent glass vessels were especially popular. He decorated them with the most familiar Art Nouveau motifs: willowy flowers and foliage, insects and marine creatures. He died of leukemia in 1904.

Gallen-Kallela in his laboratory.

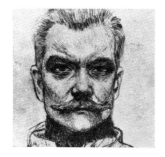

Axel Gallen-Kallela, *Self-portrait*, 1891.

GALLEN-KALLELA, AKSELI
(Pori, Finland, 1865 – Stockholm, 1931) Finnish painter

After Munch, he was the most important Scandinavian Jugendstil painter. He studied in Helsinki (1881-83) and in Paris (1884-90) and then he returned home. Influenced by the Symbolist writer Adolf Paul, who left Berlin in 1893 to visit him, he became a Symbolist. From 1895 he was involved in illustrating the Finnish epic *Kalevala* which was published in 1922. He also made tapestries and decorative panels which elaborate in an Art Nouveau style, elements of the Finnish decorative tradition.

GAUDÍ, ANTONI
(Reus, 1852 – Barcelona, 1926) Spanish architect

From a family of craftsmen, Gaudí studied in Barcelona at the School

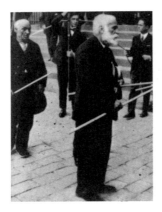

Antoni Gaudí.

of Architecture and received his degree in 1878. A great admirer of the work of Viollet-le-Duc, and briefly influenced by the fashion for historicism, he elaborated a very personal style, which combines Moorish and Gothic elements. His career was helped by the presence in Barcelona of Eusebio Güell who became his patron. He designed the Güell Palace (1885-89) and Park (1900-14).

From 1878 to 1880 he designed the Casa Vicens in Barcelona, which anticipates the influence of continental Art Nouveau style in its dynamic distribution of space and form. From 1884 to 1887 he began to build the crypt of the Church of the Holy Family in Barcelona, He resumed work there in 1903 and completely dedicated himself to it from 1910 until his death in 1926, leaving the building unfinished. He also left the chapel of Santa Colonia de Cervello (1898), probably one of his most innovative buildings, unfinished. The plan was entirely asymmetrical. His other works include the College of the Theresians in Barcelona; the house of Los Borines in Léon (1892-94); the Calvet House (1898-1904); the Villa de Bellesguardo (1900-14); the Miralles House (1901-02); the Battló House (1905-08), which has a facade covered in ceramics; and the Milá House (1905-10), with its undulating facade which anticipates Expressionist architecture.

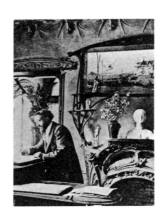

Hector Guimard in his studio.

GUIMARD, HECTOR
(Paris, 1867 – New York, 1942) French architect and designer

He studied at the Ecole des Beaux Arts and the Ecole des Arts Décoratifs in Paris (1882-86). Interested in contemporary avant-garde movements, he was particularly influenced by Victor Horta and the Belgian Art Nouveau Movement. His most famous buildings are the Castel Béranger (1894-97); a residential building with very ornate interiors; another residential building in rue de la Fontaine, Paris (1894-98); the concert hall Humbert de Romans (1902—now demolished); the synagogue built in concrete in rue Pavée au Marais in Paris (1912). Guimard is most famous for the entrances to the Paris Métro stations (1899-1904). The open metal arched entrances and light fittings are in a pure Art Noveau style. Many of these entrances have been destroyed; one of them has been acquired by the Museum of Modern Art in New York. The Art Nouveau style was sometimes called 'style Guimard' or 'style Métro' in France.

HANKAR, PAUL
(Frameries, 1861 – Brussels, 1901) Belgian architect

Until 1894 he worked in the studio of Henry Beyaert, and he borrowed some elements from him which later became characteristic of his refined, linear style. He liked to combine colours, especially white, blue-grey, and brick red, with decorative ironwork. His designs were often asymmetrical, and pointed arches, cantilevered roofs and projecting cornices often featured in his buildings. He made designs for

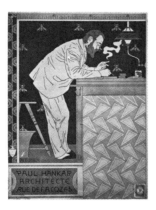

Adolphe Crispin, poster for the architect Paul Hankar, 1894.

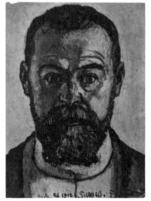

Ferdinand Hodler, *Self-portrait*, 1912.

Emil Orlik, portrait of Josef Hoffmann, 1901.

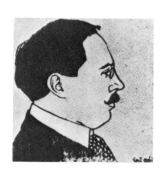

a Cité des Artistes, but they were never realized. He is, with Horta, the most interesting personality in the circle of Belgian Art Nouveau architects.

HODLER, FERDINAND
(Berne, 1853 – Geneva, 1918) Swiss painter

After a poor and difficult childhood (his father died when he was seven, his mother when he was 14), he studied in Geneva (1871-76) under Barthélémy Menn, a pupil of Ingres and friend of Corot. He travelled widely and became acquainted with the work of Holbein, Raphael, Velasquez and Dürer. In 1884 he met the Symbolist poet Louis Duchosal, an admirer of Baudelaire and Wagner. His work in the 1890s was mystical and Symbolist in content. It shows the influence of Art Nouveau in the treatment of forms. Hodler's style is characterized by monumental, symmetrical compositions and a flat, uniform use of colour. In 1896-97 he was asked to design a series of murals for the outside walls of the Zurich Landesmuseum. From 1900 he was a member of the Berlin Secession. In 1904 he exhibited his works at the Vienna Secession exhibition, and he received many commissions for mural decorations because of his success there. One of his frescoes is in the Hohenhoff building by Henry van de Velde at Hagen.

HOFFMANN, JOSEF
(Pirnitz, Moravia, 1870 – Vienna, 1956) Austrian architect

He was a pupil of Otto Wagner at the Academy in Vienna before the Secession (1897), of which he, with Gustav Klimt and Joseph Olbrich, was one of the founder members. He was a book illustrator and furniture designer as well as an architect. In 1899 he began teaching at the School of Applied Arts in Vienna. In 1903 he founded the Wiener Werkstätten with Koloman Moser, which continued until 1933. Furniture was made to a high standard of quality and taste in these workshops. This linked them with the ideals of the Arts and Crafts Movement in England.

In 1907, Hoffmann founded the Kunstschau with Gustav Klimt. His most important buildings include the Sanatorium at Purkesdorf (1904) and the Palais Stoclet in Brussels (1905-11). Hoffmann proved in this building that unrelieved shapes could be made to look monumental and lavish by means of the materials used—in this case white marble framed in bronze outside and mosaics by Klimt inside. Hoffmann's style developed from Art Nouveau linearity towards elegant, volumetric design.

In 1914 he designed and built the Austrian pavilion at the Werkbund exhibition in Cologne. In 1932 he built the Austrian pavilion for the Venice Biennale. He continued working after the Second World War.

Ludwig von Hofmann.

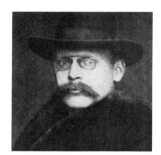

HOFMANN, LUDWIG VON
(Darmstadt, 1861 – Pillnitz, 1945) German painter

Pupil of his uncle, Heinrich Hofmann at the Academy in Dresden, he studied later at the Academy of Karlsruhe under Ferdinand Keller. In 1889 he was in Paris, at the Académie Julian, when he discovered Puvis de Chavannes and Albert Besnard. From 1890 he lived in Berlin, and was a member of the XI group formed by Max Liebermann. He was in Munich in 1892 and in Rome in 1900. He taught at the art school in Weimar (1903-08).

Victor Horta.

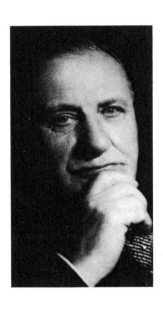

HORTA, VICTOR
(Ghent, 1861 – Brussels, 1947) Belgian architect

He studied in Paris (1878-80) and at the Brussels Academy under the Neo-Classicist Alphonse Balat. In the 1890s he designed several hotels which can be seen as Art Nouveau style at its boldest. The staircase of the Hôtel Tassel (1892-93) has exposed iron supports; the walls, floors and railings have a profusion of floral ornament. This commission was followed by the lavish Hôtel Solvay (1895-1900); the Hôtel Wissinger (1895-96); Hôtel van Eetvelde (1895); and the Maison du Peuple (1896-99, demolished), which has the first glass and iron facade in Belgium. Horta also designed the store L'Innovation (1901, now demolished); the Brugman Hospital (1906-24); and the Grand Bazaar in Frankfurt (1903), notable for their large expanses of glass.

Horta was appointed professor of the Brussels Academy in 1912, and he was the director from 1927 until 1931. He lived in the United States from 1916 to 1919. On his return to Brussels his work became more rationalist. The Palais des Beaux Arts in Brussels (1922-28) is a characteristic design of this period. Built in concrete, it is the prototype for the 'community centre' which architects and planners favoured in the post-war period.

William Holman Hunt.

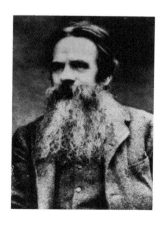

HOLMAN HUNT, WILLIAM
(London, 1827 – 1910) English painter

One of the founder members, with Millais and Rossetti, of the Pre-Raphaelite Brotherhood in 1848. He painted biblical scenes, and, encouraged by Ruskin, he went to the Holy Land and Egypt three times in 1854, 1869 and 1873 in order to make the settings of his pictures accurate. In his work he combines allegorical symbolism with a minute observation of nature. He was the only member of the Brotherhood to remain faithful to their principles.

In 1905 he published *Pre-Raphaelitism and the Pre-Raphaelite Brotherhood*, the best documented memoir of the movement.

Wassily Kandinsky.

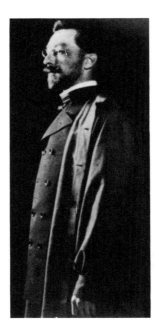

KANDINSKY, WASSILY
(Moscow, 1866 – Neuilly-sur-Seine, 1944) Russian painter

Kandinsky studied law and political economics at Moscow University. He was interested in popular Russian art and in 1896 he went to Munich to become a painter. At this stage in his career, his predilection for folklore is combined with Art Nouveau curving lines and bright colours. In 1901 he founded the association, Phalanx, in Munich, which organized exhibitions of contemporary European artists, as well as of its own members. From 1903-08 Kandinsky travelled a great deal (Italy, Holland, Tunis, Paris) and his painting gradually became more abstract. In 1910 he painted his first purely abstract work, and he was one of the inventors of abstract painting. In 1911 he was a founder member of the Blaue Reiter group.

He published a book in 1912 which was translated into English and published in 1914: *The Art of Spiritual Harmony*. He was in Russia in 1914-21 and then he returned to Germany and he taught at the Bauhaus from 1922. In 1933 he settled in France.

KHNOPFF, FERNAND
(Gremberger-les-Termonde, 1858 – Brussels, 1921) Belgian painter, engraver and critic

Khnopff first studied law at the University of Brussels. He then studied with Xavier Mellery at the Academy in Brussels. In 1877 he went to Paris where he frequented the studio of Lefèvre and the Académie Julian. He was greatly influenced by Gustave Moreau and Burne-Jones, whose names, engraved in two bronze rings, hung on the wall of an otherwise empty room in his house. He maintained contacts with Germany and Austria, particularly with Vienna; in 1898 his work was illustrated in *Ver Sacrum*, the periodical of the Vienna Secession. In 1884 he was among the founders of the Belgian group Les XX. He was friendly with many of the poets of his generation, from Maeterlinck to Verhaeren (who also wrote about his work).

His subject matter was enigmatic and full of symbolic references. He was preoccupied with the idea of woman as a mysterious and seductive figure, a sphinx from another world. The titles of his paintings often contain quotations from Symbolist poets. He took part in the first Salon de la Rose et Croix in 1892 in Paris. He also designed the furniture and decor of the Hôtel de la Ville in Saint-Gilles and of the Théâtre de la Monnaie in Brussels.

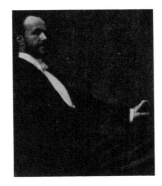

Fernand Khnopff.

KLIMT, GUSTAV
(Baumgarten, Vienna, 1862 – Vienna, 1918) Austrian painter

After following courses at the School of Decorative Arts in Vienna (1876-83) he worked with his brother Ernst and the painter Frantz Matsch on large allegorical paintings (the ceilings for the theatres in

Gustav Klimt.

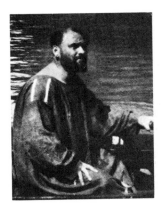

Reichenberg, Fiume, Karlsbad, as well as for the Kunsthistorisches Museum and the Burgtheater in Vienna) until the death of his brother in 1892. In 1897 Klimt became the president of the newly formed, avant-garde organization, the Vienna Secession, and contributed to *Ver Sacrum*, their journal.

Klimt's style combines both naturalistic and highly decorative elements. He was influenced by the Pre-Raphaelites as well as by Japanese art. From 1899 to 1907, Klimt worked on the designs for the ceiling of the Great Hall of Vienna University (Philosophy, Medicine, Jurisprudence), but his work was very unpopular and it was rejected. In 1905 he refused the Villa Romano prize (which he had won together with Hodler and Hübner) and he turned down the professorship at the Academy in Vienna. In 1907, after leaving the Secession, he founded the Kunstschau (with Hoffmann). In 1906 he was in Brussels working on the mosaic wall decorations for Hoffmann's Palais Stoclet (cartoons 1905-09, executed 1909-11).

Max Klinger.

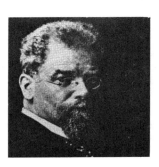

KLINGER, MAX
(Leipzig, 1857 – Grossjena, nr Naumberg, 1920) German painter, engraver and sculptor

He studied at the Karlsruhe Academy under Grussow and he went with his teacher to Berlin in 1875. In 1878 he exhibited two series of drawings at the annual exhibition of the Academy in Berlin, which were acquired by the Academy. From 1883 to 1886 he was in Paris, then he returned to Berlin. He was in Rome from 1888-93 where he worked in the studio of Arnold Böcklin. After his return to Germany he settled in Leipzig where he taught at the Academy. His home was the focal point of artistic life in the city. From 1903 he lived in Grossjena. He worked on sculpture and in graphics as well as painting – his polychrome sculpture of Beethoven (1886-1902) was well known in his lifetime. His symbolist and fantastic graphic work reflected several influences, especially Böcklin and Goya.

KOKOSCHKA, OSKAR
(Pöchlarn, 1886 – 1980) Austrian painter

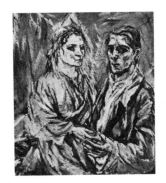

A friend of Gustav Klimt and other artists of the Secession, Kokoschka attended the School of Arts and Crafts in Vienna from 1904. He dedicated his first engravings to Klimt which were illustrations for a children's book entitled *Children's Dreams* (1908). They were full of allusions to popular art and Austrian folklore. He was also a friend of Adolf Loos, who was the first artist to break with the use of Art Nouveau ornament. Kokoschka collaborated on the magazine *Der Sturm*, which was one of the organs of the Expressionists.

Oskar Kokoschka, *Self-portrait with Alma Mahler,* 1913.

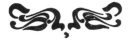

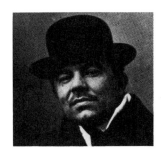

Pavel Warfolomeivitch Kousnetsov.

KOUSNETSOV, PETER WARFOLOMEIVITCH
(Saratov on the Volga, 1878 – Moscow, 1908) Russian painter

He was a pupil of the School of Painting, Sculpture and Architecture in Moscow, together with his friend Petrov-Vodkine. His work was greatly influenced by Borissov-Moussatov. Between 1902 and 1908 he was one of the most important young Russian Symbolists in the group called the Blue Rose; he was also connected with the magazine *La Toison d'Or*. In Paris Kousnetsov was a member of the jury of the Salon d'Automne. His connection with Symbolism ceased around 1910.

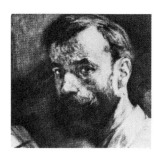

Frantisek Kupka, *Self-portrait*.

KUPKA, FRANTISEK
(Opocno, Bohemia, 1871 – Puteaux, 1957) Czechoslovakian painter

Kupka was first a saddler and then a varnisher for a craftsman who taught him colouring, and he became a sign painter. After studying in Prague at the Academy from 1887-91 and at the Viennese Academy from 1891-95, Kupka went to live in Paris, where he practised as a spiritualist medium and contributed to various satirical magazines like *Le Canard Sauvage*, *L'Assiette au Beurre* and several books including the *Lysistrata* of Aristophanes (1911).

His painting was initially inspired by the Fauves. Later he began investigating the colour theories of Newton, Chevreul and the Neo-Impressionists, and his art developed towards abstraction. In 1911 he produced his *Planes of Colour*, a series of experimental abstract colour compositions.

LALIQUE, RENÉ
(Paris, 1860 – 1945) French designer and jeweller

After studying at the Ecole des Beaux Arts in Paris, he opened a jewellery workshop (1885) and later supplied jewellery for the opening of Bing's shop, L'Art Nouveau. He reacted against the nineteenth-century taste for large cut stones. In his jewellery the settings are as important as the stones. He favoured asymmetrical patterns and he used all of the most popular Art Nouveau motifs – dragonflies, beetles, peacocks, sinuous female nudes, flowers, etc.

LÉVY-DHURMER, LUCIEN
(Algiers, 1865 – Le Vesinet, 1935) French painter

He studied at the Community School of Design and Sculpture in Paris and later followed Raphaël Collin's courses. He received a prize at the International Exhibition in Paris in 1900. He worked at first as a decorator, then in 1895 he visited Italy and became interested in Italian classical art and the Pre-Raphaelites. He exhibited at the gallery of

Georges Petit in Paris (1896) when he added his maternal name, Lévy, to his surname.

His painting is in the refined, Symbolist manner and is almost the pictorial equivalent of Jean Lorrain's writing.

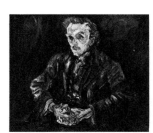

Oskar Kokoschka, *Portrait of Adolf Loos*, 1909.

LOOS, ADOLF
(Brno, 1870 – Kalksburg, 1933) Austrian architect

He studied architecture at Dresden Polytechnic. From 1893 to 1896 he was in America and visited the Chicago Exhibition. His work in Vienna was strongly influenced by Otto Wagner. His most important buildings are private houses of 1904 to 1910 (like the house on Lake Geneva and the Steiner House). They are characterized by their cubic shape, a total absence of ornament and a love of fine materials. In his journalism he was a rabid anti-ornamentalist and an enemy of the Wiener Werkstätten and of Josef Hoffmann.

His writings brought him into contact with artists and intellectuals like Oskar Kokoschka, Arnold Schönberg, Karl Kraus and Peter Altenberg. In 1906 he founded the Free School of Architecture and in 1908 published his famous essay 'Ornament and Crime'.

His architectural work includes the Museum Café in Vienna (1899) and the Café Américain. From 1920-22 he was in charge of housing in Vienna. In 1922 he moved to Paris and into the Jeanneret-Ozenfant and Dadaist circles. He built a house for Tristan Tzara in Paris (1926). Later he worked in Vienna and Prague.

Loos was not a successful architect but he was influential among some of the avant-garde in Europe.

MCNAIR, FRANCES MACDONALD
(Glasgow, 1874 – 1921) Scottish designer

She studied at the Glasgow School of Art with her sister Margaret, Charles Rennie Mackintosh, and Herbert McNair (whom she married in 1899). She was one of the Group of Four, which constituted the Glasgow School, the principal exponents of the Scottish Art Nouveau movement. They executed many decorative works as a group, and with McNair she participated in the most important international exhibitions of the decorative arts. From 1907 she taught the decorative arts at the School of Art in Glasgow.

MCNAIR, HERBERT
(Glasgow, 1870 – 1945) Scottish architect, designer and illustrator

He studied at the Glasgow School of Art, where he met Charles Rennie Mackintosh and the MacDonald sisters, with whom he started a fruitful collaboration as the Glasgow Four who introduced the newest forms of

Art Nouveau into Scotland. He often worked in collaboration with his wife, Frances MacDonald, and was the author of *Furnishings and Textile Decoration* as well as illustrating several literary works.

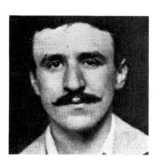

Charles Rennie Mackintosh.

MACKINTOSH, CHARLES RENNIE
(Glasgow, 1868 – London, 1928) Scottish architect and designer

He studied at the Glasgow School of Art from 1885. In 1890 he was a designer for the Honeyman and Keppie Co. in Glasgow. From 1893 with McNair and their future wives, Margaret and Frances MacDonald, they designed graphic work and metalwork in an Art Nouveau style inspired by photographs and illustrations in *The Studio* (which started publication in London in 1893) and especially by the work of Jan Toorop. He designed the revolutionary Glasgow School of Art (1897), a number of tea rooms in Glasgow for Miss Cranston (1897-1910) and several private houses notably Windyhill, Kilmalcolm (1899-1901) and Hill House, Helensburgh (1902-03)).

He began to design furniture for his own use in c. 1890 and he provided designs for the Glasgow firm of furniture makers, Guthrie and Wells. His own individual style in interior design had fully evolved by 1899 – white lacquered chairs and cupboards with decoration in metal and pink, mauve or mother-of-pearl enamel.

His designs were not particularly popular in Britain, but they were very successful on the Continent. He exhibited in Venice (1899), Vienna (1900), and Turin (1902). In 1901 he won second prize in a German publisher's competition for the 'House of an Art Lover' (Baillie Scott came first), and this consolidated his fame abroad. He was very influential in Vienna and Germany.

He was a difficult man whose erratic ways alienated him from clients. In 1913 he left the firm (Honeyman and Keppie) in which he had been a partner since 1904. He moved to Walberswick and then to London, to Port Vendres and finally back to London. He painted highly original landscapes, but he never recovered his architectural practice.

MACKINTOSH, MARGARET MACDONALD
(Glasgow, 1865 – 1933) Scottish designer and decorator

Together with Mackintosh, whom she married in 1900, she was part of the Group of Four (with her sister Frances and McNair) who introduced Art Nouveau to Scotland. Her style is similar to Mackintosh and she is particularly noted for her decorative panels. Several of her works are in metal and her many works in collaboration with Mackintosh are highly valued.

MACKMURDO, ARTHUR
(Heygate, 1851 – 1942) English architect, designer, economist

Around 1880 he was encouraged by John Ruskin (with whom he had travelled to Italy in 1874) to become an architect. In 1882, with Herbert Horne, Selwyn Image and Bernard Creswick he founded the Century Guild, a co-operative association of artists and craftsmen who were inspired by Morris and Ruskin. He devoted himself to typography, textile design and graphics. He wrote, among other things, *Wren's City Churches*, which he published in 1883. The design for the cover, with its flame-like curves, was taken up almost a decade later as a basic motif of Art Nouveau design. The furniture he designed from 1886 established him as the forerunner of Voysey in its clarity of structure, elegance and originality.

After 1884 he was editor of the magazine of the Century Guild *The Hobby Horse*. Among his architectural works are two houses in Bush Hill Park (1873-83) as well as the Mempes House (1899) and, in collaboration with H. Horne, the Savoy Hotel in London (1889). In 1904 he retired to Essex and concentrated on economic problems and writing.

Ford Madox Brown.

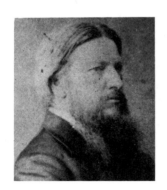

MADOX BROWN, FORD
(Calais, 1821 – London, 1893) English painter

He travelled in the Netherlands and was a pupil, in Bruges, of Gregorius (a follower of David) and in Antwerp, of Wappers. During his formative years in Paris and Rome, he was influenced by the Nazarenes, Cornelius and Overbeck, whom he had met in Rome. After his return to London in 1845 he was close to the Pre-Raphaelites (he met Rossetti in 1848) although he was never a member of the Brotherhood. He carried out large-scale decorations for the Town Hall of Manchester.

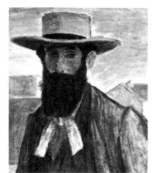

Joseph Rippl-Ronai,
Portrait of A. Maillol,
1899.

MAILLOL, ARISTIDE
(Banyuls-sur-Mer, 1861 – Perpignan, 1944) French sculptor

At the Ecole de Beaux Arts in Paris, he was the pupil of Gérôme and Cabanel. Later he went on to study sculpture at the Ecole des Arts Décoratifs. His meeting with Gauguin was momentous; after it he abandoned his academic studies and opened a tapestry workshop in Banyuls. In 1893 he came into contact with the Nabis. After an illness of the eye in 1895, he abandoned painting and tapestry and turned to sculpture. He participated in 1898 in the Brussels exhibition of Le Livre Esthétique, with a series of small terracotta sculptures. His sculpture was a reaction against the fluid contours of Rodin's work. He stressed the static and monumental qualities of the human figure, which he achieved by returning to the ideals of Greek art of the fifth century BC.

In 1903 he went to live at Marly, near Maurice Denis, who influenced him strongly. One of his most famous works, the Cézanne Monument for Aix (1912) was rejected by the city in 1925. It was later placed in the Tuileries in Paris.

MAJORELLE, LOUIS
(Toul, 1859 – Nancy, 1926) French furniture designer

After following a course of the Academy of Fine Arts in Paris, he returned to Nancy, where he took over the management of his father's (Auguste Majorelle) furniture company. At first he made reproductions in a variety of styles, particularly Rococo. Later, probably due to Gallé's influence, he turned to the linear and floral lines of Art Nouveau. His factory was almost completely burnt down in 1916, but he returned to Nancy in 1918 to rebuild it. He abandoned Art Nouveau design, which had gone out of fashion, in favour of a more classic style.

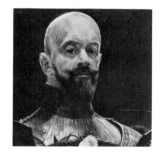

Jacek Malczweski, *Self-portrait*, 1914.

MALCZWESKI, JACEK
(Radomin, 1854 – Cracow, 1929) Polish painter

After studying in Cracow he lived in Paris from 1867 to 1877, where he attended the Ecole des Beaux Arts. Later he travelled to Asia Minor, Greece, Italy and Germany. Upon his return to Cracow he became rector of the Academy of Fine Arts. His early works were realistic treatments of the theme of national liberation against Russia. After 1890 he became a Symbolist and transformed his colour range with more expansive and lighter tones. His nostalgic references to a mythical past and to the ideals of national awakening remained his fundamental theme. He portrayed people from real life, friends and celebrities, and he located them in realistic landscapes, but he added invented and mythical images, like angels, mermaids, figures of death, to these compositions.

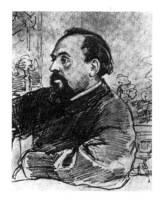

Ilya Repin, *Portrait of Savva Mamontov*, 1879.

MAMONTOV, ELIZABETH AND SAVVA
(Elizabeth, 1847 – 1909; Savva, 1841 – 1918) Russian industrialists and patrons of the arts

The Mamontovs initially aimed at forming a private opera company with a circle of artists, musicians and critics which they had drawn to Abramtsevo. This developed into a more grandiose scheme, a centre for the rebirth of Russian popular art, which was aimed at teaching crafts to the peasants. At the forefront of the paternalistic Mamontov circle were figures like Korovin, Vastnetsov and Vrubel, all of whom contributed to the diffusion of Modernism in Russian culture. The theories of Ruskin and Morris were an important starting point, but the popular forms of local tradition provided the working material.

Alberto Martini, *Self-portrait*, 1898.

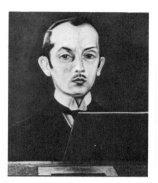

MARTINI, ALBERTO
(Oderzo, Treviso, 1876 – Milan, 1954) Italian engraver, painter and illustrator

He studied engraving in the Secessionist circle in Munich in 1898. He illustrated works which included *Il Morgante Maggiore* by Pulci and Dante's *Divine Comedy*. He expressed eroticism in an almost surreal manner; the macabre and cruel elements in his style were appropriate to his illustrations of Poe (1905-08), to Huysman's *A Rebours*; D'Annunzio's *Cronaca Bizantina* and Shakespeare's *Hamlet* and *Macbeth*. In 1904 he exhibited two series of lithographs: *The Mysteries* and *The Macabre Dance*. In the early 1920s he worked as a set designer, but in 1928 he moved to Paris and began to develop his chiaroscuro paintings.

Joseph Mehoffer, *Self-portrait*, 1898.

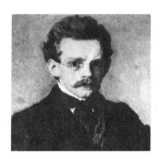

MEHOFFER, JOSEF
(Ropczyc, 1869 – Wadorvic, 1946) Polish painter

Mehoffer first studied law and then became a painter. He participated in the realization of the stained glass windows in the Church of Our Lady in Cracow. He went to Vienna and Paris and on his return he won the competition for the stained glass windows at the collegiate Church of St. Nicholas in Freiburg, and executed the windows between 1896 and 1934. As well as working in stained glass he made several frescoes, such as those for the Wavel castle in Cracow. His paintings, inspired by local folklore, are richly decorative.

MICHELAZZI, GIOVANNI
(Rome, 1879 – Florence, 1920) Italian architect

He worked mainly in France, having been influenced by the Art Nouveau of the Secessions and of the School of Glasgow. He read the theoretical writing of Otto Wagner, from *New Architecture* (1894) to all of the publications of the Wagnerschule. He succeeded in producing a series of buildings that are among the most important of the Italian Art Nouveau movement, even if they are possibly not the most well known: the small Villa Ravazzini in Florence (1907-08), the studio house in the Borgo Ognissanti close to the historical centre of Florence. Other buildings by him are the Villa Broggi-Caraceni (1911) and Villa Baroncelli (1920). No autograph drawings or documents remain. He committed suicide in 1920.

Sir John Everett Millais.

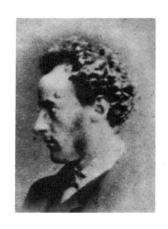

MILLAIS, SIR JOHN EVERETT
(1829-96) English painter

He was a student at the Royal Academy Schools in 1840 (when aged eleven). In 1848 he, with Hunt and Rossetti, founded the Pre-Raphaelite Brotherhood. Millais later broke away from the Brotherhood, and developed into a fashionable academic portrait- and genre-painter. He later became President of the Royal Academy and a baronet.

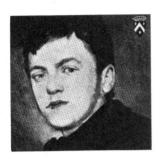

G. van de Walle, *Portrait of George Minne*, 1885.

MINNE, GEORGE
(Ghent, 1866 – Laethem-St-Martin, 1941) Belgian sculptor and designer

His father, an architect and building contractor, did not believe in the artistic talent of his son, who managed to attend the Academy in Ghent from 1882 to 1884. Between 1885 and 1889 he worked in solitude, influenced by Rodin. His friendships with the major Belgian Symbolist poets from Grégoire Le Roy to van Lerberghe and Verhaeren, accentuated his mystical sensibility. His most important works were realized in extreme solitude, almost in poverty, in Brussels, where he lived between 1895 and 1898; these are *The Kneelers*, *The Man with the Leather Bag*, and *Solidarity*. Invited in 1890 by Les XX to go to Brussels, he joined them in 1891. After his move in 1899 to Laethem-St-Martin, he became involved in the cultural life of the town. From 1912 to 1914 and from 1916 to 1919 he taught at the Academy in Ghent. His most famous work is the *Fountain of the Kneeling Youths*, 1898.

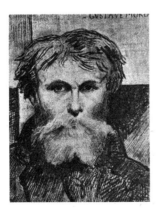

Gustave Moreau, *Self-portrait*.

MOREAU, GUSTAVE
(Paris, 1826 – 1898) French painter

The son of an architect, he studied at the Ecole des Beaux Arts in Paris under the guidance of Picot (1846-49). From 1850 to 1856 he attended the studio of Chassériau, who, along with Delacroix, was one of Moreau's favourite painters. Later he went to Italy (1857-59), where he copied the works of the Renaissance painters. He exhibited at several Salons, but led a very isolated life. He would often resume work on a painting even after a break of many years. His subject matter came from classical myths, legends and the Bible. The theme of Salomé personified his idea of woman ('bored, capricious, like an animal'). Salomé is an image to which he returned frequently in his compositions. The mystery in Moreau's paintings was admired by the Surrealists. He was one of the precursors of Symbolism. He made many illustrations for La Fontaine's stories like *Oedipus and the Sphinx*, *Hercules and the Hydra* and *The Rape of Europa*.

His house in Paris in rue La Rochefoucauld has been turned into the Musée Moreau. It contains most of his paintings and graphic work as well as wax sculpture by him.

Dante Gabriel Rossetti,
William Morris at Twenty-two Years, 1856.

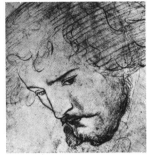

Max Beerbohm, caricature
of Morris and Burne-
Jones.

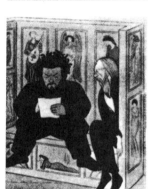

MORRIS, WILLIAM
(Walthamstow, 1834 – Hammersmith, 1896) English designer, craftsman and theorist

He was educated at Marlborough and Oxford where he studied Divinity. He became a friend of Burne-Jones with whom he formed an Oxford division of the Pre-Raphaelite Brotherhood. He began his career as an architect in the office of G. E. Street where he met Philip Webb who built the Red House for him (1860), which was decorated and furnished by Morris himself. In 1861, together with Rossetti, Burne-Jones, Madox Brown, Marshall, Faulkner and Webb, he founded the Company Morris, Marshall, Faulkner and Co., which made craft objects and furnishings. Morris believed that 'all the minor arts were in a state of complete degradation' and his company tried to improve the situation by reviving craftsmanship. He was hostile to machinery and his insistence on hand-made goods made his products far too expensive for the ordinary people. However, his textiles, wallpapers, stained glass and furniture became very popular amongst the wealthy and in 1881 the company (with the defection of Madox Brown, Rossetti and Marshall) moved to Merton Abbey. In 1881, together with others, Morris founded the Arts and Crafts Exhibition Society.

In 1890, Morris opened, again at Merton Abbey, the Kelmscott Press, which became famous for its prestigious hand-printed publications; among the most important works was an edition of *The Complete Works of Chaucer* in 1896. Morris designed a typeface especially for it. Most of his designs were based on floral patterns, a style which became richer and denser in his maturity.

He was a socialist and he founded in London *The Oxford and Cambridge Magazine.* He wrote several books including *The Dream of John Bull, News from Nowhere,* and *Socialism its Growth and Outcome.*

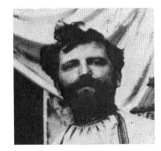

Alphonse Mucha.

MUCHA, ALPHONSE MARIA
(Ivancice, Moravia, 1860 – Prague, 1939) Czechoslovakian decorator, painter and graphic artist

Early in his career he intended to work in the theatre. In Vienna in 1877 he worked as a designer for the Theater am Ring. A patron who recognized his talent, Khuen Belassi, sent him to study in Munich, at the Academy. In Paris in 1887, with the Czech painter Masek, he attended the Académie Julian and the Académie Colarossi, and began work as an illustrator for the most famous Parisian journals. In 1898 he was commissioned to design a poster for Sarah Bernhardt, who was at the height of her success as an actress. He became famous overnight for his poster designs (e.g. the Bernhardt posters and those advertising 'Job' cigarette papers, 1898). He also designed fabrics, clothes, shop fittings and window displays. In 1901 he designed a jewellery shop for Georges Fouquet in Paris (now demolished), as well as some very elaborate jewellery. Famous world wide for his graphics, he left Paris for the United States in 1904. He returned to Czechoslovakia in 1911, and executed a number of paintings which were dedicated to Slavic Europe. He was represented at the International Exhibition of Paris by his graphic work for magazines like *La Plume*. He decorated many public buildings, notably theatres in Berlin and Prague.

MUNCH, EDVARD
(Löten, 1863 – Ekely, 1944) Norwegian painter

Educated in Norway, his formative years were spent in Paris and Berlin, where a large exhibition of his work (1892) was the formative influence on German painting. After this exhibition he was influenced by Gauguin, but his subjects deal with basic themes of love and death. His graphic work is probably more influential than his paintings. He is the precursor of Expressionism.

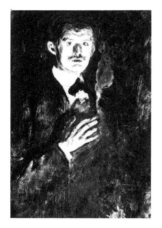

Edvard Munch, *Self-portrait*, 1895.

NERÉE TOT BABBERICH, KAREL CHRISTOPHE HENRI DE
(Huize Babberich, Zevenaar, 1880 – Todtmoos, Baden, 1901) Dutch painter

Born into a noble family, he attended the School of Commerce in Antwerp (1895-97) and immediately entered the diplomatic service, which he abandoned in 1901 because of ill health. His biography in many respects is similar to Beardsley's. Like Beardsley, he had drawn since childhood, though not professionally. Like Beardsley, illness was probably the incentive which made him develop his own particular tense and refined language. He spent his last years in one sanatorium after another. He was influenced first by the work of Toorop, whom he admired greatly. Later his engravings came close to the style of De Feure. He is the author of at least 350 illustrations, of which some 300 are preserved.

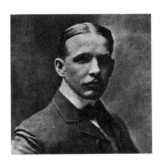

C. K. H. de Nerée Tot Babberich.

OBRIST, HERMANN
(Kilchberg, Zurich, 1869 – Munich, 1927) Swiss sculptor and designer

After attending the Faculty of Science at the University of Heidelberg, he enrolled at the Crafts School in Karlsruhe (1888). Later he continued his studies at Weimar. In Turingia he realized a series of drawings for ceramics for the Grand Duke of Saxony. He designed tapestries and the famous embroidery *Cyclamen* (1895), one of the finest examples of the whiplash line. In 1892 he opened an embroidery workshop in Florence, which he moved to Munich in 1894. In 1897 he opened a furnishing factory there. His designs are very close to early Belgian Art Nouveau.

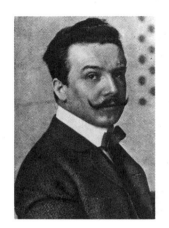

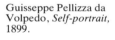
Joseph Olbrich.

OLBRICH, JOSEPH MARIA
(Troppau, 1867 – Dusseldorf, 1908) Austrian architect

At first he was a pupil of Hasenauer at the Academy in Vienna (1890-93) and then he trained under Otto Wagner. With Wagner, Olbrich built several Viennese underground stations. In 1897 he was, with Klimt, one of the founders of the Vienna Secession, and he designed their exhibition centre. Here he showed his refined taste for detail, as well as his sense for free organization of internal spaces, which could be arranged in various ways using movable walls and wings. He designed a series of villas and houses in Vienna and worked on a project for an artists' village at Darmstadt, where he lived and built his house. In the Tietz department store in Düsseldorf (1908), which was his last work, he returned to a classical style of architecture.

He died suddenly while the building was under construction. He was prolific; he left 40 executed works and approximately 28,000 drawings. Notable examples of his works are his house in Darmstadt and the Exhibition Palace and Marriage Tower in Darmstadt (1907).

Guisseppe Pellizza da Volpedo, *Self-portrait*, 1899.

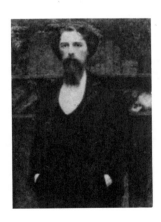

PELIZZA DA VOLPEDO, GIUSEPPE
(Volpedo, Alessandria, 1869 – 1907) Italian painter

Born into a peasant family, he first attended the Brera Academy (1883) in Milan, and later in Rome and Florence (1887-88). Initially he painted in a Divisionist style. He followed courses in literature, history and art history at the University of Florence. There, medieval and early-Renaissance painters were carefully studied by Italian as well as by Pre-Raphaelite painters. His meeting with Morbelli and his study of Morris, Engels, Marx and Tolstoy, contributed greatly to his search for social realism. He was also influenced by the Symbolism of Segantini and Previati. He was in Paris in 1889 and later in 1900, where he exhibited in the International Exhibition. There he saw the work of Monet and Seurat. The tryptich *The Love of Life* is one of the best examples of Italian Symbolism.

PERRET, AUGUSTE
(Exelles, 1874 – Paris, 1954) French architect

The son of the owner of a building and contracting firm, after studying under Gaudet at the Ecole des Beaux Arts, he and his brothers joined the firm (known from 1905 as Perret Frères). His first large job was No. 25b rue Franklin, a block of flats, which had a reinforced concrete structure with the concrete members displayed and Art Nouveau faience infilling. The garage in the rue Ponthieu expresses even more emphatically the structural concrete frame. He collaborated with van de Velde (1911-14) on the theatre on the Champs Elysées, which was originally designed by van de Velde. Because of its proudly displayed concrete skeleton, its final design is essentially Perret's.

Perret continued to experiment with the new material. In 1945 he was in charge of the rebuilding of Le Havre, using prefabricated elements. He can be seen as the architect who developed the structural inventions in the Art Nouveau period and made the transition to rationalist modern architecture.

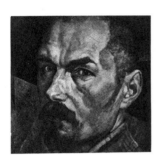

Kosma Petrov-Vodkine, *Self-portrait*, 1908.

PETROV-VODKIN, KOSMA SERGEIVITCH
(Chwalynsk on the Volga, 1878 – Leningrad, 1939) Russian painter

Petrov-Vodkine was one of the most important Russian painters of the first twenty years of this century. He studied design and painting in Saratov and in St. Petersburg, and sculpture and architecture in Moscow. He went to Munich, London, Italy and he also studied in Paris, where he returned after a journey to North Africa. He was a writer and theorist as well as an artist. He wrote a book on perspective, *Theory of Colours and Volumes*, which defined spherical perspective. He applied his theories to his Symbolist paintings, which were also inspired by the work of Puvis de Chavannes and Maurice Denis. They are characterized by a flat, dry use of colour. He was the author of plays and of two autobiographies, *Chlynowsk* (1930) and *Euclid's Space* (1932).

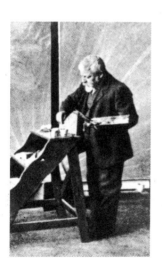

Gaetano Previati.

PREVIATI, GAETANO
(Ferrara, 1852 – Lavagna, 1920) Italian painter

After studying at Ferrara, at the School of Fine Arts, he attended Bertini's courses at the Brera in Milan and was influenced by the contemporary Scapigliatura movement in Lombard painting. After 1900 he elaborated a scientific theory on the use of colour which was inspired by Grubicy and which is evident in *The Kiss* (1887) and *Peace* (1889). The futurists saw Previati as an innovator. His technique made an impression on Boccioni, who arrived in Milan in 1907.

In c. 1890 he worked on illustrations of Poe, which were influenced by the Symbolism of Redon. After the death of Segantini, he became the major representative of Italian Divisionism, but later his style of painting was weighed down with rhetoric. Between 1909 and 1916 he published his theoretical essays *Scientific Principles of Divisionism*.

PUVIS DE CHAVANNES, PIERRE
(Lyons, 1824 – Paris, 1898) French painter

Puvis de Chavannes attempted to recreate something of the monumental Italian fresco style in his huge decorative canvases. His colour was flat and pale, giving his work a dreamlike atmosphere. His symbolism, in some decorative aspects, approaches Art Nouveau examples. He decorated many town halls and other official buildings in

France, the most famous being the Panthéon, Paris (1874-78), the Hôtel de la Ville, Paris (1889-93), and the Library in Boston (1893-95). He was admired by the Post-Impressionists as a painter of symbolical and allegorical decoration, who respected the wall surface and composed his murals in simple areas of colour with rhythmic linear patterns.

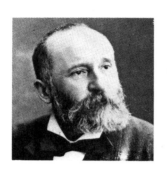

Pierre Puvis de Chavannes.

RANSON, PAUL
(Limoges, 1864 – Paris, 1909) French painter and decorator

After his education at the School of Decorative Arts in Limoges and in Paris, he entered the Académie Julian in 1888; there he came into contact with the Nabis and shared a studio with them. In 1893-94 he produced lithographs for the *Revue Blanche* and in 1895 he designed his first tapestries.

His paintings were always consistent with the ideas of the Nabis, which were based on Gauguin's ideas on colour, later reinforced by Sérusier's theories. Before his death, Ranson formed an academy where many of the Nabis, as well as other artists including Denis, taught.

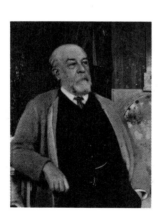

Odilon Redon.

REDON, ODILON
(Bordeaux, 1840 – Paris, 1916) French painter, engraver and writer

He was a student of the watercolourist Stanislaus Gorin in Bordeaux and later a student of Gérôme in Paris. Initially he devoted himself to engraving and later he turned to lithography. A great admirer of Moreau and a friend of the Nabis, he was one of the principal Symbolist painters. He illustrated the work of many poets, from Mallarmé to Huysmans (who was, in turn, an admirer of Redon) to Baudelaire. His work evolved in two directions. He painted colourful vases of flowers or landscapes as well as painting symbolic subjects taken from dreams, visions or nightmares. His work shows some affinity with the imagery of Art Nouveau, in the wealth of fantasy it contains. His lithographic albums include *Dans le Rêve* (1879); *Les Origines* (1883); *La Nuit* (1886); *Songes* (1891). He exhibited at the Indépendants, of which he was a founder member, in 1884. He was invited by Les XX to show his work in Brussels (1887 and 1890), at Le Livre Esthétique (1894, 1895, 1897) and in Vienna at the Vienna Secession in 1903.

RICKETTS, CHARLES
(Geneva, 1866 – 1931) English painter, sculptor and graphic designer

He spent his childhood in France. In 1882 he went to the Lambeth School of Art. Between 1889 and 1897 he directed, together with Charles Shannon, the magazine *The Dial*. Again in collaboration with Shannon he illustrated many books and designed their covers as well, in a delicate style which contributed to the revival of book design in England. These include *A House of Pomegranates* (1891) and *Daphne and Chloë* (1893) by Oscar Wilde. In 1886 he founded the Vale Press which published many books by Morris and the Pre-Raphaelites. He designed stage sets and exhibited at the International Society from 1906 and at the Grosvenor Gallery from 1921. He also designed jewellery and small bronzes. In 1922 he became a member of the Royal Academy in London.

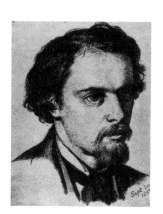

Dante Gabriel Rossetti, *Self-portrait*, 1855.

ROSSETTI, DANTE GABRIEL
(London, 1828 – Birchington-on-Sea, 1882) English poet and painter

Rossetti was the son of an Italian political refugee in London. He was taught drawing by Cotman and after a few months with Ford Madox Brown he went to Holman Hunt in 1848. Under his guidance he painted his first major work *The Girlhood of Mary*, the first picture (exhibited 1849) with the initials PRB (Pre-Raphaelite Brotherhood) which he founded with Holman Hunt and Millais in 1848. His adherence to the ideals of the Brotherhood was short-lived. His subjects were drawn mostly from Dante and medieval legend. In 1850 he met Elizabeth Siddal, who also posed for Hunt and Millais. They married in 1860; in 1862 she died of narcotics and he became a virtual recluse and eventually a chloral addict. In 1857 he was involved with Morris and Burne-Jones in the decoration of the Oxford Union and he did one painting directly on to a whitewashed wall. It perished immediately. In 1861 he was again involved with Morris in the foundation of his company, Morris, Marshall Faulkner, and Co.

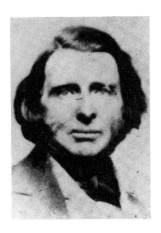

John Ruskin.

RUSKIN, JOHN
(London, 1819 – 1900) English critic and theorist

Ruskin was the most influential nineteenth-century art critic in England. In criticism he revealed the relationship between art and nature, which was crucial to the development of the Pre-Raphaelite Brotherhood and later to Art Nouveau. He was one of the first defenders of the Brotherhood. His criticism of industrial society and his praise for Gothic art was received with hostility, but nevertheless brought him great fame.

He was the first Slade Professor at Oxford and his books include *Modern Painters* (1843-60); *The Seven Lamps of Architecture* (1849); and *The Stones of Venice* (1851-53).

He was a meticulous draughtsman, particularly of architecture and plant forms, and there is a large collection of his drawings in Oxford.

A. P. Ryder, *Self-portrait*, c. 1883.

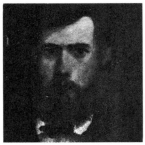

RYDER, ALBERT PINKHAM
(New Bedford, Mass., 1847 – New York, 1917) American painter

He rejected the realism which then dominated American painting and pursued his own particular vision – which was unrealistic and dreamlike and inspired by romantic literature, and, in some aspects, close to European Symbolism. He lived in New York from 1870 onwards and he studied at the National Academy of Design under Marshall. In 1875 he took part in an exhibition of dissident artists, and in 1877 was one of the founder members of the Society of American Artists. He had an unusual technique. He superimposed layers of varnished colour. The subject matter of his paintings is taken from romantic literature, the Bible and Shakespeare. Absolutely ignored in his day, he was rediscovered by artists of the subsequent generation, among them Pollock.

Eliel Saarinen in his studio.

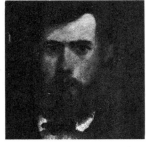

SAARINEN, ELIEL
(Rantasalmi, Finland, 1873 – Bloomfield Hills, Mich., 1950) Finnish architect

After completing his architectural studies at Helsinki, he designed many buildings in Finland, the most famous being the Railway Station in Helsinki. The style of the building is inspired by the Vienna Secession but it is highly original. Saarinen took part in the *Chicago Tribune* competition of 1922, and his design, though placed second, was much admired. As a result, he left Finland and emigrated to the United States, where his best known buildings are Cranbrook School (1925-29) and Christ Church, Minneapolis (1949).

Sant'Elia, Funi and Marinetti in the uniform of volunteer cyclists in the war of 1914-18.

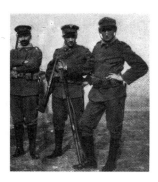

SANT'ELIA, ANTONIO
(Como, 1888 – Monfalcone, 1916) Italian architect

He studied in Como, in Milan at the Brera, and in Bologna. He completed his studies in 1912 and set up a practice in the same year in Milan. He became involved with Marinetti's Futurists and in 1914 published his Manifesto of Futurist Architecture. His vision of the future, the *Città Nuova*, was exhibited in Milan in 1914. He was killed in action in 1916.

SARTORIO, ARISTIDE GIULIO
(Rome, 1860 – 1932) Italian painter

He was initially a humanitarian socialist who tried to deal with social problems in his work. His painting *Malaria* dates from this period. In 1893 he was a member of the group In Arte Libertas, founded by Nino Costa, who, like the Pre-Raphaelites, felt the need to return to traditional forms. Sartorio collaborated with D'Annunzio on the

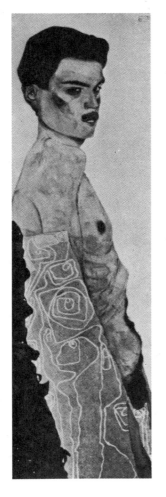

Egon Schiele, *Self-portrait with decorated fabrics*, 1909.

magazine *Il Convito* which was owned by Adolfo De Bosis and from 1895 to 1897 he taught at the Academy in Weimar. He was Professor of Painting at the Academy in Rome in 1878.

He volunteered to fight in the First World War, was wounded and taken prisoner. After his release on the Pope's intercession, he returned to the front in order to paint the war. His paintings are decorative rather than realistic, for example *The Gorgon and the Heroes* and *Diana of Ephesus and the Slaves*. His illustrations for D'Annunzio (1886) and those for *Il Convito* (1895) are characteristic expressions of the decadent taste of the period.

SCHIELE, EGON
(Dànau, 1890 – Vienna, 1918) Austrian painter

He studied at the academy in Vienna and in 1907 he met Klimt, who was then at the height of his fame. In 1911 he was one of the founders of the Neukunstgruppe (New Art Group). His art was consistently attacked during these years and the eroticism in his work led to his arrest on one occasion.

In 1910 his style was Expressionist, and his figures are distorted and emaciated. In 1915, after moving to the country, to Neulengbach, he married Edith Harms. He enjoyed a brief period of serenity and this is reflected in his work, but this was interrupted by the war. He returned from the war in 1917, but in 1918 he lost his life in an epidemic of Spanish influenza.

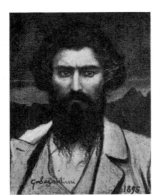

G. Segantini, *Self-portrait*, 1895.

SEGANTINI, GIOVANNI
(Arco, 1858 – Schafberg, 1899) Italian painter

After a difficult childhood, part of which was spent in a reformatory in Milan, he studied at the Brera Academy (1875-79). Later he signed a contract with Grubicy, the art dealer and critic, who later became a painter. Segantini retired to Pusiano, in the Brianza (1881-86), where he executed naturalistic paintings inspired by the landscape. In 1886 he withdrew to Savognino, in the Grigioni Hills (1886-94), and Symbolist influences began to show in his work. After 1891 he was influenced decisively by Art Nouveau. His work is steeped in literature and allegory which came from reading Tolstoy, D'Annunzio, Goethe and Nietzsche. He also admired Japanese prints and Indian painting. He managed to fuse all these influences with a conscious return to the Italian art of the fourteenth and fifteenth centuries. This is visible in *The Pagan Goddess* (1894-97).

SCOTT, MACKAY HUGH BAILLIE
(Ramsgate, 1865 – 1945) English architect and interior designer

Baillie Scott graduated from the Royal Agricultural College at
Cirencester in 1885 and began training in the office of Charles E. Davis,
an architect in Bath. In 1889 he started a practice in Douglas, Isle of
Man. Influenced by the Arts and Crafts Movement and the architecture
of Norman Shaw and Voysey, his early work derives from the red brick,
half-timbered vernacular architecture of the South of England. He was
also interested in the applied arts and designed materials, embroidery
and wallpaper. In 1897-98 he decorated the palace of the Grand Duke
of Hesse in Darmstadt. He was influential in America, where in 1901
several Arts and Crafts societies were founded. His influential *Houses
and Gardens* appeared in 1906 and Beresford brought out a second
edition in 1933.

SOMMARUGA GIUSEPPE
(Milan, 1867 – 1917) Italian architect

He studied at the Brera Academy under the guidance of the eclectic,
historicist architects Camillo Boito and Beltrami, but he was later
influenced by the Art Nouveau movement and became, with Raimondo
d'Aronco, its principal representative in Italy. His most important works
are the Castiglioni Palace in Milan (1903) and the Hotel Tre Croci near
Varese (1909), the Faccanonia Sarnico Mausoleum, as well as the
Columbus Clinic in Milan (1909) which shows a more linear decoration.

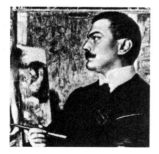

Franz von Stuck, *Self-portrait in his studio,* 1905.

STUCK, FRANZ VON
*(Tettenweis, Bavaria, 1863 – Munich, 1928) German painter and graphic
artist*

From 1881 to 1884 he studied at the School of Arts and Crafts in
Munich and in 1885 at the Academy. He was greatly influenced by
Böcklin, Thoma and Klinger. His early works are illustrations and
designs, like the humorous drawings in the *Fliegende Blätter* of Munich
and the *Allegorien und Embleme*. From about 1800 he began painting
in a Symbolist style in which he translated the classicism of von Marée
and Hildebrand into an allegorical and Symbolist idiom. In 1892 he
was, together with Trübner, one of the founder members of the Munich
Secession. In 1895 he bought the Villa Stuck, and in its decoration he
tried to realize the Jugendstil concept of the 'total work of art'. This is
his masterpiece, one in which he combined his talents for architecture,
painting and sculpture.

    He was titled in the 1890s, and he began painting portraits. He used
photographs of his sitters for his portraits.

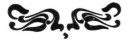

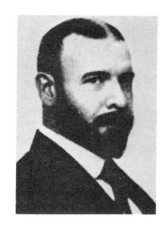

Louis Sullivan.

SULLIVAN, LOUIS HENRY
(Boston, 1856 – Chicago, 1924) American architect

Sullivan is the most interesting architect of the Chicago School. The son of immigrants (his father was Irish, his mother French-Swiss), he was born in Boston and studied architecture briefly at the Massachusetts Institute of Technology. He moved to Chicago in 1873 after spending a year in Paris. Chicago was being rebuilt after the fire of 1871 and Sullivan went to work with the engineer Frederick Baumann, with whom he gained experience of structural problems. In 1879 he went to work for Dankmar Adler, and later he became his associate (1881). The Auditorium Building in Chicago (1886-89) is the first building in their collaboration in which Sullivan's architectural style can be seen. In other works (still in collaboration with Adler) such as the Stock Exchange in Chicago (1898-99) and the Carson, Pirie, Scott and Co. Building (1899-1904), he anticipated the American rationalism and created the modern skyscraper. The Chicago World Fair of 1893 marked the end of the Functionalism of the Chicago School, and the Adler Sullivan studio had no commissions. The partnership broke up and Sullivan built several provincial buildings like the Merchants Association Bank in Grinnel, 1914; the Farmers and Merchants Union Bank in Columbus, 1919; the Peoples' Savings Association Bank in Sydney, 1917. He is the author of two books: *Kindergarten Chats and Other Writings*, 1901, and *Autobiography of an Idea*, 1922.

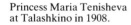

Princess Maria Tenisheva
at Talashkino in 1908.

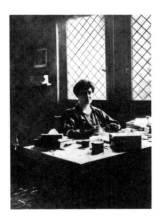

TENISHEVA, MARIA, PRINCESS OF TALASHKINO
(1867 – 1928) Patroness

Following Mamontov's example she organized a school of fine and decorative arts in Talashkino near Smolensk, where she taught orphans the rudiments of craftsmanship. The school had small workshops and a music school. In order to sell their products, Tenisheva opened a store in Moscow which unfortunately failed almost immediately. She commissioned designs from artists like Golovin, Vrubel and Miliuti. In 1905 she created a small museum of Russian crafts in Smolensk which contained items of embroidery, goldsmith work and furniture. In the same year she closed her school and moved to Paris, where she organized exhibitions of old Russian crafts at the Musée des Arts Décoratifs. The pieces she obtained in Paris she later sent to the Archeological Institute in Moscow. During her stay in Paris she became particularly interested in jewellery and she wrote a thesis on the subject for the University of Moscow in 1916. She remained in Paris after the revolution and continued to play an important role in cultural life. Near her villa she opened the 'little Talashkino', a school devoted exclusively to jewellery, which she ran until her death.

Jan Thorn Prikker.

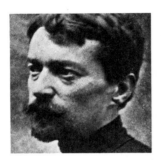

THORN PRIKKER, JAN
(The Hague, 1868 – Cologne, 1932) Dutch painter and designer

From 1883 to 1887 he attended the Academy at The Hague. His early paintings are in a Post-Impressionist and Pointillist style. From 1892 to 1895 he executed a series of religious paintings which are influenced by the Flemish old masters as well as Symbolism derived from Gauguin, van de Velde and the poet Verlaine (whom he met in 1892).

He was associated with the Belgian group Les XX and he went to Belgium where he was rather unsuccessful, but his friend H. P. Bremmer helped him and bought many of his works for the Kröller-Müller collection. Between 1892 and 1896 he corresponded with the literary symbolist Henri Borel. In 1895 he abandoned easel painting in favour of fresco' stained glass, and mosaics. In 1904 he taught at Krefeld, at the Kunstgewerbeschule; he also taught in The Hague and Essen, and later in Munich, Düsseldorf and Cologne.

TIFFANY, LOUIS COMFORT
(New York, 1848 – 1933) American designer and interior decorator

The son of the well-known goldsmith and jeweller Charles Tiffany, initially he studied painting but c. 1878 he devoted himself entirely to the decorative arts. In 1879 the Louis C. Tiffany Company of Associate Artists, an interior design and furnishing company, was founded. One of their commissions was the White House in Washington DC (1882-83).

Tiffany patented a type of hand-made iridescent glass (1880) which he called *Favrile* glass. He opened the Tiffany glass furnaces in 1892. In 1893 he designed the Chapel for the International Exhibition of Chicago, which was later located in the Church of St John the Divine in New York. He also executed stained glass windows designed by famous artists, including Vuillard, Bonnard and Toulouse-Lautrec, for Bing's shop L'Art Nouveau.

After the death of his father in 1902, Louis C. Tiffany designed jewellery and built himself a house, Laurelton Hall, on Long Island. In 1932 the Tiffany Studios went bankrupt and in 1946 the Laurelton Hall collection was sold at auction.

Jan Toorop.

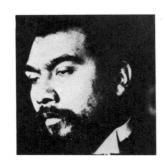

TOOROP, JAN
(Poerworedje, Java, 1858 – The Hague, 1928) Dutch painter

After going to Holland in 1869 he studied in Delft and at the Academy in Amsterdam (1880-01). He won a scholarship and he went to study at the Academy in Brussels (1882-85). He joined the Belgian group Les XX which became Le Libre Esthétique in 1894. Khnopff, Ensor, Vogels and van Rijsselberghe were all members. In 1884 he went to London with Verhaeren. In 1886 he met Whistler in London, who introduced him to the works of the Pre-Raphaelites and to the humanitarian

Henri de Toulouse-Lautrec.

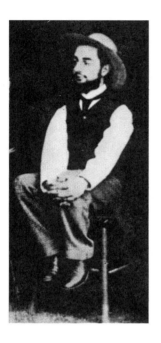

theories of Morris. On his return to Holland, he used the 'pointillist' technique and for a time he was the first in his country to do so. In 1890, through his contact with Maeterlinck and Verhaeren, he began to paint in a Symbolist manner, using pagan and Christian symbols. From 1893 he tended to envelop his compositions in a dense network of ornamental lines, which recalls Beardsley. Toorop was the greatest exponent of Dutch Art Nouveau painting.

TOULOUSE-LAUTREC, HENRI DE
(Albi, 1864 – Malromé, Gironde, 1901) French painter

He was stunted in growth because he broke both legs in childhood. In 1882 he began to study art in Paris, and by 1885 he had a studio in Montmartre. He exhibited at the Salon des Indépendants from 1889 and with Les XX in Brussels. In 1891 his first posters brought him instant fame. He made his first colour prints in 1892. In 1895 he made the first of several visits to London, where he knew Oscar Wilde and Beardsley.

By 1898 his health was deteriorating through drink, and in 1899 he spent some time in a clinic, where he worked on a series of drawings of the circus. In 1901 he broke down and died.

Félix Vallotton, *Self-portrait*, 1885.

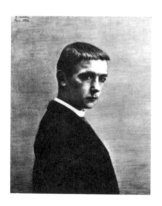

VALLOTTON, FÉLIX
(Lausanne, 1865 – Paris, 1925) French painter

Although of Swiss origin, his whole career was spent in Paris. In 1882 he went to the Académie Julian; in 1885 he exhibited at the Salon des Artistes Français and he became a constant exhibitor at the Salon des Indépendants. From 1887 he specialized in graphics and excelled in woodcut as well as in lithography and poster art. He collaborated on the *Revue Blanche* of Paris, the American periodical *Chap Book* and the German *Pan*. His style was very direct, smooth and linear. His contact with Symbolism and Art Nouveau was marginal, and it is limited to the choice of subject matter.

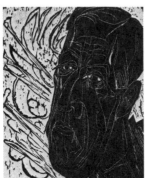

VELDE, HENRY CLEMENS VAN DE
(Antwerp, 1863 – Zurich, 1957) Belgian architect, industrial designer, painter and art critic

He studied at the Academy of Art in Antwerp from 1881 to 1883, then Paris in 1884 to 1885, where he was influenced by the Post-Impressionists and Symbolists, including Monet, Signac, Pissarro, Verlaine and Debussy. In 1885 he returned to Belgium and lived in Antwerp and Brussels where he worked as a painter and critic. In 1889 he joined Les XX in Brussels and made contact with the painter and potter Willy Finch, who introduced the English Arts and Crafts Movement to Belgium.

Ernst Ludwig Kirchner, *Portrait of Henry van de Velde*, 1917.

From 1890, under the impact of Ruskin and Morris, he turned from painting to the decorative arts and architecture. He made furniture, book decoration and panels in a purely Art Nouveau style. From 1895 he became interested in architecture and he designed his own house at Bloemenwerf near Brussels (1895); and the interior of Kunstsalon Cassirer in Berlin. Because of the enthusiasm for his work in Germany van de Velde left Brussels and went to live in Germany.

In 1902 he was called to Weimar by Archduke Wilhelm Ernst of Saxony to direct the School of Arts and Crafts which can be seen as anticipating the Bauhaus. In 1903 he furnished the Neitzsche Archive and in 1906 he designed the Industrial School of Art in Weimar. He was responsible for the interior of the Folkwang Museum at Hagen (1901-02) and the Abbe Monument at Jena (1908). He was one of the principal figures in the Werkbund for whom he built the theatre for the 1914 Cologne Exhibition. During the war van de Velde left Germany and after restless years of émigré life only settled back in Brussels in 1925. His late style is less personal, its finest example being the Kröller-Müller Museum at Otterlo in Holland.

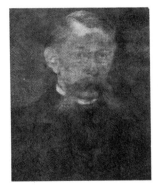

Constant Montald, *Portrait of Verhaeren*, 1903.

VERHAEREN, ÉMILE
(Saint-Amand, 1855 – Rouen, 1916) Belgian poet

As well as his commitment to poetry, Verhaeren was highly committed to the visual arts. He collaborated on a number of periodicals – *La Jeune Belgique, L'Art Moderne* – in which he defended contemporary aesthetic movements. His social commitment is evidenced in his collaboration with La Société Nouvelle. In 1892 he founded, with others, the Section d'Art at the Maison du Peuple in Brussels.

VIOLLET-LE-DUC, EUGÈNE-EMMANUEL
(Paris, 1814 – Lausanne, 1879) French architect and architectural theorist

Viollet-Le-Duc was a student of the critic E. Delécluse, and a friend of Mérimée, who from 1873 was Director of Historic Monuments in France, and under whose influence he greatly increased his knowledge of medieval French architecture. He travelled to Italy and Sicily where he studied classical architecture. He dedicated himself to the study of Gothic architecture and became an international expert on the restoration of medieval monuments. He developed new and influential ideas on the Gothic architectural style, which he believed was the national style of architecture in France.

The Gothic style to Viollet-Le-Duc was a rational style of construction based on the system of rib vault, buttress and flying buttress. These ribs are skeletons like the nineteenth-century iron are skeletons, and the webs are just infilling. These ideas were laid down in his influential *Dictionnaire raisonné de l'architecture française* (1854-68). The comparison between the Gothic skeleton and the nineteenth-century skeleton was drawn in his *Entretiens sur l'Architecture* (2 vols, 1863 and 1872).

In 1840 he began the restoration of the Eglise de la Madeleine in Vézelay, and he collaborated with Lassus on the restoration of the Sainte Chapelle and of Nôtre Dame in Paris. In 1848 he became the General Inspector of ecclesiastical buildings in France. In 1844 he began the restoration of the medieval walled city of Carcassonne.

VOYSEY, CHARLES FRANCIS ANNESLEY
(Hessle, Yorkshire, 1857 – Winchester, 1941) English architect

A pupil of Seddon and then of Devey, he set up practice in 1882. He was as interested in design as in architecture, under the general influence of Morris, and of Mackmurdo in particular. His earliest designs for wallpapers are of 1883 and they are very reminiscent of Mackmurdo. His first commissions for houses date from 1888 to 1889 and from then until the First World War he built a large number of country houses.

They are never very large, grand or representational. They are placed in intimate relation to nature and developed informally. They spread with ease and have lowish comfortable rooms. The exteriors are usually rendered with pebbledash and they have horizontal windows. Voysey designed all of the details, such as fireplaces and metalwork, and all of the furniture. The furniture too is inspired by Mackmurdo. It is reasonable and friendly.

Among his houses which had tremendous influence at home and abroad are Perrycroft, Colwall (1893); Annesley Lodge, Hampstead (1896); and The Orchard, Chorley Wood (1900-01). After the war Voysey was rarely commissioned to do any architectural work.

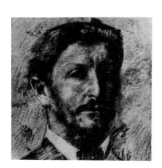

Max Vrubel, *Self-portrait*, 1904.

VRUBEL, MICHAEL ALEXANDROVITCH
(Omsk, Siberia, 1856 – St. Petersburg, 1910) Russian painter

In his childhood he showed a talent for music and design. He studied law, and in 1884 he entered the St. Petersburg Academy. Early in his career he collaborated in the restoration of a series of frescoes in the Church of St Cirillo in Kiev. He visited Italy in 1884-85, and later went to live in Moscow, where he worked in the theatre. With the help of Mamontov (the well-known industrialist who also promoted the arts), Vrubel came into contact with the painting of Nesterov, Korovin and Serov, and with modern, international art movements. He was continually inspired by the works of Pushkin, Lermontov and by the music of Rimsky-Korsakoff. His work has an abundance of decorative details which are influenced by Russian traditions. In 1896 he married the singer Nadezda Zabela. Seriously ill, he entered a psychiatric hospital, and continued painting there in his lucid moments.

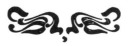

WAGNER, OTTO
(Petzing, Vienna, 1841 – Vienna, 1918) Austrian architect

He began his studies at the Technical High School in Vienna in 1857. Later he attended the Bauakademie in Berlin and from 1861 to 1863 the School of Architecture at the Viennese Academy. His early buildings are in a Neo-Renaissance style. His most famous works are the stations for the Viennese underground (1894-97); they are Art Nouveau in style and have a lot of exposed ironwork, though they are more restrained than Guimard's contemporary designs for the Paris Métro. His most 'twentieth century' achievement is the Postal Savings Bank of Vienna (1904-06) which follows the rationalist principles of the Modern Movement. It is faced with marble slabs held in place by aluminium bolts. The interior features a glass barrel vault.

Wagner was a decisive influence on the younger generation of architects in Vienna; in 1894 he became a professor at the Academy of Vienna. His courses were attended by Loos, Hoffmann and Olbrich. His book *Moderne Architektur*, published in Vienna in 1895, which in part grew out of his courses, was widely read. It was one of the principal means of the diffusion of his ideas which were especially influential in Italy.

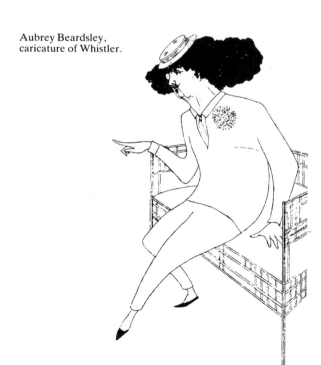

Aubrey Beardsley, caricature of Whistler.

WHISTLER, JAMES ABBOTT MCNEILL
(Lowell, Mass., 1834 – London, 1903)

Whistler attended the Military Academy at West Point. Failing there, he worked as a cartographer for the Navy Department in Washington. He moved to Paris in 1855 to study painting. He met Fantin-Latour in Paris, and Degas, and he was influenced by Courbet, whose paintings were on show in the Pavilion of Realism. When his own work was rejected by the jury of the Salon, like Courbet he exhibited privately with Fantin-Latour in Bouvin's studio (1859). In 1859 he moved to London where he discovered Japanese prints and became a passionate collector of Chinese porcelain. He shared this taste with the Pre-Raphaelites, and with English Aesthetes.

The work which he exhibited at the 1865 Salon in Paris revealed a greater interest in colour, and the juxtaposition of closely related tones. This is reflected in the titles of his paintings. In 1878 Whistler began court proceedings against Ruskin, who had referred to *Nocturne in Black and Gold* as 'flinging a pot of paint in the public's face'. Whistler won the case but lost his reputation and he sold his house and his collection of porcelain to pay his costs.

From 1870-80 he lived in Venice and then in Paris, visiting London in 1883. He wrote *The Gentle Art of Making Enemies* (London 1880) and *The Baronet and the Butterfly* (which was about a lawsuit against W. Eden).

WILDT, ADOLFO
(Milan, 1868 – 1931) Italian sculptor

A student of Grandi in Milan, he did not work in the Impressionist style which was fashionable for sculpture of the period. He often worked in marble, and his work is close to the Belgian artist, Minne, but is even more stylized. He is one of the most important Art Nouveau sculptors. His most famous work is the fountain in the garden of the Villa Reale in Milan (1912).

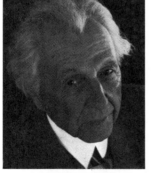

J. F. Willumsen, *Self-portrait*, 1910.

WILLUMSEN, JENS FERDINAND
(Copenhagen, 1863 – Cannes, 1958)

He studied architecture and worked as a sculptor and potter. He progressed from Naturalism, via Symbolism, to Expressionism. He visited Paris twice between 1888 and 1894 where he was in close contact with the Symbolists and the painters of Pont-Aven. Between these visits he travelled to Spain where he became an enthusiastic admirer of El Greco and Goya. He was a friend of van Gogh, and through him he met Odilon Redon (whose work was crucial to his Symbolist period). Between 1897 and 1900 he was artistic director at the Bing Gallery and the Grondahl Porcelain Factory in Copenhagen. The collection of his works is now housed in the Willumsen Museum in Fredriksund.

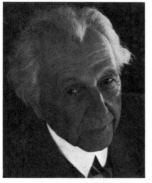

Frank Lloyd Wright.

WRIGHT, FRANK LLOYD
(Richland Center, Wisconsin, 1869 – Taliesin West, Arizona, 1959) American architect

A member of the Chicago School, he first worked for Sullivan, whom he never ceased to admire, and he was responsible for much of his domestic architecture. Early in his career the influence of the Art Nouveau spirit is present in his metalwork and furniture designs.

As an independent architect he went his own way. The first type of building he developed was the 'prairie house'. Many of these are in the suburbs of Chicago (Oak Park and Riverside). They have sequences of rooms which run into each other, the terraces merge with the gardens and the roofs project outwards. The series of designs for this type of house began in 1900 and was complete in 1905.

His work rarely ran parallel with any of the international developments, but he influenced Gropius and the Dutch De Stijl group.

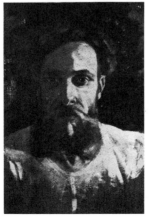

V. Zecchin, *Self-portrait*, 1903.

ZECCHIN, VITTORIO
(Venice, 1878 – 1947) Italian painter and decorator

He studied at the Academy of Fine Arts in Venice. His desire to surpass nineteenth-century realism made him adopt motifs discovered in the linear work of Toorop, which he saw at the Venice Biennale in 1895. He was also influenced by the work of Klimt, which he saw in the 1910 Biennale. Zecchin executed cartoons for tapestries, decorative panels, embroideries and stained glass windows. He worked with sensitivity and taste in all of these media.

Bibliography: Publications by the Artists

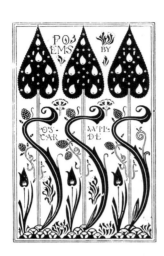

Charles Ricketts, cover for *Poems* by Oscar Wilde, 1892.

APPIA, ADOLPHE: *La mise en scène du drame wagnerien*, Paris, 1895. / *Die Musik und die Inszenierung*, Munich, 1899.

ASHBEE, CHARLES ROBERT: *A Short History of the Guild and School of Handicraft*, in "Transactions of the Guild and School of Handicraft", London, 1890. / *A few Chapters on Workshop Reconstruction and Citizenship*, London, 1894. / *On Table Service*, in « The Art Journal », London, 1898. / *An Endeavour towards the Teaching of John Ruskin and W. Morris*, London, 1901. / *Modern English Silverwork*, London, 1909.

BASILE, ERNESTO: *Per il mio progetto del palazzo di Giustizia e per l'Arte*, Rome, 1884. / *Progetto per il palazzo del Parlamento italiano; premiato al Concorso nazionale del 1889*, Rome, 1890. / *Studi e schizzi*, Turin, 1911.

BAHR, HERMAN: *Sezession*, Vienna, 1900.

BEARDSLEY, AUBREY: *The Early Work of Aubrey Beardsley*, London and New York, 1899. / *The Later Work of Aubrey Beardsley*, London and New York, 1901. / *Under the Hill*, London, 1904.

BEHRENS, PETER: *Feste des Lebens und der Kunst*, Jena, 1900. / *Ein Dokument Deutscher Kunst: die Ausstellung der Künstler Kolonie in Darmstadt*, Munich, 1901.

BENOIS, ALEXANDRE: *Istoriya-Russkoi Zhivopisi v XIX Veke*, St Petersburg, 1902. / *Reminiscences of the Russian Ballet*, London, 1941.

BERLAGE, HENDRIK PETRUS: *Over Architektur*, in « Tweemaandlijk Tijdschrift », Amsterdam, 1896, II. / *Gedanken über den Stil in der Baukunst*, Leipzig, 1905.

BING, SAMUEL: *Artistic Japan: Illustrations and Essays*, London, 1888-1891 (trans. Paris and Leipzig). / *La Culture artistique en Amérique*, Paris, 1893. / *Salon de l'Art Nouveau*, Paris, 1896. / *Wohin treiben Wir?*, « Dekorative Kunst », Munich, 1898. / *L'Art Nouveau*, in « Architectural Record », New York and London, 1902.

BRADLEY, WILLIAM: « Bradley – His Book », from 1896.

CHRISTIANSEN, HANS: *Neue Flachornamente auf Grund von Naturformen*, 1889.

COOK, TH. A.: *The curves of Life*, New York, 1914.

CRAIG, EDWARD GORDON: *The Art of the Theatre*, London, 1905. / *The Actor and the Über-Marionette*, in « The Mask », 1908. / *On the Art of the Theatre,* London, 1911. / *Toward a New Theatre*, London, 1913.

CRANE, WALTER: *The Claims of Decorative Art*, London, 1892. / *On the Decorative Illustration of Books Old and New*, London, 1896. / *The Art of W. Crane: Notes by the Artist*, in « The Art Journal The Easter Art Annual », London, 1898. / *Line and Form*, London, 1900. / *Ideals in Art. Papers of the Arts and Crafts Movement*, London, 1905. / *William Morris to James McNeill Whistler*, London, 1911.

DAY, LEWIS F.: *Everyday Art: Short Essays on the Arts not-Fine*, London 1882. / *Some Principles of Everyday Art*, London, 1890. / *L'Art Nouveau*, in « The Art Journal », London, 1900.

DELVILLE, JEAN: « L'Art et l'Idée », c. from 1890. / *Dialogue entre nous*, Brussels, 1895. / *La grande hiérarchie de l'occulte*, Brussels, 1897. / *Le frisson du Sphinx*, Brussels, 1897. / *Mission de l'Art*, Brussels, 1900.

DENIS, MAURICE: *Théories, 1890-1910*, Paris, 1913 (III ed.).

DRESSER, CHRISTOPHER: *Unity and Variety*, London, 1859. / *Rudiments of Botany*, London, 1859. / *The Art of Decorative Design*, London, 1862. / *On Decorative Art*, in « The Planet », London, 1862. / *Development of Ornamental Art*, London, 1862. / *Studies in Design*, London, Paris, New York, 1874-1876. / *Principles of Decorative Design*, London, 1880. / *Japan: Its Architecture, Art, and Art Manufactures*, London, 1882. / *Modern Ornamentation*, London, 1886. / *The Work of Ch. Dresser,* in « The Studio », London, 1898, XV.

ECKMANN, OTTO: *Der Weltjahrmarkt*, Paris and Berlin, 1900. / *Vorrede zu meiner Schrift*, Offenbach, 1900. / « Dekorative Entwürfe », Berlin, from 1907.

ENDELL, AUGUST: *Um die Schönheit. Eine Paraphrase die Münchner Kunstausstellung 1896*, Munich, 1896. / *Möglichkeiten und Ziele einer neuen Architecktur*, in « Deutsche Kunst und Dekoration », Darmstadt, 1897-1898. / *Gedanken; Formkunst*, in « Dekorative Kunst », Munich, 1898, I. / *Formeschönheit und Dekorative Kunst*, in « Dekorative Kunst », Munich, 1898, II. / *Architecktonische Erstlinge*, in

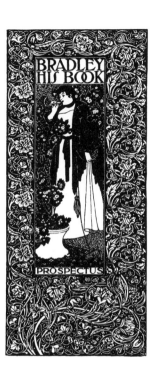

Fernand Khnopff, *On n'a que soi*, ex-libris from *Ver Sacrum*, 1892.

« Dekorative Kunst », Munich, 1900, III.

FULLER, LOÏE: *Quinze ans de ma vie*, Paris, 1908 (trans. London, 1913).

GAILLARD, EMILE: *A propos du Mobilier*, Paris, 1908.

GALLE, EMILE: « L'Etoile de l'Est », Nancy, c. 1895. / *Le Salon du Champ de Mars*, in « Revue de Arts Décoratifs », Paris, 1891-1892, XII. / *Le Décor Symboliste, discours de réception a l'Académie Stanislas*, Nancy, 1900. / *Exposition de l'Ecole de Nancy, à Paris, I série. Le Mobilier*, Paris, 1901. / *Ecrits pour l'Art, 1884-1889*, Paris, 1900.

GONCOURT, EDMOND JULES: *Journal*, 1851-1895, Paris.

GRASSET, EUGÈNE: *L'Art Nouveau*, in « La Plume », Paris, 1894, VI. / *La plante et ses applications ornamentales*, Paris, 1896. / *L'Architecture moderne jugée par Eugène Grasset*, in « L'Emulation », Brussels, 1896, XXI. / *L'Art Nouveau*, in « Revue des Arts Décoratifs », Paris, 1897, XVII. / *Eugène Grasset*, in « La Plume », Paris, 1900, XII. / *Méthode de composition ornamentale*, Paris, 1905.

GUIMARD, HECTOR: *Le Castel Béranger*, Paris, 1899. / *An Architect's Opinion of 'Art Nouveau'*, in « The Architectural Record », New York and London, 1902, XII.

HANKAR, PAUL: *L'Oeuvre Artistique. Exposition d'art appliqué*, 1895, in « L'Emulation », Brussels, 1895; XX.

HAECKEL, E.: *Kunstformen der Natur*, Leipzig and Vienna, 1899-1905.

HAMLIN, A. D. F.: *L'Art Nouveau; its Origin and Development*, in « Craftsman », Eastwood, New York, 1902, III.

HOFFMANN, JOSEF: *Der Moderne Stil*, Stoccarda, 1899-1905. / *Einfache Möbel*, in « Das Interieur », Vienna, 1901, II.

HUNT, WILLIAM HOLMAN: *Pre-Raphaelitism and the pre-Raphaelite Brotherhood*, London, 1905.

HORTA, VICTOR: *Considerations sur l'art moderne*, Brussels, 1925.

HUYSMANS, JORIS KARLS: *À rebours*, Paris, 1884.

JONES, OWEN: *The Grammar of Ornament*, London, 1856. / *The True and the False in the Decorative Arts*, London, 1863.

KANDINSKY, VASSILI: *Über des Geistige in der Kunst*, Munich, 1912. / *Klange*, Munich, 1913. / *Ruckblicke*, Berlin, 1913.

KOKOSCHKA, OSKAR: *Die Träumenden Knaben*, Vienna, 1908.

LAHORE, JEAN: *William Morris et le mouvement nouveau de l'art décoratif*, Geneva, 1897. / *L'Art Nouveau. Son histoire, l'art nouveau a l'Exposition, l'art nouveau au point de vue sociale*, Paris, 1901.

LIBERTY & CO. LTD: *Handbook of Sketches*, London, 1890. / *Cymric Sylver*, London, 1900.

LOOS, ADOLF: « L'Altro. Periodico per l'introduzione della civiltà occidentale in Austria », Vienna, 1908. / *Ins Leere Gesprochen*, 1897-1900, Paris, 1921, Innsbruck, 1932.

LORRAIN, JEAN: *Très russe*, Paris, 1886. / *Princesses d'Ivoire et d'ivresse*, Paris, 1902. / *Monsieur de Phocas*, Paris, 1910.

MACKINTOSH, CHARLES RENNIE: *Manuscripts*, University of Glasgow.

MACKMURDO, ARTHUR HEYGATE: *Wren's City Churches*, London, 1883. / *Nature in Ornament*, in « The Hobby Horse », London, 1892, VII. / *History of the Arts and Crafts Movement* (manuscript).

MADOX BROWN, F. FORD: *The Pre-Raphaelite Brotherhood*, London and New York, 1907.

MAKOVSKY, S. K.: *Talashkino. L'Art décoratif des ateliers de la Princesse Tenicheva*.

MAJORELLE, LOUIS: *Majorelle Frères & Cie., Meubles d'Art*, catalogue, Nancy.

MAUS, M. OCTAVE: *Trente années de lutte pour l'art, 1884-1914*, Brussels, 1926. / *L'art et la vie en Belgique, 1830-1905*, Brussels, 1929.

MEIER, GRAEFE J.: *Das plastische Ornament*, in « Pan », Berlin, 1898, IV. / *Entwichlungsgeschichte der modernen Kunst*, Stoccarda, 1904-1905.

MORRIS, WILLIAM: « Oxford and Cambridge Magazine », Oxford, from 1885. / *New From Nowhere*, London, 1893. / *Socialism; its Growth and Outcome*, London, 1893. / *Arts and Crafts Exhibition Society, London*, London, 1899. / *The Collected Works of William Morris*, London, 1910-1915.

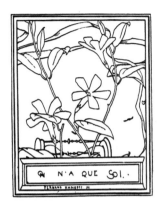

William Bradley,
frontispiece of *Bradley:
His Book,* 1896.

MORSE, EDWARD S.: *Japanese Homes and Their Surroundings*, Boston, 1889.

MOSER, KOLO: *Mein Werdegang*, in « Velhagen und Klasings Monatschefte », XXXI, II, 1916.

MUCHA, ALPHONSE: *Figures décoratives*, Paris, 1905.

MUTHESIUS, HERMANN: *Die Englische Baukunst der Gegenwart*, Leipzig, 1900. / *Der Kunstgewerbliche Dilettantismus in England*, Berlin, 1900. / *Die neiere kirchliche Baukunst in England*, Berlin, 1901. / *M. H. Baillie Scott. Haus eines Kunstfreundes. Meister der Innenkunst I*, Darmstadt, 1902. / *Charles Rennie Mackintosh. Haus eines Kunstfreudes. Meister der Innenkunst II*, Darmstadt, 1902. / *Die Kunst Richard Riemerschmid*, in « Dekorative Kunst », Munich, 1904, VII. / *Das Englische Haus*, Berlin, 1904-1905.

NIEUWENHUIS, T.: *Afbeeldingen van Werken naar ontwerpen van T. Nieuwenhuis*, Amsterdam, 1911.

NOCQ, HENRY: *Tendences nouvelles, Enquête sur l'évolution des industries d'art*, Paris, 1896.

OBRIST, HERMAN: *Wozu über Kunst schreiben*, in « Dekorative Kunst », Munich, 1900, V. / *Die Zukunst unserer Architektur*, in « Dekorative Kunst », Munich, 1901, VII. / *Luxuskunst oder Volkskunst*, in « Dekorative Kunst », Munich, 1901-1902, IX. / *Neue Möglichkeiten in der bildenden Kunst, 1896-1900*, Leipzig, 1903.

OLBRICH, JOSEPH MARIA: *Ideen*, Vienna, 1900. / *Neue Gärten*, Berlin, 1905.

PETROV-VODKINE, KOSMA S.: *Chlynowsk*, St. Petersburg, 1930. / *Lo spazio di Euclide*, Mosca, 1932.

PREVIATI, GAETANO: *Principi scientifici del Divisionismo*, Milan, 1909-1916.

RIMSKY-KORSAKOF, NICOLAI: *Trattato pratico di armonia*, St Petersburg, 1884. / *Principi di strumentazione*, St Petersburg, 1913.

ROBINEAU, ADELAIDE: *Porcelains*, in « Keramic Studio », IX, 1907.

RUSKIN, JOHN: *The Works of John Ruskin*, London, 1903-1912.

ROHLFS, CHARLES: *My Adventures in Wood-Carving*, in « Arts Journal », 1925, 21-22.

SALOMÈ-ANDREAS, LOUIS: *Nietzsche in seine Werken*, 1894. / *Ibsen Frauengestalten*, 1892.

SARGENT, IRENE: *The Wavy Line*, in « Craftsman », Eastwood, New York, 1902, II.

SEDDING, JOHN: *Arts and Crafts Essays*, in « Design », London, 1893.

SÉRUSIER, PAUL: *ABC de la Peinture*, Paris, 1942.

SERRUSIER-BOVY, GUSTAVE: *Album d'Intérieur*. Lüttich, s.d.

SHAW, RICHARD NORMAN: *Sketches for Cottages*, London, 1878. / *Architecture. A Profession or an Art*, London, 1892.

SOMMARUGA, GIUSEPPE: *L'Architettura di Giuseppe Sommaruga*, Milan, 1908.

STRINDBERG, AUGUST: *L'exposition d'Edvard Munch*, in « La Revue Blanche », Paris, 1896, X.

SULLIVAN, LOUIS H.: *Characteristics and Tendencies of American Architecture*, in « Inland Architect and Builder », 1885. / *A System of Architectural Ornament according with a Philosophy of Man's Posers*. New York, 1924. / *The Autobiography of an Idea*, New York, 1924. / *Kindergarten Chats and Other Writings*, New York, 1947.

SWINBURNE, ALGERNON-CHARLES: *William Blake, A critical Essay*, London, 1868.

TIFFANY, LOUIS: *The Art Work of Louis Tiffany*, Garden City, New York, 1914.

TOLSTOY, LEON: *Che cos'è l'arte*, 1897.

TOWNSEND, CHARLES HARRISON: *Originality in Architecture*, in « The Builder », London, 1902, LXXXII.

VELDE, HENRY VAN DE: *Notes d'art*, in « La Vallonie », Brussels, 1890, 2-3. / *Artistic Wall-Papers*, in « L'Art Moderne », Brussels, 1893, XIII. / *Déblaiement d'art*, Brussels, 1894. / *Essex and Co.'s Westminster Wall-Papers*, in « L'Art Moderne », 1894, XIV. / *Ein Kapitel über Entwurf und Bau Moderner Möbel*, in « Pan », Berlin, 1897, II. / *Die Renaissance in modernen Kunstgewerbe*, Berlin, 1901. / *Kunstgewerbliche Laienpredigten*, Leipzig, 1902. / *Gustave Serrusier-Bovy*, in « Zeitschrift für Innendekoration », Darmstadt, 1902, XII. / *Von neuen Stil*, Leipzig, 1907. / *Amo*, Leipzig, 1909. / *Saggi*, 1910. / *Formule della Bellezza architettonica moderna*, 1917. /

Formule di una estetica moderna, 1923.

VERHAEREN, EMILE: *Quelques notes sur l'oeuvre de Fernand Khnopff, 1881-1887*, Brussels, 1887.

VIOLLET-LE-DUC, EUGÈNE EMMANUEL: *Entretiens sur l'Architecture*, Paris, 1863,1872.

VOYSEY, CHARLES A. F.: *Domestic Furniture*, in « The Journal of the Royal British Institute of British Architects », London, 1894. / *Individuality*, London, 1911.

WAGNER, OTTO: *Moderne Architektur*, Vienna, 1895. / *Die Kunst der Gegenwart*, in « Ver Sacrum », Vienna, 1900, III. / *Aus der Wagnerschule*, Vienna, 1900. / *Wagner-Schule*, Leipzig, 1902. / *Einige Skizzen, Projekte und Ausgeführte Bauwerke*, Vienna, 1892-1922.

WHISTLER, JAMES MCNEILL: *The gentle Art of Making Enemies*, London, 1880. / *The Baronet and the Butterfly*, London, 1884. / *Mr Whistler's "Ten O'clock"*, London, 1885.

WILDE, OSCAR: *The Decay of Lying*, in "Complete Works", New York, 1916. / *Art and Decoration*, London, 1920.

WRIGHT, FRANK LLOYD: *In the Cause of Architecture*, in « Architectural Record », 1908, XXIII. / *On Architecture. Selected Writings, 1894-1940*, New York, 1941.

A. Beardsley, design for the frontispiece of *The Yellow Book*.

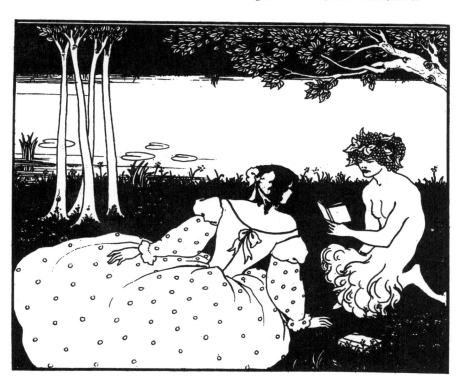

Magazines and Periodicals of the Period

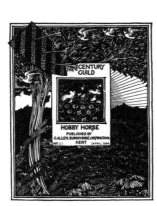

Selwyn Image, frontispiece from *The Century Guild Hobby Horse,* 1884, n.l.

AUSTRIA

« Die Graphischen Künstler », Vienna, from 1879. / « Das Interieurs », Vienna, 1900-1915. / « Kunst und Kunsthandwerk », Vienna, 1898-1921. / « Ver Sacrum », Vienna, 1898; Leipzig 1899-1903.

BELGIUM

« L'art et l'Idée », Brussels, c. from 1890. / « L'Art Moderne », Brussels, 1881-1914. / « L'Emulation », Brussels, from 1874. / « Le Réveil », Ghent, from 1891. / « Van Nu en Straks », Brussels and Antwerp, 1892-1901.

ENGLAND

« Oxford and Cambridge Magazine », London. / « The Century Guild Hobby Horse », Orpington, 1884-1886, 1892; successively « The Hobby Horse », London, 1893-1894. / « The Dial », London, 1889-1897. / « The Dome », London, 1897-1900. / « The Germ », London, 1849. / « The Pageant », London, 1896-1897. / « The Savoy », London, 1896. / « The Studio », London, from 1893. / « The Yellow Book », London, 1894-1895.

FRANCE

« Art et Décoration », Paris, from 1897. / « L'Art Décoratif », Paris, 1989-1914, 1898. / « La Plume », Paris, 1889-1913. / « La Revue Blanche », Paris, 1891-1903. / « Le Courier Français », Paris, 1886-1894. / « Le Rire », Paris. / « L'Image », Paris. / « L'Ymager », Paris. / « Renovation Esthétique », Paris, 1905-1910. / « Revue des Arts Décoratifs », Paris, 1880-1902.

GERMANY

« Avalan », Munich, 1901. / « Dekorative Kunst », Munich, 1897-1929. / « Deutsche Kunst und Dekoration », Darmstadt, 1897-1934. / « Fliegende Blätter », Munich, 1844-1928. / « Hyperion », Munich. / « Die Insel », Berlin, 1888-1901 and Leipzig, 1902. / « Jugend », Munich, 1899-1933. / « Die Kunst für Alle », Munich, 1885-1899; successively « Die Kunst », 1899-1945. / « Die Neue Rundschau ». / « Pan », Berlin, 1895-1900. / « Quickborn », Berlin. « Simplizissimus », Munich, 1896-1967. / « Zeitschrift für Innendekoration », Darmstadt, from 1890. / « Zeitschrift für Bücherfreunde ». / « Kunst und Handwerk », from 1897.

HOLLAND

« Arts and Crafts ». / « Bouw en Sierkunst », Haarlem, 1898-1902. / « En Industrie », from 1898.

ITALY

« Arte italiana decorativa and industriale », Rome and Venice, 1890-1914. / « Arte utile », from 1890. / « Edilizia moderna », from 1895. / « Emporium », Bergamo, from 1896. / « Flegrea », from 1899. / « Hermes », Florence, from 1904. / « Italia che ride », Bologna, 1900. / « La casa », Rome, from 1908. / « La Lettura », from 1901. / « L'Ambiente moderno », from 1910. / « L'Architettura italiana », from 1905. / « L'Arte », Rome, 1898-1901. / « L'Arte aristocratica », from 1902. / « L'Arte decorativa moderna », Turin, from 1902. / « L'artista moderna », Turin, from 1902. / « Il giovane artista moderno ». / « L'Eroica », from 1911. / « L'illustrazione italiana », from 1900. / « Novissima », Milan and Rome, from 1900. / « Per l'Arte », from 1909.

POLAND

« Chimera », Warsaw. / « Czas », Cracow. / « Nats Kray », Lemberg.

RUSSIA

« Apollon », St. Petersburg. / « La Toison d'or », Moscow, from 1906. / « Mir Iskusstva », St. Petersburg, 1899-1904.

Doboujinsky, frontispiece from *Mir Iskusstva,* 1904.

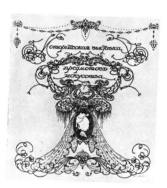

SPAIN
« Joventut », Barcelona, 1900-1903.

THE UNITED STATES
« Handicraft », Boston, from 1902. / « House Beautiful », Chicago, from 1896. / « House and Garden », Philadelphia, from 1901. / « Interiors », New York, from 1888. / « Ceramic Studio », Syracuse, from 1899. / « Ladies' Home Journal », from 1901. / « The Architectural Record », New York and London, from 1891. / « The Chap-Book », Chicago, 1894-1898. / « The Craftsman », Syracuse, 1901-1916. / « The Evergreen », Edinburgh, Philadelphia, 1895-1897.

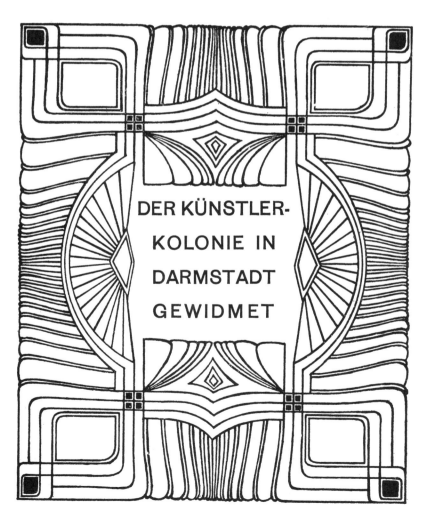

P. Behrens, page for *Feste des Lebens und der Kunst,* 1900.

Selection Bibliography

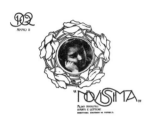

Ornamental inset not
identified

F. ALISON, « Charles Rennie Mackintosh as a Designer of Chairs », London, 1974. / M. AMAJA, « Art Nouveau », London-New York, 1966. /E. ASLIN, « The Aesthetic Movement. Prelude to Art Nouveau », London, 1969. / AUDSLY, « Designs and Patterns from Historic Ornament », New York, 1968. / E. BAIRATI, R. BOSSAGLIA, M. ROSCI, « Italia Liberty », Milan, 1973. / R. BARILLI, « I Preraffaelliti », Milan, 1967; « Il Simbolismo », Milan, 1967; « Il Liberty », Milan, 1966. / G. BAZIN, « The Evolution of Art », London-Milan, 1962. / J. BLOCH-DERMANT, « L'Art du verre en France, 1860-1914 », Freiburg, 1974. / O. BOHIGAS, « Architettura modernista », Barcelona, 1968, Turin, 1969. / F. BORSI, P. PORTOGHESI, « Horta », Rome, 1969. / R. BOSSAGLIA, « Il Mobile Liberty », Novara, 1967; « Il Liberty », Florence, 1974. / R. BOSSAGLIA, X Il Mobile Liberty Y, Novara, 1967; X Il Liberty Y, Florence, 1974. R. BOSSAGLIA, A. HAMMACHER, « Mazzucotelli », Milan, Tubingen, 1971. / M. BUCCI, R. BENCINI, « I Palazzi di Firenze », Florence, 1971. / O. CAMERANA, « Linea FIAT », Turin, 1966. / J. CASSOU, E. LANGUI, N. PEVSNER, « The Sources of Modern Art », London, 1962. / A. CIRICI PELLICER, J. GOMIS, « Barcelona 1900 », Barcelona, 1967. / I CREMONA, « Il tempo dell'Art Nouveau », Florence, 1964. / C. CRESTI, *Liberty a Firenze*, in « Antichità viva », n. 5, Florence, 1970; *Villa Ruggeri a Pesaro* (Rilievi di Gugnali-Paganelli-Vannini), in « Bollettino degli Ingegneri », n. 11, Florence, 1970; *Un edificio Liberty a Firenze*, in « Bollettino degli Ingegneri », n. 11, Florence, 1972. / A. DEL GUERCIO, « Le avanguardie russe e sovietiche », Milan, 1970. / C. DE MAEYER, « Paul Hankar », Brussels, 1963. / F. R. FRATINI, « Turin 1902, Polemiche in Italia per l'arte nuova », Turin, 1970. R. Goldwater, *Symbolism*, London, 1979. / C. GRAY, « The Russian Experiment in Art, 1863-1922 », London, 1962. / M. HOWELLS, « Lost examples of Colonial Architecture », New York, 1931. / W. HOFMANN, U. KULTERMAN, « Architettura moderna », Essen, Novara, 1969. / H. H. HOFSTÄTTER, « Jugendstil Drukkunst », Baden-Baden, 1869. / G. HUGHES, « Modern Jewellery », London 1963. / P. JULLIAN, « Dreamers of Decadence », London, 1971; « The Symbolists », London, 1973; « The Triumph of Art Nouveau – Paris Exhibition 1900 », London, 1974. / KOCK, « Louis C. Tiffany, Glass-Bronze-Lamps », New York, 1961. / M. LUZI, « L'Idea Simbolista », Milan, 1960. / R. MACLEOD, « C. R. Mackintosh », Middlesex, 1968. / MADSEN, « Sources of Art Nouveau », Oslo, 1956. / MANFREDI-NICOLETTI, « D'Aronco », Milan, 1955. / M. MANIERI-ELIA, « William Morris e l'ideologia dell'architettura, moderna », Bari, 1976. / MARILLIR, « The early Works of Audrey Beardsley », New York, 1899, 1967. / G. MASSOBRIO, P. PORTOGHESI, « Album del Liberty », Bari, 1975. / J. MILNER, « Symbolists and Decadents », London, 1971. / M. MONTGOMERY, « America's Arts and Skills », New York, 1957. / J. MUCHA, M. HENDERSON, A. SCHARF, « Mucha », London, 1961. / NICOLL, « The Pre-Raphaelites », Suffolk, 1970. / N. PAGLIARA, « Appunti su Otto Wagner », Naples, 1968. / V. PICA, « L'Arte decorativa all'Esposizione di Torino del 1902 », Bergamo, 1903. / N. PONENTE, « Le Strutture del Mondo moderno, 1850-1900 », Geneva, Milan, 1965. / M. PRAZ, *Art Nouveau* (in J. B. Hodin, « European Critic, A tribute on his 60th birthday »), London, 1965. / B. READE, « Aubrey Beardsley », New York, 1967. / M. RHEIMS, « L'Art 1900 », Paris, 1965; « L'Objet 1900 », Paris, 1964. / A. RIEGL, « Stilfragen », Berlin, 1893. / H. R. HITCHCOCK, « Architecture: nineteenth and twentieth centuries », Harmondsworth, 1958, 1968. / R. SCHMUTZLER, « Art Nouveau », London, 1978. / V. SCULLY, « Frank Lloyd Wright », New York, Milan, 1960. / H. TEIRLINCK, « Henry van de Velde », Brussels 1959. / S. TSCHUDI-MADSEN, « Fortuna dell'Art Nouveau », Milan, 1957. / P. VERGO, « Art in Vienna, 1898-1918 », London, 1975./ G. VERONESI, « Josef Hoffmann », Milan, 1956. / H. VEVER, « La Bijouterie française au XIX siècle », Paris, 1906. / H. VOSS, « Franz Von Stuck », Munich, 1973. / T. WALTERS, « Art Nouveau Graphics », London-New York, 1971.

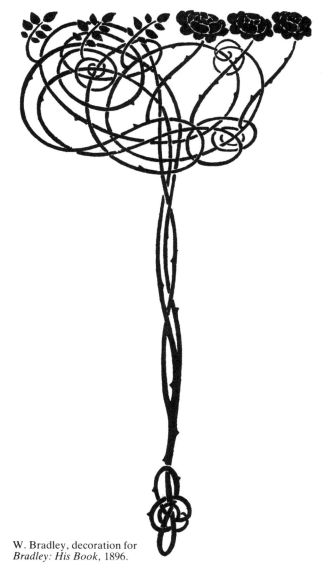

W. Bradley, decoration for
Bradley: His Book, 1896.

« Van de Velde », Zurich, Kunstgewerbemuseum, 1958. / « Morris and Company, 1861-1940 », London, The Arts Council, 1961. / « Gustav Klimt », Graz, Neuegalerie am Landesmuseum Joanneum, 1962. / « Antonio Sant'Elia », Como, 1962. / « Art Nouveau Sampler », The University of Michigan, 1962-63. / « Henry van de Velde », Brussels, 1963. / « Un Maître de l'Art Nouveau: Alphonse Mucha », Paris, 1966. / « Mucha », Milan-Rome, Galleria del Levante, 1966. / « Johan Thorn Prikker », Krefeld, Kaiser Willhelm Museum, 1966. / « Léon Bakst », Milan-Rome-Munich, Galleria del Levante, 1967. / « Alberto Martini », Odessa, 1967. / « La grafica boema nel periodo dell'Art Nouveau », Rome, Calcografia Nazionale, 1968. / « Kolo Moser », Graz, Neuegalerie am Landesmuseum Joanneum, 1969. / « Hector Guimard », New York, The Museum of Modern Art, 1970. / « Charles A. Voysey », Santa Barbara, California University, 1970. / « Henry van de Velde », Brussels, 1970. / « Symbolismus in Belgien », Milan-Munich-New York, Galleria del Levante, 1970-71. / « Tiffany », Tallahasse, University Art Gallery, 1972. / « Architettura Liberty a Milano », Milan, 1972/ « Galileo Chini », Salsomaggiore, 1974. / « Duilio Cambellotti », Rome, Emporio Floreale, 1975. / « Tiffany », Sarasota, Florida, 1975.

Location of the Works of Art

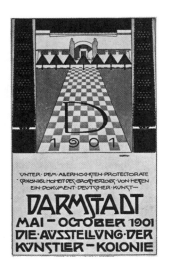

J. Olbrich, poster for the exhibition of the Colony of Artists in Darmstadt, 1901.

502, 508 Oslo, Kommunes Kunstsamlingen
Munch Museum
509, 510, 511 Munich, Staatliche Graphische
Sammlung
512 Vienna, Kunsthistorische Museum
513 Schweinfurt, coll. George Schäffer
514 Munich, Bayerische Staatgemäldesammlungen
515 Berlin, National Gallery
516 Darmstadt, Hessische Landesmuseum
519 Ratzeburg, coll. Barlach
521 Vienna, Albertina
522, 546, 547 Darmstadt, Hessische Landesmuseum
558, 571 Vienna, Österreichisches Museum für
Angewandte Kunst
582 Munich, Bayerische Staatgemäldesammlungen
583 Vienna, Österreichisches Museum für
Angewandte Kunst
584 Venice, Galleria d'Arte Moderna
586 Vienna, Österreichisches Museum für
Angewandte Kunst
587 Soleure, Private Collection
588 Prague, Narodni Galerie
589 Graz, coll. Fritz Böck
590, 591 Vienna, Österreichisches Museum für
Angewandte Kunst
596, 597 Vienna, coll. Rudolf Leopold
599 Linz, Wolfgang Gaulitt Museum
601 Vienna, Österreichische Museum für
Angewandte Kunst
602 Basle, Kunstmuseum
603 Rome, coll. Paul E. Geier
607 Berne, Kunstmuseum
608 Zurich, Kunsthaus
609 Berne, Kunstmuseum
612, 614 Basle, Kunstmuseum
615 Leipzig Museum der Bildener Kunst
616 Berlin, Staatliche Museum Preussischer
Kulturbesitz
617, 618 Basle, Kunstmuseum
619 Dresden, Staatliche Kunstsammlungen
669 Cracow, Museum Narodowe
670, 676 Warsaw, Museum Narodowe
685 Belgrade, National Gallery
694 London, Grosvenor Collection
708 Prague, Narodni Galerie
710 Oslo, National Gallery
711 Prague, Narodni Galerie
713 Paris, Musée du Louvre
732 New York, coll. Rothschild
740 Talashkino Museum
741 Leningrad, State Museum
742 Moscow, Pushkin Museum
743, 744 Milan, Galleria del Levante
746 Leningrad, State Museum
747 Moscow, State Tretyakov Gallery
749 Paris, Musée des Arts Décoratifs
752 Moscow, Tretjakovskaja Gallery
763 Lithuania, Kaunas Museum
767 Berlin, Staatliche Kunstgewerbemuseum
772 Moscow, now the Gorky Museum

775 London, Tate Gallery
780, 781 Chicago, School of Architecture
784, 786, 790, 791 New York, The Metropolitan
Museum of Art
801, 803, 804, 805 Chicago, The Art Institute
806 Chicago, The University Collection
812 Cincinnati, Art Museum
841 Washington, Smithsonian Institution
843 Cleveland, Museum of Art
844 Paris, Musée des Arts Décoratifs
845 Washington, National Gallery of Art
855 New York, Museum of Modern Art
858 Chicago, coll. Mr. & Mrs. Sidney Lewis
908 Milan, coll. Pellini
909 Prato, Galleria Falsetti
911 Leghorn, Museo Fattori
915 Florence, coll. Lunardi-Gheradini
924 Trieste, Museo Revoltella
925, 926 Zurich, Kunsthaus
927 Berne, Kunstmuseum
928 Piacenza, Galleria d'Arte Moderna
929 Brescia, Museo Civico
933 Turin, Galleria Civica d'Arte Moderna
935 Turin, coll. Forti
936 Piacenza, Galleria Ricci-Oddi
937 Velletri, coll. Sartorio
938 Florence, coll. Crestini
940 Florence, coll. Gherardini
942 Milan, Civica Raccoita Bertorelli
944 Milan, Private Collection
945 Mestre, coll. Aristide Coin
946 Milan, coll. Martini
948 Turin, coll. Martano
949 Paris, Musée Nationale d'Art Moderne
950 Venice, Private Collection
951 Milan, coll. Ricordi
952 Parma, coll. Ranza
961 Rome, Museo Barracco di Scultura antica
964 Como, Museo di Villa Olmo
965 Milan, Galleria Civica d'Arte Moderna
968 Paris, Musée Nationale d'Art Moderne
971 Milan, coll. Accetti
980 New York, Museum of Modern Art
982 New York, Guggenheim Museum
983 Pennsylvania, coll. H. Gates Lloyd
985 Milan, coll. Panza di Biumo
986 The Hague, Gemeentemuseum
987 New York, Willard Gallery
988 London, Tate Gallery
991 Detroit, Institute of Art
993 London, Marlborough Collection
994 New Canaan (Connecticut), coll. A. Ault
996 Buffalo, Albright-Knox Art Gallery
997 Milan, Private Collection
999 Vienna, Österreichisches Museum für
Angewandte Kunst
1001 Milan, Private Collection
1004 New York, The Museum of Modern Art
1005 Florence, coll. Cesaroni-Venanzi

Index